Name Dependent territories of Commonwealth states (in brackets) SCALE 1 : 88,000,000

1. First find the large towns and cities. What do you notice about their position? What does this tell you about where most Australians live? Why do you think this is?
2. Which place names sound British? Which ones do you think are 'original Australian' names? Why do you think so many names sound British?
3. What does the map of the English speaking world tell you about Australia's place in the world? Compare it with the position of the country you live in. (Think of the climate, seasons, the country's nearest neighbours …) What could this mean for Australians?

Learning English

Red Line new 5

Unterrichtswerk für Realschulen

von

Stephanie Ashford, Claudia Finkbeiner,
Rosemary Hellyer-Jones, Marion Horner,
Peter Lampater, Peter Pasch
und Gunther Volk
sowie Alice Beile-Bowes
und Werner Beile

Ernst Klett Verlag
Stuttgart Düsseldorf Leipzig

MIRJAM MAIER 9A

Learning English

Red Line New 5

für Klasse 9 an Realschulen

von
Stephanie Ashford B.A., Villingen-Schwenningen; Prof. Dr. Claudia Finkbeiner, Heilbronn; Rosemary Hellyer-Jones M.A., Ehingen (Donau); Marion Horner M.A., Cambridge; Peter Lampater, Ehingen (Donau); Prof. Dr. Peter Pasch, Tübingen; Gunther Volk, Villingen-Schwenningen

sowie: Alice Beile-Bowes M.A. und Prof. Dr. Werner Beile, Wuppertal und Iserlohn

Beratende Mitarbeit
Wolfgang Froese, Oldenburg; Christoph Kunz, Bietigheim-Bissingen; Franziska Lehmann-Lezmi, Lahr; Wolfgang Weber, Lebrade

Visuelle Gestaltung
Christian Dekelver, Weinstadt (Grafiken, Layout)

Kassetten und CDs zu diesem Band

SB *Begleitkassette zum Schülerbuch* für zu Hause und für den Unterricht mit Topictexten, Liedern, Ausspracheübungen (Klettnummer 546458).
Die *Begleit-CD zum Schülerbuch* mit demselben Inhalt hat die Klettnummer 546491.
Lieferung durch jede Buchhandlung oder, wo dies auf Schwierigkeiten stößt, zuzüglich Portokosten per Nachnahme vom Verlag.

HV *Kassette zum Hörverstehen* für den Unterricht mit den Hörverstehenstexten aller Werkteile (Klettnummer 546459).
Die *CD zum Hörverstehen* für den Unterricht hat die Klettnummer 546492.
Lieferung direkt an Lehrerinnen und Lehrer, Schulstempel erforderlich.

Software

Passend zu diesem Band gibt es einen Grammatik- und Vokabeltrainer mit abwechslungsreichem Übungsmaterial, intelligenten Fehlerrückmeldungen, integriertem „sprechendem" Wörterbuch und Lernstatistik u.a.

1. Auflage A 1 9 8 7 6 5 | 2006 2005 2004 2003 2002

Alle Drucke dieser Auflage können im Unterricht nebeneinander benutzt werden, sie sind untereinander unverändert.

Die letzte Zahl bezeichnet das Jahr des Druckes.

Internetadresse: http://www.klett-verlag.de

Redaktion: Roland Behnke, Joanne Popp B.A.

Herstellung: Franz Wanka
Umschlaggestaltung: Christian Dekelver, Weinstadt
Satz: DTP-Verlag und Lihs, Satz und Repro, Ludwigsburg
Reproduktion: Repro Maurer GmbH + Co, Tübingen
Druck: Druckerei Wirtz, Speyer
ISBN: 3-12-546450-1

9 783125 464506

INHALT

Der fünfte Band von *Red Line New* ist anders aufgebaut als die Bände 1-4.

Statt *Units* und *Workshops* gibt es nun **Topics** (Themeneinheiten). Bis auf *Topic 4* besteht jede *Topic* aus drei **Modules** (Modulen): 1. das *Text Module*: Hier konzentriert ihr euch auf die Arbeit mit Texten. 2. das *Language Module*: Hier macht ihr Wortschatzarbeit (*Vocabulary*), lernt neue Grammatik (*Grammar*) und wiederholt bekannte Grammatik (*Revision*). 3. das *Test Yourself Module*: Hier wiederholt ihr den Stoff der neuen *Topic*.

Außerdem gibt es in jeder *Topic* 1-2 **Strategy pages,** die euch neue Lern- und Arbeitstechniken beibringen oder bekannte Techniken vertiefen.

Neben den Texten im *Text Module* findet ihr eine große Auswahl an weiteren Texten zu jeder *Topic* in **Further Reading**. Diese fakultativen Texte können zusätzlich zu den Texten im *Text Module* gelesen werden oder gelegentlich auch einen dieser Texte ersetzen.

Im *Text Module* findet ihr Verweispfeile → *LM 15.1* auf einzelne Übungen im *Language Module.* Sie weisen auf Übungen hin, die besonders gut zu den einzelnen Texten passen und direkt im Anschluss an diese gemacht werden können. Eure Lehrerin oder euer Lehrer kann sie aber auch erst zu einem späteren Zeitpunkt einsetzen.

Zu jedem neuen Grammatikpensum und zu den Wiederholpensen findet ihr ab S. 98 Regeln und Erklärungen im Grammatikanhang.

Das Vokabular ab Seite 123 ist in der Reihenfolge angelegt, wie die sechs *Topics* im Buch erscheinen. Bei vielen authentischen Texten wird dort nur der Lernwortschatz aufgeführt. Den Rest des neuen Wortschatzes findet ihr in der Alphabetischen Wortliste ab Seite 157 mit einem Gesamtverzeichnis aller neuen Wörter von **Red Line New Band 1-5.**

Hier sind noch die im Buch verwendeten Symbole:

SB	Begleitkassette bzw. CD zum Schülerbuch
HV	Kassette bzw. CD zum Hörverstehen
→ E	Mit dieser Übung kannst du dich besonders gut auf die Abschlussprüfung vorbereiten.
D	Bei dieser Aufgabe solltest du ein Wörterbuch verwenden.
→ *LM 15.1*	verweist auf eine passende Übung im *Language Module* (hier z. B. Seite 15,Übung 1)
⟨ ⟩	wahlfreie Aufgaben
[ ]	fakultativ für Bundesländer, in denen die Behandlung in Kl. 9 nicht vorgesehen ist
	schwierigere Aufgaben, die wahlfrei sind
	Diese *Topic* bietet Material für fächerübergreifenden Unterricht.

Module *Lernschwerpunkte* *Seite*

1 AUSTRALIA

1 Down under

G'day! I'm Tricia, and I come from Sydney. It's the biggest city in Australia, with about 4 million inhabitants now. I really love the Opera House and the Harbour Bridge.

Aussies love surfing! Most of us live in the cities round the coast anyway, so the kids learn to surf quite early. The waves 'surfies' ride on can be ten to twenty feet high!

This is the longest fence in the world – the dingo fence. It's over 5,000 km long. It was made to keep out dingoes. They're wild dogs that live in the outback. Farmers hate them because they kill thousands of sheep every year. Bushmen started building the dog fence about 100 years ago.

An American friend said everything here was the wrong way round – or upside down! The further north you go here in Oz, the hotter it gets. And when you go south, it gets colder! If you come here in January, it's summer – and if you're here in July, it's winter. He even said: "You Aussies drive on the wrong side of the road." Well, OK – but we got that idea from the Poms.

This didgeridoo player is from Yothu Yindi – a very popular Aborigine rock group.

Australia is the hottest continent – and the driest, too. Not many people actually live in the outback, except people that work on the huge sheep and cattle stations. Aussies call the loneliest parts of the outback the 'never-never land'.

A lot of our animals look really sweet – like koala bears and kangaroos. But we have some pretty nasty ones, too – sharks and saltwater crocodiles, for example.

Have you heard these?

- What do you get if you cross a kangaroo with an elephant?
- Big holes all over Australia.

- What do you call a kangaroo in Antarctica?
- Lost.

1 Australia

a) *Talk about these pictures of Australia. What contrasts do you notice?*

b) *What is 'upside down' or 'the wrong way round' in Australia? Why is this? What else is different?*

c) *Look at the map of Australia at the front of your book.* → LM 15.1

2 → E Listening practice: Australians

a) *First just listen to the recording. Try to get used to the Australian accent.*

b) *Listen again. This time take notes about*
- *where Ken, Julie and Frank live.*
- *what it is like there.*
- *details you find interesting.*

2 Facts about Australia

a) *First read these statements through. Say if you think they are true or not – or if you aren't sure.*

b) *Now find their 'other halves' below. Then you'll see if you were right – and you'll find out more!*

c) *Choose five 'fact pairs' that you find most interesting and write them down. Try to find pictures from magazines, brochures or the Internet to go with them. Add more information if you can.*

1. Australia is the world's largest 'island'.
2. Australia is about the same size as the USA (without Alaska and Hawaii), but only about 18 million people live there.
3. Australia is the home of 150 million sheep.
4. Most Australians live in the big cities on the north coast.
5. Melbourne is the third largest 'Greek' city in the world.
6. Most immigrants to Australia today come from Asia.
7. The first inhabitants of Australia, the Aborigines, came from the north by raft or boat.
8. From 1980 to 1990 sharks killed eleven people in Australia.
9. The first European settlement in Australia was for convicts.
10. For millions of years, the continent of Australia was isolated from the rest of the world. So its plants and animals developed differently.
11. Only 10% of today's Australians are Aborigines.
12. Aussies love surfing.
13. In June and July, Sydney is great for beach parties and barbecues.
14. You can do winter sports in the Australian Alps in New South Wales.

a) Many of them are from Vietnam.

b) Even fewer! Only about one in a hundred people are Aborigines.

c) After Athens and Thessalonica.

d) That's only about two people per square kilometre.

e) Kangaroos, koala bears – even budgies – are examples of this.

f) True! Then you could even fly north to Queensland and go surfing the same day.

g) The prisons in Britain had become so crowded that the government sent ships full of convicts to start a colony on the 'new' continent. They arrived in 1788.

h) This was perhaps about 60,000 years ago – or even earlier.

i) There's a city on the east coast of Queensland that's called Surfers Paradise.

j) Think again! Christmas is summer-time down under. (Then you can really enjoy Bondi Beach – and over thirty others!)

k) It is also the world's smallest continent.

l) So it's no surprise that Australia exports more wool than any other country in the world.

m) True. But on the other hand, traffic accidents killed 32,000 during those ten years!

n) Most of the big cities are on the south east and east coasts. Only about one in seven people live in the country.

→ LM 16.1

3 A story from Australia

1 Before you read

The text you are going to read is about an Australian boy who moves from the country to a big city. *Imagine what problems* ***you*** *might have if you and your family had to move to a different place. (Think of friends, activities, school, weekends ...)*

2 Thomas

'You are not the only person who has ever had to move school,' Thomas's mother said. 'C'mon, love. It'll get better. You will make friends, you know.'

'So why did you come to Sydney?' Five of them were sitting with their desks together. Problem solving, Ms Kelly called it. She'd told Thomas to go with them, Troy, Pete, Rodney and Andrew. They looked over the top of their pieces of paper at him.
'Mum got a job. Dad reckons he's got more chance of a job down here.'
'Where d'you come from?'
'Dungog.'
'Where's that?'
'Up the bush.'
'Did you live on a farm?'
'No. In town.' Not a farm, but an empty block next door and kids everywhere. Always kids. His friends. Stacey's friends. Kids playing, eating, sleeping over, disappearing all day and no one worried. Not like now. A small house with no spare room. Empty. Quiet. Just Mum and Dad and Stace.
The others were quiet after that. Maybe he should have said a farm. Could've talked about horse riding or a four-wheel drive. Trouble was, he'd never ridden anything but a bike, unless you counted a Shetland pony at the Show when he was five.
Back home he and Dad had bred budgies. They'd built cages all along one side of the shed and they'd calculated the chances of getting certain colours from different pairs. Every day Thomas had raced home to check if there were eggs, if they had hatched, if the babies were flying. He'd fed and watered and cleaned. And then Dad lost his job.
Thomas scribbled on his sheet. Maths problems were easy. He could manage problems on paper.

At the weekend, Thomas sat on the back step, flopped on the sofa in front of the television or lay on his bed.
'If you want to go to a friend's place,' his mother said, 'that's fine by me.'
'I haven't got any friends.'
'Why don't you invite someone here then?'
'Because I don't like any of them.'
'How do you know till you've tried? You've never had to try before.'
'It's all right for you.' His voice was rising. 'You knew the people you were coming down to work with. It's easy for you. It's not fair! I hate this place. Bloody Sydney. I hate, hate, hate it.' He was screaming.

a) *What do you find out from the text about Thomas's life before the family moved?*
b) *Talk about how you think Thomas feels at different times in the story – and why:*
1. before school starts; 2. in his new class; 3. when he does work for school; 4. at weekends; 5. when he talks to his mother; 6. when he compares Sydney with his old home.

Example: I think Thomas feels worried before school starts in Sydney because ...

bored? | (un)sure of himself? | worried? | ...?

Thomas slowly gets to know the other kids a little. Then one day at school, there's a note on his desk – with an invitation to go to a rock concert with the others.

They all met up at the station on Saturday. Thomas stood for the fifteen minutes in to town.
It was the first time he'd been on a suburban train. He hadn't even seen a double-decker train before the move.

They heard the music from the station exit. A heavy, thundering bass. Guitar. Keyboard. Drums. The huge crowd carried them up the steps from underground, across College Street and down Art Gallery Road. They could see thousands and thousands of people, on the grass, standing, watching, dancing to the music. The crowd started to run. They ran, too. Thomas felt his hands grabbed, one by Pete and the other by Cass. She grinned at him. He hadn't held hands with a girl, with anyone, since folk dancing in sixth grade.
He smelt the Harbour salt and felt the wind and the warm sun on his face.
They bought cold drinks and then pushed their way closer to the front.
Wall-to-wall people. More than the whole of Dungog and all in one place. He was singing along. He was dancing. He was grinning. With Rebecca. With Cass, Fran, Cathy.

The heat went out of the sun. Finally the stage lights went down and didn't come back up again.
'We can't go home yet. Every station's going to be chock-a-block,' said Cathy. 'Let's go down through the Gardens.'
'Where's that?' said Thomas.
'Don't you know anything?' said Rebecca. 'It's kindergarten excursion stuff.'
'Come on, let's take him.' Cathy grabbed one of Thomas's hands. Troy grabbed the other one.
'Hey, where are we going?'
'You'll see.'
'You're all crazy,' said Thomas. But he laughed and ran again with them, to the wall around the Harbour. Ahead was the Opera House.
'Let's go round to the bridge,' said Cathy. They stopped on the grass by one of the huge southern pylons. Cars, buses and trains roared above them. The wind blew cool off the water.
Cathy pulled them into a circle to hear her above the noise. 'I've always wanted to do this,' she said, and as the next wave of vehicles thundered above them, she spread her arms wide and screamed. The others watched for a moment, and then Cass and Pete, Troy and Rebecca began. Thomas watched. He dropped down on his back on the grass and looked up at the dark underbelly of the Bridge.
He spread his arms and legs. The others dropped to the grass with him. They all held hands, in a circle of cutout dolls. Thomas felt the cool grass, the warm air, the sounds of machines above and friends all around. He opened his mouth and hurled to the world a long, long, wild and joyful cry.

(From 'Love Me, Love Me Not' by Libby Gleeson, adapted)

c) *Collect words from the text that show positive feelings. Write a list – or make a mind map.*
Example: to invite, warm sun …
Try to explain how Thomas's feelings change.

→ LM 15.2 → LM 16.2

4 English – a language for all?

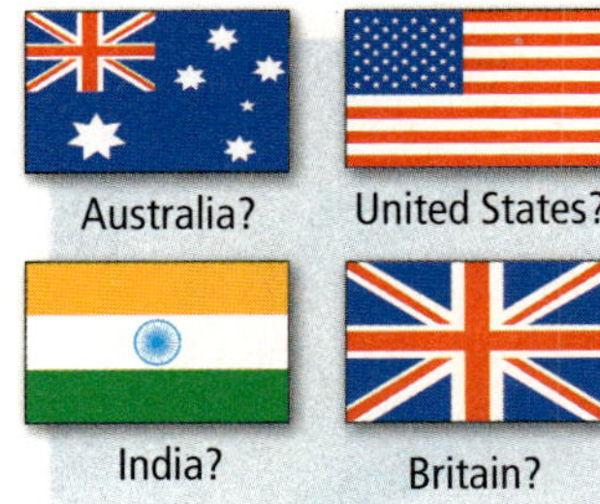

1 Listening practice: At Sydney's International Airport

You will hear the voices of four different people on the recording. They all speak English, but they are from different countries, so they have different accents.

a) *Listen carefully and guess where the speakers are from.*

b) *What is each of the speakers doing at Sydney Airport? Say what you think.*
Example: I think the … speaker has just … . He/She probably … Maybe …

2 Why English?

Why do people in so many different countries speak English? The main reason lies in Britain's history. Britain once had a huge empire, with colonies in all corners of the earth. English became the main language in countries where English-speaking people settled – like North America or Australia. And in parts of the Empire where the British lived as rulers but did not settle permanently – like India – it became an official language. This is still a great advantage, as the people of India, for example, speak a large number of different languages, and English helps them to understand each other.
The influence of the United States in the world has made English more important than ever. Now that the world has got 'smaller', it also needs a language that people from all the different countries can use for communication. And English is the one!

English is …

- … the mother tongue of more than 400 million people, most of them in North America.
- … an official language for another 400 million people, most of them in countries that were British colonies.
- … a second language for about 1 billion other people.
- … learnt by four-fifths of Europe's young people.
- … learnt by more people all over the world than any other language. It can be used by nearly a third of the world's population.
- … used for 85 % of all messages on the Internet.

Look at the map at the front of the book. Make a list of the countries where English is spoken. Why is English the mother tongue in some of them, but only an 'official language' in others?

3 English around the world

Now think about these points.

1. In what ways has the world got 'smaller'? (Think of things that are possible now – with today's technology, for example – but which weren't possible a century ago.)
2. English is often very useful in people's work. If you work for an airline, for example, you'll need English. How many other kinds of work can you think of? *Make a list. Make a list of words you think would be useful in the world of work.*
3. English has worked its way into other languages, too. In German, for example, you often see and hear English words. How many can you find? *Try to think of German words that you could use instead. (This may not always be easy!)*

5 STRATEGIES Giving a talk

Giving a talk can be fun – especially if you work in groups. These two pages will give you tips about how to prepare your talk and how to present it. "Australia" is just an example. You will find the tips useful for whatever subject you choose to talk about.

1 Collecting ideas

What do you find most interesting about Australia? The climate and types of landscape? The animals? City life? …
*First make a list of interesting topics. Then decide which one **you** are most interested in. From now on people with the same interests can work together.*

2 Looking for information

Now it's time to look for information on the topic you've chosen.

Places to look: • book shops • your local library • the Internet • the school library • … ?

Things to look for: • cassettes • magazines • atlases • … ?

TIP Organization is important! Decide:

- **Who** is going to get **what**?
- **When** must everything be ready?

3 Picking out the interesting points from texts

Make photocopies of important texts. Then look for key words and mark them. After that you can make notes. This example – from a text about diving on the Great Barrier Reef – shows how this can be done.

TIP Remember the strategies you have learnt about understanding difficult texts. Talk about them in class before you start working.

Diving on the Great Barrier Reef

Cairns is the scuba diving capital of the Barrier Reef.

Most people look for a course which takes them to the outer Barrier Reef. Some places give you more time on the reef than others – but you may prefer an extra day in the pool and classroom before venturing out. A chat with people who have already done a course can tell you some of the pros and cons. A good teacher can make all the difference to your confidence and the amount of fun you have. Another factor is how big the groups are – the smaller the better if you want personal attention.

The most common and popular courses last five days and lead to a recognized open water certificate. These five day courses usually involve two days' pool and classroom tuition, followed by three days on the reef, with one or two overnight stays on board out there. Normally you have to swim 200 metres and tread water for 10 minutes before you start a course.

Prices differ little between schools. Expect to pay around $300 for the five day course. For your money you can expect transport to and from the training sites, use of all equipment, and meals while you're out on the reef. The only hidden extra is a medical, which most schools arrange for you and costs $10.

X Cairns – diving capital of G.B.R.
X Talk – people who've done course – pros and cons
X Good teacher important – more fun!
X Small groups best!
X Courses usually 5 days: 2 in pool + classroom; 3 on reef

Now decide on the most interesting points in the rest of the text. Then make your own notes.

4 Getting information from a German text

This short text from a German travel brochure gives some general information about the Great Barrier Reef. Don't try to translate German texts word for word!
Just use the most interesting information – and say it in English in **your own words**!
The examples below the text will give you ideas.

> **TIP** If you're using a German text, mark the key words in it, then try to put the main ideas into notes in English. Use your dictionary and ask your teacher for help, too.

QUEENSLAND ERLEBNIS

GREAT BARRIER REEF

Australiens Great Barrier Reef ist einzigartig in der Welt. In Millionen von Jahren entstand hier aus winzigen Korallenpolypen das größte Riff der Erde. Es erstreckt sich über 2 500 km entlang der australischen Ostküste und schützt die dahinterliegende Lagune mit hunderten verträumter tropischer Inseln. Abgeschirmt vom offenen Ozean entstand hier ein wahres Paradies mit Palmen und sandigen Buchten. Das Seefahrerlabyrinth, das bereits James Cook durchfuhr, hat auch heute noch nichts von seinem Reiz verloren.

• einzigartig in der Welt	• There's no other reef in the world like the G.B.R.!
• In Millionen von Jahren entstand hier …	• It's taken millions of years to grow.
• aus winzigen Korallenpolypen	• made of coral (very small animals that live in the ocean)
• Es erstreckt sich über 2.500 km entlang der australischen Ostküste	• It's 2,500 km long and it's near the east coast of A.
• mit hunderten verträumter tropischer Inseln	• hundreds of islands on the reef

5 Getting it all together

Decide on the best order for these 'steps' and make a flow chart.

- Practise the talk with your friends.
- Use transparencies to present important information. (Remember to write large enough.)
- Make a handout. (Write a summary with the most important points in your talk that you can give to your listeners.)
- Write notes for your talk.
- Collect your information.
- Find headings for different sections.
- Make a list of new words.

You can start like this:

Collect your information → [ ] → …

6 Giving your talk

- *Give everyone in the group something to do – and something to say.*
  (It's more fun if you all work together and more interesting for your listeners, too.)
- *Try to speak freely.*
  (Don't read a long text word for word. It's easier to stay 'in touch' with your listeners if you just use notes and look up as often as you can.)
- *Let people ask questions.*
  (Tell your listeners they can interrupt if they have important questions. Or tell them they can ask at the end of the talk.)

1 Vocabulary

1 A mind map

Make a mind map for Australia. Here's an example of how you could start. (You can add more words as you do more work on this topic!)

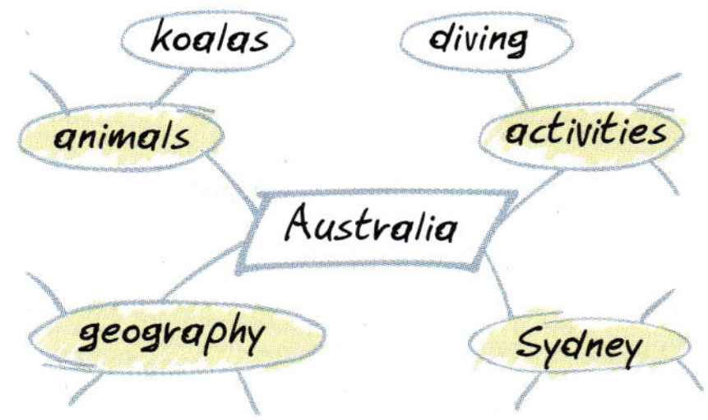

2 Words you can use in several ways

a) These words – all from the 'Thomas' text – can be used in two ways – as nouns and as verbs. *Decide which you can use to complete the sentences. (Careful! If you use a word as a verb, you may have to change its form.)*

•race •sleep •ride •work •move •thunder •grin •show •heat •roar •drive •sound

1. "My dad's lost his job. But maybe he'll find … here in Sydney." 2. In cold climates, a lot of energy is used to … people's homes. 3. "There was an awful storm last night! Did you hear the …?" 4. "Have you seen our new car? It's a four-wheel …" – "Hey, that … great!" 5. "Our hotel was in the city centre. We could hear the … of traffic all night." 6. "Have you ever … a horse?" – "No, only a pony at a … when I was six!" 7. When Thomas lived in Dungog, he … home after school every day. That was before the … to Sydney. 8. "I'm dead tired! I didn't get any … last night." 9. Thomas felt happy at last. There was a big … on his face!

b) *Now make your own sentences and use the words again – the 'other way round'.*
Example: (work) – "My father **works** in Sydney now."
(In **a)**, 'work' was a noun. Now it's a verb.)

3 Organizing new vocabulary

a) It can be much easier to remember words if you think of them in groups. Which kind of group does each box of words belong to?

Group 1: Words that belong to the *same context*
Group 2: *Examples* of a more general word
Group 3: Words that mean (nearly) *the same*
Group 4: Words with *opposite* meanings
Group 5: Words that belong to the same *word family*

ANIMAL
kangaroo
elephant
sheep

air
airline
open-air
airport

language
to speak
mother tongue
translation
to understand

to reckon
to calculate

to rise
to fall

b) *Now look at these words and try to organize them in the same way. (List them in five different groups. Find a suitable heading for group 2.)*

bass – saltwater crocodile – smile – drums – four-wheel drive – drive-in – koala bear – summer – outback – driver's license – winter – desert – grin – keyboard – bush – guitar – sheep station – drive

2 REVISION Tenses and relative clauses

1 When Europeans came to Australia

Look at this information about Australia's history. Read it carefully. Then write a text in the past tense. Start like this: In the 17th century Dutch explorers **landed** on the north and west coasts of Australia. They ...

17th century: Dutch explorers land on north and west coasts. They call 'new' continent New Holland but do not settle.
1770: Captain Cook claims east coast for England. Meets native Australians, calls them 'Ab-Origines'.
May 1787: English Government sends first settlers to Australia, over 700 of them are convicts from English prisons. 11 ships sail together from England. Journey (12,000 miles by sea) takes 8 months. Many become ill. Some die of disease.
January 1788: Ships arrive. Place where they land has natural harbour. Settlers start colony and call it Sydney.

2 What has happened?

Look at each situation. Talk about what you see, how you think Thomas feels – and why. (What has happened to make him feel like this?)
Example: 1. Thomas is grinning here! I'm sure he feels happy because one of the budgies **has laid** some eggs. I think he'**s** probably **come** home from school. He'**s** just **looked** in the nest and **seen** the eggs.

3 There's always a reason

When things go wrong, there's always a reason!
Look at the example. Now make dialogues with a partner. Tell him or her what has happened. Then explain what the reasons were. (Before you start, write down a few ideas.)

lose – budgie/purse/keys/...
break – leg/arm/(sun)glasses/...
someone – steal – bike/bag/camera/...
ticket for .../... – disappear

We've lost our budgie!

Oh dear! I'm sorry to hear that. How did it happen?

Well, my mother let him out of his cage yesterday, and she didn't notice that the window was open.

That's too bad. I hope you find him again.

4 People and things in Australia

Put the right sentence parts together – with a suitable relative pronoun.

1. The kangaroo is an animal
2. Captain James Cook was the man
3. Yothu Yindi are a rock group
4. The Australian Open is a big tennis event
5. Most of the first white settlers were convicts
6. There are about 400 Australian birds
7. Australia is the only continent
8. Most of the world's pullovers are made of wool

- the British government had sent to Australia.
- comes from Australian sheep.
- carries its babies in a 'pocket'.
- people are one nation.
- claimed Australia for England.
- music became popular in the 1990s.
- are not found anywhere else in the world.
- takes place in Melbourne every year.

5 What visitors say

a) People who come to Australia for the first time are often fascinated by the experience. *What do these visitors say?*

Example: 1. Kangaroos are very strange animals! (see)
– In fact, they're the strangest animals I've ever seen!

2. The Australians are really friendly people! (meet)
3. Alice Springs is a terribly hot place! (visit)
4. The birds we saw in the outback yesterday were so colourful! (see)
5. That barbecue last night was very good! (have)
6. That Aborigine picture I got is really beautiful. (buy)
7. The waves here are fantastic for surfing! (know)

b) *Now say something about some of your own experiences – places you've visited, things you've seen, pop groups you've heard, people you've met …*

Example: Istanbul is the most fascinating city I've ever visited!
– Well, I've never been to Istanbul. But I think Berlin is the greatest city I've ever visited!

6 It's a thing you use …

Can you explain in English what these German words mean? Use relative clauses without a relative pronoun.

Examples: What's a *Mofa*? – It's a very small **motorbike you can ride** without a licence.
What's a *Telefonkarte*? – It's a little **plastic card you** …

1. *Nachtisch* 2. *Monatskarte* 3. *Haargel* 4. *Aprilscherz* 5. *Attest (vom Arzt)*
6. *Reiseproviant* 7. *Taucherbrille* 8. *Heimtrainer* 9. *Mietwagen* 10. *Strafzettel*

3 Grammar

1 Same holiday – different opinions

These people have both been on a trip to the far north of Australia. But their experiences were quite different.

We stayed **at** very nice hotels.
We went **to** some very interesting places.
We shared our 4WD vehicle **with** some very friendly people.

The hotels *we* stayed **at** were terrible!
The places *we* went **to** weren't interesting at all!
The people *we* shared our vehicle **with** were very unfriendly.

Can you go on? What might the unhappy tourist say about these things?

1. We slept in really comfortable beds. – The beds *we* …
2. We walked through some beautiful parts of the rainforest. – The parts of the rainforest *we* …
3. We went on a very exciting 'crocodile boat trip'. – …
4. We looked at some really fascinating Aborigine rock paintings. – …
5. We travelled in a new four-wheel drive – and it was very clean inside. – …
6. We went with a very experienced guide. – …

2 Living in Australia for thousands of years

Whites have been living in Australia since the 18th century. But the Aborigines, of course, have been living there for much, much longer! Although many of them have moved to the big cities, there are others who prefer to keep up their old traditions.

Big Bill Neidje is an Aborigine from Kakadu, in northern Australia. He is talking to a group of tourists.

Which is right: 'for' or 'since'?

Bill **has been talking** to us *for half an hour/since ten o'clock.*

	for / since	
Aborigines have been living in Australia		60,000 years or more.
My own people have probably been living in Kakadu		40,000 years.
Kakadu National Park has been attracting tourists		the film 'Crocodile Dundee' made it so famous.
The whites have been talking of building an airport here		a while now.
I've been teaching young Aborigines about our traditions		quite a long time.
I've been speaking our language to my son, John,		he was a little boy.
He's been working as a ranger here		last summer.
In our own way, we Aborigines have been looking after this beautiful wilderness		we first came here!

1 Word power

a) *Put these words into five groups. Find a good heading for each group.*

raft
surfing four-wheel drive
diving Sydney
shark ship
wilderness bush winter sports
koala bear budgie
Perth outback Melbourne

b) *Choose a word from each group, and use it in a sentence about Australia.*

Example: raft: The Aborigines probably came to Australia by raft or boat.

c) *Try to add at least one more word to each group.*

2 Going to Australia in 1788

Imagine those eleven ships that took the first 1530 settlers to Australia.
Say it differently!

Example: 1. The settlers sailed in ships that weren't very big.
The ships the settlers sailed in weren't very big.

2. They went by a route which was long and dangerous. – The route they …
3. They had to sail through weather that was often terrible. – The weather they …
4. The convicts had to live on food that was unhealthy and sometimes bad. – The food the convicts …
5. They lived in parts of the ship that were dark and dirty. – The parts of the ship they …
6. They were all going to a continent which was 12,000 miles away from home. – The continent they …
7. They had to start a colony in a land that was wild and strange. – The land they …

3 [How long?]

Use the present perfect progressive to explain these situations in a different way.

Example: 1. John started work on the sheep station three months ago. He is still there. (work)
– John **has been working** on the sheep station for three months.

2. The Haritonidis came to Australia in 1993. They've got a flat in Melbourne. (live)
3. The Jacksons arrived at Sydney Airport four hours ago. Their flight still isn't ready to leave. (wait)
4. It's a long drive through the outback from Darwin to Adelaide. The Müllers left Darwin on July 2nd. Now it's July 6th, and they haven't arrived in Adelaide yet. (travel)
5. The Australian Open is on TV. Sue started watching the tennis at 2 o'clock. Now it's 5 o'clock – and she's still in front of the TV! (watch)
6. Mr Wilson's hobby is breeding budgies. He built his first cage six years ago now. (breed)

brownie

2 FROM SCHOOL TO WORK

1 The world of work

A

B

Looking for work

Making things work

Voluntary work

C

D

Teamwork

E

All work and no play?

F

Work and play

Working for pocket money

G

1 What are they saying?

a) *Work in pairs. Imagine what the people in these photos are saying to each other. Take notes and tell the class about your ideas.*

b) *Listen and match the four dialogues you hear with the photos. Compare them with your ideas.*

c) *Now use your ideas from a) and write short dialogues for the other three photos.*

2 Working for pocket money

a) *Have you ever done a job in your free time? Or have you done 'work experience' as part of school yet? Describe the job and its good and bad points.*

b) *Now read the advertisements. Which job would you apply for? Explain why.*

ASSISTANT wanted for chip shop. Fun working atmosphere, good pay. Part-time only. Tel. 01753/238908

Young person required for **paper round**, mornings and evenings. Apply within.

HORSE LOVERS WANTED
Help needed at stables. Sorry, no wages, but *free riding lessons* for cleaning out stables, and looking after the horses.
Tel. 01628/98765, or come and see us at Snowball Farm, Taplow

We are looking for a friendly and reliable **BABYSITTER** for one evening a week. References required. Tel. 01628/12345

*Earn **£3 an hour** for walking my dog twice a day. Call Mildred Spencer, 01628/54321*

Saturday assistant needed for busy hairdressers. No experience necessary. Phone for details. 01753/224488

c) *What are the good and the bad points of 'after school jobs'? Discuss.*

→ LM 25.1

2 Choosing a career

1 Before you read

a) *Make a mind map of things that can make a job 'perfect'.*

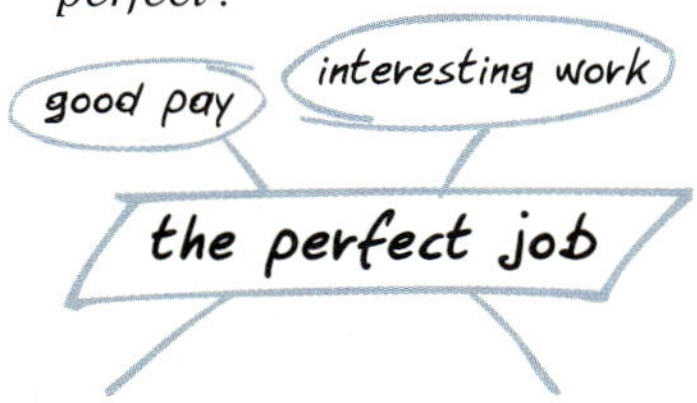

b) *Which three points are the most important to **you**?*

2 Looking at the text

*Read about Mark's job and find out if it has any of the points on your mind map. What would you **not** like about his job?* → LM 25.2

3 Going further

a) *Look back at page 20 and 21. For each of the jobs, say which of these qualities one would need to do the job well.*

good at languages – fit – a good leader – friendly – good at working in a team/on your own – tidy – good with numbers – good at organizing things – *anything else?*

b) *Talk about what you can do after leaving school.*

- start training for a job
- go on to another school/ to college
- do military service or community service
- …

What are the good and bad points of these things?

careering

Window dresser

Mark Upstone, 21, is a window dresser at a London home furnishings store.

Did you always want to be a window dresser? I've always been interested in window displays. When I did art at school, I loved making 3D models and building big, window-like constructions filled with objects.

Did you go to college? Yes. I went to West Thames College for two years and got a BTEC diploma in Display.

Working week? I work from 9.30am to 6pm five days a week. At busy periods like Christmas, I sometimes come in at weekends. I work on both the windows and displays inside the shop. The window-dressing is normally done in a team, but we all do displays on our own, too. Mondays are usually spent tidying up the shop after busy weekends. I'll also help do the flowers, which I always buy from flower markets. We start the window displays on Tuesday – the bigger ones usually take a month to do. Once a month, we also rearrange all the furniture in the shop and think of new colour schemes.

Best bit: Doing smaller displays, like table settings. I prefer working on my own displays as you've got more freedom.

Worst bit: Changing the flowers and tidying up. A lot of customers walk into the window displays by mistake and mess them up.

In ten years' time? I hope to be still working here as I love it. Hopefully, by then I'll have become the display manager.

Holidays: Four weeks a year. And I get some time off if I've been working at weekends.

Pay? You have to love the job as there isn't much money in it, even though my salary isn't bad.

(From The Times 1015, abridged)

learning vocabularies !

CLERK, CUSTOMER SERVICE

DOUBLE QUICK is a UK parcel service offering fast and reliable deliveries worldwide. We have just opened a new office in Berlin and have vacancies for clerks in the Customer Service Department.

Applicants should:
- be fluent in English and German
- have a basic knowledge of French
- have the Mittlere Reife (or equivalent)
- have experience in selling

We offer:
- on-the-job training
- an attractive salary plus perks

Apply to: Jill North, Personnel Manager, Kleiststr. 115 b, 10787 Berlin
by 30th August.

We are an equal opportunities employer.

Krokusweg 82
13994 Berlin

Jill North
Personnel Manager
DOUBLE QUICK
Kleiststr. 115 b
10787 Berlin

15 August 1999

Vacancy in Customer Service Department

Dear Ms North,

I am writing to apply for the job as clerk in your Customer Service Department, as advertised in today's *Berliner Tagesspiegel*.

As you can see from my enclosed CV, I am of German nationality. I did my Mittlere Reife at Gutenberg-Realschule in Berlin-Wedding. After that I started an apprenticeship in retailing at Megamarkt in Berlin-Mitte. I will be finished with that by the end of August.

I have taken several language courses in England and I am also doing evening classes in Business French.

The position you offer is just what I am looking for. I enjoy working with people and would also like to have a job where I can use my languages.

I would be pleased to be invited for a personal interview, and look forward to hearing from you.

Yours sincerely,

Julia Maier

Julia Maier

Enclosed: CV and certificates

3 Applying for a job

1 Finding the right job

Make a list of ways you can find out about available jobs.

2 That can't be right

Correct the wrong statements below with information from the advertisement and the letter.

1. The pay DOUBLE QUICK offers isn't very good.
2. DOUBLE QUICK only delivers to customers in Europe.
3. Women have a better chance of getting a job there than men.
4. Julia found out about the job last week.
5. Jill North wants the applications no later than 15th August.
6. Julia hasn't got the right qualifications for the job.

lernen!

3 The curriculum vitae

*Which of these things does Julia **not** put in her CV?*
Would you put them in yours?
Why, or why not?

1. Details about her family.
2. Where she has worked.
3. The date she was born.
4. The salary she would like to get.
5. A photo of herself.
6. Prizes she has won.
7. Names of people who can give information about her.
8. Her religion.

→ *LM 25.3* → *LM 25.4*

Robert Thompson, © The Spectator

'Hobbies. Swimming...eh...'

Curriculum Vitae

Personal details:

Name:	Julia Maier
Address:	Krokusweg 82 13994 Berlin
Tel. no.:	030/8614
Nationality:	German
Date of birth:	21 January, 1980
Marital status:	Single

Education and Training:

1986–1992:	Wedding Grundschule (primary school)
1992–1996:	Gutenberg-Realschule Wedding (secondary modern)
1996–1999:	Apprenticeship in retailing at Megamarkt Berlin-Mitte

Qualifications: Mittlere Reife

Languages: English and German: fluent
French: good working knowledge

Work experience:

1998 (summer):	Voluntary work with children at the Stadtranderholungsheim Wannsee
From June 1999:	Shop assistant at Megamarkt Berlin-Mitte

Interests: Cooking, tennis, skating

References:

Herr Bernd Henschel Manager Megamarkt Berlin-Mitte	Frau Waltraut Schöppner Stadtjugendamt Berlin-Mitte

4 Listening practice: After the interviews

Jill North and her colleague Steve are talking about two people they have interviewed for the same job Julia applied for.

a) *Copy the grid and take notes while you listen.*

b) *Compare your notes with someone else. Then listen again and check.*

c) *Who do you think **won't** get the job? Why not?*

	Simon	Miriam
Character		
Education		
Work experience		
Hobbies		
Languages		

1 Vocabulary

1 Which job?

A word is missing from each sentence. Find a possible word and write the sentence with the word in the right place. Say whether the word is a noun, a verb, an adjective, a preposition or an article.

Example: I need a haircut before starting my job. What's that new like?
I need a haircut before starting my job. What's that new **hairdresser** like?
('Hairdresser' is a noun.)

1. Are you going to apply the job?
2. They gave me good because they liked my work.
3. They are for an assistant.
4. You are right person for this job.
5. I like the job but the is pretty low.
6. Is it to have some experience for this job?

2 Same but different

Check the meaning of the marked words and phrases. Translate the sentences, if necessary.

1. We **spend** all day tidying up.
   Don't **spend** all your money.
2. They walked in **by mistake**.
   They **made a mistake**.
3. It was a lot of **work**.
   It was a **work** of art.
4. The display **took** a month.
   Mark **took** a photo of it.
5. I need it **by** Monday.
   I go **by** train.
6. He **changed** the flowers.
   He **changed** trains.

3 The right person for the right job

a) *Jill North has to do these things when she is looking for someone for a new job. Work out the right order of the steps, and make a flow chart.*

write to the applicants who weren't chosen – interview the applicants – make a list of suitable applicants – advertise the job – offer the applicant the job – read the applications – invite them for an interview – decide who is the person for the job – write a job description

write a job description ➪ [ ] ➪ …

b) *Imagine you are Jill. Use the flow chart to describe how you find the right person for the right job.*
"First we write a job description. Then we … After that … Next … And finally …"

4→E Applying for a job

Find words and phrases that mean more or less the same.

1. regular payment for work (s…)
2. a job you can apply for (v…)
3. chance (o…)
4. at your place of work (o…-t…-j…)
5. without a husband or wife (s…)
6. work you choose to do without any pay (v… w…)
7. a report about your character or work (r…)
8. company car, free lunch, etc. (p…s)
9. sending something with a letter (e…)
10. exams you have passed, certificates, etc. (q…s)

2 STRATEGIES Using a grammar book

1 The 'language of grammar'

Check how well you know the 'language of grammar'. (The grammar list on page 119 will help you.) *Look at the text 'Window dresser' on page 22 and do these tasks:*

1. Find two **adjectives** and at least two **prepositions** in lines 1–7.
2. Find one example of the **present perfect**, and three examples of the **simple past**.
3. What **tense** is used in 'Working Week'? List the **adverbs of time** that appear with the tense.
4. Find a **noun** in 'Working Week' that is uncountable in English, but countable in German.
5. How many examples of the **passive** can you find?

TIP

A grammar book is useful if:
- you want **to check** something you are not sure about.
- you have made a mistake and want **to find out why**.
- you want to look up and learn **new grammar**.
- you want to see reliable **examples** of a rule in context.

2 How to use a grammar book

a) Your grammar book can help you to answer questions like these. *First try to answer them **without** using a grammar book.*

1. Is it 'look forward to see' or 'look forward to seeing?'
2. When do I say 'good', and when do I say 'well'?
3. Is the sentence 'We meet you at the station tomorrow' wrong?
4. Can I say 'They go every day to school'?
5. Why is it 'I saw her yesterday' and not 'I have seen her yesterday'?
6. I know 'an information' and 'informations' are wrong – so what can I say instead? Are there more examples like this?

b) *Look at the box on the right and find a key word for each question.*

c) *Check your grammar book to see whether your answers to 1–6 were right.* (The key words may be in German.)

TIP

The quickest way to find information you need is to look up a **key word** in the **index**. The index lists the grammar points with the page(s) you should look at.

adjectives and adverbs – word order – present perfect or simple past? – future time – countable/uncountable nouns – gerunds and infinitives

3 Practice

Imagine someone in Class 6 asks you these questions:

1. Wann benutzt man 'How **much**', und wann benutzt man 'How **many**'?
2. In diesem Text steht: "Could I have some sugar, please?" In Fragen muss man doch 'any' benutzen, oder?
3. Was ist der Unterschied zwischen '**I wear**' und '**I am wearing**'?

Check what your grammar book says about these points. Decide what the key words are, and then look up the information. How would you explain the rule in German?

TIP

These tips will help you to remember the grammar points you look up:
- Copy them and try to arrange them in a different form – as a list, as a grid, as a mind map … whatever you find suitable.
- Try to find more examples in authentic texts.
- Try to explain the rule(s) to someone else.
- Make your own examples. You could even try to write an exercise for your class.

3 Grammar

1 Just like a child!

Martin is talking to his friend Heather on the phone.

"... They really treat me like a child! ... Well, they always expect me to tell them where I'm going and who with ... It makes me so angry. This morning I was still sleeping when Mum banged on the door and ordered me to get out of bed ... Because she wanted to clean my room ... Well, maybe *you* think I'm lucky, but I didn't ask her to do it. I even had to remind her *not* to tidy up my room – she always puts my things where I can't find them ... Of course I've thought about what I'm going to do after school! ... I'd like to train as a store manager ... Birmingham? No, that's too far from home ... No, I'd prefer to stay here ... Because it's cheaper, and I won't have to do all my own washing and cooking. The problem is that Mum and Dad want me to move out and find my own flat ... Huh? What do you mean, you aren't surprised? ..."

to ask/tell/remind/order s.b. (not) to do s.th.
to want/expect s.b. to do/not to do s.th.

a) *Find out:*

- two things Martin's parents expect or want him to do. (They **expect him to tell** them .... They also **want him to ...**)
- what his mother ordered him to do this morning, and why.
- whether he had wanted her to do this.
- what he often tells his mother not to do.
- what he usually expects her to do.

b) *What should Heather tell Martin to do?*

2 → E Do this, do that

Heather has got a part-time job in a restaurant. Not all her customers are friendly.

Be careful with the pronouns in reported speech. Quite often you have to change them. (See §3 in the grammar section on page 100.)

What does she tell Martin?
"First **he asked me to give him** a table by the window. Then he told me to ..."

3 A fax to the editor

To: Jo Lawson (Editor)
From: Jeff Pitt
Date: 24 July
Subject: Our report on young people and jobs

I interviewed a fifth year class at Taplow High this morning. Here's what I found out.
They told me they had talked to the careers officer last year, but some of them still didn't know what to do. However most wanted to go on to college or do an apprenticeship.
When I asked about the jobs they wanted to do, I got some surprising answers. One boy said he was going to be a nurse and several girls said they had applied to do engineering or technology – the traditional roles are changing.
One girl said she was thinking of becoming a reporter.
I told her she could apply at our paper, but getting an interview with you wouldn't be easy!

Yours, Jeff

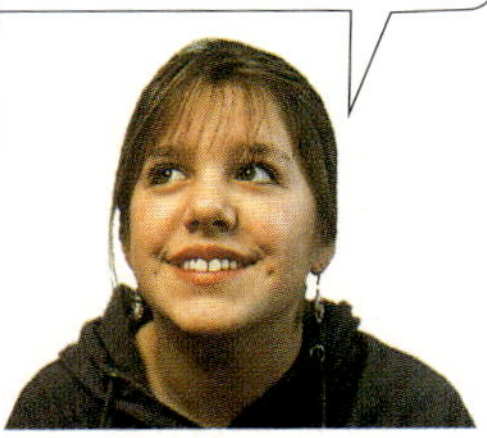

Reporting what they said

am/are/is	->	**was/were**
can	->	**could**
will	->	**would**
have applied	->	**had applied**
talked	->	**had talked**
was/were	->	**had been**

Look at what these people say and how Jeff reports it. What changes do you notice? Compare what you found out with §5 on 'Reported speech' on page 102 in the grammar section. You can also use a grammar book.

4 What Martin told Heather

When Martin started his new job, he loved it. This is what he told Heather after his first day.

A few days later he's disappointed. *What does Heather say when Martin tells her these things?*

1. The boss shouted at me today.
2. She was angry about my phone calls to you.
3. I don't get on with the other shop assistants.
4. I've got to work until 8 o'clock on Fridays!
5. I can't live on just £3 an hour!
6. I'll have to work through July and August.
7. My office hasn't got any windows!
8. The cafeteria meals are too expensive.

5 A call from Chang

The next time Heather meets Martin, he's a lot happier.

Martin: Guess what! I had a call from Chang. Do you remember him?
Heather: Of course! Has he still got that little shop in King Street?
Martin: Yes, but it's a giant supermarket now. Anyway, he asked me whether I was enjoying my job. I couldn't say much because the boss was listening, so I asked him why he wanted to know.
Heather: What did he say?
Martin: He said he needed an assistant to help him in the office, and he thought of me!
Heather: Well, what sort of work is it exactly? And how much is he going to pay you?
Martin: I couldn't ask him on the phone, but I'm sure it'll be good. I'm going to take the job!
Heather: Look, I know Chang's a nice guy, but find out a bit more about the job before you decide.

a) *Look at the dialogue. Can you find two indirect questions?*
b) *Report what Heather and Martin asked each other.*
– Martin asked Heather if … – Heather wanted to know …

> **Indirect questions:**
> ask/want to know +
> whether/if/question word:
> Martin **asked** Heather **if** she **remembered** Chang.

6 Reporting an interview

a) Yesterday Jeff interviewed people who do interesting jobs. *Write sentences that start:* He wanted to know …

Example: 1. He wanted to know whether they had always wanted to do their job.

1. wanted/had/they/to do their job/whether/always
2. when/they/how old/had been/started/they
3. their/had chosen/they/job/why
4. they/earned/money/how much
5. job/if/happy/were/they/their/with
6. they/like/their/what/about/job/didn't
7. hours/worked/they/per week/how many
8. their/had needed/they/if/special training/job/for

b) *What do you think Jeff actually asks? Write the questions in direct speech.*

Example: Have you always wanted to do this job?

7 ⟨Just for fun⟩

'I told you if we didn't tie him up he'd follow us'

8 Finding a parking space

This man doesn't know where to park his car.

This man doesn't know where to park his car either. But he knows how to ask!

Direct: Where **can** I park? Indirect: Can you tell me **where to park**?

9 Could you tell me ...?

It's Martin's first day in his new job. He still has a lot of questions.

Could you tell me ... I don't know ... I'm not sure ...	where how whether when what who	to + infinitive

Example: Where can I get a cup of coffee? – Could you tell me where to get a cup of coffee?

1. Where do I have to put the folders?
2. How do I get to the cafeteria from here?
3. Who shall I give the copies to?
4. What do I tell Mr Cooper if he calls?
5. Should I give the report to Mike or Sue?
6. When can I have my lunchbreak?
7. How do I send a fax?
8. Should I call Ms Morgan by her first or her second name?

10 A customer's story

One of Chang Wong's customers is telling him a story.

"Yesterday I found a mouse in a bag of rice I bought at your supermarket! I got the rice last week and even used some of it. Then when I started cooking dinner last night, I saw the mouse in the bag. Have you ever found mice in your rice, Mr Wong? No? Well, don't worry – this one was alive! My son's pet mouse escaped from its cage two days ago and probably got hungry. It's back in its cage now and we gave it some more rice today. – Now, could you recommend a good bottle of wine, please? My relatives are coming for a meal tomorrow."

How does Chang tell the story to Martin a few days later? (The box shows how you can change time adverbs in reported speech.)

last week	-> **the week before**
yesterday	-> **the day before**
today	-> **that day**
tomorrow	-> **the next day**
two days ago	-> **two days earlier**

Start like this: One of our customers came into the store some days ago. She said that the day before she had found a ...

1 → E Word families

*Complete the sentences with the **noun** form of the verbs on the right.*

1. Please fill in the **application** form and send it to us by 15th October.
2. I've got an (...) to an interview.
3. You need a good working (...) of Spanish for this job.
4. The personnel manager gave us a short (...) to the firm.
5. Jill North wrote a job (...) for the vacancy.
6. Julia read the (...) for the job in the *Daily News*.
7. Do you know anything about the (...) of department stores?

introduce
describe
apply
advertise
manage
know
invite

2 → E Interview tips

A careers officer gave a school class some tips about job interviews. One of the pupils, Emma, wasn't at school that day so she asks her friend Peter to tell her what the careers officer said. *Look at the tips, and say what Peter tells Emma.*

1. Practise job interviews with a friend. It will help you to get used to difficult questions.
   (The careers officer **advised us to practise** job interviews with a friend. She said it **would ...**)
2. Prepare some questions about the job. You can ask about on-the-job training, for example.
3. Don't wear jeans! You should wear more formal clothes.
4. Find out as much as possible about the company before the interview.
5. Don't be late, of course. Try to arrive a few minutes early.
6. Don't tell lies about your qualifications. Nobody is perfect.
7. Remember to be polite and friendly! Don't look down at the floor all the time.

3 → E Some difficult questions

Julia was asked some difficult questions during her interview for the job at DOUBLE QUICK. *Report what she told her parents after the interview.*

Start like this: The personnel manager asked me why I thought ...

4 Trainees

Steve from DOUBLE QUICK also helps young people in his department who are doing their training. *Read what they told him and say how he helped them.*

Rajiv: I have to programme the fax machine, but I don't know how.
Elizabeth: I want to throw away these plastic bottles, but I'm not sure where.
Karen: I need to copy something onto a transparency. Can you show me how?
Paul: I have to ring Mr Jones. It's one of these two numbers, but I'm not sure which.
Samira: I should do this course on Business French but I don't know when.

Example: Steve showed Rajiv how to programme the fax machine.

3 THE WORLD AROUND US

1 Helping the environment

1 ... with music

The Australian band 'Midnight Oil' have written a lot of songs about the environment. Here is one of them.

Earth and Sun and Moon

In the morning we will wake up and take to the air
Look back at the planet – I'm glued[1] to my chair
Southern half is burning as we climb through the sky
Sea-birds softly falling, smoke 'way up high

There's the contours[2] of the mountains, the deserts and plains
And a hurricane is blowing, and it turns once again
Now there's oil spills[3] in the water where Columbus once sailed
And there's history and mystery and it's rolling away

I wish you could see this great mystery
Earth and sun and moon human tribe, thin blue line
Earth and sun and moon will survive

Sediment[4] is flowing from river to sea
Now where are the mighty nations, no lines to be seen
An axe upon the broken ground, the sigh[5] of the trees
And it's floating in the ether[6], it brings me to my knees

Too messed up to care, anyone got a wing and a prayer[7]

In the blink[8] of an eye thank you and good night

Earth and sun and moon human tribe, one thin blue line
Earth and sun and moon will survive, will survive, we will survive

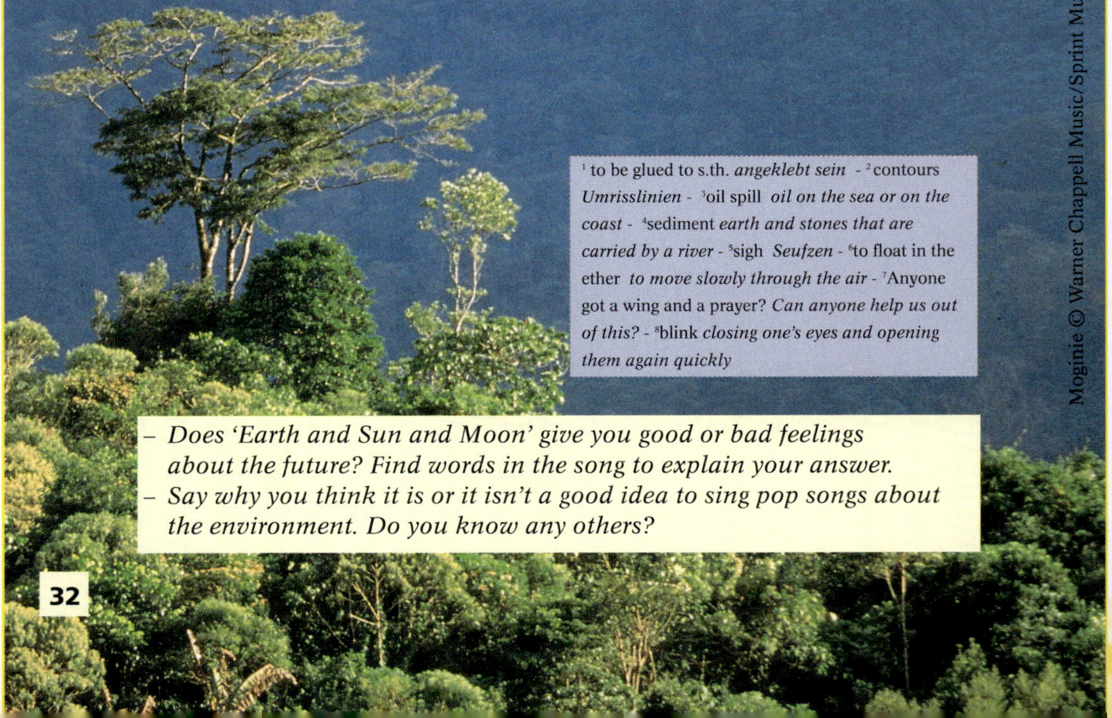

[1] to be glued to s.th. *angeklebt sein* - [2] contours *Umrisslinien* - [3] oil spill *oil on the sea or on the coast* - [4] sediment *earth and stones that are carried by a river* - [5] sigh *Seufzen* - [6] to float in the ether *to move slowly through the air* - [7] Anyone got a wing and a prayer? *Can anyone help us out of this?* - [8] blink *closing one's eyes and opening them again quickly*

- *Does 'Earth and Sun and Moon' give you good or bad feelings about the future? Find words in the song to explain your answer.*
- *Say why you think it is or it isn't a good idea to sing pop songs about the environment. Do you know any others?*

2 ... through an organization

FRIENDS OF THE EARTH
Age: It was formed in the USA in 1969 and in Britain in 1971.
Aims: To protect the environment and the natural resources of the world.
Campaigns: The world's rainforests are disappearing, air and water pollution are becoming worse, and global warming is a danger to everyone. Friends of the Earth campaigns in all these areas.
What you can do: Join Friends of the Earth. Organize an event to make money. Make your lifestyle more environmentally friendly.

Marathon Bike Ride – April 20th
Please help to make LOTS of money for Friends of the Earth. Get details from Jez Taylor (11BD)

- *How is Jez trying to help Friends of the Earth?*
- *Talk about how we can make our lifestyle more environmentally friendly.*

What other environmental groups have you heard of? Find out about one of them, make a fact card and present the group to your class.

3 ... in your own area

What are the people in the photo protesting about? Why do you think they are taking part in the protest?

4 ... on a personal level

Everybody knows that cattle ranching has destroyed large parts of the rainforests, Stella. And in our own country animal farming is the biggest cause of water pollution.

So you've decided to go veggie and save the world, eh? Get real, Carrie! What difference do you think one more vegetarian is going to make?

- *Explain what Carrie has decided to do, and why.*
- *How does Stella react? Imagine you are Carrie and find a good answer to Stella's question.*

→ LM 39.2

2 Enough for everyone?

1 Food

Meat eating is:

A Waste of Resources

Eating meat adds to the problem of world hunger. A piece of land that can feed ten people on a vegetarian diet can feed only one person if the land is used to grow food for animals and we then eat the animals.

(From an 'Animal Aid' leaflet)

FACT BOX

- There are over 3 million vegetarians in the UK, or about 4.5% of the population.
- Around 12% of all young British people are vegetarians and 24% of teenage girls no longer eat red meat.
- Every week 2,000 more people give up meat.

(Information from 'Animal Aid')

a) *What does Animal Aid want people to do, and why?*

b) *Collect more reasons why people might be vegetarians. (These headings from the same Animal Aid leaflet will give you some ideas.)*

A Waste of Life

An Environmental Nightmare

A Waste of Health

c) *Talk about the information in the Fact Box. Why do you think more young people than old people are vegetarians? Check how many percent of pupils in your class are vegetarians. (More or less than in the UK?)*

HV **d)** *Listen to the recording. Take notes about why the two speakers think it is all right to eat meat.*

e) *What do you personally think about eating meat? Give reasons for your opinion.*

2 Energy

a) *Look at the CD-ROM quiz on the right. Match the words on the screen with the photos. Some of them are new, but you can probably guess them. Now say what kind of power the texts are about. Try to do it after you have read only the first sentence of each text. Then read on to check if you are right.*

b) *What kind of power do you use in your home? What is it used for? Imagine what it would be like if these power sources ran out. Explain what you would miss most and why.*

electricity?
gas? ...?

dishwasher?
washing machine?
...?

c) *Choose **one** source of power and write a paragraph about it. Give information about its advantages and disadvantages. Use your dictionary if necessary.*

3 ⟨Project: A poster⟩

Work with a partner and make a 'Save Energy' poster. You can write tips or Do's and Don'ts, and you can use pictures or graphics. Try to think of a good heading for your poster.

→ LM 39.1 → LM 40.3

E IS FOR ENERGY AND THE ENVIRONMENT

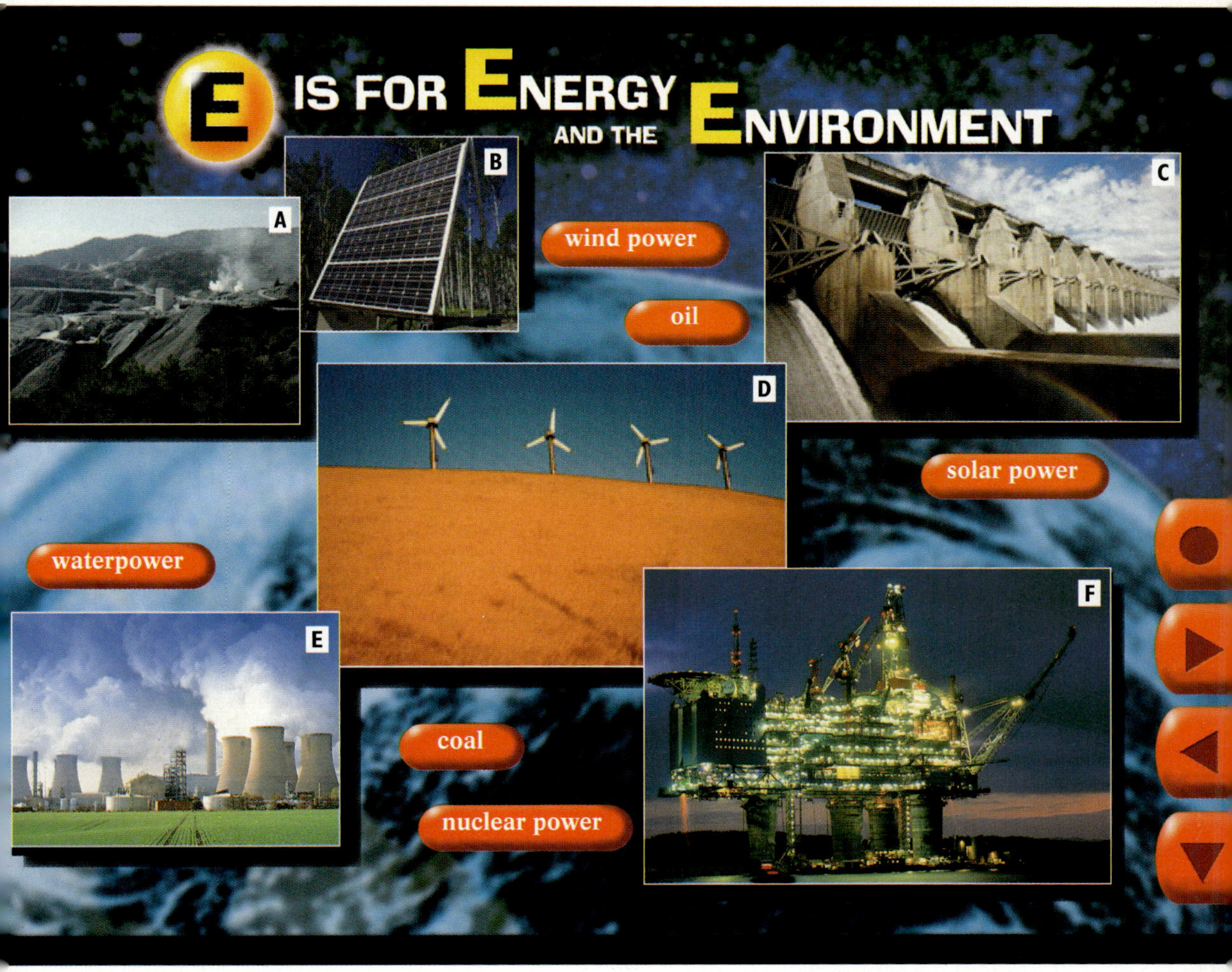

1 A lot of people have protested about the dangers of this kind of power. It has been used since the 1950s to produce electricity. Knowing where to put the waste is a big problem.

2 It is natural and environmentally friendly, but you can't depend on it in northern Europe! It was first developed by American space scientists. Perhaps it powers the calculator you use.

3 This is one of the oldest sources of energy – just think of sailing ships! But some people say that the turbines make too much noise, and that they are an eyesore in beautiful countryside.

4 No one is sure how long the UK's reserves under the North Sea will last.
We depend heavily on it for transport, but it causes water and air pollution.

5 This helped to create the Industrial Revolution. But today it is too expensive to mine in Europe. Another disadvantage is that burning it is one of the biggest causes of global warming.

6 Across the world it is the most widely used renewable source of energy.
It is clean and does not produce dangerous waste. But making reservoirs and building power stations can damage the environment.

3 Airport argument

1 Before you read

Collect ideas about why a city like Manchester might want to have a big airport.

– make travel easier for local people?
– become an international city?
– make the North of England more important? …?

2 The Bollin Valley campaign

This text is about events that really happened …

AROOGA!

'Arooga! Arooga!' It was 3.45 in the morning when the alarm call came.

Jackie woke in her tent with a shock. She was already in her clothes. She and the other protesters always slept like that. They knew that sooner or later the bailiffs would arrive to try and evict them from the six camps they had set up in the Bollin Valley woods. The old woods were where Manchester Airport was planning to build a second runway.

'Arooga! They're hitting Ziontree camp! Jimi Hendrix will be next!'

As quickly as she could, Jackie crawled out of the tent. She ran to a rope ladder which was hanging from a tree. A minute later she was high above the ground in one of the treehouses in the Jimi Hendrix camp. She waited until Kate and Mick, two other protesters, had climbed up beside her. Then she pulled up the rope behind them all.

From their tree they could hear noises and shouts which were coming from Ziontree.

'What do you think is going on?' asked Jackie. This was the first time she had ever taken part in anything like this. Kate and Mick had both been in action before, in other environmental campaigns.

'Hard to say exactly,' answered Kate. 'I just hope that everybody had time to get into the trees or the tunnels.'

Jackie shivered when she thought of the tunnels which some protesters had dug in the woods. They had enough food and water to stay down there for weeks. She would never be able to lock herself away under the ground like that. But she wanted to help, too. That was why she had decided not to start her nursing course in London and had come north to Manchester. That was why she was now waiting nervously in a tree in the woods …

She did not have to wait long.

'Here they come!' shouted Mick. His words were lost in the noise of engines as a group of bailiffs came through the trees on four-wheel motorbikes. They jumped off and grabbed a few protesters who were still on the ground. The others shouted and whistled from the trees.

In the meantime a second group of men had arrived with climbing equipment. One of them started to climb the tree Jackie and her friends were in. 'Come down!' the man shouted. 'We don't want anyone to get hurt.'

'Quick! Get to another tree!' yelled Kate. She led the way across a rope bridge to the next tree. All the trees were linked in this way so that the protesters could cross from one tree to another and escape.

But the bailiffs had planned carefully, too. As soon as they saw that a tree was empty, they switched on their powerful saws. They cut through the main branches, and the treehouses and the ropes were brought down. Then the protesters could not use that tree again.

At last all the links were broken, and the protesters were left isolated in only a few trees. Some were able to climb down themselves. Some, like Jackie, were helped by the bailiffs to get safely down to the ground.

It was the end of Jackie's campaign. Together with the other protesters she was led away. As they passed through the gate in the airport fence they were met by television cameras and reporters. Some local people who had already heard what was happening that morning had come to watch, too.

'Well done!' came a voice from the crowd. 'Thanks for trying to save our valley.'

'Thanks for nothing!' shouted someone else. 'Green hypocrites! Go home and leave us alone!'

3 → E The facts

1. What were the campaigners protesting against? Why? 2. What information does the text give you about the action they took? 3. Did all the local people support the campaign? Which words tell you this?

4 The arguments

a) *Look at these statements. Which support the protesters? Which are against them? Explain the reasons.*

'Think of the extra noise and pollution!'

'Soon we won't have any more beautiful countryside.'

'There was a full discussion about the plans two years ago. You can't break the law just because you don't agree with something.'

'They've damaged the woods themselves with their camps and their tunnels!'

'The woods are part of the history of this area.'

'I'm out of work – like a lot of people around here. But maybe we'll soon have the chance of a job.'

b) *Make a dialogue with a partner. Take the roles of the two people who speak at the end of the text. Start:* 'Those wonderful young people! We should say a big thank you to them.' – 'What for? They …'

5 What about you?

Think what you feel strongly about. Would you take part in a campaign? Say why or why not. What would you do or wouldn't you do?

Example: I would take part in a campaign to stop the pollution of the air. I would go on a big protest march.

- a new motorway
- a nuclear power station
- the dumping of dangerous waste
- damage to the world's rainforests
- the transport of live animals
- …

?

- go to a public meeting
- write a letter to your MP/local councillor/a newspaper …
- set up a camp
- boycott certain companies
- …

?

4 STRATEGIES Creative writing

© The Spectator

'Take it easy, dear – it's only an answering machine message, after all.'

1 Different kinds of texts

a) *What kinds of texts can you write?*
Start: Diaries, reviews, ... *Go on.*

b) *Explain what you write about in different kinds of texts.*
Example: In a diary you write down what has happened to you that day, and how you feel.

2 A newspaper article

Write an article about the end of the Bollin Valley campaign for a newspaper the next day. Use the information in part 3 of this module. This is what you should do:

- *Think of a good headline to make the reader interested.*
- *The reader wants to know the facts right away. So start with a sentence that gives a short summary of what happened yesterday.*
- *Now it's time to go into detail. Explain what the campaign was about, arguments for and against, what action the protesters took, how it ended.*
- *Find a good ending to the article. Reporters often finish with people's comments about the situation.*

When you have finished your article, don't forget to check it for mistakes together with a partner.

TIP
A newspaper article should answer these questions: What? Who? When? Where? Why? How?

3 Other ideas

a) *Look at these other ideas some young people had when they heard about the Bollin Valley campaign. Match their ideas to the beginnings of the texts they wrote.*

1. "I'll write a description of a lovely wood."
2. "I'll imagine I'm living in a tunnel."
3. "I can write a letter to a newspaper."
4. "I think I'll write a 'protest poem'."

A It is three days since I locked myself away down here. I am writing this diary by the light of a candle.

B The sun smiles down into the wood, as the birds welcome the new day with their morning song.

C Sir,
I feel I must protest about the protesters in Bollin Valley.

D Leave us our land
It is our history
Leave us our trees
They are beautiful

TIP
Think what kind of words and phrases are needed for the different texts:
description: verbs, adjectives, adverbs, ...
story: verbs, 'feelings' words, ...
protest letter: phrases for formal letters, phrases for discussions (In my opinion ...)
protest poem: words that sound good together (leave us our land)
Collect suitable words and phrases before you start writing your text.

b) *Choose one of the ideas from a), and go on with the text. Use your imagination!*

1 Vocabulary

1 Putting words together

a) *Find verbs and nouns that you can put together. (Sometimes more than one link is possible.)*
Start: to listen to advice, …

to listen to — the past — to see — a difference — to take part in — lifestyle — to change — damage — to solve — to learn from — the danger signs — to make — problems — a campaign — advice — to cause

b) *Show how you can use the phrases you made in sentences about the environment.*
Example: We should listen to advice about saving energy.
or: Pollution will get worse if people don't listen to advice about the environment.

2 → E Making words

a) *How can you make adjectives from all these nouns? Write them down and mark the endings. Be careful with the spelling and check the pronunciation.*

centre – environment – industry – music – nature – person – tradition

Example: centre – central

b) *Complete these sentences with the adjectives from a).*
1. Friends of the Earth is a famous … organization. 2. We should try to use the … resources of the world more carefully. 3. Everyone can help on a … level. 4. It would save energy if we turned down our … heating. 5. … lifestyles are better for the environment than our modern way of life. 6. Pollution is worse in … areas than in the countryside. 7. 'Earth and Sun and Moon' is a … statement about the environment.

c) *Find a beginning or ending which goes with all the words in each group. What new words can you make? (If necessary, use a dictionary to check.)*

dis- un- re- super- -able -less

1. man, market, human, star
2. drink, depend, reason, renew
3. appear, agree, advantage, like
4. do, tidy, lucky, friendly
5. sleep, use, life, hope
6. tell, view, write, cycle

d) *Explain how the beginnings or endings in c) change the meaning of the words. Example:* A **super**man has **greater** powers than a normal man.

© Ken Pyne

3 Saying words

a) *Even when words belong to the same word family, you don't always stress the same part of the word.*
Example: en**vi**ronment – environ**ment**al [ɪn'vaɪərnmənt] – [ɪnˌvaɪərn'mentl]
Find the related words in these sentences. If you aren't sure how they are stressed, check in the Alphabetical word list. Then read the sentences out loud.

1. Vegetarians eat lots of vegetables.
2. Mining became an important industry during the Industrial Revolution.
3. Organizing fun events can make money for your organization.
4. The information in the leaflet will inform you about Animal Aid.
5. We went on a protest march to protest about the new road.

b) *These English words look similar to German, but they are pronounced differently. Practise saying them. Be careful with the sounds and with the stress.*

technology – energy – electricity – nuclear – revolution – international – discussion – article

4 Guessing new words

Read what someone has written to a newspaper. The new words are all marked. Try to guess what they mean, and explain how you guessed.
Example: 'Planners' must mean *Planungsbehörden*. It belongs to the same word family as 'plan'. It also makes sense in the context.

TIP

Remember: If you don't know a word, ask yourself ...
- Does it look similar to a German word?
- Does it belong to a word family I already know?
- What meaning makes sense in the context?

(If you still can't guess, use a dictionary.)

Sir,
Why do **planners** allow so many new housing **developments** in the countryside? I **accept** that new houses are needed, but surely a better **alternative** would be to build on **wasteland** in the cities. **Disused** factories are standing empty everywhere. We should knock them down and **replace** them with houses. This would help to **preserve** the countryside for future **generations**. It would also help to make the inner cities more **attractive**. It might even **result in** less pollution from cars, as city **dwellers** use public transport more often than people who live in the country.
Yours sincerely,
Martin Golightly

5 ⟨A game: Reacting to words⟩

Play a game in class or in groups.
Take turns to say a word. Say whatever you first think of when you hear the word which the person before you says. Go on for 30 seconds. Can you go back to the beginning again and remember all the words?
You can start with one of the words on the right – or a different word.

pollution
car
sun
reservoir
turbine
green
campaign

Example:

car – road – journey – long – short ...

2 REVISION The passive voice

1 Is it made with meat?

Explain what vegetarians can or can't eat.

Examples: They can eat soup **if it is made with** vegetables.
They can't eat hamburgers **because they are made with** beef.

more ideas?

is/are made with
fruit/fish/potatoes/beef/sausages/vegetables/
chicken/ham/cabbage/cheese/...

2 Animals in the news

a) *Find the animals in each headline and use them to complete the correct sentences.*
Start: 1. ANIMAL RIGHTS GROUP TAKES LABORATORY DOGS. The dogs were ...

1. ANIMAL RIGHTS GROUP TAKES LABORATORY DOGS	... was hit by a car on a forest road.
2. VET SAVES DEER'S LIFE	... was thrown in the water and left to die by its owner.
3. MAN STOPS SHOW WITH CIRCUS HORSE	... were not fed or watered during the whole journey.
4. FARMER ANGRY ABOUT TRANSPORT OF LAMBS	... were probably killed by pollution.
5. GIRL RESCUES CAT FROM POND	... were used by scientists for their experiments.
6. TIDE WASHES UP DEAD SEALS ON BEACH	... was forced to jump through rings of fire.

b) *Change the story. Find other animals that are suitable in the context. You can use the words in a) to write down what happened, but don't forget to change the tense in the headlines.*

Example: An animal rights group took some mice from a laboratory. The mice were used by scientists for their experiments.

Read out your ideas in class so that you can see what animals you all thought of.

3 [When the rainforests are damaged]

What does Carrie tell Stella about the rainforests? Use passive forms.

Start: It usually starts when hardwood trees are cut down in the rainforests. They're used for furniture, for example.
1. When hardwood trees **are taken out,** roads **are built**.

1. hardwood trees/take out – roads/build
2. region/open up by roads – huge areas of rainforest/cut or burn down
3. millions of trees/burn – air/pollute
4. rare plants/destroy – source of new medicines/lose
5. land/clear – ranches and plantations/create
6. rainforest/turn into farmland – tribal land/take away
7. land/use for ranches or plantations – soil/gradually wash away
8. huge areas of rainforest/destroy – climate/change
9. changes like this/make – damage/do forever

3 Grammar

Mal

Huh! Money given to those people is money thrown away.

Lee

I don't agree. I think they should be supported. I mean, if the environment isn't looked after, it will be worse for us all. And most environmental groups have to ask for money because they aren't given any official help. – Hm. I think I'll give them a pound myself. It isn't much, but maybe it can be used to do something positive.

Please help the environment!

1 The words they use

Answer the questions with words from the speech bubbles.
1. What does Mal say about money given to environmental groups? 2. Why does Lee think environmental groups should be supported? 3. Why do most groups have to ask for money? 4. What does Lee say about the money he gives?

2 Stop and think!

a) *Put the right parts together to make sentences for an environmental leaflet.*

1. Lights left on in empty rooms …	– waste petrol and cause extra air pollution.
2. Newspapers thrown out with the rubbish …	– has to be replaced in the reservoir.
3. Water wasted in the home …	– is an eyesore in the street.
4. Cars used for short journeys …	– are a waste of energy and money.
5. Drinks sold in cans …	– is a polluted piece of land.
6. A garden sprayed with chemicals …	– should be left on the supermarket shelves.
7. Rubbish dropped on the ground …	– mean the death of more trees.

b) *What can or should be done? Use the ideas below to make more sentences about the things in a).*
Start: 1. Lights should be turned off when you leave a room. 2. Newspapers can be … *Go on.*

can be … should be …	put in a bin or taken home · treated naturally · turned off · left in the garage · used as carefully as possible · bought in glass bottles · collected for recycling

3 All for Friends of the Earth

to · of (2 x) · at · about · after · for

Read what a member of Friends of the Earth *says.*
Find the right prepositions to finish the passive forms.

1. It's important that the environment is looked … 2. Our group's work is paid … with money that people give. 3. But sometimes we make money ourselves – all kinds of crazy activities are thought … 4. I was laughed … by some people last year when I decided to crawl a mile on all fours. 5. But I collected a lot of money, and my 'crawlathon' was written … in the newspaper – with a photo, too. 6. The next day I was spoken … by lots of people in the street. 7. So you see, I've been famous for a day – even if I'm never heard … again!

1 →E What are they called?

Say what these things or people are called. You have learned all the words in the text and language module. Example: 1. Something that looks very ugly is called an **eyesore**.

1. something that looks very ugly
2. a machine that does the washing-up
3. people who don't eat meat
4. a walk when people want to protest about something
5. the time when machines were developed in the 18th and 19th centuries
6. a lake where water is collected
7. a building where electricity is produced

2 Word power

a) *Find an adjective on the right that you can use with all the nouns in each group.*
Start: 1. You can say 'nuclear power', 'nuclear waste' and 'nuclear weapon'.

clean
environmental
modern
natural
nuclear
political
public

1. power – waste – weapon
2. resources – science – environment
3. air – source of energy – street
4. opinion – meeting – transport
5. leader – campaign – argument
6. way of life – industry – technology

b) *Write down the adjective which you did not use in a). Then write down three nouns that you can describe with this adjective.*

3 How can it be made better?

a) *Listen to the recording. Some pupils are suggesting what can be done to make their town more attractive. Find out and write down what they think:*

1. more rubbish bins
2.

1. … should be put in the streets.
2. … ought to be washed off the walls.
3. … can be repaired and painted.
4. … should be picked up in the playground.
5. … can be planted on the roundabouts.
6. … ought to be knocked down.
7. ... can be created on that piece of land.

b) *Find answers for the teacher's last question.*

[**c)**] *Suggest what can/ought to/should be done where you live.*

4 ⟨Just for fun⟩

If you put these lines in the right order, you can make a limerick.

When asked to explain

She said, "The sun powers my brain

When it's cloudy I just have to wait."

Whose homework was always done late

There was a young student called Kate

4 THE NORMAN CONQUEST

1 The Battle of Hastings

In 1066 Edward the Confessor, king of England, dies. The country is left without a ruler.

The English noblemen choose Harold as their new king.

And there is another person who doesn't like it – Harald Hardraada, king of Norway. He sails to the North of England with hundreds of ships.

When Harold hears about this he marches north with a big army. He meets Harald and his soldiers near York.

In the meantime William crosses the English Channel with an invasion fleet from France.

When news of the invasion in the South reach Harold and his men they hurry down to Hastings.

Harold and his army meet William near Hastings. The Anglo-Saxons take position on a hill and fight back the attacking Normans.

After some time the Normans retreat. The Anglo-Saxons leave their hill and run after them.

But the retreat of the Normans is only a trick. Now that the English have left their hill the Normans can attack them from both sides. Harold is killed and the Anglo-Saxons lose the battle.

William marches to London and is crowned king of England on Christmas Day 1066. But the Anglo-Saxons don't want a Norman ruler. In 1069 there is a rebellion against the Normans in Yorkshire. William puts it down brutally. By 1086 nearly all of the country is under Norman control.

Write a short text of about 120 words about the Norman Conquest. You can:

a) *write a text for a history book.*
b) *imagine you are William and write a letter to your wife.*
c) *write a speech for William's crowning.*
d) *imagine William and Harold talked to each other before the Battle of Hastings and write a short dialogue.*
e) "William won the Battle of Hastings because he was lucky." *Comment on this.*

2 The Normans in control

William believed that the whole of England belonged to him. He gave the land that he had taken from the English noblemen to the men from Normandy who had fought with him at Hastings. Norman castles were built all over the country. William gave all the important jobs in the government and the Church to the Normans. Then he ordered a huge survey of the land that he had conquered. An Anglo-Saxon monk of the time wrote: 'The king sent his men over all England into every county to find out how much land there was and how much tax should be paid from each county. This was done so carefully that there was not a single ox, cow or pig that was left out.'

1 The feudal system

The Normans had brought a new form of society to England – the feudal system. There were four 'classes' of society.

a) *Put them in order – from top to bottom – and explain how the feudal system worked.*

b) *What was the role of women in the feudal system?*

→ LM 48.1 → LM 48.2 → LM 48.3

3 The development of the English language

The English language of today has been formed by the different groups of people who have settled in Britain over the centuries.

The Britons

From 600 to about 200 BC

They came over to Britain from Europe in various waves. Even today some people in Wales and Ireland still speak languages that are similar to the language of the Britons.

The Romans

From 43 to about 400 AD

They drove the Britons to the west (Wales) and the north (Scotland). There are only a few words that the Romans left. What do you think 'strata', 'tabula' and 'vallum' mean in English?

The Angles and Saxons

From about 450 AD

They came from North Germany when the Romans had left. That is why many of the Anglo-Saxon words in English look like German words. 'Word' itself is an example. Can you think of any others?

The Vikings

From about 800 to about 1000 AD

They came again and again, fought against the Angles and Saxons, stole gold and sailed back to Denmark and Norway.

But some stayed in the north of England. There are a lot of words that came with the Vikings. 'Egg', 'sky' and 'happy' are a few examples.

prison – couleur – soldat – bœuf – forêt – fleur – gouvernement

The Normans

1066

William was the last foreigner to conquer England. Do you know the English words that are like the French words on the left?

1 Animals and meat

a) *Look at the list of Modern English words and match them with the Old English and Old French words in the boxes.*

b) *Compare the meanings of the words in the Modern English list. What is the difference between them? Can you explain this? (Remember that the Normans in England were noblemen and most of the Anglo-Saxons poor peasants.)* → LM 49.4

Old English		Modern English		Old French
oxa	⇒	ox		
		beef	⇐	
		calf		
		veal		
		sheep		
		mutton		
		pig		
		pork		

Old English

cealf – sceap – oxa – picga

Old French

veel – mouton – bœuf – porc

1 Vocabulary

1 Organizing new words

When you want to remember new words, it is useful to learn them in groups. *Put these words into the five groups below.* (Some can be verbs or nouns. They can go into more than one group. If you aren't sure which group, use a dictionary.)

army attack battle lead castle class conquer crown the English fight gold build the Normans invasion government king knight land monk nobleman order rebellion ruler control cross lose put down survey

1. individual person	**2.** a group of people	**3.** what they do	**4.** objects (things you can touch)	**5.** feelings, ideas, events ('things' you can't touch)
king	*army*	*to attack*	*castle*	*attack*
…	…	…	…	…

2 Using words in contexts

You know that it is more helpful to learn words together in phrases like "the English fought a battle" or "the Normans attacked from the sides." *Look at your five lists of words and finish these sentences. Use words from groups 3–5. Write in the past tense.*

Example: William **built** many **castles** (4).
or: William **led** (3) the first **attack** (5).

1. The English noblemen …
2. The king of Norway …
3. The Normans …
4. The Anglo-Saxons …
5. The Norman rulers …
6. William …

3 Words in action

a) What can you 'do' with these things? *Choose from the verbs on the right. Think of more verbs if you can.*

build pay understand spend paint invade fight speak count win buy attack collect lose …

1. a castle 2. a country 3. a battle 4. money 5. rent 6. a language 7. a picture

Example: 1. castle: You can **build** a castle. You can **attack** a castle. Or you can **defend** it …

b) *Now think of nouns or phrases you can use with the verbs in a).*

4 → E The growth of the English language

a) *Copy this diagram into your exercise book. Then listen to the recording and fill in the missing words. Use the diagram to explain how the English language developed.*

b) *Can you find the right endings for these sentences?*

1. The history of the English language started a) in 1066 b) a long time before 1066 c) in the 14th century.
2. Old English is a) very similar to b) almost the same as c) quite different from Modern English.
3. The English peasants a) spoke Old English and French b) spoke only Old English c) spoke Old English but could read French.

The Anglo-Saxons spoke ... ...

Those two languages took ... to develop into ...

By the end of ..., when more people could ... books were written in ...

In the last centuries words like ... have come from ...

Modern English

5 At the museum in Bayeux

The Bayeux Tapestry was probably made for William's brother and shows the story of 1066. It can be seen in a museum in Bayeux in Northern France.

You are on holiday and visit this museum. Another tourist comes up to you. He asks you in English if you can explain what is happening in this scene from the tapestry. What do you tell him? (You can do this with a partner and make a dialogue.)

5 YOUR CHOICE

1 What's in a magazine?

THIS WEEK'S CONTENTS ...

page 4

REGULARS

COOL CLOTHES 8
Want to change your image? See what a fashion makeover can do for you.

PICTURE STORY 12
Carrie and Dave continue to try and break into the world of entertainment.

CONSUMER CORNER 20
We check out which personal stereos give you the most for your money.

DON'T MISS IT 23
The best of next week's TV and radio choice.

FUN TIME 24
More hot tips on where to go with your friends.

HELP! 26
Cindy and Nick offer their advice on your problems.

REVIEW ROUNDUP 32
New films, music, games …

AND MUCH MUCH MORE!

page 8

page 20

page 24

page 22

FEATURES

page 28

1. *Imagine someone gave you this magazine. Explain*
   – *which page you would turn to first and why.*
   – *which other articles you would or would not want to read.*

(not) interested in … might give me ideas for … sounds important/stupid/boring …
prefer to choose my own … a waste of time

2. *List the articles under the three headings below and comment on what you find out from your lists. (Some articles may go in more than one list.)*
   INFORMATION – ENTERTAINMENT – ADVERTISING

3. *Talk about magazines you read. (Maybe you can bring some to school.)*
   – *What kinds of topics are the articles about?*
   – *Find examples of information/entertainment/advertising.*

4. *Discuss different ways magazines can influence their readers.*

'create' stars help people with their personal problems

present advertising as information …

→ LM 57.1

2 Critical consumers

These letters are from the teenage pages of 'The Times' newspaper, '1015'.

Dear 1015,
I think that adverts for beauty products are cheating the public. They show beautiful girls putting on cream and saying things like, 'You'll look younger by the minute.' Why can't they show somebody who has not yet used the product, get them to use it and show what they looked like afterwards, so you can judge?
Holly Leadham, Wigston, Leicester

Dear 1015,
In answer to Rebecca McCracken's letter on the dangers of alcoholic drinks which look and taste like juice. I don't think people are too stupid or ignorant to be able to read the side of a can or bottle and check the alcohol content. I, like most people, can do this without any trouble.
James Clark, Ruislip, Middlesex

1 Dear 1015

a) 1. *Say why Holly criticizes adverts for beauty products.*
2. *Comment on her suggestion about how adverts should be made.*
3. *Explain the point that James makes in his letter.*
4. *Give your opinion on who you think is right: James or Rebecca.*

b) 1. *Write Rebecca McCracken's letter to 1015.*
2. *Are you a critical consumer? Try to write a critical letter about some product to 1015.*

2 The 'right' trainers

a) 1. *Explain the idea behind the advert.*
- *What has happened to the spider?*
- *Is the result what you would expect?*
- *What 'message' does this give you?*

2. *Say what you think of this advert.*

(not) good because … unusual/silly/funny/…

b) 1. *There are a lot of adverts for trainers. Collect ideas about the reasons for this.*
2. *Discuss why some trainers have a better image than others. What is your opinion on wearing the 'right' trainers?*
3. *Talk about other clothes or things young people have which count as status symbols.*

3 Advertising strategies

A good advert is an advert you notice – and remember.
Talk about adverts you know. Bring adverts from magazines to school, or describe adverts on TV. Explain what advertising strategies are used. Here are some ideas and words to help you:

good headline famous person humour improved product
image (fun/'the good life'/...) tell a story bright colours catchy music
unusual picture clever slogan important message (your health/your future/...)

4 Consumer power

At Blackpool Pleasure Beach, a huge theme park in the north of England, the managers decided to set up a teenage committee. The group meet three times a year.

a) *Say why you think the teenage committee was set up. (You can check if you are right in part* **b)***!)*

HV **b)** 1. *Listen to the beginning of a committee discussion. Take notes about what the girls and boys say.*
2. *Collect more ideas about what might be important for young people visiting a theme park.*

5 ⟨Project: Make your own consumer report⟩

Work in groups for this. Decide what products or places you want to test. (You don't need to spend money if you already know about different trainers/magazines/ stereos/cinemas/ ...)
Discuss what information consumers might want to know and make a list.
Think of a good way to present the results. (Written comments? A grid? Marks out of 10? Order from best to worst?)

look/taste good?
price? sound?
comfortable? clean?
interesting films/articles?
friendly? ...?

3 STRATEGIES Listening

If you don't understand something an English-speaking person says, you can often ask him or her to explain or to speak more slowly. But in some situations this is not possible ...

1 Recorded telephone information

TIP

It's a good idea to make a checklist of information you need before you dial.

a) *Note down what information you need if you want to go to the cinema.*

b) *Listen to some recorded cinema information. Find out which button you press*
- *to start the information service.*
- *for details of the film 'Trapped'.*
- *to find out about the next film.*
- *for the booking office.*

Films are given certificates – for example:
'U' – for everyone
'12' – not for people under 12
'18' – not for people under 18

c) *Now listen again, and also to some more details about 'Trapped'. Take down the important information while you listen. Your notes from a) will help you.*

d) *Have you got all the information you need? If not, what can you do?*

2 Announcements

In public places you sometimes suddenly hear announcements. You want to be able to understand them – they might be for you!

Listen to these announcements in a theme park. Sum up who they are for, and what action the people should take.
Start: 1. This announcement is for someone who has lost ...
He or she should ...

TIP

Try to listen only to the voice making the announcement (not to other voices and noises around you). – The main information is often repeated, so don't worry if you don't catch everything the first time.

3 Identifying what you hear on the radio

If you're planning to listen to a certain programme on the radio, you know which radio station you want. But sometimes you 'surf' from station to station to find out what's on ...

a) *Listen, and make a list of what you can hear on different radio stations. The ideas on the right will help you with some of the programmes (but not all).*

advert drama interview comedy news ...?

b) *Compare your lists. Check if you all wrote down the same. Talk about what clues you used to identify what you heard (what was said? the tone of the voice(s)? other sounds or noises in the background? ...?).*

TIP

Listen to 'real' English (radio, TV, pop songs) as often as you can. Practice makes perfect!

4 War of the worlds

'Sunday evening at home in New York City. As usual at eight o'clock I turn on the radio for the Charlie McCarthy Show. I normally enjoy the program, but the music isn't so great tonight. Some new singer I never heard of before. I listen for a few minutes, then I decide to look for a better program on a different radio station.

I change to CBS and catch the end of the weather forecast. 'This weather report comes to you from the Government Bureau. – We take you now to the Meridian Room at the Hotel Park Plaza in downtown New York where you will be entertained by the music of Ramon Raquello and his orchestra.'

Some unexciting dance music follows. I'm just going to change stations again when the program is interrupted by a news report. Several explosions on the planet Mars have been reported, and now it seems there are clouds of gas approaching earth at great speed. Unusual news. I think I'll stay with CBS.

We go back to the music for a while. It stops again for an interview with a famous astronomer at Princeton Observatory. A message arrives that a shock as strong as an earthquake has been recorded near Princeton. The astronomer says it probably has nothing to do with the explosions on Mars. To me it all seems very strange.

More music follows. It breaks off for another CBS announcement. This confirms that a huge burning object has fallen on a farm at Grovers Mill, New Jersey. What is going on? I want to hear more, but we get the music again. I have to wait.

The next report comes direct from the scene at Grovers Mill. The atmosphere is – well, I'm not sure. I'm confused by all the sounds in the background. The reporter gives a description of a huge metal object he can see. I can hear the police trying to hold back a crowd of people. I guess they're local people who heard the news on the radio, like me, and want to see what's happening for themselves. I feel nervous although I don't know why.

Now the reporter talks of strange noises coming from the object. I can hear the noises over the radio. I don't like them. They sound scary. The reporter says the object is opening up. I go cold as he describes horrible creatures appearing. I can hear people shout and scream. The creatures are attacking and killing them. I listen in horror to the reporter's frightened voice. '... spreading everywhere – coming this way now – about twenty yards from my right –' Suddenly his words are cut off. Then silence.

I feel helpless. The calm music makes me feel worse. Not knowing what is happening is terrible. I try to call CBS, but I can't get through. The lines are jammed. It's the same when I try to dial other radio stations and newspapers.

I stay sitting next to my radio. What else can I do? At last a man's voice says, 'Ladies and gentlemen, I have a grave announcement to make.' He gives the terrible news that the creatures in New Jersey are part of an army from Mars. I jump up in a blind panic. The Martians have landed. They are going to kill us all. I run screaming out into the street ...'

The experience which is described above really happened! The date was October 30th, 1938. – Hard to believe?
You'll find out more on the next page.

On October 30th, 1938, Americans across the country started to panic as they heard on CBS radio how the Martians had come to conquer the world. The word spread quickly, as people phoned their neighbours and relatives to tell them of the danger. In the cities restaurants emptied. Buses and taxis were full as people tried to get home to their families. Roads were jammed with people trying to escape to the hills by car.

What all these panicking people did not know was that they had been listening to a radio play – 'War of the Worlds' by H. G. Wells! Many listeners had missed the introduction at the beginning of the play because they had been listening to the Charlie McCarthy Show on another radio station. They did not find out their mistake because they left their radios in fear before the end of the drama.

Orson Welles and his Mercury Theater of the Air had worked especially hard to make 'War of the Worlds' exciting. The ratings for their Sunday evening drama series on CBS were always very low because most Americans listened to the Charlie McCarthy Show on a rival station. Welles knew that he had to win over listeners if he wanted to save his series. He thought that acting the play as live news reports might make it more realistic. And he was right. Listeners who changed to CBS because they were bored with the McCarthy Show took everything they heard for fact.

Surprisingly Welles himself did not realize the effect his play had had on people until he left his apartment the following morning and saw the headlines. 'Orson Welles Causes Panic'. 'Attack from Mars puts Thousands in Fear'. Newspapers said he had been irresponsible with his play, but CBS were happy. Now everybody was talking about their radio station.

1 The mistake

a) *Explain what mistake lots of Americans made on October 30th 1938. Why did so many people not realize they were listening to a radio play?*

b) *Say how you think these people felt the next day, and why.* 1. Orson Welles 2. the CBS bosses 3. listeners who had heard all the play 4. listeners who had panicked

c) *Discuss whether you think the same mistake could happen today.*

2 The radio play

a) 1. *Why did Orson Welles work so hard to make his play realistic?*
2. *Look back at page 55 and list the different 'news reports' in the play.*
3. *What did the listeners hear between the news reports? Say what effect you think this had. (There are some clues in the text.)*

b) *Listen to the recording. You are going to hear a scene from Orson Welles' radio play. This is an old recording, so the quality is poor. But don't worry. Just try to get an idea of what's going on. Say which lines on page 55 describe the scene you hear. Talk about the atmosphere in the scene. (What is it like? What helps to make it like this?)*

3 Entertainment today

Today lots of people watch TV for entertainment at home.
Find out which programmes or series get the highest ratings in your country. Say why you think people enjoy watching them.

1 Vocabulary

1 Participles as adjectives

a) *You can use some participles – present and past – as adjectives. Choose the correct participles and nouns to complete the information from a magazine contents page.*

1. TV tips – we tell you about … next week.
2. … write to us about their problems.
3. Find out about the latest … at Alton Towers theme park.
4. Meet the schoolgirl who won the … in a new musical.
5. Can a … really make a difference to your life?
6. 'Just say no.' A look at the … about drugs.
7. No more … – learn how to cook the perfect meal!
8. Exam time will be here again soon. The way to get … at school.

leading role
improved grades
changed image
exciting ride
burnt sausages
entertaining programmes
worried readers
frightening facts

b) *Here are some more participles which are often used as adjectives. Think of suitable nouns, and make your own sentences.*

surprising – frightened – broken – winning – lost – shocking – caring – written

2 Describing things

Different consumers have different ideas about what products should be like. What do these things mean to you? What words or phrases can you use to describe them more exactly?

Example: For me a good book is a story I don't want to put down. It's got interesting characters and …

a good book — lovely food — a super magazine — cool music — a fantastic video — great clothes

3 Describing people

a) *Read the description on the right. Use examples from it to talk about the different kinds of things you can include when you describe someone.*
You can say where someone comes from. The text says the man 'comes from another planet'.
You can explain … *Go on.*

b) *Think of a famous **real** person – from the world of music or films, sport, politics, … Write a description of the person, but don't include the name. (If you need new words for your description, look them up in a dictionary.) Read your text to a partner. How quickly can he/she guess who you are describing?*

2 Grammar: Participles Part A

Mel is telling her friend Hannah that she saw a TV actor in a music store …

Mel: I saw this guy looking at CDs, you see. And he looked familiar, but he had dark glasses on and I just couldn't think who it was. So I stood watching him for a while –
Hannah: Did he notice you standing there?
Mel: No, I was very careful. Anyway, then he picked up a CD and took it to the counter. So I followed him over – not too quickly, of course. But when I got near enough to hear him talking to the assistant – well, then I knew. I mean, anybody would recognize the way he speaks.
Hannah: Did you ask him for his autograph?
Mel: Of course I did. But he said I'd made a mistake and went hurrying out of the place as fast as he could …

I **saw** him look**ing** at CDs.

1 A different point of view

a) *Put the right parts together to tell the story from the assistant's point of view.*
Start: 1. Well, I'd already seen a guy in dark glasses **looking** at CDs. 2. But then … *Go on.*

1. I'd already seen a guy in dark glasses …
2. But then I also noticed a girl …
3. After a while I noticed the guy …
4. And I saw the girl …
5. It seemed as if she wanted to hear him …
6. After he had paid for his CD I noticed the two of them …
7. I couldn't hear what they were saying, but I saw the guy … – I've no idea what it was all about.

… talking to me. … coming over to me.
… watching the guy. … following him over.
… shaking his head. … looking at CDs.
… talking to each other.

b) *Why do you think the actor told Mel she had made a mistake?*

2 I saw a star!

Imagine that you saw some famous people doing everyday activities. What do you tell your friends?
Example: I saw Martina Hingis **doing** the shopping the other day. I followed her/asked …

- wait for a bus
- take the dog for a walk
- visit a zoo
- do the shopping

- sit in a traffic jam
- buy an ice-cream
- play minigolf in the park
- *any more ideas?*

3 It isn't easy

A supermodel is talking on the radio about what it is like to be famous. Complete the sentences with the pairs of verbs. Use the participle form of the second verb in each pair.

come/jump out — stand/wait for — come/run — hang around/hope — run away/scream — come out/smile — sit/hide ✓ — go/hurry

1. It isn't easy, you know. Sometimes I just want to **sit hiding** behind closed doors.
2. I don't really mind the fans who … autographs outside my house.
3. But there are always reporters who … to get some story.
4. And wherever I go, photographers … with their cameras.
5. Of course in the end I always … at everybody, like people expect.
6. I try to be friendly to people who … up to me in the street.
7. I mean, they look so disappointed if I just … past them.
8. But like I said, at times I could … because it all gets too much.

4 In the headlines again

a) *Read the newspaper article. Find the sentences which tell you how Susan used the money she won.*
Start: 'I had a dream house built.'
'I paid to have all …'
She … …

b) *Explain the difference between these two sentences.*
I have done everything.
I have everything done.

[c)] *Say what kind of things* **you** *would or wouldn't have done if you had the money.*
Examples:

I would have a swimming pool built.

I wouldn't have my face changed.

LOTTERY WINNER GIVES AWAY MONEY

Hairdresser Susan Smith became famous when she won £10 million in the lottery two years ago. Now she is in the headlines again because she has decided to give most of her money away.

'At first it was great,' she says. 'I had a dream house built, and I didn't do any work, even at home. I paid to have all my housework done and I had all my meals cooked for me, too.'

For a time she spent money like water. She had a trip around the world organized for her in a private plane. She had expensive clothes made by the top names in fashion. She also paid for an operation to have her nose made smaller, but she didn't like her new nose, so she had it changed back again.

Now Susan has decided that she prefers not only her old nose, but her old lifestyle, too. 'Having everything done for me became very boring,' she explains. 'And I wasn't sure if my friends liked me for myself or for my money. I'm not stupid – I've kept a little money in the bank for a rainy day. But I've gone back to my job and I'm having all the rest of my money divided between my favourite charities.'

3 Grammar: Participles Part B

The people sitting round the table work for an advertising agency. A software company wants them to advertise 'Star Trip', a new computer game coming onto the market soon …

The people	who are sitting sitting	round the table …

1 A team talk

Complete what the team leader is saying.
Find the correct participle phrases to finish the sentences.

Start: 1. OK, as you know, there are a lot of computer games **competing** for kids' money.

2. So we have to create a powerful campaign for the software company …
3. The main advert in the campaign will be seen by kids …
4. But there will also be adverts …
5. Forget about boring pictures like someone just …
6. What we need is an unusual image …
7. All the information you need about the game is in the folder …
8. Remember – 'Star Trip' must become number one on the list for anyone …

lying on the table
appearing in magazines
suggesting something different
selling this game
buying a computer game
competing for kids' money
watching TV
playing the game

2 New adverts

These drawings are suggestions for new adverts. What kind of products do you think the people in the pictures are advertising? Use participles to identify the people.

Example: I think the girl **running** up the mountain is advertising trainers (… an energy drink).

the children holding up … | the boy lying on … | the woman looking in …
the girl running up … | the child putting money in … | the people dancing with …

1 Word power

Find pairs to make compounds. Write a sentence explaining the meaning of each compound you make. (If you aren't sure whether your compounds exist, check in a dictionary!).
Example: A **consumer report** gives people information about products or services they can buy.

consumer radio symbol office personal report booking
drama makeover station series status stereo fashion

2 [Oops! It's live!]

Sometimes people appearing on live TV or radio programmes aren't ready, so mistakes happen. Explain what viewers or listeners can see or hear happening in the following situations.

Example: 1. Viewers can **see someone putting on** lipstick. 2. Listeners can hear someone …

talk about
read put on
eat spray
laugh

3 The 'Sizz' story

a) *Put the sentences in the right order to find out what happens in a TV advert for 'Sizz', a lemonade drink.*
Start: A thirsty marathon runner …

In shock, most of the crowd just stand watching her.
The advert ends with a can of SIZZ wearing a gold medal.
The hot sun beating down is too much for her, and she falls.
The runner sits drinking the boy's SIZZ for a few seconds.
A thirsty marathon runner comes lurching along the road.
Then she jumps up and goes flying down the road.
But a little boy holding a can of SIZZ comes to the rescue.

b) *Think of your own little story for a TV advert. Write down a few sentences describing what happens.*

6 THE INDUSTRIAL REVOLUTION

1 Changes in society

In British history the time from about 1750 to about 1850 is known as the Industrial Revolution. It was a time in which the way people lived together and worked together changed completely.

A

Before the revolution

This picture was painted in the middle of the 18th century. The women are spinning cotton by hand.

During the revolution

This is a picture of a cotton factory at the beginning of the 19th century. The machines are driven by a steam engine, the most important invention of the Industrial Revolution.

B

1. *Compare the two pictures. Talk about:*
   • who you can see • what these people look like (clothes, expressions on their faces, etc.) • what they are doing • what their relation to each other might be
2. *What do you imagine living and working conditions were like in Picture A and Picture B? (Think of where people lived and worked, working hours, meals, etc.)*
3. *What developments and changes probably happened between 1750 and 1850?*
4. *Work in groups. Imagine you could ask one of the people in Picture B five questions about life in 1850. What would you ask? Keep your questions and look at them again when you are finished with this topic. Can you answer them now?*

2 The Industrial Revolution

Up to the middle of the 18th century people had worked at home. Anyone who made goods for sale made them in a workshop in or near his own house. People used to work very long hours, but everybody could work at their own speed. In the new factories, however, it was the machine that set the speed. The workers had to learn to work by the clock.

The factories that made cloth were called mills because they used to run on water power before the steam engine had been invented.

For the mill owners it was cheaper to employ women and children. In 1833 the cotton mills employed about 60,000 men, 65,000 women and 84,000 young people, half of them boys and girls under 14. Ten years later, of 420,000 workers, less than a quarter were men over 18 and 242,000 were women and girls.

Rows and rows of grey houses were built around the grim factories with their tall chimneys. But these gloomy industrial towns made Britain “the workshop of the world”.

Look at the picture of Manchester in 1851. What impression of the city do you get?

1 The workshop of the world

Match these sentence parts correctly and you get the ‘story’ of how Britain became the workshop of the world.

1. In the middle of the 18th century the population in Britain started to grow very quickly,
2. Before 1750 people had only known animal, wind and water power,
3. The early steam engines were very big and expensive
4. The new factories were built in the towns,
5. You need coal to produce steam and iron,
6. The steam engine was also used to drive locomotives,
7. By the late 18th century Britain had become the world’s leading trading nation

a) so the speed of travel changed enormously.
b) and British ships carried goods all over the world.
c) so people who were looking for work had to leave their home in the country.
d) so far more people needed food, clothes and houses.
e) so mining became an important industry.
f) so they could only be used in large factories.
g) but with the invention of the steam engine big machines could be used.

What negative effects did the Industrial Revolution bring about? Were there any positive effects?

→ LM 65.1

1 STRATEGIES Word building

1 → E Making nouns with -ion

You know quite a few verbs that you can make into nouns by adding **-ion**. *Complete these sentences with the matching verbs. (Be careful: sometimes you have to do more than just take off* **-ion**!*)*

Example: The introduct**ion** of new laws in the 19th century changed the working conditions of young people in England.
In the 19th century the government **introduced** new laws that changed the working conditions of young people in England.

TIP

Whenever you revise your words and come across a noun, think: Do I know the verb? Do I know the adjective? Do I know other related words? You can also do it the other way around, of course (verb > noun, verb > adjective, etc.).

1. With the invention of the steam engine by James Watt machines could be used instead of animal power. When James Watt …
2. Big cities with lots of factories had a huge attraction for unemployed people from the country. People from the country felt … to …
3. Competition for jobs was hard because so many people were looking for work. A lot of people were looking for work and … for …
4. Some authors give a very good description of working conditions in the coal-mines. Some authors … very well.
5. The pollution of the rivers running by the mills was terrible. The rivers running by the mills … terribly …
6. The discussion of life in the mines in Parliament led to new laws. Parliament … and this …

2 → E Making adjectives with -al

You know that you can make adjectives from some nouns by adding **-al**: industry – industri**al** (but be careful: often you have to make other changes, too). *Can you find 6 nouns in this text that can be made into an adjective by adding -al? Use each of them in a sentence or try to write a short text with them.*

During the Industrial Revolution traditions changed quickly. One of the most important people of the time was James Watt, the inventor of the steam engine. Britain was the first nation to use it.
People moved from the country to the big cities, the centres of development. Most people worked in factories; only very few people worked in offices in those days.
Life in the cities was hard. Some of the rivers were badly polluted and clouds of black smoke hung over the cities. But people didn't have time to worry about nature. Most of them were poor and found it difficult enough to stay alive. Those who couldn't find work sometimes had to steal to survive. Then they were sent to prison in England or to faraway places on the other side of the globe.

TIP

What other word building patterns do you know? (*Example*: noun + ful, verb + ment). Make a list and find word families for each of them.

TIP

Most grammar books have a list of word building patterns. Find this list in your grammar book. Make a file card for each pattern and add new words as you learn them.

2 Vocabulary

1 [What life used to be like]

Imagine what life used to be like at the time of the Industrial Revolution.
Example: People **used to walk** to work. Most children **didn't use to go** to school.

a) *Think of these things and say what life must have been like for many people.*

- lots of people lived together in small grim houses
- lots of them caught diseases because of this
- people didn't earn enough to pay for a doctor
- women and children worked in factories and mines
- people worked very long hours
- they were badly paid
- factories were very dangerous places, lots of accidents happened
- people didn't have much free time

b) *Try to think back some years. Say what things used to be like for you. (Think of school, hobbies, sport, where you lived and so on.)*

Example: When I was a kid, I used to watch a lot of TV, but now I prefer surfing the Internet.

2 Who or what am I?

You know that you can make nouns from verbs by adding **-er** or **-or** (to paint > painter).
Complete these sentences and say whether the missing nouns end in **-er** *or* **-or**.

1. I help you in your Maths lesson and with your Maths homework. I am a pocket ...
2. I've got ideas for new things that help to make life easier. I'm an ...
3. People work for me and I pay them for it. I am their ...
4. I took England in 1066 because I was promised the English crown. My name is ...
5. Whenever there's something interesting happening in the world, I am there to write about it. I am a ...
6. You can see me in movies, in the theatre or on TV. I'm an ...
7. In Britain people usually call me 'lift', but Americans say ...
8. Millions of people live in this city but I don't. I've just come to see the sights. I am just a ...

3 REVISION Reported speech

1 → E Are you interested in history?

Paul Cooper wrote a report for his school magazine – after he had interviewed a number of people in the lunch break. Here's what three of them said:

1. *Thomas:* I'm not interested in history at all. I think it's boring. I don't want to know about what happened to people hundreds of years ago.
2. *Sophie:* I'm enjoying History at school at the moment. We're learning about the Industrial Revolution, and I find that really interesting. I can't see much interest in kings and queens!
3. *Jack:* I never read history books. But there are a lot of exciting films about life in the past. I've seen at least three Robin Hood films and they were all good. The advantage of films is that you can see it all happening. They make history come to life. In books it all seems dead!

Can you write this part of Paul's report? Start like this:
Thomas **told me** he wasn't interested … He said he thought it … He said he didn't …

2 → E Children at work in the 19th century

In the industrial towns in the North of England, life for most of the population was terrible. Before the Factory Acts of the 1840s became law, inspectors were sent by the government to make reports. They saw a lot of children working, and talked to some of them.

1. In a cotton mill:
Inspector: How old are you, boy?
Boy: I'll be ten at Christmas, sir.
Inspector: And how many hours do you work?
Boy: I usually work about twelve hours a day.
Inspector: Do you ever have a holiday or a day off work?
Boy: Only on Sundays, sir. I don't have to work then.
Inspector: What kind of work do you do?
Boy: Well, at the moment I'm cleaning the moving parts of one of the machines. Before that I cleaned up the floor.

2. In a coal mine:
Inspector: Aren't you too young to be down here?
Girl: I don't know. I'm eight. A lot of the others are younger. My sister is six – and she's going to start work down in the mine soon.
Inspector: What time do you start in the morning?
Girl: I left home at four this morning. Sometimes it's earlier.
Inspector: And when will you go home tonight?
Girl: They usually let us go at five.
Inspector: Do you feel frightened here in the dark?
Girl: Sometimes I do. Then I sing a bit – so I don't feel so lonely.

Can you write these parts of the inspector's report? Start like this:
First I went to one of the cotton mills and talked to a small boy who was working there. I asked him how old …

1 → E Synonyms

Synonyms are words with the same (or nearly the same) meaning as other words, so *terrible* and *awful* are synonyms. *Replace the underlined words in these sentences by synonyms.*

1. During the Industrial Revolution, machines were powered by steam for the first time. 2. Life for most of the people, especially in the North of England, changed quickly. 3. The factory owners gave work to thousands of women and children – because this was less expensive. 4. Many of these factories were cotton mills, where cloth was produced. 5. Mining became one of Britain's most important industries, because coal was needed in the factories. 6. The dark and dirty industrial towns of the North made Britain "the workshop of the world". 7. But the poor people who worked in all the factories and mines, got very little money, and lived in very bad conditions. 8. Some of the new buildings for the factory workers didn't even have floors or windows.

2 → E Opposites

Complete these sentences using opposites of the underlined words.

1. Today most goods are produced by machines, but before the Industrial Revolution things were made ... . 2. For centuries, country people's way of life had more or less stayed the same. Then suddenly things began to ... . 3. The mills were built with large windows, so that even on short winter days it would be light inside from morning till evening. But in the coal-mines where ... children had to work ... hours, it was always ... . 4. Employers in those days did little to make conditions safe for their workers. Factories were very ... places to work in. 5. But it was better for the children in the mills than in the coal-mines. There conditions were even ... . 6. High prices made it difficult, too. Even when whole families were working, ... wages meant that it still wasn't ... to survive.

3 Odd one out

The 'odd one out' is something or someone that is different from the rest of a group.
Example: people – soldier – population – class – army. 'Soldier' is the 'odd one out' because a soldier is an individual person and not a group of people.

a) *Find the 'odd one out' in these groups and try to explain why it doesn't belong to the rest of the group. (Use a dictionary for the picture.)*

1. century – year – month – history – age
2. ship – locomotive – truck – mill – train
3. rebellion – revolution – conquest – invention – invasion
4. steam – oil – wind – water – factory
5. ox – mutton – calf – cow – pig
6. miserable – overworked – gloomy – beautiful – grim
7. king – monk – engineer – nobleman – peasant
8. to walk – to march – to drive – to run – to crawl

b) *Can you make an 'Odd one out' exercise for your class?*

1 Dingo

From all the dogs roaming the world, unwanted, unloved, I had to give my affection to a dingo, the wild dog of the Australian outback. As a pup she showed no sign of the killer instinct of the dingo, the reason they are hated, hunted, trapped and poisoned on the big cattle and sheep stations. Call a man a dingo down under and he'll feel wounded for life; it's the most terrible insult.

Riding in the Georgina country, I came upon this pup. Mine was a lonely job but a good one, that is if you enjoy the wide open spaces of outback Australia, which I did. I got to know and love every tree: the Coolibar, Gum, Box. Flowers would not survive the heat, but birds, budgerigars, parrots, gave colour and life as they flew around or rested on the trees.

Happily I rode the paddocks, repairing broken fences; reporting to the station manager movement of cattle; herding small mobs back to the paddock if they had strayed. I carried my tucker in the saddle bag, bread, meat, tea, and at noon, after a hard morning's riding, boiled my pot over a bushman's fire.

My home was a hut, ten miles from the station. I rode out six days a week, happy in the freedom of my life, the blue skies, the peacefulness.

I'd sat down to enjoy my break when I saw this pup. There was movement among some bushes, and a small bundle of fur came through the bush. Apart from birds and cattle, animal life in that vast countryside was rare. I called her to me and after a while she came and let me stroke her. I fed her cooled tea, which seemed to go down well. 'You're lucky,' I told her, 'you wouldn't have survived long in this heat.'

So Lucky she became. I put her on my saddle, and rode for home. I became the loving slave of my Lucky, and watched her grow. She was all a cattle dog should be, which was strange, but that's the way it goes sometimes. She was always by my side when I rode out. I fed her the best, plenty of meat and big bones. She repaid me with her love; my shadow by day, sleeping beside me at night.

She was only ten months old when the boss drove over early one morning to my hut. Lucky growled as he stood in the doorway.

We talked for a few minutes about the work in hand, and then 'Get those cleanskins in Adelaide paddock,' he told me, 'and drown that bloody dingo.' Aussies are like that, especially in the great outback. Station life is hard, serious, there's no time for playing about. If the boss gives an order it is carried out at once.

I should have known my dingo pup would never be tolerated on that cattle station; now I had to face the results of my foolishness.

Of course I couldn't do it; I could no more hurt her, drown her, shoot her, than jump off Sydney Bridge. She was everything to me. The boss, I told myself, was being very unreasonable. I climbed slowly into the saddle and rode for Adelaide paddock. Lucky ran beside me, coming to me when I whistled.

I found the cleanskins in Adelaide paddock; I approached them slowly, Lucky beside me; one false move and they'd be gone with the wind. I was excited; in that vast country you were not always lucky enough to come upon them. As I approached, they moved on. I had them now; riding, I moved them towards home. I looked for Lucky, couldn't see her. She was still a pup, it had been a long hard day, I was expecting too much from her. My work must come first.

But my eyes searched the far paddocks as I rode; I looked for movement, any sign of my pup. The paddock had no bush or tree to hide her from me. My Lucky never returned. Sadly I rode the trail to my lonely hut.

Life went on; station work is hard. My days were busy; but the hours to bedtime were long. I missed her all the time.

Life on an outback station

pup	a young dog
paddock	a piece of land where cattle or sheep are kept
tucker	Australian for 'food'
cleanskin	a young bull or cow
milker	a cow that produces milk

I was out looking for the station milkers, a small mob of Jerseys and Friesians. They'd gone through the home paddock fences, heading for that vast wilderness of far west Australia. I found them, and at the sight of me they turned and headed for home. I was moving them along when I noticed the yellow shadows behind the stragglers; a pack of dingoes who looked thin and hungry.

At a distance they circled now; this was something I'd never experienced before, although I knew the savagery of those wild dogs when hungry. They were waiting for the right moment to attack.

And then I saw my Lucky. Thinner, full grown, she ran with the mob! So she'd gone to the pack! I whistled, the old whistle she'd known so well, telling her to come to me. I fell from my saddle, holding her as she jumped into my arms, licking my face.

It was my job to protect the milkers, to get them safely home. And yet I believe, in that great moment of joy at finding my pet again, I would have left the cows for the love of that dog.

Then a group of riders galloped towards me. They were my mates from the station; now, seeing the danger, they were riding to help me.

Scared by the horses, the dingoes raced away, following their leader. I looked for Lucky, whistled as I saw her running to join the pack. Soon she was up with the leader, heading for the never-never land of far west Australia.

(F. Bennett – abridged and slightly adapted)

1 Reacting to the story

a) Did you *enjoy* reading the story? Try to give reasons for your opinion.
b) Look at the *setting*. Find details that give a picture of the Australian outback.
c) Look for words and phrases in the text that show the narrator's *feelings*. What do these feelings tell you about him?
d) Find the moments of *decision* in the story. Explain who makes the decisions, why, and what the decisions show about their characters.

2 Reading between the lines

a) 'I became the loving slave of my Lucky' (l. 45). Why does the narrator use the word *slave* here?
b) 'She was all a cattle dog should be' (l. 47). Imagine the kind of work Lucky does.
c) 'Lucky growled' (l. 55). Why?

2 From Empire to Commonwealth

Australia's ties with Britain

Modern Australia is a country of many different ethnic groups and cultures. Even though Australia has orientated itself away from Europe and more towards South East Asian and Pacific countries, it is still easy to see that it was once a British colony. The colonial influence can be seen in the names of many of the places, in the system of government and the law, and of course in the language spoken there – English. Australia has been a member of the Commonwealth of Nations since the beginning of the Commonwealth in 1926. Lately, there has been a growing movement for changing Australia from a monarchy with the British king or queen as its head of state into a republic. But even if this movement succeeds, Australia's ties with Britain will remain.

From Empire to Commonwealth

In the 17th century Britain was the greatest sea power in the world, and began to take colonies. Some of the first important colonies were in North America. Later, in the 18th and 19th centuries, parts of Africa and Asia, all of Australia and New Zealand, and many smaller islands all over the world became British. Although the American colonies had broken away in 1776, the British Empire was huge.

The Commonwealth developed naturally as Britain gave up this worldwide Empire. First, countries with a mainly British population, like Canada or Australia, were given self-government. They decided to keep their ties with the mother country. Then, when countries with people of a different ethnic background became independent – India was first, in 1947 – many of them decided to do the same. Today, 48 independent states, a quarter of the world's people and countries, belong to the Commonwealth. They are all different in size, wealth, ethnic background and culture. But because of their history, they have much in common: experiences, traditions and the English language – either as a main or a working language. Britain's monarch is recognized by all of them as Head of the Commonwealth, although he or she is head of state in only some of them. The leaders of all member countries meet every two years to discuss international problems. Just as important as the meetings between politicians, however, are the meetings between other groups of people – business and professional people, for example, or writers and artists. Sportsmen and women meet every four years at the Commonwealth Games – the 'Friendly Games' as they call them.

1. *What does modern Australia still have in common with Britain?*
2. *How did the Commonwealth develop out of the British Empire?*
3. *Do you know any typically British sports that are played in many Commonwealth countries?*
4. *Look at the Commonwealth countries on the map at the front of the book and choose one of them. Try to find some information about this country and present it to the class.*

3 Australia: A song and a recipe

1 A song: Treaty

Well I heard it on the radio,
And I saw it on the television
Back in 1988.
All those talking politicians.

Words are easy, words are cheap
Much cheaper than our priceless land
But promises can disappear
Just like writing in the sand.

Treaty, yeh. Treaty now. Treaty, yeh. Treaty now.
(Nhima Djatpangarri nhima walangwalang
Nhe Djatpayatpanhima gaya nhe
Matjini … Yakarray – nhe Djat'pa nhe walang
Gumurrtjararrk Gutjuk)

This land was never given up.
This land was never bought and sold.
The planting of the Union Jack
Never changed our law at all.
Now two rivers run their course
Separated for so long,
I'm dreaming of a brighter day
When the waters will be one.

Chorus
(Nhema Gayakaya nhe gaya nhe …)
Treaty, yeh. Treaty now. Treaty, yeh. Treaty now.
Promises disappear,
Priceless land, destiny.
Well I heard it on the radio,
And I saw it on the television,
But promises can disappear
Just like writing in the sand.

Chorus

1. What is the 'message' of the song?
2. Why was 1988 a special date in Australia's history?

2 Pavlova

This wonderful recipe is very popular in Australia and New Zealand. It's great for parties – and very easy to make!

You will need (for 6 people):

- 3 large eggs (egg whites only)
- 180 g very fine sugar
- 350–400 g soft summer fruits (raspberries, strawberries, redcurrants)
- 300 g whipped cream
- Baking paper

Beat the egg whites until they are stiff. (To test: Turn the bowl upside down. If the egg whites are stiff enough, they'll stay in!)
Now slowly add the sugar – one spoon at a time. Beat well each time, until all the sugar is in.
Spread the mixture on the baking paper, in the form of a circle (Ø 20 cm).
Make it flat in the middle, but make little 'mountains' all the way round the sides.
Heat the oven to 150° (fan oven: 120–130°). When it is hot, put the Pavlova in, and immediately turn the heat down to 140° (fan oven: 110–120°). After 1 hour, turn the oven off, but leave the Pavlova in the oven until it is cold. (This way, it will dry out well – it mustn't be sticky inside!) If you make it the day before your party, leave it in the oven all night (after you've turned it off).
To serve: Take the Pavlova off the baking sheet and put it on a plate. Fill it with whipped cream, and put the fruit on top. Cut into pieces – like a cake.
(Or you can make 'mini' Pavlovas – one for each person. The method is exactly the same.)

1 How's the job then?

Graeme, 16, has left school and has started his training in a big supermarket.

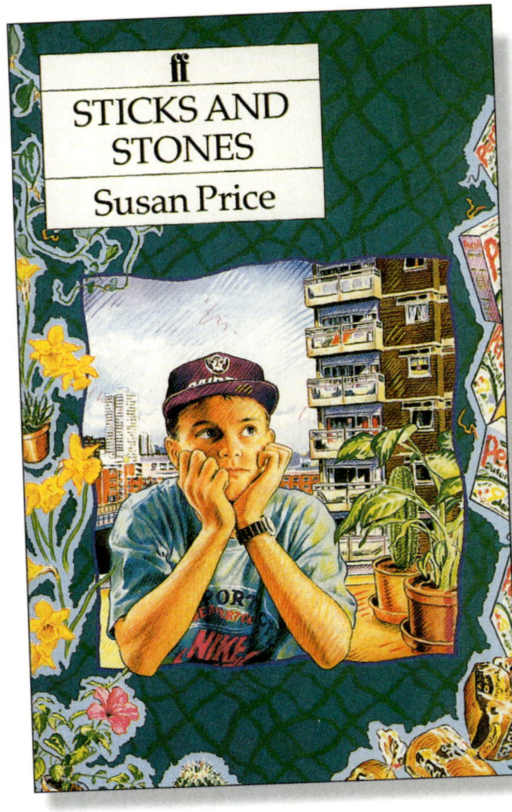

The firm's own soap-powders were on special offer, and the boss wanted a big display of them. I opened a box, and priced them, and I stacked them up. I looked at my watch. Five past eleven. Roll on twelve. Or, better still, five o'clock.

I don't like this job much. I like the people – but I'm not so strong on the job. Almost everything I do, I could do without thinking, and that means I have to think of something else, which is fine if you have something else.

If you haven't, you get bored.

Dad keeps saying it'll be better when I've passed the exams, and I'm qualified to be a manager, but that isn't all the training you get. That just gets you ready for the next stage, if you're chosen for that. After I pass the exam, if I pass, I'll still be a sixteen-year-old kid, and I'll be stuck with stacking soap-powders.

I might never get a job as a manager.

I opened another box. I'd never wanted this job. Only I'd left school and had no job to go to. The Labour sent me after two jobs I didn't get, and then Dad came home and said he'd rung up the manager of Bancroft's, the supermarket, and I was to go the next day for an interview. It took me about ten minutes to get the job and I've been here ever since. I never fancied it – but I had to get a job. And after I'd got it – well – Dad doesn't approve of people who keep changing their jobs. He doesn't like it. I know I'd better not get any ideas about changing my job.

At work, I always feel sleepy. There are no windows except at the front of the shop. Where I work, up at the other end, if they switch the lights out at mid-day, it's pitch-black. And the building's all concrete and tiles. Like being buried alive eight hours a day. You forget what daylight's like and you're surprised when you go out. And then you get this feeling that it'll be dark soon and all the day's gone while you've been shut up in there, and that all your life's going the same way – in working.

I had been going to eat my sandwiches up here, but now I thought I'd go to the park. It's just across the road, behind the shop. The gardener was there. He looked up.

"Hello. Haven't seen you for a week or two, have I? How's the job then?"

"Oh, it's all right," I said. "There's worse. I've been stacking soap-powders all this morning."

"Oh, that sounds like boring work to me."

"I do get a bit fed up sometimes. It's all sort of shut in, see. It's dark – all electric light. Makes your eyes tired."

He chewed his egg sandwiches. "What you want is a job in the open. Wouldn't you like to work outside?"

"Well – yeah – I would … I wouldn't know what to do. Well – I wouldn't want to work on a building-site – that'd be as bad as stacking soap-powders – and – well, what else is there?"

He sat up suddenly. "I work outside, don't I?"

"Well, I couldn't get a job as a gardener."

"Why not? Have you got greenfly?"

I rolled over on my back, laughing. "No – I don't think so – but, you know, I wouldn't know where to go or anything –"

"Just go to the Labour and tell them you'd like to be a park gardener – they'll help you out. I used to have an assistant, but he left. Job's been open for months now. They don't like it, you see, these youngsters, the money's not much. You can earn more in a factory."

"Gardening – that'd be great."

"Well," he said. "It's worth thinking about. If you don't like that job."

"I don't." I thought about it. "My dad wouldn't like it," I said. "He doesn't like people to change their jobs. He'd stop me."

"He couldn't once you're eighteen."

"That's two years."

"Isn't long to wait."

Wasn't long to wait? Two years. It was endless. I could be dead.

I should never have gone to the park. After being in the sunshine I couldn't settle to working in the stock-room.

Park gardening. I really liked that idea. I couldn't think why it hadn't come to me before. I could have said, "I want to be a park gardener." But I don't suppose Dad would have let me. But there's me – I've been growing date-stones and orange-pips in cups since I was six. But I never thought of being a gardener. I suppose it's because you don't expect to enjoy your work.

I suppose if I'd told that careers officer that I liked growing things, he'd have said, "What about being a park gardener, then?" But I didn't tell him. He didn't seem to be the kind of bloke who'd be interested in rosemary in pots in the kitchen. And I wasn't interested in any of his ideas. They sent me to see him five times. We just talked round in circles, never getting anywhere. And then he'd say, "Well, go away and think about it." And away I'd go, thankful to have got him off my back again. So it's partly my fault I'm stuck in this job.

Not that I think Dad would have let me be a park gardener – not for a thousand careers officers.

(From: Susan Price, *Sticks and Stones*)

a) *Finish the sentences.*

1. Graeme has just started his … in a …
2. Although he likes the …, he finds the job …
3. He could become a manager if he …
4. When he is at work he feels … because …
5. He got the job because his father …
6. Graeme's father won't be pleased if …
7. One day, Graeme goes to the … to eat his …
8. The gardener says he should …
9. Graeme thinks the idea is …
10. The careers officer couldn't help Graeme because …

b) *Work in pairs. Write a dialogue between Graeme and his father. Start like this:*

Graeme: Dad, I've got something important to tell you.

2 Are you obsessed with your work?

Can you handle the pressure or do you crack?

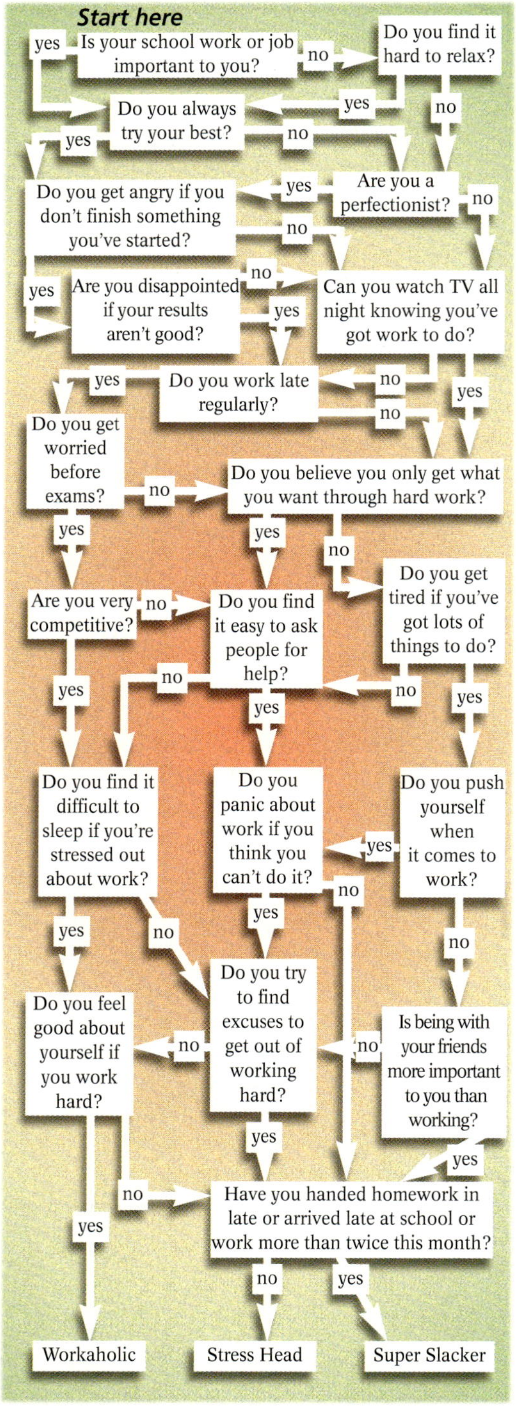

From: *Bliss* (slightly adapted)

WORKAHOLIC
You are obsessed with getting the best results, but this means you spend too much time working and not enough time having fun.
Action plan: Relax and enjoy yourself more. You don't have to be perfect all the time!

"STRESS HEAD"
You worry too much about work.
Action plan: When you're not working, you should try to think of something else. Do as much work as you can in the time you've got, and then forget about it.

"SUPER SLACKER"
Hard work is just not important for you, is it? Be careful, or life will pass you by.
Action plan: Set yourself some goals. If you go on being lazy, you're never going to get what you want or where you want to be.

3 Carol Raymond, a ferry worker

This is an authentic interview made on a Channel ferry.

What's it like working on a Channel ferry?

I run the coffee shop now. I order beverages, sandwiches and other foods and make sure that everything is fresh. I also make the coffee and the tea, serve the customers and keep the shop clean. When it's very busy someone helps me.
I work 84 hours a week. My working week goes from Thursday to Thursday, and I work 12 hours a day. I live on the ferry during this time. I have my own room and there are sports and entertainment facilities, although I'm usually too tired at the end of my shift to do anything. Then the next week I'm off work. I always work one week and then I'm off one week. I have a small place in Dover now, although I'm actually from London. Well, and I live in Dover when I'm not on the ferry. Having a whole week off every other week is great although at first I was a bit lost. You see, all my friends were on board – we're a very close group. But now I have a set of friends on shore, too. My boyfriend is on board, though, and there can be problems when we're not on the same shift. In fact, a lot of married people who've done this kind of work for a number of years get divorced.

Do you need any special skills for this kind of work?

Not really. You just have to be willing to work hard and put up with this lifestyle. But of course it does help if you know a foreign language like French or German. The only real training I received was in life saving and survival. We had to go through the whole survival training programme. That was really something.

What about the pay?

Well, one good thing about this job is that I'm in the UK for only half a year. The rest of the time I'm on board. So I don't have to pay any tax. They deduct it, but I get everything back at the end of the year. So all in all, the pay is pretty good.
Another good thing is that I get cheap travel in my time off. Next week I'm going to Alicante, and it will only cost me £25. The company will pay the rest. Pretty good, isn't it? I guess I really like this kind of work, but if I ever want to have a family, I'm not so sure I'll keep on doing it.

1. What are the good points and the bad points about Carol's job?
2. What personal qualities and what qualifications must one have to do Carol's job?

4 A song: Money

Money, getaway
Get a good job with more pay and you're OK
Money it's a gas
Grab that cash with both hands and make a stash
New car, caviar, four star daydream,
Think I'll buy me a football team
Money get back
I'm all right Jack keep your hands off my stack
Money it's a hit
Don't give me that do goody-good bullshit
I'm in the hi-fidelity first class travelling set
And I think I need a Lear jet
Money it's a crime
Share it fairly but don't take a slice of my pie
Money so they say
Is the root of all evil today
But if you ask for a rise it's no surprise that they're giving none away

1 Coal

a) The development of industry during the nineteenth century made Britain rich. But the factories depended on coal, and for the poor people who worked long hours in the coal-mines life was terrible. Underground it was hot and dark, and the air was full of dust. Miners often had to walk more than a mile to get to the coal face. There they had to work on their knees with picks and shovels.

Usually ponies were used to pull the waggons of coal through the galleries of the mine. But if a gallery was too low for ponies, women and children had to drag the waggons along the railway lines instead. Many people lost their lives in accidents or in earth falls in the mines. Even if they were not killed in this way, working in such terrible conditions nearly always meant bad health and an early death.

SB **b)** *During the first part of the twentieth century miners tried to improve their conditions. But working in the old coal-mines remained a hard and dangerous job, as this story from the 1950s shows ...*

Somewhere in the half mile of rock, earth and coal which lay between the Elbow gallery of the Johnson coal-mine and the surface of the earth there had been a subsidence. It did not show on the surface. Up there everything was normal. The women were hard at work sorting the coal. They were talking happily because it was Saturday morning and very soon they would finish for the weekend.

The Elbow gallery was the oldest gallery in the mine. It had never been possible to mechanise it. Hundreds of tons of rock were now pressing very heavily on part of it.

Further down the gallery six men were putting coal into waggons, while a seventh man, Jud, was getting his pony Moses ready to take away some more waggons that were already full. Moses pulled, and slowly the wheels began to turn over the railway lines.

Jud stepped on ahead, and the shadows jumped as his lamp moved. It was like any other of the many thousands of journeys they had made together until they reached the Elbow. Here, where the gallery turned right, Jud suddenly stopped and looked back.

'What's wrong with you?' he asked, and lifted his lamp to look back at his pony. Moses had stopped, and his ears were laid back, while his eyes rolled as if he was scared. 'Come on, boy.'

But Moses did not move, and when Jack tried to lead him, the pony grabbed Jud's arm in his teeth.

'Ow ...!' As Jud pulled away there was suddenly a roar. Jud threw himself backwards. Dust flew in the air, and the ground shook as hundreds of tons of rocks crashed down into the Elbow gallery.

For what seemed hours the roar went on. Really it was only minutes. Jud lay on his back. When he had thrown himself backwards he had hit his head against one of the coal waggons. His lamp had been broken and he lay in complete darkness.

From the coal face came shouts. Jud began to sit up. Lights were dancing and jumping as his six workmates ran up.

'Jud … Jud … where are you? JUD!' Their faces were like ghosts in the light of their helmet lamps. They were relieved when Jud got slowly to his feet.

'Another step or two, Jud, and you'd have had it,' one of the men said. He shone his lamp on the rocks which were blocking the gallery. 'What an escape, eh?'

'I wouldn't be here if Moses hadn't stopped me. He must have known something. Maybe he heard it. He bit me! First time he's ever done that. He didn't want me to go on into the Elbow.'

'Well, he's all right.' One of the others was kneeling by the side of Moses 'He's got a stone on his leg … but there's nothing else wrong with him.'

Jud went across to his pony. Water was flooding into the gallery now as they moved the stone and lifted Moses to his feet. A black river was racing out from under the rocks. The others went back to the coal face for picks, shovels and their coats. There was bad news when they came back. The big pipe which brought fresh air to the gallery had been broken by the fall in the Elbow. No more air was coming in. They were cut off in every way. Even if the water did not drown them, they would not last very long down there without fresh air.

'Of course they'll soon start digging for us,' someone said. 'Till then let's do a bit for ourselves.'

Three of the six lamps were switched off to save the batteries, and the men took it in turns to attack the rock. They stopped every few minutes to listen for sounds on the other side, but several hours had passed before they heard the far-off sound of a pick.

Excitedly they stood and listened while the oldest man there tapped with his pick on a large stone. Sound travels well through the earth, and they had to get news to the other side that they were still alive. It took half an hour of tapping to get a message from the rescue team. When that message was translated, the faces of the men grew even more serious. The fall blocked a large part of the Elbow. Ninety feet of rock and earth lay between them and safety. All the time the water was getting deeper …

(From 'Half a Mile Down' by Arthur Catherall, adapted)

- *Talk in class about how the story might go on. Think of different endings. Then listen to the recording to find out how the author ends his story.*
- *Write a newspaper article about what happened. Choose the author's or your own ending. (Remember what you learned on page 38 about writing an article.)*

2 North Sea oil

Britain started to extract and export North Sea oil in 1975. On the whole, this has been very positive for Britain's economy, especially for the economic development of Scotland. In the region around Aberdeen lots of new jobs have been created. Roads, housing and all kinds of facilities have been improved or newly built.
But, of course, the extraction of oil has its problems, too. What to do with used oil platforms, for example? Environmental activists still remember the fight about the Brent Spar in 1995 ...

a) *May 1st 1995*

PROTESTERS OCCUPY OIL PLATFORM

Four Greenpeace protesters occupied a North Sea oil platform 120 miles northeast of Shetland yesterday. The action is part of a campaign to stop the dumping of the platform at sea. The Brent Spar, which belongs to Shell, was used to store oil from the Brent field. Now the oil is piped ashore, and the platform has not been used since 1991.
Greenpeace says that the platform contains toxic materials, and that the four protesters will stay on board 'until September if necessary'.
A spokesperson for Shell said, 'They have made their protest. Now the group should leave.'

(From 'The Times', 1.5.1995)

b) *February 23rd 1998*

Brent Spar, the oil platform that has become a symbol of the fight between environmental protesters and the oil industry, will finally come to rest in Norway. The 14,500 ton platform will be taken to pieces and used as part of a new harbour for a ferry.
It has taken more than two years to find a final resting place for the platform since Greenpeace forced Shell to drop plans to dump it at sea. The company was boycotted in parts of Europe. Opposition was especially strong in Germany.
Taking the Brent Spar out of service has cost £20 million. Cutting up the platform will cost a further £26 million.

1. Why do you think Shell wanted to dump the Brent Spar at sea?
   - Why didn't Greenpeace want them to do this?
   - What happened to the Brent Spar in the end? Why?
2. Think what other environmental campaigns you have heard/read about. Choose one campaign and prepare a short talk.
   - Explain what the campaign is (was) about.
   - Describe what action the campaigners took (are taking).
   - Report if the campaign was (or you think it will be) successful.

3 Poem: 'The Battery Hen', by Pam Ayres

Pam Ayres writes humorous poems. She comes from the southwest of England, where some people speak English differently from the way you have learned it. Watch out for strange verb forms – for example, 'you has', 'I lays', 'they rolls' – and also for 'me' instead of 'my'.
Sometimes the word order is different from usual, too.

Oh, I am a battery hen,
On me back there's not a germ,
I never scratched a farmyard,
And I never pecked a worm.
I never had the sunshine
To warm me feathers through.
Eggs I lay. Every day,
For the likes of you.

When you has them scrambled,
Piled up on your plate,
It's me what you should thank for that.
I never lays them late,
I always lays them reg'lar,
I always lays them right,
I never lays them brown,
I always lays them white.

But it's no life for a battery hen.
In me box I'm sat,
A funnel stuck out from the side,
Me pellets comes down that.
I gets a squirt of water,
Every half a day,
Watchin' with me beady eye,
Me eggs roll away.
I lays them in
a funnel,
Strategically
placed,
So that I don't kick 'em
And let them go to waste.
They rolls off down the tubing
And up the gangway quick,
Sometimes I gets to thinkin',
'That could have been a chick!'

I might have been a farmyard hen,
Scratchin' in the sun,
There might have been a crowd of chicks
After me to run.
There might have been a cockerel fine
To pay us his respects,
Instead of sittin' here,
Till someone comes and wrings our necks.

I see the Time and Motion clock
Is sayin' nearly noon.
I 'spec me squirt of water
Will come flyin' at me soon,
And then me spray of pellets
Will nearly break me leg,
And I'll bite the wire nettin'
And lay one more bloody egg.

In a chicken battery	
funnel	Trichter
pellet	a small round object (*here:* chicken food)
squirt (of water)	Spritzer (Wasser)
tubing	(Verbindungs-)Röhre
gangway	Kanal, in dem die Eier abtransportiert werden
wire netting	Maschengitter

On a farmyard	
to scratch	scharren
chick	a baby chicken
cockerel	woman <-> man hen <-> ~

1. *Use details from the poem to compare the life of a battery hen with the life of a farmyard hen.*
2. *Do you think it is good to write a humorous poem about a topic like this?*

Hereward at King William's court

There are a lot of stories about Hereward, a young Englishman who leads a rebellion against William the Conqueror. Hereward is from the Fens, the flat, wet area of Eastern England. In this story he is in Ely, which was then an island. King William attacks the island, but is beaten off.

William made sure that it was quite impossible to enter or leave the island. Hereward's people were frightened, not knowing what was going to happen, or how William might attack them next. They decided to send a man to Brandon, where the king and all his men were, to see what he could find out. Hereward wanted to go himself, although they all said it was too dangerous. But he started off, taking with him his horse, Swallow. Swallow looked ugly and awkward, but was very fast. Before Hereward left, he changed his clothes, cut his hair and beard and put on an old cloak. He was sure no-one would recognize him. Along the way he met a potter. Hereward gave him some money for all his pots and the man helped him to put them on Swallow. Hereward made his way to Brandon and looked for somewhere to sleep. He came to the house of an old woman. There was another old woman there as well. That night Hereward heard them discussing in French how they were going to use witchcraft to destroy the English in Ely. (They thought Hereward was a poor, simple man and did not understand the French language. He understood them, and he wasn't so simple that he believed in their witchcraft.)

Early next morning Hereward put the pots on Swallow again and went to the king's court. He called out, "Pots, pots, good pots! All first-class pots!" After a while some servants led him into the kitchen to show his pots there. By bad luck a man from the town was there, too. He shouted that he had never seen a man who looked so much like Hereward, the famous fighter. Other people came to look at this potter. He was even led into the king's hall among the knights, so they could see him. This was getting dangerous! The knights looked at him closely, but some of them said that this man couldn't be brave and daring like Hereward: he wasn't tall enough! One knight asked the potter if he had ever seen the real Hereward. Hereward replied: "I wish I had him here among us now! I hate him! He stole my cow, four sheep, and everything I had, except for my pots and my old horse!"

Now orders were given for the king's dinner to be prepared, and Hereward returned to the kitchen, where he felt safer. After dinner the servants, cooks, and kitchen-boys drank a lot of wine and they decided to have some fun with this potter who looked like the famous Hereward. They all stood close around him and some of them tried to cut off his hair. Hereward was beginning to get worried. He just wanted to get out of there alive. Then they thought of something better. Before Hereward knew what was happening they had put a blindfold on him. He couldn't see what they were doing but he heard the sound of pots being put down. The kitchen-boys, full of wine and not very safe on their feet, were putting his unsold pots on the floor all around him.

"Here, potter," one of the cooks called. "Here's a pot of wine for you. Come over here." They all laughed.

Hereward knew that if he moved he would break some of the pots, and that a real potter would not want to do that. They kept shouting to him, but Hereward did not move. When he didn't want to play this game with them, one of them came and hit him hard. This was too much for Hereward, who took off the blindfold and hit him back. Then the man's friends all attacked him together. Grabbing a piece of wood from near the fire, Hereward defended himself against them all. But in the end he was caught and taken prisoner.

One of the guards came up to him carrying his sword in one hand and iron chains in the other. Hereward grabbed the guard and attacked him with his own sword. Free again, he ran into the lower yard of the house, where he found Swallow. As he jumped on the horse's back and rode out of the gate, the guard at the gate shouted to the king's servants to follow him. But they were too slow, and Swallow was so fast that, travelling through the night by the light of the moon, Hereward reached Ely early the next morning.

Hereward continued to fight against William, but in the end the English lost. In 1083 the Normans began to build a new cathedral on the island of Ely.

1 What the story doesn't tell us

The story tells us what happens, but it doesn't always tell us what people were thinking and why they did things. What do you think?

1. Why did Hereward want to go to Brandon himself?
2. In Brandon, Hereward found out about the witches. Why didn't he then go back to Ely?
3. Why didn't Hereward just say "No, I haven't" when he was asked if he had ever seen the real Hereward? Why does he say "I wish I had him here among us now …?"
4. Hereward could have left the kitchen while the dinner was prepared. Why did he stay there?
5. Why didn't Hereward fight when they put the blindfold on him?

2 Cooking for an army

William the Conqueror invaded Britain with an army. They brought with them not just horses and swords but food and drink and people to cook for them. *Look at these pictures from the Bayeux Tapestry and say what and how they cooked.*

1

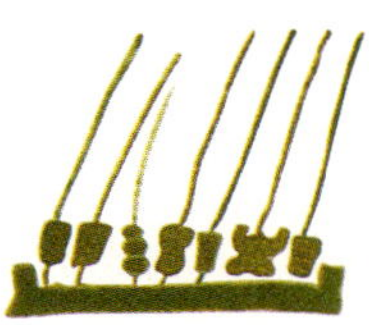

2

3

4

1 What kind of reader are you?

Write down your answers to this questionnaire for British pupils in your exercise book – to find out exactly what kind of reader you *are.*

What kind of reader are you?

1 When did you last read a book?
(a) a long time ago
(b) within the last month
(c) within the last week

2 Who was it by?
(a) I don't know
(b) I can't remember
(c) I can tell you

3 What was it about?
(a) I don't know
(b) I vaguely know
(c) I can tell you in detail

4 Why did you read it?
(a) told to read it at school
(b) given it as a present
(c) I wanted to

5 Did you finish it?
(a) no
(b) I pretended I had
(c) yes

6 Did you enjoy it?
(a) Not at all
(b) it was OK
(c) yes

7 Do you have a favourite author or authors?
(a) no
(b) I used to have
(c) yes

8 How many books do you own?
(a) one or two
(b) at least five
(c) ten or more

9 If someone gave you a £5.00 book token today would you ...?
(a) try to sell it for £2.50
(b) have a vague idea of what you might buy
(c) buy something you know that you want to get

10 How do you read newspapers and magazines?
(a) look at the pictures
(b) flip through and read what catches my eye
(c) start at the front and read all the way through

11 What reading do you do in other subjects?
(a) as little as possible
(b) what I'm told to
(c) I use reading to find extra information

12 Do you have a hobby or interest which encourages you to read?
(a) no
(b) I have had in the past
(c) yes

13 Do the rest of your family read much?
(a) no
(b) occasionally
(c) regularly

14 When did you last visit your local library?
(a) can't remember
(b) in the last year
(c) in the past month

How did you score?

If most of your answers were (c)s: you're probably too good to be true! It shows that you often read, and enjoy reading – two important things. You need to make sure that you don't get 'stuck' in one kind of reading.
If most of your answers were (a)s: you don't enjoy reading and you don't see why you should read. You may find reading difficult as well. Finding the right books to start with is going to be your next problem: your teacher should be able to advise you.
If most of your answers were (b)s: you're a lazy reader. You need to find a few really good stories to read and then start to enjoy reading.

2 Rap music

Like many other styles of popular music, rap was originally black American music. The first rappers were young blacks in New York. Their music was the folk music of the street in the late 1970s and the early 1980s. They came from a background of soul, disco and African-Caribbean music, but then they started to use jive-talk and rhymes, with the result that they created a whole new style and sound. The city rap grew as part of the hip-hop culture, which had started with black teenagers in the ghettos of New York. Soon young people in other places heard it, too, and rap began to spread …

Because rap started with young city people in poor areas, the MCs often delivered a social 'message'. But there are several different categories of rap. Here is how Kurtis Blow, one of the first successful rappers, describes them:

'There's the ego-trip rapper who tells you how bad they are.'

'The inspirational rapper offers a message with his rap – positive messages.'

'There's gossip rap where they talk about each other.'

'There's the party-time rapper.'

'There's the political-message rapper.'

'There's the informative rap, which basically gives out information about a subject like basketball.'

- *What rappers and rap music do you know? Maybe you can bring some rap music to school and play it in class. Talk about what category of rap it is.*
- *Make your own rap. Find suitable music and write lyrics to go with it.*

3 Spotlight on sport

The text on these two pages is from a book by Dennis Rodman, an American basketball star with a 'crazy, bad boy' image ...

1. *What impression of Rodman do you get from the text? Try to explain your opinion – it might help to pick out words or phrases from the text.*

sees things realistically?

has a high opinion of himself?

crazy?

irresponsible?

cool?

only wants money?

...?

I make $2.5 million a year. Nobody is going to feel sorry for me because of that, and nobody should. But the people also need to understand the kind of money out there. The NBA is a billion-dollar business. They're filling arenas all over the place. Walk into any mall in any city in the United States and you'll see at least three stores selling NBA jerseys, shorts, baseball caps. The money is there for some people, but for others the door is closed. I make a lot of money, but I'm way in the back of the NBA's money train.

I've learned something through all the years of diving for balls: People want excitement, enjoyment, and a winning team. They also want something different. From the first time I colored my hair, I knew that. I walked out onto the court in San Antonio with bleach-blond hair, and right away I saw how much those **PEOPLE LOVED WHAT DENNIS RODMAN WAS GIVING THEM**. The excitement was right there, right now. That's what this game is all about, and all I ask is that somebody see it and appreciate it.

I feel **I've been used for the past four or five years** to provide entertainment to the fans and money to the league owners. They used me for marketing in San Antonio, because they knew I was popular with the fans. Other teams did the same thing. When we were on the road, you could watch the commercials for the other team and hear them telling people, 'Come out and watch Dennis Rodman and the San Antonio Spurs.' Same thing on the radio.

They didn't have a problem with me being *WILD AND CRAZY* when it came time to fill the arenas.

They don't think I'm the right kind of **family man** or **role model** or **LOCKER-ROOM LEADER**.

There's something in that I don't understand.

I thought all along I was a basketball player.

I thought that was the only thing that mattered. You don't pay me to be a guardian angel, to go to team picnics and kiss everbody's kids. You pay me to play this game. If I do that, it should be good enough.

With me it never is good enough. **I'M NOTHING MORE THAN A SPORTS SLAVE.** If it's going to be all about money, then I might as well try to get what I'm worth. Some guys take the NBA's money for their soul. Sorry, but I can't do it that way.

It seems the one time other players want to talk to me is when they decide it's time to preach to me.

The ridiculous thing about these 'NBA stars' worrying about the example I set for kids is the response I get from the kids. It's the complete opposite of everything I hear from the league and its so-called important players.

Kids tell me, 'I think you're so cool.'

I don't hear, 'I think you're a great basketball player.'

To me it means they're getting something from me that isn't completely or only about basketball.

I'm not trying to be a role model. I know I'm in a position where I should be one, but I'm not. I can't put myself up there and tell kids they should do things the way I do them. I know my way isn't for everybody, and **I would hope that everybody has an easier road to success than I had.** I figure the only thing I can do is show that I care about people and that you can be in the public spotlight and still be true to yourself.

(from: *Bad as I wanna be* by Dennis Rodman)

2. *Talk about other famous sports stars you know of.*
   – *Give examples to show if it is necessary to be 'wild' or 'crazy' to hit the headlines, or if success is enough.*
   – *Comment on how an image like Rodman's can be an advantage or a disadvantage.*

3. *Discuss whether sports stars should try to be good role models.*
   – *Think who else in the public spotlight has an influence on young people. In what way?*

1 Child labour in factories and mines

At the time of the Industrial Revolution only very few children went to school. By the age of seven children were expected to work. Working conditions were particularly bad in the coal-mines. In the early 1830s there were several government investigations. This is what some people told the parliament inspectors:

My boy, Edwin, was well known for being lively and straight before he went to the mill. And after three years he was weak in his knees and it was so bad that he could hardly walk. Many people told me to take him away but I was a poor man with a large family and needed the wages.

I push tubs of coal. The bald place on my head is made by thrusting the tubs. I push the tubs a mile and more underground and back; they weigh three hundredweight; I push eleven a day. The coal-diggers that I work for beat me with their hands if I am not quick enough. I am the only girl in the pit. There are about twenty boys and fifteen men.

They are called 'trappers'. They sit in a little hole and open and shut doors. They are in the pit the whole time it is worked, frequently about twelve hours a day. They sit in the dark, often with a damp floor. Their ages vary from five to ten years.

Gradually Parliament passed a series of laws to improve working conditions:

1833	**TEXTILES**	**No child workers under 9 years of age.**
1842	**COAL-MINING**	**No women or children may work underground.**
1844	**TEXTILES**	**Children 8–13 years may work six-and-a-half hours a day.**
1847	**TEXTILES**	**Women and children under 18 years of age may not work more than ten hours a day.**
1867	**AGRICULTURE**	**No child may be employed under the age of 8 years.**
1901	**ALL INDUSTRIES**	**Minimum working age: 12 years.**

In present-day Britain it is illegal to employ children under the age of thirteen. Once they are thirteen, children are allowed to do small jobs like paper rounds, babysitting etc. But they have to stay at school until they are sixteen. After that, they can take up a full-time job.

1. *Describe what the children had to do in the mills and factories. Why did they have to work?*
2. *Can you imagine why laws were made that gradually improved working conditions?*
3. *Try to find out what the law says about child labour in Germany.*

2 And today?

"Dust from the chemical powders and strong vapours in both the storeroom and the boiler room were obvious … We found 250 children, mostly below the age of ten working in a long hall. Row upon row of children, some barely five years old …"

A report about child labour during the Industrial Revolution, in Britain? No, it's from a 1990 report on the matchstick-making industry in India. But the reasons why these children work are the same: Their families are large and poor, and they have to earn their share of the family income.

For employers it is cheaper to give work to children, especially to girls, who earn even less than boys. And children aren't organized in trade unions which could defend their rights and fight for better working conditions.

In some countries, children have to work to pay for their school. But sometimes these schools are so bad that the children prefer working instead of going to school.

Quite often it is very difficult to get reliable data on child labour: Lots of children aren't registered when they are born, so it is hard to tell how old they are when they start working. And lots of children, especially girls, work in private homes – as housemaids, for example. Working conditions are particularly hard for those children. There aren't any statistics for that kind of labour, so it's difficult to do anything about it.

1. *Look at the photos of children at work. Can you explain what jobs they are doing?*
2. *What do you think can be done to stop child labour in the world?*

1 Tenses

1 The way the Aussies do it

a) *Put in the right tenses of the verbs.*

present tense | past perfect | past tense | will-future | present perfect

There ... once a British farmer who ... the UK and ... to live in Australia. There he ... a small sheep farm, which ... about the same size as the farm he ... back home. After some time ..., he ... an Australian citizen. "Right," he ..., "I ... here for quite a long time now, and I ... to feel like a real Aussie. From now on I ... everything the way the Aussies ... it!"

Next day he ... a big Australian sheep-shearing company that he ... of, and ... them to send some men out to shear his sheep. The voice on the other end of the phone (a very Australian voice) ..., "Yeah, well, we ... pretty busy at the moment. The 'A' team (our 24-man team) ... out on the Riverina. They still ... another 22 thousand to shear, so it ... them two weeks or so yet. And the 'B' team (our 19-man team) ... just ... on the Darling Downs, with 13 thousand to shear. But I ... sure we ... it somehow. Now, let's see – er, how many sheep ... there on your station?"

"42."

"Thousand?"

"No – individual sheep."

The voice at the other end ... at first. Then the man ..., with a break in his voice, "Can I have their names?"

be – leave – go
start – be
have
pass – become – think – be
begin
do – do
phone
hear – ask
say – be
work
have – take
start
be – manage
be
not answer – say

(From: P. Shindler, 100 Favourite After-Dinner Stories)

b) *How well can you remember the story? Close your book and try to retell the story to a partner. Be careful with the tenses.*

2 Experiences you've had

Find out about each other's experiences. Work in groups. First prepare a list of questions you'd like to ask. Then interview the others in your group. Make a note of the answers. Then give the class the results of your survey. Example:

1. 'Have you ever stayed up all night?'
   'Yes, I have. It was when I went to a rock concert near Frankfurt with some friends. We drove all the way back after the concert – and didn't go to bed at all that night.'

I bet you've never ...! | Have you ever ...? | Have you ... yet?

Results: Our first question was: Have you ever stayed up all night? Two of the people in our group said yes. One of them went to a rock concert, the other ...

2 Conditional sentences

3 The new golf course

PLANS FOR NEW GOLF COURSE OFF RIGBY ROAD

When people saw this in their local newspaper, they didn't all react in the same way. *Match the sentence parts below and say which of these people said what.*

1. Owner of a local hotel 2. Golfer 3. Local farmer 4. Nature lover 5. Dog owner 6. Woman who lives in Rigby Road 7. Unemployed gardener

Example: 1. The owner of a local hotel said: "If more visitors **come** to this area, it'**ll be** good for business."

If	a really great course/be built	there/be work for people like me
	people/park their cars outside my house	a lot of wild animals/probably disappear
	more visitors/come to this area	I/make a lot of money
	they/want to keep the course in good condition	I/put up a 'No Parking' sign
	I/be able to sell some of my land	I/join the new club
	the public footpaths in the area/be closed off	it/be good for business
	those fields/be made into a golf course	we/not be able to go for walks there

4 Excuses

a) Everyone knows how important it is to keep fit. But it's so easy to find excuses!
Try to finish these people's excuses for them.

Example: 1. If I **had** more time, I **would go** jogging every day.

1. If I had more time, … 2. If there was a club near here, … 3. If I was good at ball games, … 4. If I didn't get tired so easily, … 5. If I had someone to go with me, … 6. If I had the money, … 7. If the swimming pool wasn't so far away, … 8. If we lived in the country, …

b) 'Healthy living' is important, too. But here again, people find excuses.
Can you finish these people's excuses, too?

1. I would eat more salads if … 2. We would grow our own vegetables if … 4. I'd buy food at the health shop if … 4. I would have a proper breakfast every day if … 5. I would use my bike more if … 6. I would go to bed earlier if …

5 Different situations – different forms

Examples: 1. Hurry up! If we **leave** now, we'**ll get** to the station in time.
2. I'm too old! If I **was** 2 years younger, **I'd take** part in the junior play.

3. Great weather! If it … (be) still hot on Saturday, I … (go) to the beach. 4. Sorry I can't come. If I … (have) time, I … (spend) the day with you. 5. Too expensive! If these jeans … (be) cheaper, I … (buy) them. 6. Let's go to the cinema. If you … (like) love stories, you … (enjoy) this film! 7. I can't speak French. If I … (understand) the language, I … (love) to go to France. 8. I really feel ill! If I … (not feel) better tomorrow, I … (stay) in bed.

3 '-ing'-forms

6 What's the difference?

Talk about what you can see in the pictures. What differences are there?

There is .../There are .../You can see ... + -ing

Example:
In picture 1 there are two children feeding the ducks. In picture 2 you can only see one child feeding them.

In the park ...

Ten minutes later ...

7 Lovely!

Say what you can see, hear or smell.

Example: 1. It's lovely out here in the garden. I can hear the birds singing!

1. It's lovely out here in the garden. (*hear*) 2. Aha! I know what's for breakfast! (*smell*)
3. What a view! (*see*) 4. It's great to be in the Alps! (*hear*) 5. We'll be off in a minute! (*see*)
6. Oh dear, that's *not* so lovely ... (*smell*)

8 What are you scared of?

We all have fears, it's quite normal. Here is a list of some of the fears lots of people have.

Talk about the fears, and how you feel about them. You can talk about people you know, too.

Making decisions	Being alone
Going for interviews	Getting old
Using the telephone	Being ill
Making new friends	Leaving home
Driving	Taking exams
Flying	Walking home in the dark
Speaking in front of a lot of people	Using lifts

Examples:
– I'm not usually afraid of making decisions.
– I really enjoy using the telephone! But my grandma hates using the telephone.

be afraid of | like | hate | enjoy | look forward to | think about

be scared of | feel nervous about | feel worried about

4 Reported speech

9 Who expects what?

a) Could this be YOUR parents/English (...) teacher/sister/brother/friend?

Please make your bed! Don't leave your things all over the floor! Switch the TV off! Don't have your music on so loud! Please do your homework right away. Don't use my shampoo! Will you come and help me, please? Don't be late! Learn the words for homework. Practise every day if you can. Can you lend me your new CD? Please be quiet while I'm talking!

Example: "Don't leave your things all over the floor!" – That sounds like my mother! She often tells me not to leave my things on the floor. expect tell ask ... (not) to ...

b) *Write down three or four other things that people you know often say. Then compare notes with a partner, like this:*

You: "Please help me with my Maths!" That's what my sister often says.
Partner: Really? *My* sister never **asks** me **to help** her with her Maths.

10 How disappointing!

People sometimes promise something, and later they change their minds. Here are examples.

1. *Dad:* We're going to have a great holiday this year. I've been to the travel agent's. I think we may go to Spain. Maybe we can go to the hotel Uncle Bill stayed at last year. I saw it in a catalogue. It isn't expensive.
(*Later:* Sorry, all of you, but I don't think we can afford a holiday this year ...)
2. *Friend:* I want to go to the rock concert next weekend. It'll be great. Rick will take us in the car – I've already asked him. And we can spend the night at a camping site.
(*Later:* Sorry, but I'm not going to that concert at the weekend ...)
3. *Shop assistant:* I'll be able to order the CD for you. It's no problem. It may take a little while. But we'll have it for you in ten days or so, OK?
(*Later:* Sorry, but that CD is no longer available ...)

I feel so disappointed! I can't believe it! How unfair! But why? Oh no! You can't be serious! Do you really mean it?

How would you react to these disappointing situations? Tell people how you feel – then remind them of what they said!

Example: But Dad! You can't be serious! You said we were going to have ... You told me you ...

11 After the interview

Here are some of the questions Emma was asked when she went for an interview for a part-time job in a café.

1. How old are you? 2. Have you ever worked in a café before? 3. Are you still at school? 4. Where do you live? 5. Have you told your parents about the job? 6. Will you be prepared to work on Sundays? 7. How did you hear about the vacancy? 8. Can you cook at all? 9. Do you enjoy working with other people? 10. Is this the only job you've applied for?

Later she told her boyfriend about the questions she was asked.

They asked me how old I was. And they wanted to know ... *Go on.*

⟨TRANSLATION PRACTICE⟩

1 STRATEGIES Using a dictionary

Visitor Guide **Kakadu National Park**

Crocodiles

Saltwater crocodiles are superbly adapted predators

Freshwater and saltwater crocodiles are present in the Park. Both species can be dangerous, in particular the saltwater crocodile. Consequently, you should not swim or paddle in natural waterways or allow children to play near the water's edge.

You could be placing yourself and others at risk if you clean fish or leave food waste near water. Crocodiles are known to be disturbed by dogs. People in boats should keep away from crocodiles and not harass them.

present[1] ['preznt] **I.** *adj.* **1.** (*räumlich*) anwesend, zugegen; vorhanden **2.** (*räumlich u. zeitlich*) gegenwärtig **3.** (*zeitlich*) augenblicklich, momentan **4.** vorliegend; laufend; **at the ~ time** gegenwärtig; **in the ~ case** im vorliegenden Fall; **up to the ~ time** bis zum heutigen Tage, bis heute; **be ~ at s.th.** bei e~r S anwesend, zugegen sein, e~r S beiwohnen; **all ~** alle Anwesenden *pl*; **be ~ at s.th.** bei etw (anwesend) sein; **~ company excepted** Anwesende ausgenommen; **poisonous substances ~ in the atmosphere** in der Atmosphäre vorhandene Giftstoffe; **in the ~ circumstances** unter den gegenwärtigen [*o* gegebenen] Umständen; **~ tense** Präsens *n*, Gegenwart *f*; **~ participle** Partizip *n* Präsens; **~ perfect (tense)** Perfekt *n*, zweite Vergangenheit **II.** *s* **1.** Gegenwart *f* **2.** (GRAM) Gegenwart *f*, Präsens *n*; **at ~** zur Zeit, im Augenblick; **for the ~** vorerst, vorläufig

present[2] [prɪ'zent] **I.** *tr* **1.** übergeben, überreichen **2.** schenken (*s.o. with s.th.* jdm etw) **3.** vorlegen, (vor)zeigen; aufzeigen; (*Vorschlag*) unterbreiten **4.** (*Sicht, Möglichkeit, Angriffsziel*) bieten **5.** (*Menschen*) vorstellen **6.** (RADIO, TV) präsentieren; moderieren; (THEAT) zeigen **7.** (*Gewehr*) zielen (*at* auf); **~ one's compliments to s.o.** jdm Grüße, ein Kompliment ausrichten lassen; **that ~s us with a problem** das stellt uns vor ein Problem; **~ arms!** präsentiert das Gewehr! **II.** *refl* erscheinen; (*Gelegenheit, Problem*) sich ergeben; **~ o.s. for an exam** zur Prüfung erscheinen **III.** ['preznt] *s* Geschenk *n*; **make s.o. a ~ of s.th.** jdm etw schenken; **birthday/Christmas ~** Geburtstags-/Weihnachtsgeschenk *n*

from: PONS Kompaktwörterbuch Englisch-Deutsch, Deutsch-Englisch

TIP

- Always look at the *context* carefully before you decide which meaning is correct.
- Before you look a word up, think what 'kind' of word it is: A noun? Verb? Adjective? …?
- Watch out for false friends! If you aren't sure, look it up!
- *Looking up compounds and phrases*: You'll find 'national park' under 'n' **and** 'p'. But with 'at risk', look under 'r' first.

1 Finding the right meaning

First read the information about crocodiles in Kakadu National Park. Then look especially at these words in the text.

1. present You already know two meanings for this word. What are they? Now look at the dictionary entry on the left to find out what 'present' means here. (*Think first:* Is it used as a noun or an adjective? Or as a verb even?)
2. species Use your dictionary to find out how to pronounce the word. What is the singular form? Which German word translates it best here?
3. in particular Find the meaning of this phrase. (Should you look it up under 'i' or under 'p'?)
4. paddle You can imagine what this means. But careful! It may have another meaning! Look it up and decide which German word is suitable in this context.
5. edge This word can be translated with a number of different German words. Find out which is the correct meaning here.
6. disturbed Is this a verb form? Or an adjective? Check in your dictionary which meaning fits here.
7. keep away 'Keep' has many different meanings. First guess what it means here, then look it up to check if you were right.
8. harass You can probably guess from the context what this must mean. But you'll need a dictionary for the pronunciation.

2 Same word – different meanings

Find good translations for these sentences. Your dictionary will help.

1. Sorry, I can't help you at all. I'm rather busy **at present**.
2. Just imagine! My uncle was **presented** to the Queen last week!
3. Don't bring your dog into the house, please. My mother's very **particular**.
4. I'm interested in your new models. Please send me **particulars**.
5. Their new house is on the **edge** of Sherwood Forest.
6. What on earth's the matter with Dad? He's terribly **on edge**!
7. Private: **Keep out**!
8. Your English is getting better and better. **Keep it up**!

3 Easy to understand – not so easy to pronounce

These English words look a lot like German words you know – but how are they pronounced? Guessing won't help you much! *Look them up in your dictionary, then say each word carefully. Listen to the recording to see if you got them right.*

1. kilometre 2. civilization 3. comeback 4. subtropical 5. product 6. culture 7. multimedia 8. yacht 9. final 10. basis 11. deodorant 12. technical 13. derby 14. commercial 15. vitality 16. evolution 17. budget 18. neutral

TIP
To make sure you've found the right word, doublecheck: Look up the English word you've chosen and check the meaning again.

4 Finding the right word in English

a) *What is the correct word for the context?*
As you know, one word in German sometimes has two or more meanings – and for each meaning there is a different word in English! For example, 'Platz' can be a **seat** (in a bus), a **square** (in a town), a **court** (for tennis) – or …
Use your dictionary to translate these sentences into English.

1. Bitte nehmen Sie **Platz**! 2. In der Garage ist **Platz** für zwei Autos. 3. Ich kann mir nicht **vorstellen**, was passiert ist. 4. Wir müssen uns den neuen Nachbarn **vorstellen**. 5. Mir ist **übel**. 6. Dieser Käse schmeckt nicht **übel**. 7. Die Übung ist **leicht**. 8. Keine Sorge – der Kuchen ist ganz **leicht**! 9. Er ist sehr **geschickt**. 10. Er hat uns nach Hause **geschickt**.

b) *What preposition is right in English?*
Phrases with prepositions can be difficult to translate. Very often a different preposition is used in English. *Use your dictionary to find the right prepositions. (First decide* ***which word*** *in the sentence to look up! It may be a verb, a noun, or an adjective.)*

1. Ich interessiere mich **für** Sport. 2. Meiner Meinung **nach** ist die deutsche Mannschaft stark. 3. Das ist typisch **für** dich! 4. Er sagte es nur **aus** Spaß. 5. Ich wohne noch **bei** meinen Eltern. 6. Ich warte **auf** dich – du kannst dich **auf** mich verlassen. 7. Fährst du **mit** dem Bus? Ich gehe **zu** Fuß.

c) *Careful with German compounds!*
You can't always translate German compounds word for word!
Look up these in your dictionary.
1. Staubsauger 2. Handschuhe 3. Brieftasche 4. Hörspiel 5. Katzensprung 6. Freibad 7. mutterseelenallein 8. Bombenstimmung

2 Translation exercises

5 (after Topic 1) What's hot, dry and big? Australia's outback

Translate the text into German for a travel magazine.

The road ahead is flat, the same as the road behind. On each side the grass is the colour of dried straw. This is the outback, a huge area that covers over 70 percent of Australia. Where the outback begins is open to interpretation. Several towns call themselves the gateway to the outback. One thing is certain: country that counts as outback has to be hot, dry and big. So big, in fact, that there are still a lot of places no one has been to. The cattle and sheep stations are enormous; deep into the outback, they become larger because it takes more land to feed each animal. The biggest station is bigger than the whole of Texas, or so Aussies say.

In an average year, 400,000 people visit Ayers Rock, the giant red rock the Aborigines call 'Uluru'. Famous as the world's largest rock, it sits in the red centre of the country. Compared with the many millions of visitors that travel to the Grand Canyon in Arizona each year, the numbers are small. One reason is, of course, its remote position; until only a few years ago many of the roads were unpaved, and the airport visitors could fly to was suitable only for small planes.

The outback, also called the bush and the never-never land, plays an important role in Australian life, although few Australians actually visit it. Bookstores are full of books about the outback, stories of life on remote cattle stations, or people who have found new personal energy by 'going bush.' City people buy bush-style clothes because of the lifestyle they suggest. Many of the people architects plan houses for ask especially for a bush look with natural wood and even tin roofs.

The outback is wild and strange. And that is something most people are fascinated by.

Margin notes:
- ahead: You can guess this from 'to go ahead'.
- straw: The German word sounds almost the same.
- covers: Guess this from the context.
- open to interpretation: Use a 'free' translation here!
- gateway: A 'gate' is a kind of door.
- places: Which German word fits best here?
- takes: Careful! – 'take' has several meanings.
- sits: What sounds best in German?
- only … only: Two different meanings!
- actually: Careful! A false friend!
- by 'going bush': You can guess what this means.
- suggest: Another word with more than one meaning.
- architects plan houses for: Another relative clause.
- roofs: Look this one up!

(adapted from an article in *The Christian Science Monitor*)

6 (after Topic 2) How about working as a model?

HV

You are listening to a British radio station. A magazine's fashion assistant is answering young people's questions. – The same afternoon, you're sitting with your friends in a café. They start talking about modelling. How would you answer – in German, of course! – what they say about it? Use the information you have 'picked up' from the recording.

- Ich glaube, man kann als Model ganz schön Geld nebenbei verdienen.
- Ich möchte gern an so einem Wettbewerb teilnehmen, hab' aber keine Ahnung, was ich für die Fotos anziehen soll!
- Meine Eltern würden ausflippen, wenn ich als Model arbeiten würde. Meine Noten sind jetzt schon schlecht genug!
- Model? Ein Traumjob! Aber wenn man nicht in der Großstadt lebt, geht das natürlich nicht!

7 (after Topic 3) The world war against nature

Translate this newspaper article into good German.

Imagine you switched the TV on this evening and heard this on the news:
"Today 55,000 hectares of rainforest were cut down. In the last 24 hours the world's deserts have grown by another 20,000 hectares. 100 different species of animal and plant life have disappeared forever. Millions of tons of greenhouse gases have entered the air. Today 100,000 people have died of hunger."

The sad fact is that reports like this could be made every day. This is what we are doing to our world – day after day. Energy is wasted, the air is polluted, tons of meat are eaten by the rich countries of the world, while people in the poorer countries are dying.

Sooner or later the lifestyle we have become used to will have to change. Alternatives will have to be found. This can be seen from the example of countries that have begun to develop very quickly – like China. If China ever became so rich that the amount of energy used per person reached US levels, its population would need more oil per day than the world produces!

Not so long ago people interested in saving the environment were laughed at. Now more and more people accept that the small world we live in must be well looked after.

Think a moment: What tense is best in German?

You need a different preposition in German.

Think how to say this in German.

A 'greenhouse' is a glass house for plants – so you can guess this!

Careful! It's part of a passive form.

Try 'antun' here.

A different preposition in German!

Careful here! Look it up if necessary.

Can you find a German noun for this phrase?

Use a relative clause in German.

8 (after Topic 4) Visiting Battle Abbey

People who want to visit the place where the Battle of Hastings was fought must go to the small town of Battle – just a few miles outside Hastings …

Look up the marked words in your dictionary. Then answer this German visitor's questions about Battle.

1. Warum wurde die Abtei gebaut?
2. Warum wird der Hochaltar besonders erwähnt?
3. Gibt es hier Führungen?
4. Erfährt man auch etwas über die Schlacht bei Hastings?

Battle Abbey was built by William the Conqueror to atone for the terrible slaughter of the Battle of Hastings, in 1066. On the day of the battle William vowed that he would build a church on the site if God gave him victory. The high altar was built on the very spot where Harold fell. Interactive exhibitions bring alive the history of this fascinating site, while a new interactive audio tour takes you around the full length of the battlefield itself, vividly recreating the sounds of this famous historic battle.

ENGLISH HERITAGE

Explore England's
History

Battle Abbey

9 (after Topic 5) In a clothes shop

You are looking at the jeans in a new clothes shop in town when you notice a girl standing at the counter. She seems to be English, and she is having a bit of trouble because the assistant can only speak German.

TIP
Just try to give the gist in your own words – so the other person can understand the situation!

You: Can I help at all?
Girl: Oh, that'd be nice. You see, I bought this T-shirt here on Monday, and I want to change it.
You: …
Assistant: Kein Problem. (*She looks at the T-shirt.*) Aber Sie haben's ja schon getragen! Dann kann ich's natürlich nicht mehr umtauschen. Tut mir leid.
You: …
Girl: But wait a minute. That's just the problem! I washed it yesterday and when I looked at it afterwards, I just couldn't believe it. Look! It's shrunk to about half the size. It *was* size 38, but it's so small now, I can't possibly wear it. I'm normally not so critical, but – well, judge for yourself.
You: …
Assistant: Sie haben's bestimmt zu heiß gewaschen. Gerade bei Baumwolle muss man ja sehr vorsichtig sein.
You: …
Girl: No, I looked at the washing instructions carefully, and I even washed it by hand.
You: …
Assistant: Also, so was dürfte normalerweise nicht passieren – da haben Sie schon Recht. Es ist tatsächlich ganz schön eingelaufen. Haben Sie den Kassenzettel dabei?
You: Have you got the piece of paper with … ?
Girl: Oh, the sales slip? Yes – here you are.
Assistant: Danke. Möchten Sie ein anderes T-shirt aussuchen, oder möchten Sie lieber Ihr Geld zurückhaben?
You: …
Girl: Well, I think if I've got the choice, I'd rather have my money back, please.
You: …
Assistant: Bitte schön.
Girl: Thanks a lot! (*to you*) Thanks for your help. I could never have explained all that in German.
You: …

10 (after Topic 5) Joyriding*

Can you translate this for a German teenage magazine?

Kirsten, 15, lives in Manchester. She often goes joyriding with her boyfriend …

"Barry's great at breaking into cars. He's got this big keyring full of keys and they fit most locks. Some nights he lets me pick out what car I want, then he breaks into it and off we go. If an alarm goes off, we just run away. We make sure we leave the car somewhere at the end of the night, so it isn't really stealing.

Emma, 16, lives in Leeds. Three months ago her little sister Kate was knocked down by a car driven by joyriders …

"I was walking home with Kate. She was running in front of me when I heard a car approaching. I looked round, and there was a black car coming round the corner – fast.
I could see 3 or 4 young boys sitting in it. Before I could reach out and grab Kate, the car hit another car – and then it hit Kate. It didn't stop, though, it just went roaring away down the road. When I saw Kate lying on the road, I thought she was dead. I panicked and screamed, and suddenly there were lots of people hurrying towards us. Then an ambulance arrived and took Kate to hospital. Her right leg was badly damaged. Poor Kate! She's only three!

**Read the text, then you'll understand what 'joyriding' mean*

What I like most about it is the excitement. You know, when we get the car door open, start the engine and go driving off! I really don't see what the problem is. We're just having a bit of fun ..."

Afterwards I described the car to the police. They told me they'd found it on a piece of wasteland. But they never found out who'd done it. Those idiots in that car! How can anyone be so irresponsible? I still have frightening dreams about the accident – and wake up crying ..."

(from SHOUT magazine, adapted)

JOYRIDING – KNOW THE FACTS

- Joyriding is stealing.
- If you are caught in a stolen car, even if you are not driving, the police can charge you.
- Hundreds of people are killed or badly hurt by joyriders every year. Don't imagine it's harmless fun.

11 (after Topic 6) Child labour

Child labour: a UNICEF report

„Bangkok: Bei einer Gasexplosion in einer Streichholzfabrik in Thailand kamen sechs junge Frauen ums Leben. Sie waren noch keine 14 Jahre alt." Diese Nachricht war den Medien in Deutschland gerade drei Zeilen wert. Und doch wirft sie ein Schlaglicht auf eine bittere Lebenswirklichkeit vieler Kinder: Kinderarbeit ist in Asien, Afrika, Lateinamerika und zunehmend auch wieder in Europa an der Tagesordnung. Weltweit müssen schätzungsweise 250 Millionen Kinder zwischen fünf und 14 Jahren unter Bedingungen arbeiten, die ihrer Entwicklung schaden. Kinder werden schon früh zu schwerer körperlicher Arbeit eingesetzt. Sie nähen Billigtaschen und T-Shirts in Bangkok und Seoul, fertigen Fußbälle in Peshawar, arbeiten in Indien, Pakistan und Nepal in der Teppichindustrie. Sie verkaufen sich als Prostituierte, Müllsammler und Schuhputzer. Es sind Kinder, die Verantwortung für sich und ihre Geschwister tragen müssen. Solange den Eltern der gerechte Lohn für ihre Arbeit verwehrt bleibt, werden sie weiterhin ihre Kinder in die Fabrik statt in eine Schule schicken, damit sie durch ihre Arbeit zum Überleben der Familien beitragen.

a) Daniel's English friend Matthew is staying with him in Germany. He picks up a UNICEF leaflet and reads this article about child labour – but he doesn't understand everything. *Can you answer his questions?*

1. What's this bit about a gas explosion in Thailand? I don't understand 'ums Leben'.
2. How awful! 'Medien' is the media – so was it in the headlines?
3. It says something about 250 million children between five and fourteen – but what's the meaning of 'unter Bedingungen arbeiten'?
4. Here it says they make bags and T-shirts – but what about footballs? Doesn't 'fertig' mean 'ready'?
5. 'Teppichindustrie' is the carpet industry, and 'Prostituierte' must be prostitutes. But what are 'Müllsammler' and 'Schuhputzer'?
6. I understand this bit about 'Verantwortung' – that children have to take responsibility. But why? What's 'der gerechte Lohn'? And I've never seen the word 'verwehrt' before.

b) *Don't try to translate the text, but write about 50–70 words in English about child labour, using information from the leaflet. Only use a dictionary if you get stuck.*

GRAMMAR

In diesem Teil deines Buches findest du wieder die **grammatischen Strukturen**, die dir beim Lernen und Vertiefen der englischen Sprache helfen sollen. Der Grammatikanhang ist so aufgebaut, dass die neuen grammatischen Gebiete jeweils **den einzelnen Topics des Buches zugeordnet** sind. Du kennst diese Art von Aufbereitung schon.
Neu ist, dass ein **Wiederholungsteil** am Schluss des grammatischen Anhangs steht. Er soll dir helfen, Dinge in größeren Zusammenhängen zu sehen und zu wiederholen.
Versuche überhaupt die jeweiligen grammatischen Gebiete in **größeren Übersichten** zu erfassen, wozu dir auch eine **Nachschlagegrammatik** helfen könnte:

- Dort könntest du z. B. ein grammatisches Gebiet nachschlagen, bei dem du dir nicht (mehr) ganz sicher bist.
- Eine Nachschlagegrammatik könnte dir auch verdeutlichen, warum du einen Fehler gemacht hast und ihn vermeiden helfen.
- Meist hat sie auch eine Reihe von Beispielsätzen, die eine zusätzliche Merkhilfe sein können.
- Vielleicht wird eine Regel etwas anders als in deinem Englischbuch erläutert, was eine gute Ergänzung sein kann.

Weitere Hinweise zum Gebrauch einer Nachschlagegrammatik kannst du der Seite 26 entnehmen **(Strategies: Using a grammar book)**.

Auch in diesem Band gibt es gelegentlich **kleine Aufgaben** für dich.
Immer, wenn du „am Ball bist", findest du dieses Symbol.

Viel Spaß bei der Arbeit!

1 AUSTRALIA

§ 1 Die Verlaufsform des present perfect
The present perfect progressive

past	present	future
It began to rain at two o'clock. 	Now it's five o'clock. It's still raining. 	?

It **has been raining** for three hours.

- Mit dem *present perfect progressive* kannst du etwas beschreiben, das in der Vergangenheit anfing und noch nicht beendet ist.
- Das *present perfect progressive* wird gebildet aus *have been/has been* und der *-ing*-Form: *I/you/we/they have been waiting … He/she/it has been waiting …*
- Im Deutschen benutzen wir meist das Präsens und betonen die Dauer des Vorgangs mit **‚schon':**
It has been raining for three hours. Es regnet **schon** seit drei Stunden.

‚for' und ‚since'

For und *since* sind dir schon aus Band 4 bekannt. Sie werden häufig mit dem ***present perfect progressive*** verwendet.

How long?

Thomas	**has been living**	in Sydney **for only a few weeks.**	... erst **seit** wenigen Wochen.
His dad	**has been looking**	for a job **for some time now.**	... schon **seit** einiger Zeit.

Since when?

White people	**have been coming**	to live in Australia since the late 18th century.	... kommen schon **seit** Ende des 18. Jahrhunderts ...
My cousin	**has been working**	in Melbourne since last May.	... arbeitet schon **seit** letzten Mai ...

- **For** bezieht sich auf den **Zeitraum,** den eine Handlung bereits andauert: **For** two hours, **for** a long time, **for** twenty minutes, ... etc.
- **Since** bezieht sich auf den **Zeitpunkt,** an dem die Handlung begann: **Since** three o'clock, **since** last week, **since** May, **since** 8 o'clock, ... etc.

Schau dir diese Situation an und beschreibe sie mit einem Satz mit ‚since' und einem Satz mit ‚for'.

§ 2 Präpositionen im Relativsatz Relative clauses with prepositions

Wie du schon weißt, wird das Relativpronomen im Englischen meist weggelassen, wenn es Objekt des Relativsatzes ist.

	object	subject	
Sydney was the name	**which/that**	the English settlers	chose for the new colony.
	–	the English settlers	chose for the new colony.
Dingoes are dogs	**which/that**	the Aborigines	brought with them to Australia.
Dingoes are dogs	–	the Aborigines	brought with them to Australia.

	relative clause		
Sydney is a city	that/which	lots of tourists go **to.**	
Sydney is a city		lots of tourists go **to.**	
The aunt	who	I stayed **with**	is Australian.
The aunt		I stayed **with**	is Australian.

Wird in solchen Relativsätzen mit oder ohne Relativpronomen eine Präposition gebraucht, steht sie hinter dem Verb. Sätze dieser Art werden im Englischen sehr häufig verwendet.

	relative pronoun		
This is the place		we stayed **at.**	... der Ort, **an** dem ...
Here is a photo of the car		we travelled **in.**	... **in** dem wir fuhren.
The friends		we went **with** were from Melbourne.	... **mit** denen wir fuhren ...

Ergänze bitte die folgenden Sätze:

1. The photo you are looking ... shows Sydney.
2. Here is the restaurant we went ... yesterday.
3. Is that an Australian song you are listening ...?
4. The glass you are drinking ... is a souvenir from Australia.

1. at 2. to
3. to 4. from

2 FROM SCHOOL TO WORK

§ 3 Direkte und indirekte Rede Direct speech and reported speech

Wenn man berichten möchte, was jemand sagt oder gesagt hat, verwendet man gewöhnlich nicht die direkte, sondern die indirekte Rede.

direct speech	reported speech
I'm looking for a new job. A computer firm has invited me for an interview. I had answered their advert and they wrote back last week.	Sarah says (that) she's looking for a new job. She says (that) a computer firm has invited her for an interview. She says (that) she had answered their advert and (that) they wrote back last week.

- Die indirekte Rede besteht aus einem einleitenden Hauptsatz *(Sarah says …)* und einem davon abhängigen Nebensatz *(… that she's looking for a job).*
- Anders als im Deutschen steht zwischen diesem Einführungssatz und der indirekten Rede **kein Komma.**
- Das einleitende *that* kannst du weglassen.
- Personalpronomen und Possessivpronomen werden häufig verändert, um sie dem Standpunkt des Berichterstatters anzupassen: I ⇛ she, me ⇛ her, they ⇛ them, etc.
- Steht das Verb im Einführungssatz im *present tense,* so wird in der indirekten Rede die gleiche Zeitform verwendet wie in der direkten Rede.

§ 4 Die Verben ‚ask', ‚tell' und ‚want' zum Ausdruck indirekter Aufforderungen und Wünsche

The verbs 'ask', 'tell' and 'want' to express reported commands and wishes

direct speech	reported speech			
		verb	object	infinitive + to
His parents <u>want</u> Martin <u>to do</u> what they tell him:				
"Turn down the music in your room, please."	They	**ask**	**him**	**to turn down** the music in his room.
"Open the windows."	They	**tell**	**him**	**to open** the windows.
"Take the dirty glasses to the kitchen."	They	**want**	**him**	**to take** the dirty glasses to the kitchen.
"Put your clothes away in the cupboard, please."	They	**ask**	**him**	**to put away** his clothes in the cupboard.
"Please tell us where you are going and who with."	They	**want**	**him**	**to tell** them where he is going and who with.

Mit den Verben *ask, tell* und *want* kannst du berichten, dass jemand etwas wünscht oder fordert.

Diese ***object + infinitive construction*** kannst du auch nach den Verben *expect, remind, order* und *advise* verwenden.

Pass auf: *Ask* heißt hier *bitten* und nicht *fragen:* Vergleiche: They <u>asked</u> me to help them.
= Sie <u>baten</u> mich, ihnen zu helfen.
They <u>asked:</u> "Could you help us?"
= Sie <u>fragten</u> …

Bitte übersetze die folgenden Sätze ins Englische:

1. Willst du, dass ich den Brief lese?
2. Ich möchte, dass ihr alle an meinem Geburtstag da seid.
3. Ich erwarte, dass ihr eure Schuhe auszieht.
4. Meine Mutter erinnerte mich daran, die Hausaufgaben zu machen.
5. Unsere Lehrerin riet uns, eine Mindmap anzufertigen.

1. Do you **want** me to read the letter? 2. I'd **like** you all to be there on my birthday.
3. I **expect** you to take off your shoes. 4. My mother **reminded** me to do my homework.
5. Our teacher **advised** us to make a mind map.

§ 5 Indirekte Rede: Verb im Einführungssatz im past tense
Reported speech: Introductory verb in the past

direct speech	reported speech
"My new job **is** wonderful." "The people I work with **are** very helpful." "I **don't know** everyone in the department yet."	Sarah **said** (that) her new job **was** wonderful. She **said** (that) the people she worked with **were** very helpful. She **said** (that) she **didn't know** everyone in the department yet.
present tense ⇛ past tense	
"**I've** only **been** there for a week, but **I've** already **learned** a lot." "I **haven't sent** an e-mail yet."	Sarah **told me** (that) she **had** only **been** there for a week, but (that) she **had** already **learned** a lot. Sarah **said** (that) she **hadn't sent** an e-mail yet.
present perfect ⇛ past perfect	
"I **worked** with the new software on the very first day." "I **didn't have** any trouble with it at all."	Sarah **said** (that) she **had worked** with the new software on the very first day. She **said** (that) she **hadn't had** any trouble with it at all.
past tense ⇛ past perfect	

direct speech	reported speech
"I **won't** be in the same office next week." "**I'll** be in a different department then."	She **said** (that) she **wouldn't** be in the same office the following week. She **told** me (that) she **would** be in a different department then.
will ⇛ would	
"I **can** walk to work in the mornings."	She told me (that) she **could** walk to work in the mornings.
can ⇛ could	
"Eating in the cafeteria **may** be a bit of a problem."	Sarah said (that) eating in the cafeteria **might** be a bit of a problem.
may ⇛ might	

Steht das **einleitende Verb im *past tense*** *(said, told me)*, so ändern sich die Zeiten. Die Verbform in der indirekten Rede wird gegenüber der Verbform in der direkten Rede um eine Zeitstufe in die Vergangenheit zurückversetzt. Man spricht deshalb auch von einem ***backshift of tenses*** (Rückverschiebung der Zeiten).

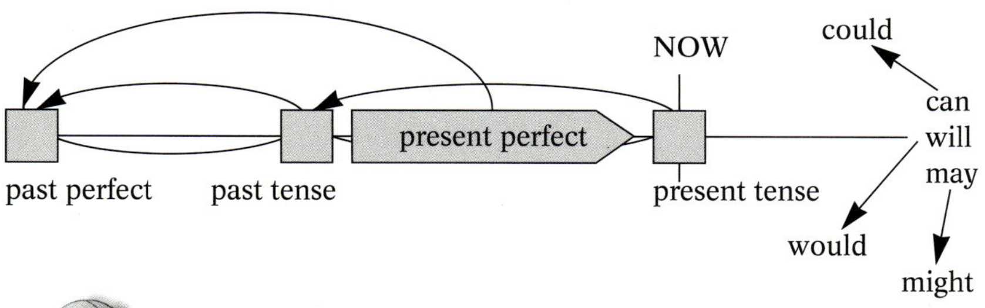

Schau dir dieses Diagramm an. Kannst du es erklären und für jeden der Pfeile einen Beispielsatz finden?

Pass auf: **say und tell:** She **said** that she lived in Scotland.
She **told him** that she lived in Scotland.

Nach *tell* folgt immer ein Objekt (= die Person, mit der jemand spricht).

§ 6 Fragen in der indirekten Rede Questions in reported speech

direct speech	reported speech
"**How** do you like your new job, Martin?"	Heather wanted to know **how** Martin liked his new job.
"**What** sort of job is it exactly?"	She asked **what** sort of job it was exactly.
"**When** do you start work in the morning?"	She wanted to know **when** he started work in the morning.
"**Why** didn't you call me from work this afternoon?"	She wanted to know **why** he hadn't called her from work that afternoon.

- Steht in der direkten Rede ein Fragewort (*how, what, why, when* etc.), so wird es in der indirekten Rede beibehalten.

"Do you like your new job, Martin?"	Chang wanted to know **if** Martin liked his new job.
"Have you tried the food in the cafeteria yet?"	Chang asked Martin **whether** he had tried the food in the cafeteria yet.

- Steht in der direkten Frage **kein Fragewort,** so wird der Nebensatz in der indirekten Rede mit ***if*** oder ***whether*** eingeleitet. (Im Deutschen: … ob …)

§ 7 Zeitangaben in der direkten und indirekten Rede
Expressions of time in direct and reported speech

Monday, May 10th (in the morning) | Monday, May 10th (in the afternoon) | Friday, May 13th

- Zeitangaben wie *today, this month, next year* usw. werden in der indirekten Rede beibehalten, wenn man noch am gleichen Tag, im gleichen Monat oder Jahr berichtet, was jemand gesagt hat. Ist der Tag (der Monat, das Jahr) jedoch vorbei, so verändern sich die Zeitangaben in der indirekten Rede.

Die folgenden Zeitangaben sind in der indirekten Rede üblich – welche Zeitangaben entsprechen ihnen in der direkten Rede?

1. the next day 2. the month before 3. three weeks earlier
4. the day before 5. that day 6. four days before 7. that year
8. the week before

1. tomorrow 2. last month 3. three weeks ago 4. yesterday 5. today 6. four days ago 7. this year 8. last week

Kannst du auch herausbekommen, welches Wort *there* in der direkten Rede entspricht?

here

§ 8 Der Infinitiv nach Fragewörtern
The infinitive after question words

	indirekter Fragesatz
Could you tell me …	**where I can get a ticket?**
	where to get a ticket?
	Fragewort + Infinitiv

- Der Infinitiv mit *to* nach Fragewörtern (*when, which, how,* etc.) kann indirekte Fragen ersetzen, die ein modales Hilfsverb (*can, must, should,* etc.) enthalten. Diese Infinitivkonstruktion wird häufiger verwendet als ein entsprechender Nebensatz.

Kannst du bei der folgenden Mini-Aufgabe die indirekten Fragesätze mit dem to-Infinitiv ersetzen?

People who travel by plane for the first time often have no idea …

… where they should put their bags.
… what they can do if they feel ill.
… how they can use their headphones.

… where to put their bags.
… what to do if they feel ill.
… how to use their headphones.

"I don't know how to say this, Jones, but you're fired*."
"Fired? I always thought slaves were sold."

* entlassen

3 THE WORLD AROUND US

§ 9 Review: The passive voice

Passivsätze findet man häufig in sachlichen und historischen Berichten, Reportagen und Zeitungsartikeln.
Sie betonen, **was** getan wird. Die Handlung selbst steht im Vordergrund, während in Aktivsätzen betont wird, **wer** etwas tut. Du kannst Passivsätze also vor allem dann verwenden, wenn du nicht genau weißt oder wenn es nicht wichtig ist, wer die entsprechende Handlung ausführt.

Das Passiv wird gebildet aus einer Form von ***be + past participle*** (3. Verbform).

simple present passive:	Millions of tons of oil **are burnt** every day. Millionen von Tonnen … werden jeden Tag verbrannt.
present perfect passive:	Nuclear energy **has been used** since the 1950s. Kernenergie wird seit den 50er Jahren genutzt.
simple past passive:	During the Industrial Revolution a lot of coal **was mined** in Britain. Während der Industriellen Revolution wurde … gefördert.
past perfect passive:	Before the Industrial Revolution wind and water power **had been used.** Vor der Industriellen Revolution waren … eingesetzt worden.
future passive:	More and more energy **will be needed** in the future. In Zukunft wird immer mehr Energie gebraucht werden.

§ 10 Der Infinitiv des Passivs The passive infinitive

How **can** the environment	**be protected?**	Wie kann man die Umwelt schützen?
Environmental groups **should**	**be supported.**	Man sollte … unterstützen.
Pollution **must**	**be stopped.**	Die … muss gestoppt werden.
More waste **has to**	**be recycled.**	Wir müssen noch mehr … wieder verwerten.
Alternative technologies **ought to**	**be developed.**	Man sollte alternative … entwickeln.
	be + past participle (3. Verbform)	

- Nach modalen Hilfsverben (*can, should, ought to,* etc.) steht im Aktivsatz der Infinitiv Aktiv *(do, support): How **can** we **protect** the environment? – We **ought to support** environmental groups.*
- Im Passivsatz steht der Infinitiv Passiv *(be done, be supported)*. Er wird gebildet aus ***be + past participle:** What **can be done?***
- Nach *can, must, may, should* wird der Infinitiv ohne ***to*** gebraucht, die Ersatzverben *(have **to**, be able **to**, be allowed **to**)* verwenden wir mit ***to***.

§ 11 Das Passiv bei Verben mit Präpositionen
Verbs with prepositions in passive sentences

active	**subject**	**verb + preposition**	**object**
	The protesters	***shouted at***	the policemen.
	The policemen	***were shouted at***	by the protesters.
passive	**subject**	**verb + preposition**	**by-agent** *(von wem?)*

- Verb und Präposition stehen im Passivsatz zusammen.
- Bei der Übersetzung ins Deutsche werden häufig Sätze mit ‚man' verwendet.

Versuche die folgenden Passivsätze mit Präpositionen ins Deutsche zu übersetzen.
(Wo stellst du im Deutschen die Präpositionen hin?
Oft gibt es mehrere richtige Lösungen.)

1. The environment must be looked after. 2. The development of new technologies must be paid for. 3. This problem has not been thought of. 4. In the past environmental groups were often laughed at.

1. Man muss sich/Wir müssen uns um die Umwelt kümmern. 2. Die Entwicklung von neuen Technologien muss bezahlt werden./Für die Entwicklung von … muss man bezahlen. 3. Man hat an dieses Problem noch nicht gedacht./An dieses Problem ist noch nicht gedacht worden. 4. In der Vergangenheit hat man oft über Umweltgruppen gelacht./In der Vergangenheit wurde oft über Umweltgruppen gelacht.

§ 12 Das Passiv bei Verben mit zwei Objekten
The passive of verbs with two objects

Mit Verben wie *give, offer, promise, sell, send, show, tell* kannst du das so genannte „persönliche Passiv“ bilden.

		indirect object („Personenobjekt“)	direct object („Sachobjekt“)	
active:	They offered	***him***	a lot of money	for the book.
passive:	***He*** **subject**	was offered a lot of money.		

Wenn du solche Passivsätze ins Deutsche übersetzen möchtest, verwendest du am besten einen Aktivsatz mit ‚man‘ oder ‚jemand‘.

Kannst du das bei diesen Sätzen versuchen?

1. Greenpeace was given a lot of help. 2. I have been sent a long letter.
3. She has been offered a very interesting job. 4. We were told a funny story.

1. Man hat Greenpeace sehr geholfen. 2. Jemand hat mir einen langen Brief geschickt. 3. Man hat ihr eine interessante Stelle angeboten. 4. Man hat uns eine lustige Geschichte erzählt.

§ 13 Verkürzung von Relativsätzen mit dem Passiv
Shortening relative clauses with passive forms

Wie du schon weißt, wird das Passiv in Zeitungsüberschriften und ähnlichem oft verkürzt verwendet:

Rainforests **cut down** in Brazil. – Rainforests **are cut down** in Brazil.
Greenpeace boat **attacked** by oil company. – A Greenpeace boat **has been/was attacked** by an oil company.

Auch in den folgenden Beispielen verkürzen Passivformen ***(past participles)*** die Sätze:

Money **given** to environmental groups is money well spent.	= **... which is given ...**
Trees **cut** down in the rainforests are gone forever.	= **... which are cut** down ...
People should not buy drinks **sold** in cans.	= **... which are sold ...**
The protesters **led away** by the police had set up camps in the woods.	= **... who were/had been led away ...**

- Das *past participle* wird in diesen Sätzen verwendet, um einen Relativsatz zu verkürzen.
- Wenn du solche Sätze übersetzt, nimmst du am besten einen Relativsatz im Deutschen: Cars only **used** for short journeys ... – Autos, **die** nur für kurze Fahrten **benutzt werden,** ...

Achtung: Achte darauf, im Deutschen die richtige Zeitform zu verwenden.

5 YOUR CHOICE

§ 14 Partizipien als Adjektive
Participles used as adjectives

present participle (-ing-Form)	**past participle** (3. Form des Verbs)
I thought the film was very **exciting.** I didn't find it **boring** at all. The **sinking** ship looked very realistic. The **leading** role was played by Douglas Harrison.	I was **shocked** to see so many **injured** people – and all the **frightened** children. Only a few passengers were picked up from the **damaged** lifeboats.

- Du kannst viele *present* und *past participles* als Adjektive verwenden, und zwar sowohl als Beifügung zum Substantiv *(the **sinking** ship)* als auch als Ergänzung zum Verb *(didn't find it **boring**)*.
- Das ***present participle*** hat **aktive Bedeutung:** *the **sinking** ship = the ship was sinking* (Das sinkende/untergehende Schiff = Das Schiff sank/ging unter.)
- Das ***past participle*** hat **passive Bedeutung:** *the **frightened** children = the children were frightened* (die verängstigten/erschrockenen Kinder = die Kinder wurden erschreckt/verängstigt.)

Kannst du diese *present* und *past participles* richtig in die Sätze „einbauen"?

boring/bored   exciting/excited   frightening/frightened   interesting/interested

1. The last English lesson was very ..., no ... texts, only stupid grammar. I felt really ... . 2. I've got a new, terribly ... computer game, 'Death on Mars'. I was so ... when I had played it that I couldn't sleep. 3. There is a ... scene, when the Mars Monster catches this ... girl. 4. Are you ... in computer games, too, or don't you find them ...?

1. boring, interesting/exciting, bored 2. exciting/interesting, excited 3. frightening, frightened 4. interested, interesting/exciting

§ 15 Partizipien nach Verben der Wahrnehmung
Participles after verbs of perception

	verb	direct object	participle	
I	**saw**	this huge object	**flying**	through the clouds.
I	**saw**	it	**coming**	towards the earth.
I	**noticed**	the doors	**opening**	slowly.
I	**saw**	some creatures	**crawling**	out of the thing.
I	**could hear**	them	**talking**	in this funny language.
		They looked like huge insects. – I ran …		

- Verben wie *hear, notice, see* drücken eine Wahrnehmung aus. Nach ihnen steht häufig ein direktes Objekt *(this huge object)* und ein *present participle (flying)*.
- Im Deutschen drückst du dies am besten mit einem Infinitiv oder mit einem Nebensatz mit **wie** aus. (Ich sah dieses riesige Ding durch die Wolken fliegen, oder: Ich sah, wie dieses riesige Ding durch die Wolken flog.)

Kannst du die restlichen Beispiele auch übersetzen?

Ich sah, wie es auf die Erde zukam. Ich bemerkte, wie sich die Türen langsam öffneten. Ich sah, wie einige Wesen/Kreaturen aus dem Ding herauskrochen. Ich sah … herauskriechen. Ich konnte hören, wie sie in dieser komischen Sprache redeten./Ich konnte sie … sprechen hören.

§ 16 Partizipien nach Verben, die Ruhe oder Bewegung ausdrücken
Participles after verbs expressing rest or movement

He **stood waiting** for her outside the cinema.	Er stand vor dem Kino und wartete auf sie.
She **came running** up to him.	Sie kam und rannte auf ihn zu.
They **sat holding** hands.	Sie saßen und hielten sich an der Hand.
They **stayed sitting** there long after the film was over.	Sie blieben noch lange sitzen nachdem …

- Verben wie *lie, stay, sit, stand* drücken eine Ruheposition aus; Verben wie *arrive, come, go, leave* drücken Bewegung aus.
- An diese Verben kannst du direkt ein *present participle* anfügen. Diese Konstruktion drückt dann aus, dass die beiden Handlungen gleichzeitig ablaufen.
- Im Deutschen kannst du dies mit zwei Verben und **und** wiedergeben. (Er **stand … und wartete** auf sie.)

§ 17 Das Partizip nach *have* in der Bedeutung „veranlassen"
The participle after *have* meaning „veranlassen" in German

	have	object	past participle	
She always	**has**	her car	**washed.**	She never does it herself.
Last year they	**had**	their house	**painted.**	
Have you	**had**	your hair	**cut?**	No, I did it myself.
But next time **I'll**	**have**	it	**cut**	by a hairdresser.

Mit ***have* + *object* + *past participle*** kannst du ausdrücken, dass jemand etwas machen lässt.
She always ***has*** *her car* ***washed.*** = Sie **lässt** ihr Auto immer **waschen.**

Wie würdest du die anderen Beispielsätze übersetzen?

Letztes Jahr ließen sie ihr Haus streichen.
Hast du dir die Haare schneiden lassen? Nein, ich habe es selbst gemacht.
Aber nächstes Mal lasse ich sie von einem Friseur schneiden.

VORSICHT!
Have + direct object + past participle kann man leicht mit dem *present perfect* verwechseln:

present perfect	**have + object + past participle**
I have washed the car.	I have the car washed.
(Ich habe das Auto gewaschen.)	(Ich lasse das Auto waschen.)

Vielleicht kannst du dir eine Regel ausdenken, um diese Konstruktionen nicht zu verwechseln. Schau dir einmal an, wo das Objekt steht.

§ 18 Das Partizip statt eines Relativsatzes
Participles instead of relative clauses

	Relativsatz			
		Partizip		
The girl	**who is**	**sitting**	over there	is a famous model.
The girl		***sitting***	over there	is a famous model.
Most of the people	**who are**	**working**	on this project	have a lot of experience.
Most of the people		***working***	on this project	have a lot of experience.
Many adverts	**which**	**appear**	on TV these days	are pretty stupid.
Many adverts		***appearing***	on TV these days	are pretty stupid.

- Anstelle von Relativsätzen kannst du auch Partizipien verwenden. (Im Relativsatz ist das Relativpronomen – *who/which* – Subjekt.)
- Im Deutschen kannst du solche Sätze mit einem Relativsatz übersetzen:
  The man ***standing*** *at the door* … Der Mann, **der** an der Tür **steht …**

- Diese Konstruktion funktioniert genauso wie die Verkürzung von Relativsätzen mit dem Passiv in **§13,** Seite 108. Es gibt allerdings einen Bedeutungsunterschied:
  Worin besteht wohl der Unterschied zwischen *The fish* ***serving*** *in this restaurant is very nice.* und *The fish* ***served*** *in this restaurant is very nice.*?

The fish serving ... bedeutet, dass der Fisch selbst etwas tut: er serviert.
The fish served ... bedeutet, dass mit dem Fisch etwas passiert: er wird serviert.

6 THE INDUSTRIAL REVOLUTION

§ 19 used to

When I was small I **used to eat** lots of sweets.	**Früher,** als ich klein war, habe ich ...
My parents **used to tell** me to eat healthier food.	Meine Eltern haben mir **immer** gesagt ...
But I simply **didn't use** to worry about what I ate.	Aber ich machte mir einfach keine Gedanken.

- Mit ***used to*** + **Infinitiv** kannst du ausdrücken, dass früher etwas Bestimmtes war oder geschah. In der Gegenwart gibt es diese Gewohnheit oder diesen Zustand nicht mehr.
- Von ***used to*** gibt es nur die *past tense*-Form, keine *present tense*-Form.
- Im Deutschen kannst du ***used to*** durch **früher** oder **immer** wiedergeben. Manchmal wird es auch nicht übersetzt.
  (Neben ***used to*** gibt es noch ***would*** + **Infinitiv** zum Ausdruck früherer Gewohnheiten:
  My grandfather ***would get up*** *very early every morning and* ***would work*** *very long hours.*
  Mein Großvater stand [gewöhnlich] jeden Morgen sehr früh auf ... .)

Kannst du den Unterschied erklären zwischen:

I **used to live** in a big city.
Now I'm **used to living** in a small town.

I used to live in a big city. = Ich wohnte (immer) in einer großen Stadt.
Now I'm used to living in a small town. = Jetzt bin ich es gewöhnt, in einer Kleinstadt zu wohnen.

REVIEW

§ 20 Die Zeiten The tenses

Active Voice

	simple	progressive
present	I always **take** lots of pictures when I'm on holiday. The trip to Sydney usually **takes** 20 hours. Does she **take** sugar in her tea?	Don't move, I'm **taking** a picture of you. She's **taking** her dad to the airport next Saturday.
past	Yesterday I **took** a day off. **Did** you **take** the steaks off the barbecue?	While he **was taking** the dog for a walk, it started to rain.
present perfect	I **have taken** care of our flights. Dad **hasn't taken** his medicine yet.	We **have been taking** didgeridoo lessons for three months now.
past perfect	Our friends liked the pictures we **had taken** of the outback.	
will-future	I **will take** pictures of all the sights in New Zealand. I **won't take** a ride in this old 4WD again!	
going-to-future	We **are going to take** the train tonight.	
conditional	If I had enough money, I **would take** six months off and go to Australia.	
conditional perfect	If she hadn't been to Australia she **wouldn't have taken** a diving course.	

Passive Voice

present	Lots of pictures **are taken** of Ayers Rock.	
past	We **were taken** on a tour of Kakadu National Park.	
present perfect	Look, the posters of the Great Barrier Reef **have been taken** off the wall.	
will-future	We won't have to pick up our bags, they **will be taken** to the hotel.	

§ 21 Das Perfekt und die einfache Vergangenheit
The present perfect and the simple past

present perfect	simple past
Bill **has broken** his leg. He is not able to play football now.	He **broke** it in the match **last Saturday.**
Jenny **has made** tea. We can have it now.	She **made** it **five minutes ago.**
Have you **ever seen** a kangaroo?	Yes, I **saw** some kangaroos at London Zoo **last year.**
I've never been to Australia.	But I **was** in New Zealand **last August.**

Wenn du ausdrücken willst, dass etwas in der Vergangenheit stattgefunden hat, musst du im Englischen entweder das *simple past* oder das *present perfect* verwenden.

- Mit dem *present perfect* kannst du ausdrücken, dass sich etwas in der Vergangenheit abgespielt hat, was jetzt noch aktuell ist.
- Das *present perfect* kannst du auch verwenden, wenn du einen Zeitraum beschreiben möchtest, der von der Vergangenheit bis in die Gegenwart reicht. Signalwörter sind *ever, never, already, often, yet.*

- Mit dem *simple past* kannst du ausdrücken, dass etwas in der Vergangenheit stattgefunden hat und abgeschlossen ist.
- Daher wird das *simple past* häufig von Signalwörtern begleitet, die sich mit ‚wann' erfragen lassen, z. B. *yesterday, last week, the day before yesterday, on Monday,* etc.

Hast du den Unterschied verstanden? Dann versuch doch gleich mal, den folgenden Satz ins Englische zu übersetzen:
Ich *habe* gestern eine Pizza *gegessen.*

Lösung: I ate/had a pizza yesterday.

Kannst du erklären, welche Zeitform du verwendet hast und warum? Kannst du weitere Beispielsätze finden – auch für die andere Zeitform?

§ 22 Bedingungssätze Conditional sentences

Wie du weißt, bestehen die Bedingungssätze aus einem if-Satz *(if-clause)* und einem Hauptsatz *(main clause)*.

Typ I

if-Satz *(if-clause)*	Hauptsatz *(main clause)*
If they pay me £3 an hour Wenn Sie mir £3 pro Stunde zahlen,	**I'll** take the job at the fish 'n' chip shop. nehme ich den Job im Fish-'n'-chips-Laden.
simple present	**will-future**

- Beim Typ I drückt das *simple present* im *if*-Satz aus, dass es tatsächlich dazu kommen kann, dass die Bedingung also erfüllbar ist. Im Hauptsatz steht das *will-future.*

Typ II

if-Satz *(if-clause)*	Hauptsatz *(main clause)*
If I **had** a million pounds, Wenn ich eine Million Pfund hätte, **If** I **found** a purse, Wenn ich einen Geldbeutel fände, **If** we **had** a car, Wenn wir ein Auto hätten,	I **would give** some of it to other people. würde ich anderen Menschen etwas davon geben. **I'd take** it to the police. würde ich ihn zur Polizei bringen. we**'d take** you home. würden wir dich nach Hause bringen.
past tense	**would + infinitive**

- Beim Typ II drückt das *past tense* aus, dass es unwahrscheinlich oder sogar unmöglich ist, die Bedingung zu erfüllen. Im Hauptsatz steht das Konditional *(would + infinitive)*.

Typ III

if-Satz *(if-clause)*	Hauptsatz *(main clause)*
If he **had hurried,** Wenn er sich beeilt hätte, **If** I **had been** on the ferry, Wenn ich auf der Fähre gewesen wäre,	he **would have caught** the train. hätte er den Zug erreicht. I **would have got** seasick. wäre ich seekrank geworden.
past perfect	**would + have + past participle (3. Form)**

- Beim Typ III weiß der Sprecher, dass die im *if*-Satz genannte Bedingung nicht mehr erfüllt werden kann: Man stellt sich bloß vor, was gewesen wäre, wenn …
  Beispiel: If the British **hadn't settled** in Australia, … (But it's a fact that they did – das ist die Wirklichkeit!)

§ 23 Modale Hilfsverben Modal auxiliaries

Mit modalen Hilfsverben kannst du Wünsche oder persönliche Einstellungen zu einer Sache ausdrücken.

- Modale Hilfsverben werden immer zusammen mit einem anderen Verb verwendet. (Ausnahme: *short answers*).
- Sie haben immer dieselbe Form. (Es gibt keine **-s**-Endung, keine **-ed**-Form für die Vergangenheit und keine **-ing**-Form.)
- Nach modalen Hilfsverben steht der **Infinitiv ohne *to*** (Ausnahme: *ought to*).
- Die meisten modalen Hilfsverben kann man nur im *present tense* verwenden. Für die anderen Zeiten muss man auf so genannte Ersatzverben zurückgreifen.

Du kannst modale Hilfsverben verwenden, um

• zu sagen, dass jemand etwas tun kann oder nicht tun kann **can/can't/cannot/could** Ersatzverb: **be able to**	**Can** you do this exercise? No, I **can't.** I **couldn't** decide what to do last night. Sorry, I won't **be able to** come to your party.
• zu sagen, dass etwas möglich erscheint **can/could/may/might**	A lot **can** happen in 2 weeks. You **could/may/might** be right.
• zu sagen, dass jemand etwas nicht tun darf **may not/must not** Ersatzverb: **not be allowed to**	I'm sorry, but you **may not/must not** eat ice-cream on the bus. We **weren't allowed** to leave the airport.
• eine Bitte auszudrücken **will/would/can/could/may**	**Will/Would** you shut the window, please? **Can/Could** I use your telephone? **May** I come in?
• zu sagen, dass etwas notwendig ist, bzw. getan werden muss **must** Ersatzverb: **have to**	I really **must** go now. Do we **have to** do this exercise?
• zu sagen, dass etwas nicht notwendig ist, nicht getan zu werden braucht **needn't** Ersatzverb: **don't have to**	You **needn't** help me. I can do it myself. We **won't have** to send him a fax, he's got e-mail.
• jemand einen Rat zu geben **should/ought to**	We **ought to** help people in need. You **shouldn't** only think of yourself.
• zu fragen, ob man jemand helfen kann oder um einen Vorschlag zu machen **shall I/shall we**	**Shall I** carry those bags for you? **Shall we** go for lunch on Sunday?

VORSICHT: Pass auf, dass du *mustn't* und *needn't* nicht verwechselst.

I don't think it'll rain.
We ***needn't*** take our anoraks.
⇛ **not necessary**

Grandma is sleeping.
You ***mustn't*** make so much noise.
⇛ **not allowed**

§ 24 Adjektive und Adverbien Adjectives and adverbs

Im Deutschen haben Adjektive und Adverbien meist die gleiche Form. Im Englischen dagegen gibt es verschiedene Formen.

ADJECTIVE

This is **easy.** It's really an **easy** exercise.

Adjektive beschreiben, wie eine Person oder Sache **ist.**
Sie stehen vor einem Substantiv oder hinter dem Verb *be.*

ADVERB

We can do this **easily.**

Adverbien beschreiben, **wie** jemand etwas **tut** oder wie etwas geschieht.
Adverbien gehören oft zu einem Verb und sagen etwas über dieses Verb aus.

Vergleiche mit Adjektiven und Adverbien

Manchester is **as big as** Liverpool.
But it isn't **as interesting as** London.
London is **bigger than** Liverpool.
And it is **more exciting than** Liverpool, too.

Of course, London is **the biggest** and **most interesting** city in Britain.

You can get to Manchester almost **as easily as** to London.
With the Channel Tunnel you can get to England **more quickly** now.
You can travel **more comfortably** by train **than** by car.
But you get to England **most quickly** and you travel **most comfortably** if you fly.

unregelmäßige Formen

good – better – best
bad – worse – worst

well – better – best
badly – worse – worst

adjective = adverb
hard – harder – hardest
fast – faster – fastest

Adjektive nach bestimmten Verben:
What about some tea? – That **sounds great.**
That cake **looks nice.**
And it **smells lovely.**
I really **feel hungry** now.
Let's hope it **tastes** as **good** as it looks.

Nach Verben der Wahrnehmung stehen im Englischen Adjektive.

Stellung von Adverbien – 1. Adverbien der Art und Weise

subject	adverb	verb	object	adverb
They		looked at	each other	**nervously.**
A strange figure	**slowly**	passed	the window.	
Someone		opened	the door	**secretly.**

2. Adverbien der Häufigkeit

subject	auxiliary	adverb	verb	
We		**often**	go	to Scotland in the summer.
I	have	**always**	liked	holidays in the mountains.
I	will	**never**	forget	the day when we climbed Ben Nevis.

GRAMMAR LIST

Deutsch/Latein	Englisch	Englisches Beispiel	§
Adjektiv	adjective	nice, terrible	24
Steigerung mit -er/-est	comparison with -er/-est	big, bigger, biggest	
Steigerung mit ‚more'/‚most'	comparison with 'more'/'most'	important, more important, most important	
Adjektiv nach bestimmten Verben	adjectives after certain verbs	This soup tastes nice.	
Adverbien	adverbs	sometimes, often	24
Adverbien der Art und Weise	adverbs of manner	How does he drive? – He drives carefully.	
Steigerung des Adverbs	comparison of adverbs	slowly, more slowly, …	
Vergleiche mit Adverbien	comparisons with adverbs	as slowly as … more slowly than …	
Apostroph (Auslassungszeichen)	apostrophe	Where's Martin?	
Artikel	article		
bestimmter Artikel	definite article	… the life of …	
Namen im Plural		The Chicago Bulls are great.	
mit *of-phrase*		The Statue of Liberty is in New York.	
unbestimmter Artikel	indefinite article	a house, an apple	
Zeit-/Mengenangaben		55 km an hour, £1 a bottle …	
nach ‚quite' und ‚such'		quite a good story, such a cold winter	
Bedingungssätze	conditional sentences		22
Typ I (erfüllbar)		If it rains tomorrow, I won't play football.	
Typ II (theoretisch)		If someone offered her a role in a film, she would feel lucky.	
Typ III (nicht mehr erfüllbar)		If he had hurried, he would have caught the bus.	
‚Each other'	each other	Sue and Josh love each other.	
Einzahl (Singular)	singular	one house	
Futur	future		
Going-to-Futur	going-to-future	I'm going to watch a film.	
Will-Futur	will-future	Carrie will be 16 next year.	
Gegenwart (Präsens)	present tense		
einfache Form	simple present	I like tennis.	
Verlaufsform	present progressive	He's watching TV.	
Present progressive zur Wiedergabe der Zukunft	present progressive with a future meaning	I'm meeting Heather in the evening.	

Deutsch/Latein	Englisch	Englisches Beispiel	§
Gerund	gerund	reading, cooking	
als Objekt	as object	I love swimming.	
als Subjekt	as subject	Reading is fun.	
nach ‚what about'/ ‚it's no good'/ ‚I can't stand'	after 'what about'/ 'it's no good'/'I can't stand'	What about going to the shops?	
nach Präpositionen	after prepositions	I'm thinking of learning French. Are you good at working with ...?	
Grundform (Infinitiv)	infinitive	to see, to do, etc.	
Infinitiv nach bestimmten Verben	the infinitive after certain verbs	Don't forget to write.	
Infinitiv nach Fragewörtern	the infinitive after question words	Could you tell me how to use this discman, please?	8
Grundzahlen	cardinal numbers	1,045,986	
Hilfsverb (modales)	modal auxiliary		23
‚Be allowed to'	be allowed to	We're allowed to sit here.	
‚Have to'	have to	I have to do my homework.	
‚Mustn't'	mustn't	You mustn't play here!	
‚Needn't'	needn't	You needn't stay in bed.	
‚Must' und ‚needn't' und die Ersatzform ‚have to'	'must' and needn't' and the substitute form 'have to'	We must leave now. You don't have to go yet.	
‚Mustn't' und die Ersatzform ‚not be allowed to'	'mustn't' and the substitute form 'not be allowed to'	You aren't allowed to play football here.	
‚Can/could' und die Ersatzform ‚be able to'	'can/could' and the substitute form 'be able to'	Can I ask you a question? I wasn't able to call you.	
Bitte, Wunsch	will you?, would you?	Will you shut the door, please?	
Vorschlag, Angebot	shall I?, should we?	Shall I open the window?	
Rat, Ermahnung	should, ought to	You should ask Tricia ...	
Indirekte und direkte Rede	reported speech and direct speech	"I went to the cinema." Tom says (that) he went to the cinema.	3
Fragen in der indirekten Rede	questions in reported speech	Peter wanted to know why I hadn't told him earlier.	6
indirekte Aufforderungen und Wünsche	reported commands and wishes	My parents expect me to be back soon.	4
Verb im Einführungssatz im *past tense*	introductory verb in the past	Sally said (that) she hadn't seen my brother.	5
Zeitangaben in der direkten u. indirekten Rede	Expressions of time in direct and reported speech	My parents said they would visit me the next day.	7

Deutsch/Latein	Englisch	Englisches Beispiel	§
Infinitiv (Grundform)	infinitive	to watch, to go, to look, etc.	
Mehrzahl (Plural)	plural	two women, five dogs	
Mitlaut (Konsonant)	consonant	b, p, k, l	
Nebensätze mit ‚when'	clauses with 'when'	When Stella is seventeen, she'll learn to drive.	
Objekt	object	Heather has got a car.	
Partizip der Gegenwart	present participle	smiling, shouting, damaging	
Partizip der Vergangenheit	past participle	asked, found, thrown	
Partizipien als Adjektive	participles used as adjectives	the winning team, the exciting match, the chosen players	14
Partizipien nach *have* in der Bedeutung „veranlassen"	participles after *have* meaning „veranlassen" in German	The Millers had their car repaired last week.	17
Partizipien nach Verben, die Ruhe oder Bewegung ausdrücken	Participles after verbs expressing rest or movement	She stood waiting on the corner.	16
Partizipien nach Verben der Wahrnehmung	participles after verbs of perception	I saw the man running down the street.	15
Partizipien statt Relativsätzen	participles instead of relative clauses	The girl standing at the bar is my sister.	18
Passiv	the passive voice		9
einfache Gegenwart	simple present passive	… damage is done …	
einfache Vergangenheit	simple past passive	… mountains of rubbish were left …	
Infinitiv des Passivs	the passive infinitive	The tickets can be collected tonight.	10
Passiv bei Verben mit Präpositionen	verbs with prepositions in passive sentences	Protesters are often laughed at.	11
Passiv bei Verben mit zwei Objekten	the passive of verbs with two objects	I was offered a lot of money.	12
Passiv zur Verkürzung von Relativsätzen	shortening relative clauses with passive forms	You shouldn't buy drinks sold in cans.	13
Past perfect	past perfect	They had always wanted a farm.	
Präposition	preposition	in, on, under	
Present Perfect	present perfect	I have known her	
mit ‚for' und ‚since'	with 'for' and 'since'	for two months/since July.	1
regelmäßige Formen	regular forms	He has cooked lunch.	
unregelmäßige Formen	irregular forms	We've eaten it.	
Fragen, Verneinung und Kurzformen	questions, negative sentences and short forms	Have you ever seen a monster? No, I haven't.	

Deutsch/Latein	Englisch	Englisches Beispiel	§
Verlaufsform	present perfect progressive	I have been looking for my keys for 20 minutes.	1
Reflexivpronomen (-self, -selves)	reflexive pronouns (-self,-selves)	myself, themselves	
Relativsätze	relative clauses	This is the boy who won the race.	
Relativpronomen	relative pronouns	who, which, that, whose	
Relativsätze ohne Relativpronomen	relative clauses without relative pronouns	This is the story I like best.	
Relativsätze mit Präpositionen	relative clauses with prepositions	Australia is the country I will go to next summer.	2
Selbstlaut (Vokal)	vowel	a, e, i, o, u	
‚Some' und ‚any'	'some' and 'any'	Have we got any bread?	
Zusammensetzungen	compounds	something, anything	
‚Some' in Fragen	'some' in questions	Would you like some cake?	
Subjekt	subject	The man was old.	
Substantiv (Nomen)	noun	dog, teacher, bike	
Used to		My father used to smoke a lot.	19
Verb	verb	to go, to see	
Verb+Objekt+Infinitiv (mit und ohne ‚to')	verb+object+infinitive (with or without 'to')	I want you to read the text at home. He made us write the text.	
Verben mit Präposition oder Adverb	phrasal verbs	look after, turn up, take out	
Verben mit zwei Objekten	verbs with two objects	I gave the kids some money.	
Vergangenheit	past		
einfache Vergangenheit von ‚to be' und ‚to have'	simple past of 'to be' and 'to have'	It was cold yesterday but I had fun in the snow.	
regelmäßige Formen	regular forms	Martin called Heather.	
unregelmäßige Formen	irregular forms	Steve went skating.	
Fragen mit ‚was' und ‚were'	questions with 'was' and 'were'	Were you on holiday last week?	
Fragen mit ‚did'	questions with 'did'	Did you like the film?	
Verlaufsform der Vergangenheit	past progressive	Tricia was watching TV.	
‚whose'	'whose'	We found a poor cat whose leg was broken.	
Zeiten	the tenses		20

VOCABULARY

a) Aufbau des Vokabulars

Das Vokabular ist genau wie in deinem Buch vom letzten Schuljahr aufgebaut:
In der linken Spalte findest du die englischen Wörter in der Reihenfolge, in der sie in dem Themenbereich vorkommen. Dahinter steht die Lautschrift in eckigen Klammern. Wie du die Lautschrift lesen musst, steht unten auf dieser Seite.

In der mittleren Spalte stehen Beispielsätze oder kleine Zeichnungen sowie wichtige Hinweise, die dir beim Lernen helfen.

In der rechten Spalte findest du eine deutsche Übersetzung des englischen Wortes. Vergiss aber nicht, dass sich Wörter aus einer Sprache nicht einfach in die andere übersetzen lassen. Deshalb werden manchmal mehrere deutsche Übersetzungsmöglichkeiten angeboten.
Wie im Buch vom Vorjahr findest du Tipps zum Vokabellernen. Außerdem findest du *vocabulary boxes*, die Wörter und Wendungen wiederholen und zusammenfassen. Du lernst sie am besten in Gruppen.

b) Abkürzungen und Zeichen

(pl)	Plural, Mehrzahl
(sg)	Singular, Einzahl
s.th.	something
s.o.	someone
umg.	umgangssprachlich
(AE)	American English
(BE)	British English

=	ist gleich
→	ist verwandt mit
⟷	ist das Gegenteil von
°	Bei Wörtern mit diesem Zeichen frag bitte deine Lehrerin oder deinen Lehrer, ob du sie lernen musst. (Erläuterungen hierzu finden sich auf Seite 157.)

c) Lautschrift

Wie die englischen Wörter ausgesprochen werden, lernst du im Unterricht. Die Lautschrift im Vokabular hilft dir, die Aussprache und Betonung eines Wortes nachzusehen. Sie benutzt einige normale Buchstaben und einige besondere Zeichen. Die Aussprache der einzelnen Zeichen kannst du dir anhand eines einfachen Wortes merken. Die Betonung eines Wortes wird durch einen Betonungsstrich **vor** der betonten Silbe gezeigt: [ˈ] zeigt den Hauptakzent des Wortes, [ˌ] den Nebenakzent. Der Bindebogen [‿] zeigt, dass zwei Wörter in der Aussprache miteinander verbunden werden.

Konsonanten		**Vokale**		**Doppellaute**	
[ŋ]	morni**ng**	[ɑː]	f**a**ther	[aɪ]	**I**, m**y**
[r]	**r**ed	[ʌ]	b**u**t, **u**nder	[aʊ]	n**ow**, h**ou**se
[s]	cla**ss**	[e]	p**e**n	[eə]	th**ere**, p**air**
[z]	i**s**	[ə]	**a** sist**er**	[eɪ]	n**a**me, th**ey**
[ʒ]	televi**sion**	[ɜː]	g**ir**l	[ɪə]	h**ere**, id**ea**
[dʒ]	**G**ermany, pa**ge**	[æ]	**a**pple	[ɔɪ]	b**oy**
[ʃ]	**sh**e	[ɪ]	**i**t	[əʊ]	**o**ld, hell**o**
[tʃ]	**ch**air, lun**ch**	[iː]	**ea**sy, sh**e**	[ʊə]	y**ou're**
[ð]	**th**e	[ɒ]	g**o**t, **o**n		
[θ]	**th**anks	[ɔː]	b**a**ll		
[v]	**v**ideo, ha**ve**	[ʊ]	b**oo**k		
[w]	**w**ord, **o**ne	[uː]	t**oo**, tw**o**		

Alle anderen Zeichen werden genau so ausgesprochen, wie sie im Deutschen geschrieben werden [j, k, …].

1 AUSTRALIA

TEXT MODULE

1 Down under

Places in Australia

Adelaide ['ædəleɪd]
Alice Springs ['ælɪs 'sprɪŋz]
Cairns [keənz]
Darwin ['dɑ:wɪn]
Dungog ['dʌngɒg]
Melbourne ['melbən]
Surfers Paradise [ˌsɜ:fəz 'pærədaɪs]
Sydney ['sɪdnɪ]
Bondi Beach ['bɒndaɪ ˌbi:tʃ]
the **Botanical Gardens** [ðə bə'tænɪkl 'gɑ:dnz]
Harbour Bridge ['hɑ:bə ˌbrɪdʒ]
Opera House ['ɒprə ˌhaʊs]

New South Wales [ˌnju: saʊθ 'weɪlz]
Queensland ['kwi:nzlənd]

Kakadu National Park ['kækədu: 'næʃənl 'pɑ:k]

Great Barrier Reef [ˌgreɪt bærɪə 'ri:f]

down under [daʊn‿'ʌndə]	a popular expression to describe Australia (or the part of the world Australia is in)	*umg.:* Australien; Ozeanien
°**G'day** [gə'deɪ]		Guten Tag *(austr. Begrüßung)*
inhabitant [ɪn'hæbɪtənt]	S.o. who lives in a city or town, for example, is an ~ of it.	Einwohner/in
fence [fens]	like a wall, you can build it between your land and your neighbour's	Zaun
dingo, dingoes *(pl)* ['dɪŋgəʊ]	a wild dog from Australia	*Hundeart*
kilometre (= km) ['kɪləʊˌmi:tə]	1 ~ = 1,000 metres	Kilometer
to **keep out** [ki:p‿'aʊt]	The dingo fence *keeps out* dingoes.	draußen halten
outback ['aʊtbæk]	areas of Australia far away from towns and cities	*austr. Hinterland*
bushman ['bʊʃmən]	s.o. who lives in the wilderness, especially in the outback	jmd. der im Busch lebt und arbeitet
Aussie ['ɒzɪ]		*umg.:* Australier/in
°**surfie** ['sɜ:fɪ]		*austr. umg.:* Wellenreiter/in
the wrong way round [ðə ˌrɒŋ weɪ 'raʊnd]		falsch herum
upside down [ˌʌpsaɪd 'daʊn]	to turn ~ 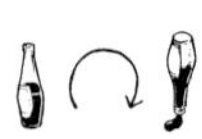	auf dem Kopf
the ... **the** ... ['ðə ... ðə ...]		je ... desto ...
Oz [ɒz]		*umg.:* Australien
Pom [pɒm]		*austr. umg.:* Engländer/in
module ['mɒdju:l]	parts or units of a book, a computer, ...	Modul
°**didgeridoo** [ˌdɪdʒerɪ'du:]		Didgeridoo *(Musikinstrument der Aborigines)*
Yothu Yindi ['jɒtu: ˌjɪndɪ]		*Name einer austr. Popgruppe*
Aborigine [ˌæbə'rɪdʒəni:]	the earliest inhabitants of Australia	*austr. Ureinwohner/in*
continent ['kɒntɪnənt]	Africa, Antarctica, Asia, Australia, Europe, North America, South America	Kontinent, Erdteil
actually ['æktʃʊəlɪ]		eigentlich; tatsächlich

except [ɪk'sept]	Everybody wanted to go to the outback ~ me.	außer
station ['steɪʃn]	In the outback there are huge cattle and sheep ~s.	*Vieh-/Schaffarm im austr. Outback*
lonely ['ləʊnlɪ]	When you are alone you may feel ~.	einsam
° **never-never land** [nevə‿'nevə ˌlænd]	the loneliest parts of the outback	*austr. Ausdruck für weit abgelegene Gegend*
koala bear [kəʊ'ɑːlə‿ˌbeə]	~s can climb up high in trees.	Koalabär
kangaroo [ˌkæŋgə'ruː]	~s can jump a long way. 	Känguru
pretty ['prɪtɪ]	Swimming in the sea can sometimes be ~ dangerous.	*hier:* ziemlich
shark [ʃɑːk]	 ~s can swim fast.	Hai
saltwater [sɔːlt'wɔːtə]	Seas have ~, lakes do not.	Salzwasser
salt [sɔːlt]	~ and pepper	Salz
crocodile ['krɒkədaɪl]	See you later alligator, in a while ~.	Krokodil
° to **cross** [krɒs]		kreuzen; überqueren
1 **contrast** ['kɒntrɑːst]	A ~ is the difference between things when you compare them.	Gegenüberstellung; Gegensatz, Kontrast
border ['bɔːdə]		Grenze; Rand
gas [gæs]	Achte auf die Aussprache!	Gas
desert ['dezət]	A dry area where nothing much grows.	Wüste
reef [riːf]		Riff
territory ['terətərɪ]		Gebiet, Territorium
ocean ['əʊʃəʊn]	An ~ is bigger than a sea.	Ozean
Brisbane ['brɪzbən]		*Stadt in Australien*
Perth [pɜːθ]		*Stadt in Australien*
Tasmania [tæz'meɪnjə]		Tasmanien
position [pə'zɪʃn]		Position, Stelle; Ausgangspunkt

2 Facts about Australia

Internet ['ɪntənet]	You need a computer to get into the ~.	Internet
Hawaii [hə'waɪiː]		*US-Bundesstaat*
raft [rɑːft]	water transport: ~, boat, ship, canoe, hovercraft	Floß
convict ['kɒnvɪkt]	s.o. who is a prisoner 	Strafgefangener/ Strafgefangene
to **be isolated** ['aɪsəleɪtɪd]	to be separate, not with others	isoliert sein
to **develop** [dɪ'veləp]	– What ~s? – Plants, animals, industry, …	(sich) entwickeln
Vietnam [ˌvjet'næm]	~ is an Asian country.	Vietnam
Athens ['æθɪnz]	~ is the capital of Greece.	*Hauptstadt Griechenlands*
Thessalonica [ˌθesələ'naɪkə]	~ is a Greek city, too.	*Stadt in Griechenland*
square kilometre ['skweə 'kɪləʊˌmiːtə]	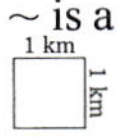 1 ~ is 1 kilometre wide and 1 kilometre long.	Quadratkilometer
prison ['prɪzn]	*prison* → prisoner	Gefängnis
to **export** ['ɪk'spɔːt]	Australia ~s lots of wool to the rest of the world.	exportieren
on the other hand [ɒn ðɪ 'ʌðə ˌhænd]	– He's a nice guy. – True, but ~ he can be quite nasty sometimes.	auf der andere Seite

3 A story from Australia

You will find all the new words from this text in the Alphabetical word list; here are the most important ones.

2	**the only** [ðɪ‿ 'əʊnlɪ]	Australia is ~ country in the world where kangaroos live in the wild.	der/die/das einzige
	to **solve** [sɒlv]	to find an answer to a problem	lösen
	Ms [məz]		Frau *(Anrede für Frauen, ob verheiratet oder nicht)*
	to **reckon** ['rekən]	to think that s.th. will happen	*hier:* glauben, damit rechnen
	bush [bʊʃ]	The Australian ~ is far away from the cities.	Busch *(freies oder offenes Land)*
	next door [ˌnekst 'dɔː]	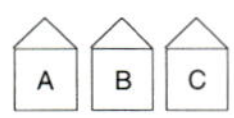 A lives ~ to B, he does not live ~ to C.	nebenan
	spare room ['speə‿ ruːm]	a room that is not in use at the moment	Gästezimmer
	spare [speə]		Ersatz-
	four-wheel drive (= 4WD) [ˌfɔːwiːl 'draɪv]		Fahrzeug mit Allrad-antrieb
	but [bʌt]	There was nothing to see ~ rocks and earth.	*hier:* außer, abgesehen von
	unless [ən'les]		es sei denn; außer
	show [ʃəʊ]	There are ~s at the theatre, at the cinema, ~s where you can buy things, …	Schau; Ausstellung
	back home [bæk 'həʊm]	*back home* ⟷ away from home	zu Hause (damals)
	to **calculate** ['kælkjʊleɪt]		(aus)rechnen, kalkulieren
	certain ['sɜːtn]	You get a ~ colour when you mix yellow and blue.	sicher, bestimmt
	to **water** ['wɔːtə]	water → *to water*	zu trinken geben; gießen
	sheet [ʃiːt]	a ~ of paper, a ~ of glass	Blatt; Scheibe; Laken
	back step [ˌbæk 'step]	*back step* ⟷ front step	Stufe am Hintereingang
	to **come down** [kʌm 'daʊn]		*hier:* hierher kommen
	to **be fair** [feə]	It is important to ~ in sport and games.	fair, gerecht sein
	to **get to know s.o.** [get tʊ‿ 'nəʊ]	It takes time to ~ well.	jdn. kennen lernen
	exit ['eksɪt]		Ausgang; Ausfahrt
	°to **thunder** ['θʌndə]	to make a loud noise like thunder	donnern
	°**bass** [beɪs]	A ~ guitar makes a very low sound.	Bass
	keyboard ['kiːbɔːd]	a *keyboard* →  ← *drums*	Keyboard
	°**drum** [drʌm]		Trommel, (*Pl.* Schlagzeug)
	to **grin** [grɪn]	Dieses Wort ist dem Deutschen ähnlich: **grin**sen	grinsen
	harbour ['hɑːbə]	A ~ is for ships and boats what a station is for trains and buses.	Hafen
	heat [hiːt]		Hitze
	kindergarten ['kɪndəˌgɑːtn]	Dies ist dasselbe Wort wie im Deutschen.	Kindergarten
	excursion [ɪk'skɜːʃn]	a short trip	Ausflug, Exkursion
	ahead [ə'hed]		vorne; vorwärts
	southern ['sʌðən]	south → *southern*	südlich
	to **roar** [rɔː]	lions make this sound	brüllen; *hier:* donnern
	to **blow, blew, blown** [bləʊ, bluː, bləʊn]	– It's hot! – Yes, but the wind is *blowing* nicely off the sea.	blasen
	cool [kuːl]	*cool* ⟷ warm	kühl
	vehicle ['vɪəkl]	car, motorbike, lorry, bus, motorhome	Fahrzeug

to **spread, spread, spread** [spred, spred, spred]	It is easy to ~ your fingers, but it is difficult to ~ your toes.	sich verbreiten; sich ausbreiten; *hier:* ausbreiten
back [bæk]		Rücken
°to **hurl** [hɜːl]	= to throw	schleudern
joyful ['dʒɔɪfʊl]	Laughing is a ~ sound.	freudig, froh
adapted [ə'dæptɪd]		vereinfacht; angepasst
positive ['pɒzətɪv]		positiv

4 English – a language for all?

speaker ['spiːkə]	speak → *speaker*	Sprecher/in
once [wʌns]	Australia was ~ a British colony.	(früher) einmal
The British Empire ['empaɪə]		das Britische Weltreich
ruler ['ruːlə]	The king or queen of a country is the ~.	Lineal; *hier:* Herrscher/in
permanent ['pɜːmənənt]	Your home address is your ~ address.	ständig, dauerhaft
official [ə'fɪʃl]		offiziell
influence ['ɪnflʊəns]		Einfluss
mother tongue ['mʌðə ˌtʌŋ]	the language you learn as a baby and a young child	Muttersprache
tongue [tʌŋ]	The soft part inside your mouth you use for tasting and speaking.	Zunge; Sprache
billion ['bɪljən]	a thousand million	Milliarde
a third [θɜːd]	~ of 9 is 3.	ein Drittel
population [pɒpjʊ'leɪʃn]	all the people who live in a country, area or place	Bevölkerung
airline ['eəlaɪn]	Lots of ~s do direct flights to London.	Fluggesellschaft, Fluglinie

5 *STRATEGIES* Giving a talk

strategy ['strætɪdʒɪ]	Learning *strategies* help you to learn better and faster.	Strategie, Vorgehensweise
to **prepare** [prɪ'peə]	Sorry, I can't go out tonight, I have to ~ for an exam.	(sich) vorbereiten, zubereiten
to **present** [prɪ'zent]	Before you ~ a talk, you must prepare it.	präsentieren, vorstellen
topic ['tɒpɪk]	= subject	Thema
local ['ləʊkl]	Our ~ hospital is two miles away.	örtlich, hiesig, lokal-
atlas ['ætləs]	a book full of maps	Atlas
to **pick (out)** [ˌpɪk‿'aʊt]	You will find all the new words from this text in the Alphabetical word list; here are the most important ones.	(her)aussuchen, herausholen; herauspicken
photocopy ['fəʊtəʊˌkɒpɪ]		Fotokopie
°**scuba diving** ['skuːbə‿ˌdaɪvɪŋ]	an underwater sport	Tauchen
to **have a chat** [tʃæt]	*to have a chat* with s.o. → to talk to s.o.	sich unterhalten, plaudern
pros and cons [ˌprəʊz‿ənd 'kɒnz]	~ = ++++ and ----	Vor- und Nachteile
confidence ['kɒnfɪdəns]	The course will help to build your ~.	Vertrauen; *hier:* Selbstvertrauen
an amount of [ə'maʊnt‿ˌɒv]	~ of sugar, ~ of money, …	eine (bestimmte) Menge an
°**personal attention** [ˌpɜːsnl ə'tenʃn]	In classes of fifty there is not much ~.	persönliche Betreuung
common ['kɒmən]	Dingoes are very ~ in Australia.	gemeinsam; *hier:* häufig, weit verbreitet
°to **recognize** ['rekəgnaɪz]	Good quality is ~d worldwide.	*hier:* anerkennen
certificate [sə'tɪfɪkət]		Bescheinigung, Nachweis

	°**tuition** [tjuːˈɪʃn]		Unterricht
	°**on board** [ɒn ˈbɔːd]	to be on a ship or a boat	an Bord
	°to **differ** [ˈdɪfə]	*to differ* → different, difference	sich unterscheiden
	around [əˈraʊnd]	= about	ungefähr
	°**training site** [ˈtreɪnɪŋ ˌsaɪt]		Übungsplatz
	to **arrange** [əˈreɪndʒ]	to plan, to organize for s.o.	arrangieren, organisieren
4	°**coral** *(sg + pl)* [ˈkɒrəl]	The Great Barrier Reef is the world's largest ~ reef.	Koralle(n)
5	**flow chart** [ˈfləʊ tʃɑːt]	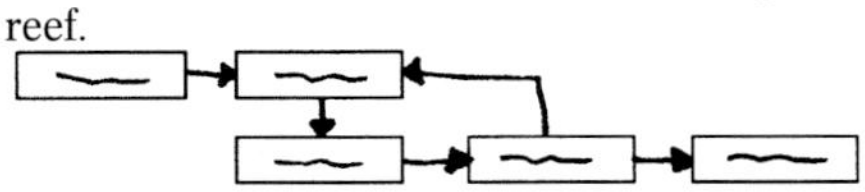	Flussdiagramm
	transparency [trænsˈpærənsɪ]	You use *transparencies* to present important information in a talk.	Folie
	handout [ˈhændaʊt]	Yes, and you can write a summary on a ~.	*zusammenfassendes Papier, Handout*
6	to **stay in touch with** [ɪn ˈtʌtʃ]		*hier:* in Verbindung bleiben mit
	to **interrupt** [ˌɪntəˈrʌpt]	to stop s.o. when he/she is talking so that you can talk	unterbrechen

LANGUAGE MODULE

1 Vocabulary

2	**grin** [grɪn]		Lächeln, Grinsen
	roar [rɔː]		Gebrüll; Donner
3	**general** [ˈdʒenərəl]		allgemein

2 *REVISION* Tenses and relative clauses

1	**explorer** [ɪkˈsplɔːrə]		Forscher/in
	to **land** [lænd]	Dutch explorers ~ed in Australia in the 17th century.	landen; *hier:* an Land gehen
	New Holland [njuː ˈhɒlənd]		*Name für Australien im 17. Jahrhundert*
	Captain Cook [ˌkæptɪn ˈkʊk]		*Personenname*
	to **claim** [kleɪm]	In 1770 Captain Cook ~ed the east coast of Australia for England.	Anspruch erheben auf, beanspruchen
	native [ˈneɪtɪv]	A ~ Australian is s.o. born in Australia.	einheimisch, Einheimische/r, Eingeborene/r, Ureinwohner/in
	natural [ˈnætʃrəl]	*natural* → nature	Natur-, natürlich
2	**nest** [nest]	Birds live in ~s.	Nest
4	**The Australian Open** [ðɪ ɒˌstreɪljən ˈaʊpən]	– I want to go to the ~. – What is it? – A big tennis tournament.	*austr. Tennisturnier*
5	to **be fascinated by s.th.** [ˈfæsɪneɪtɪd]		von etw. fasziniert sein
	Istanbul [ˌɪstænˈbʊl]		*Stadt in der Türkei*

3 Grammar

	to **share** [ʃeə]		teilen
	comfortable [ˈkʌmfətəbl]	It's good to wear ~ clothes for mountain climbing.	bequem

	rainforest ['reɪnˌfɒrɪst]		Regenwald
2	to **keep up** [ˌki:p 'ʌp]		aufrechterhalten, beibehalten
	to **attract s.o.** [ə'trækt]	*to attract* → attraction	jdn. anziehen

Australia words

Aborigine	*austr. Ureinwohner/in*	**kangaroo**	*Känguru*
Aussie	*umg.: Australier/in*	**koala bear**	*Koalabär*
bush	*Busch (freies oder offenes Land)*	**never-never land**	*austr. Ausdruck für weit abgelegene Gegend*
bushman	*jmd. der im Busch lebt und arbeitet*	**outback**	*austr. Hinterland*
didgeridoo	*Didgeridoo (Musikinstrument der Aborigines)*	**Oz**	*umg.: Australien*
		Pom	*austr. umg.: Engländer/in*
dingo	*Hundeart*	**station**	*Bauernhof; Ranch*
down under	*umg.: Australien; Ozeanien*	**surfie**	*austr. umg.: Wellenreiter/in*
G'day	*Guten Tag (austr. Begrüßung)*		

"I wasn't born here but I've adapted to the life in Australia quite well!"

2 FROM SCHOOL TO WORK

TEXT MODULE

1 The World of Work

	voluntary ['vɒləntərɪ]	When you do ~ work you get no money.	freiwillig
	teamwork ['ti:mwɜ:k]	work you do in a group or a team	Teamarbeit
2	**work experience** [ˌwɜ:k ɪk'spɪərɪəns]		Praktikum
	to **apply for** [ə'plaɪ ˌfɔ:]		sich für etw. bewerben

pay [peɪ]	to pay → *pay*	Bezahlung
to **do a paper round** ['peɪpə ˌraʊnd]	You deliver newspapers to people's houses when you ~.	Zeitungen austragen
within [wɪð'ɪn]		*hier:* innen
wage, wages (*pl*) [weɪdʒ, weɪdʒɪz]	the money you get for doing a job	Lohn
to **clean out** [ˌkliːn‿'aʊt]	We need s.o. to ~ the stables.	sauber machen; *hier:* ausmisten
reliable [rɪ'laɪəbl]		zuverlässig
reference ['refrəns]		Empfehlungsschreiben, Referenz
to **earn** [ɜːn]	People go to work to ~ money.	verdienen
hairdresser ['heəˌdresə]	A ~ washes and cuts your hair.	Friseur/in
necessary ['nesəsərɪ]	You needn't help. It isn't ~.	nötig

Jobs

assistant	*Helfer/in, Assistent/in*	**guide**	*Führer/in*
author	*Autor/in*	**hairdresser**	*Friseur/Friseurin*
babysitter	*Kinderbetreuer/in, Babysitter/in*	**lifeboatman/ woman**	*Seenotrettungs- mann/frau*
careers officer	*Berufsberater/in*	**manager**	*Geschäftsführer/in*
cashier	*Kassierer/in*	**nurse**	*Krankenpfleger/ Krankenschwester*
clerk	*Büroangestellte/r*		
coastguard	*Küstenwache*	**police officer**	*Polizist/in*
courier	*Bote/Botin; Kurier*	**ranger**	*Aufseher/in, Ranger/in*
doctor	*Arzt/Ärztin*	**reporter**	*Reporter/in, Journalist/in*
editor	*Herausgeber/in; Redakteur/in*	**soldier**	*Soldat/in*
		teacher	*Lehrer/in*
engineer	*Ingenieur/in*	**vet**	*Tierarzt/Tierärztin*
farmer	*Bauer/Bäuerin*	**window dresser**	*Schaufenster- dekorateur/in*
firefighter	*Feuerwehrmann/frau*		

2 Choosing a career

	career [kə'rɪə]	the course of one's working life	Berufsweg, Karriere
2	**window dresser** ['wɪndəʊ ˌdresə]	Look at that fantastic window. They must have a good ~.	Schaufensterdekorateur/ in
	°**home furnishings** [həʊm 'fɜːnɪʃɪŋz]		Inneneinrichtung
	to **furnish** ['fɜːnɪʃ]	My new flat is furnished, there is a bed, chairs, a table, …	einrichten, möblieren
	window display ['wɪndəʊ dɪˌspleɪ]		Auslage, Schaufenster- dekoration
	display [dɪ'spleɪ]		Ausstellung; Anzeige
	°**window-like** ['wɪndəʊ ˌlaɪk]		fensterähnlich
	construction [kən'strʌkʃn]		Bau, Konstruktion
	object ['ɒbdʒɪkt]	cars, books, candles, toys, …	Gegenstand, Objekt
	college ['kɒlɪdʒ]	kindergarten school *college* university	College, Hochschule
	°**BTEC diploma** ['biːtek dɪ'pləʊmə]		Fachabitur
	diploma [dɪ'pləʊmə]		Diplom
	period ['pɪərɪəd]	The time from November to February is usually a ~ of cold and wet weather.	*hier:* Zeit
	both … **and** ['bəʊθ … ənd]	I like *both* drawing *and* painting.	sowohl … als auch

°**window-dressing** ['wɪndəʊ ˌdresɪŋ]	Good ~ makes a shop look nice.	Schaufenster dekorieren
°**I'll also help** … [help]		Normalerweise helfe ich auch dabei …
to **rearrange** [ˌri:əˈreɪndʒ]	to arrange s.th. again or differently	umstellen
furniture *(sg + pl)* ['fɜ:nɪtʃə]	chairs, tables, cupboards, …	Möbel
°**colour scheme** ['kʌlə ˌski:m]		Farbzusammenstellung
best bit ['best bɪt]		das Beste
table setting ['teɪbl ˌsetɪŋ]	the way you arrange plates, glasses, knives, forks and spoons on a table	Tischdekoration
worst bit ['wɜ:st bɪt]		das Schlechteste
by mistake [baɪ mɪˈsteɪk]		aus Versehen
to **mess s.th. up** [mes‿ˈʌp]	to make a mess of s.th.	etw. durcheinander bringen
to **get some time off** [taɪm‿ˈɒf]	to get a period of time when you do not have to go to work	frei bekommen
salary ['sælərɪ]	People usually get paid their ~ once a month.	Gehalt
fit [fɪt]		fit
military service ['mɪlɪtərɪ ˌsɜ:vɪs]	In Germany men have to go to do ~ at the age of 18.	Wehrdienst
community service [kəˈmju:nətɪ ˌsɜ:vɪs]	Or they have to do ~ instead.	Zivildienst

3 Applying for a job

customer service [ˌkʌstəmə ˈsɜ:vɪs]	a service which shops and companies offer	Kundenservice, -dienst
parcel service ['pɑ:sl ˌsɜ:vɪs]		Paketdienst
parcel ['pɑ:sl]		Paket, Päckchen
delivery [dɪˈlɪvərɪ]		Lieferung
worldwide ['wɜ:ldwaɪd]	A company that offers deliveries ~ usually has many offices.	weltweit
vacancy ['veɪkənsɪ]		offene/freie Stelle
department [dɪˈpɑ:tmənt]	We have a Language ~, a Science ~, a …	Abteilung
applicant ['æplɪkənt]	to apply → *applicant*	Bewerber/in
to **be fluent (in a language)** [bi:‿ˈflu:ənt]	to speak a language very well	(eine Sprache) fließend sprechen
knowledge ['nɒlɪdʒ]	information about a topic which you get through experience and study	Kenntnis(se), Wissen
equivalent [ɪˈkwɪvələnt]	being more or less the same	Gleichwertiges, Entsprechendes
experience in selling [ɪkˈspɪərɪəns‿ ɪn ˌselɪŋ]	S.o. who has been selling things for some time has got ~.	Verkaufserfahrung
on-the-job training [ˌɒn ðə‿ dʒɒb ˈtreɪnɪŋ]	training while you are working	Schulung bei der Arbeit
training ['treɪnɪŋ]	to train → *training*	Ausbildung, Schulung
attractive [əˈtræktɪv]		*hier:* reizvoll
plus [plʌs]		und, plus
°**perk** [pɜ:k]	s.th. extra which a company gives its workers	Vergünstigung
°**personnel manager** [ˌpɜ:səˈnel ˈmænɪdʒə]	s.o. who is responsible for all the people in a company	Personalleiter/in
equal opportunities employer ['i:kwəl ˌɒpəˈtju:nətɪz ɪmˈplɔɪə]		Arbeitgeber/in, der/die Chancengleichheit bietet
opportunity [ˌɒpəˈtju:nətɪ]	the chance to do s.th.	Gelegenheit, Chance
employer [ɪmˈplɔɪə]		Arbeitgeber/in

	to **advertise** [ˈædvətaɪz]	A company can use billboards, newspapers, magazines, etc. to ~.	Werbung/Reklame machen, werben, ausschreiben
	CV (= Curriculum Vitae) [siː ˈviː = kəˌrɪkjələm ˈviːtaɪ]		Lebenslauf
	to **be of German nationality** [biː‿ ɒv ˈdʒɜːmən ˌnæʃəˈnælətɪ]		deutscher Staatsangehörigkeit sein
	nationality [ˌnæʃəˈnælətɪ]	Some people have two *nationalities.*	Nationalität, Staatsangehörigkeit
	apprenticeship [əˈprentɪʃɪp]	a period of time when you learn a job	Lehre
	°**retailing** [riːˈteɪlɪŋ]		Einzelhandel
	°**evening class** [ˈiːvnɪŋ ˌklɑːs]	a class you go to in the evening	Abendschule, Unterricht am Abend
	Business French [ˌbɪznɪs ˈfrentʃ]		Wirtschaftsfranzösisch
	personal interview [ˌpɜːsnl ˈɪntəvjuː]	a face to face interview	persönliches Vorstellungsgespräch
	personal [ˈpɜːsnl]		persönlich
	application [ˌæplɪˈkeɪʃn]	to apply → *application*	Bewerbung
	qualifications [ˌkwɒlɪfɪˈkeɪʃnz]	What ~ do I need for this job?	Qualifikationen; *hier:* Abschluss
3	**date of birth** [ˌdeɪt‿ əv ˈbɜːθ]	the day you were born	Geburtsdatum
	marital status [ˌmærɪtl ˈsteɪtəs]		Familienstand
	single [ˈsɪŋgl]	I've not got a husband or wife, I'm ~.	einzeln; *hier:* ledig
	secondary modern (school) [ˈsekəndərɪ ˌmɒdən]		*brit. Schultyp, entspricht etwa einer Realschule*
	good working knowledge [ˈgʊd ˌwɜːkɪŋ nɒlɪdʒ]		gute Grundkenntnis
4	**colleague** [ˈkɒliːg]		Kollege/Kollegin

Job advert words

to advertise	*Werbung/Reklame machen, werben, ausschreiben*	**experience**	*Erfahrung*
advice	*Rat(schlag)*	**firm**	*Firma, Unternehmen*
applicant	*Bewerber/in*	**interview**	*Vorstellungsgespräch*
application form	*Bewerbungsformular*	**knowledge**	*Kenntnis(se), Wissen*
to apply for	*sich für etw. bewerben*	**opportunity**	*Gelegenheit, Chance*
apprenticeship	*Lehre*	**pay**	*Bezahlung*
business	*Geschäft*	**perk**	*Vergünstigung*
career	*Berufsweg, Karriere*	**personnel**	*Personal-*
company	*Firma, Unternehmen*	**position**	*Position, Stelle*
copy	*Kopie*	**qualifications**	*Qualifikationen, Abschluss*
CV	*Lebenslauf*	**reference**	*Empfehlungsschreiben, Referenz*
department	*Abteilung*	**salary**	*Gehalt*
to earn	*verdienen*	**training**	*Ausbildung, Schulung*
employer	*Arbeitgeber/in*	**vacancy**	*offene/freie Stelle*
		wage(s)	*Lohn*

quiet = ziemlich
probably = wahrscheinlich
at all = überhaupt

LANGUAGE MODULE

1 Vocabulary

whether [ˈweðə]	Achtung! whether – weather	ob

2 STRATEGIES Using a grammar book

task [tɑːsk]	My ~ every week is to think of good window displays.	Aufgabe
countable [ˈkaʊntəbl]		zählbar
passive [ˈpæsɪv]		passiv
gerund [ˈdʒerənd]		Gerundium
authentic [ɔːˈθentɪk]	S.th. that is real is ~.	authentisch; echt

3 Grammar

to **bang** [bæŋ]	My mum ~ed on the door to wake me up.	schlagen
to **order s.o. to do s.th** [ˈɔːdə]		jdm. befehlen etw. zu tun
to **remind s.o. to do s.th.** [rɪˈmaɪnd]		jdm. daran erinnern etw. zu tun
to **move out** [ˌmuːv‿ˈaʊt]	to go to live somewhere else	ausziehen
reported speech [rɪˌpɔːtɪd ˈspiːtʃ]		indirekte Rede
editor [ˈedɪtə]		Herausgeber/in; Redakteur/in
careers officer [kəˈrɪəz ˌɒfɪsə]	s.o. at school or college who gives you advice about your career	Berufsberater/in
however [haʊˈevə]		jedoch, aber
engineering [ˌendʒɪˈnɪərɪŋ]	Achtung! Die Bedeutung ist anders als im Deutschen.	Technik; Maschinenbau
traditional [trəˈdɪʃənl]		traditionell
boss [bɒs]	The No. 1 in a team or a company.	Chef/in, Vorgesetzte/r
to **live on s.th.** [lɪv‿ɒn]		von etw. leben
Guess what! [ges ˈwɒt]		Rate mal!
indirect [ˌɪndɪˈrekt]		indirekt
sir [sɜː]	*sir* ⟷ madam	*höfliche Anrede für einen Mann*
copy [ˈkɒpɪ]	to copy → *copy*	Kopie
lunchbreak [ˈlʌntʃˌbreɪk]		Mittagspause
rice [raɪs]		Reis
alive [əˈlaɪv]	*alive* ⟷ dead	lebend
to **escape** [ɪˈskeɪp]	~ from prison or ~ from a cage	entkommen, entfliehen

TEST YOURSELF

trainee [treɪˈniː]	to train → *trainee*	Auszubildende/r

CV (= Curriculum Vitae) words

activities	*Tätigkeiten; Aktivitäten*	**high school (AE)**	*Gesamtschule*
apprenticeship	*Lehre*	**hobbies**	*Hobbys*
certificate	*Urkunde, Bescheinigung*	**language**	*Sprache*
college	*College, Hochschule*	**marital status**	*Familienstand*
community service	*Zivildienst*	**marks (BE)**	*Noten*
		military service	*Wehrdienst*
comprehensive school (BE)	*Gesamtschule*	**nationality**	*Nationalität, Staatsangehörigkeit*
course	*Kurs, Lehrgang*	**primary school**	*Grundschule*
date of birth	*Geburtsdatum*	**qualification**	*Qualifikation; Abschluss*
diploma	*Diplom*	**secondary modern**	*Realschule*
driver's license	*Führerschein*		
grades (AE)	*Noten*	**trainee**	*Auszubildende/r*

"Can Jennifer come out and work?"

3 THE WORLD AROUND US

TEXT MODULE

1 Helping the environment

Energy words

coal power	*Kohlekraft*	**power station**	*Kraftwerk*
electricity	*Elektrizität, Strom*	**resources**	*Mittel, Ressourcen*
energy	*Energie*	**solar power**	*Sonnen-/Solarkraft*
mine	*Bergwerk*	**water power**	*Wasserkraft*
nuclear power	*Kern-/Atomkraft*	**wind power**	*Windkraft*

Word	Example	German
1 **Midnight Oil** ['mɪdnaɪt ˌɔɪl]	You will find all the new words from this text in the Alphabetical word list; here are the most important ones.	*Name einer Popgruppe*
moon [mu:n]	Day: sun Night: stars and ~	Mond
planet ['plænɪt]	The Earth is called 'The blue ~'.	Planet
to **be glued to s.th.** [bɪ 'glu:d]	When Susan heard the noise she did not move. She felt like she was ~ the chair.	an etw. (fest-)geklebt sein
to **climb** [klaɪm]	~ a mountain, ~ the stairs, ~ a wall	*hier:* steigen
sky [skaɪ]	The ~ can be blue, red and dark.	Himmel
soft [sɒft]		weich; leise
°**plain** [pleɪn]	A ~ is a very flat area.	Ebene, Flachland
to **turn** [tɜ:n]	You ~ a page, a key, a steak, …	(sich) drehen, wenden
once again [wʌns ə'gen]	– This key doesn't fit! – Try it ~!	noch einmal
to **roll away** [ˌrəʊl ə'weɪ]	I dropped my ring and it *rolled away.*	wegrollen
to **wish** [wɪʃ]	I ~ I could find it again.	wünschen
thin [θɪn]	This book only has a few pages; it is very ~.	dünn
nation ['neɪʃn]	The US and Great Britain are English speaking nations.	Nation
axe [æks]	– How are you going to cut the tree down? – I'm going to use an ~.	Axt, Beil
upon [ə'pɒn]	'upon' is a formal word for 'on'	auf
°**sigh** [saɪ]		Seufzen
°to **float** [fləʊt]	An empty bottle ~s on water.	schweben; schwimmen; treiben
to **care (about)** [keə]		sich kümmern (um)
°**blink** [blɪŋk]	opening and closing your eyes very fast	Blinzeln
2 **Friends of the Earth** ['frendz‿ əv ðɪ ˌɜ:θ]		*Name einer Umweltgruppe*
aim [eɪm]	It's the ~ of Friends of the Earth to protect nature.	Ziel
natural resource [ˌnætʃrəl rɪ'sɔ:s]	Water, oil and coal are ~s.	(natürliche) Rohstoffe, Bodenschätze
resources [rɪ'sɔ:sɪz]	Books are a very good ~ for learning.	Mittel, Ressourcen
campaign [kæm'peɪn]	planned activities to reach an aim	Kampagne, Feldzug
pollution [pə'lu:ʃn]	pollute → *pollution*	Umweltverschmutzung
global warming ['gləʊbl ˌwɔ:mɪŋ]		globale Erwärmung, Treibhauseffekt
danger ['deɪndʒə]		Gefahr
to **campaign** [kæm'peɪn]		sich einsetzen, sich stark machen
environmental [ɪnˌvaɪərən'mentl]	It is important that many people campaign for an ~ly friendly lifestyle.	Umwelt-
3 **runway** ['rʌnweɪ]	The part of an airport where planes land.	Start-/Landebahn
protest ['prəʊtest]		Protest
4 **cattle ranching** ['kætl ˌrɑ:ntʃɪŋ]	~ destroys parts of the rainforests because the trees have to be cut down.	Rinderzucht
animal farming ['ænɪml ˌfɑ:mɪŋ]	~ needs a lot of natural resources like water and land.	Viehzucht
°to **go veggie** ['vedʒɪ]		*umg.:* Vegetarier/in werden
°**Get real!** [get 'ri:əl]		*etwa:* Komm auf den Boden!
vegetarian [ˌvedʒɪ'teərɪən]	A ~ eats vegetables but no meat.	Vegetarier/in

2 Enough for everyone?

1	**waste** [weɪst]	Most souvenirs are a ~ of money.	Verschwendung
	hunger ['hʌŋgə]	hungry → *hunger*	Hunger
	diet ['daɪət]		Ernährungsweise; Nahrung; Diät
	Animal Aid ['ænɪml ˌeɪd]		*Name einer Tierschutzgruppe*
	°**aid** [eɪd]		Hilfe
	no longer [nəʊ 'lɒŋgə]	I am a vegetarian, I ~ eat meat.	nicht mehr
2	**CD-ROM** [siː diː 'rɒm]	You use ~s in computers.	CD-ROM
	wind power ['wɪnd ˌpaʊə]	~ is a natural way to produce energy.	Windkraft
	power ['paʊə]		Kraft; Stärke; Macht; Energie
	solar ['səʊlə]	~ power is environmentally friendly.	Sonnen-, Solar-
	nuclear ['njuːklɪə]	Achte auf die Aussprache.	Kern-, Atom-
	to **produce** [prə'djuːs]	We have to ~ more and more energy in this modern world.	produzieren
	electricity [ˌɪlek'trɪsətɪ]	Computers, TVs, fridges: everything needs ~.	Elektrizität, Strom
	to **depend on s.th.** [dɪ'pend‿ɒn]	We ~ energy in everyday life.	abhängig sein von; sich verlassen auf
	northern ['nɔːðn]	southern ←→ *northern*	nördlich
	space [speɪs]	People cannot live in ~ yet.	Weltraum, All
	scientist ['saɪəntɪst]	Einstein was a famous ~.	Wissenschaftler/in
	to **power** ['paʊə]	Solar energy is an environmentally friendly way of ~ing things.	antreiben, betreiben
	calculator ['kælkjʊleɪtə]		Taschenrechner
	source [sɔːs]	The sun is a ~ of energy that is free!	Quelle
	°**turbine** ['tɜːbaɪn]		Turbine
	°**eyesore** ['aɪsɔː]	The graffiti on this beautiful building is an ~.	Schandfleck
	reserve [rɪ'zɜːv]		Reserve
	to **last** [lɑːst]		(noch) reichen; dauern
	to **cause** [kɔːz]	No more oil in the world would ~ problems!	verursachen
	to **create** [kriː'eɪt]		schaffen, verursachen; kreieren
	Industrial Revolution [ɪn'dʌstrɪəl ˌrevə'luːʃn]	Coal was an important source of energy in the ~.	Industrielle Revolution
	industrial [ɪn'dʌstrɪəl]	~ means related to industry.	Industrie-, industriell
	revolution [ˌrevə'luːʃn]		Revolution
	to **mine** [maɪn]		fördern, abbauen
	cause [kɔːz]	the person or thing that makes s.th. happen	Ursache
	across the world [əˌkrɒs ðə 'wɜːld]		weltweit
	renewable [rɪ'njuːəbl]		erneuerbar
	reservoir ['rezəvwɑː]	a natural or manmade lake for keeping water in	Stausee, Reservoir
	power station ['paʊə ˌsteɪʃn]	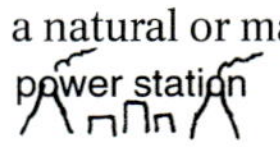	Kraftwerk
	to **run out** [ˌrʌn 'aʊt]		zu Ende gehen, ausgehen
	dishwasher ['dɪʃˌwɒʃə]	A ~ needs electricity and water.	Spülmaschine
	washing machine ['wɒʃɪŋ məˌʃiːn]	So does a ~.	Waschmaschine

3 Airport argument

1	**travel** ['trævl]	~ is made easy with cars, trains and planes.	Reisen
2	**Bollin Valley** [ˌbɒlɪn 'vælɪ]		*Name eines Tals bei Manchester*

event [ɪ'vent]		Ereignis
tent [tent]		Zelt
protester [prə'testə]	to protest → *protester* 	Protestierende/r, Demonstrant/in
sooner or later ['su:nər‿ɔ: ˌleɪtə]	Global warming will cause problems ~.	früher oder später
°**bailiff** ['beɪlɪf]		Vollzugsbeamter/-beamtin
°to **evict** [ɪ'vɪkt]		zur Räumung zwingen
to **set up camp** [set‿ʌp 'kæmp]		ein Lager aufschlagen, lagern
wood [wʊd]		Holz; Wald
to **hit** [hɪt]		*hier:* angreifen
Ziontree ['zaɪəntrɪ]		*Name eines Lagerteils*
Jimi Hendrix [ˌdʒɪmɪ 'hendrɪks]		*hier: Name eines Lagerteils*
to **crawl out** [krɔ:l‿'aʊt]	The hole was so small I had to ~.	herauskriechen
rope ladder [rəʊp 'lædə]		Strickleiter
to **hang, hung, hung** [hæŋ, hʌŋ, hʌŋ]	The rope ladder *hung* in the big old tree.	hängen
to **pull up** [pʊl‿'ʌp]		hochziehen
What's going on? [wɒts ˌgəʊɪŋ‿'ɒn]		Was geht hier vor?
to **shiver** ['ʃɪvə]	to shake with cold or fear	zittern, erschauern
to **dig, dug, dug** [dɪg, dʌg, dʌg]	They *dug* a big hole in the ground.	graben
nursing course ['nɜ:sɪŋ ˌkɔ:s]	A ~ is a training programme for nurses.	Krankenschwester/ -pflegerausbildung
to **whistle** ['wɪsl]	Sometimes the wind ~s in the trees.	pfeifen
in the meantime [ɪn ðə‿'mi:ntaɪm]		in der Zwischenzeit
to **get hurt** [hɜ:t]	When you climb trees or mountains you must be careful not to ~.	sich weh tun, sich verletzen
to **yell** [jel]		*umg.:* schreien, brüllen
to **link** [lɪŋk]		verbinden
saw [sɔ:]		Säge
branch [brɑ:ntʃ]	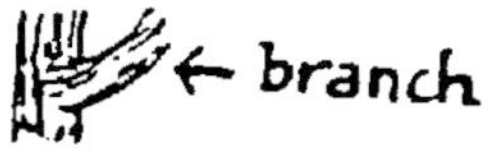	Ast, Zweig; Filiale, Zweigstelle
gate [geɪt]		Tor
°**hypocrite** ['hɪpəkrɪt]	~s say one thing, but do another.	Heuchler/in, Scheinheilige/r
to **take action** [teɪk 'ækʃn]		Schritte unternehmen
to **support** [sə'pɔ:t]	The protesters ~ the campaign against the runway.	unterstützen
argument ['ɑ:gjʊmənt]		Argument, Begründung
to **break the law** [ˌbreɪk ðə 'lɔ:]		das Gesetz brechen
law ['lɔ:]	Stealing is against the ~.	Gesetz
protest march ['prəʊtest ˌmɑ:tʃ]		Protestmarsch, Demonstration
to **dump** [dʌmp]	to drop or put down in a careless way	abladen, fallen lassen
public meeting [ˌpʌblɪk 'mi:tɪŋ]	A ~ is organized by a city or a state; it is not private.	öffentliche Versammlung
MP (= Member of Parliament) [ˌem 'pi: = ˌmembər‿ɒv 'pɑ:ləmənt]	~s decide on things that are linked to the state or country.	Abgeordnete/r *(im Parlament)*
°**local councillor** [ˌləʊkl 'kaʊnsələ]	~s decide on things that are linked to a city or area.	Stadtrat/Stadträtin
°to **boycott** ['bɔɪkɒt]	to stop buying s.th. or doing s.th. as a protest	boykottieren

4 STRATEGIES Creative writing

2	**headline** ['hedlaɪn]	Look at that headline: 'Nuclear waste dumped in river'	Überschrift, Schlagzeile
3	to **welcome** ['welkəm]	I'd like to ~ you all to our meeting today.	begrüßen, willkommen heißen
	discussion [dɪ'skʌʃn]	to discuss → *discussion*	Diskussion, Besprechung

LANGUAGE MODULE

1 Vocabulary

1	**link** [lɪŋk]	to link → *link*	Verbindung
	to **recycle** [ˌriː'saɪkl]	to use waste material to make new things	wiederverwerten
3	to **stress** [stres]		betonen
	stress [stres]	In the word 'recycle' the ~ is on 'cy'.	Betonung; Stress
	similar ['sɪmɪlə]	nearly the same	ähnlich
4	**development** [dɪ'veləpmənt]	to develop → *development*	Entwicklung
	to **accept** [ək'sept]	– I'm so happy. They ~ed me as a member of their band.	akzeptieren, annehmen
	alternative [ɔːl'tɜːnətɪv]	– They didn't have any ~. You're the best singer in town!	Alternative, andere Möglichkeit
	generation [ˌdʒenə'reɪʃn]	Mother and daughter are two ~s.	Generation
	attractive [ə'træktɪv]	attraction → *attractive*	schön, anziehend, attraktiv

2 REVISION The passive voice

2	**laboratory (= lab)** [lə'bɒrətərɪ]	You can learn languages in the language ~.	Labor
	owner ['əʊnə]	This house is mine. I'm the ~.	Besitzer/in
[3]	hardwood ['hɑːdwʊd]		Hartholz
	to clear [klɪə]		*hier:* roden
	ranch [rɑːntʃ]		Ranch, Viehfarm
	plantation [plæn'teɪʃn]	On a ~ there are many plants of the same kind.	Plantage
	to turn s.th. into s.th. ['tɜːn ˌɪntʊ]		… in etwas verwandeln
	soil [sɔːl]		Erde

3 Grammar

1	**speech bubble** ['spiːtʃ bʌbl]		Sprechblase
2	**chemical** ['kemɪkl]		Chemikalie; chemisch
	to **replace** [rɪ'pleɪs]		ersetzen
3	to **crawl** [krɔːl]		krabbeln

TEST YOURSELF

2	**natural science** [ˌnætʃrəl 'saɪəns]	I'm interested in all ~ subjects.	Naturwissenschaft
⟨4⟩	limerick ['lɪmərɪk]		Limerick *(Gedichtform)*
	brain [breɪn]	Use your ~ and think!	Gehirn

verb ➡ noun

to describe	*description*	**to paint**	*painting*	**to interview**	*interview*
to discuss	*discussion*	**to record**	*recording*	**to lift**	*lift*
to examine	*exam(ination)*			**to mine**	*mine*
to inform	*information*	**to calculate**	*calculator*	**to park**	*park*
to introduce	*introduction*	**to compare**	*comparison*	**to pay**	*pay*
to invite	*invitation*	**to enter**	*entry*	**to race**	*race*
to organize	*organization*	**to know**	*knowledge*	**to report**	*report*
to pollute	*pollution*	**to produce**	*product*	**to scream**	*scream*
to suggest	*suggestion*			**to shout**	*shout*
		to barbecue	*barbecue*	**to show**	*show*
to advertise	*advertisement*	**to call**	*call*	**to smile**	*smile*
to develop	*development*	**to change**	*change*	**to sound**	*sound*
to involve	*involvement*	**to crash**	*crash*	**to step**	*step*
to settle	*settlement*	**to dance**	*dance*	**to telephone**	*telephone*
		to drink	*drink*	**to test**	*test*
to build	*building*	**to film**	*film*	**to throw**	*throw*
to feel	*feeling*	**to force**	*force*	**to trick**	*trick*
to mean	*meaning*	**to form**	*form*	**to view**	*view*
to meet	*meeting*	**to group**	*group*		

"I see the pollution levels are up again"

4 THE NORMAN CONQUEST

TEXT MODULE

Norman ['nɔːmən]		Normanne/Normannin, normannisch
conquest ['kɒŋkwest]	to conquer → *conquest*	Eroberung

1 The Battle of Hastings

to **be left without s.th.** [bɪ left wɪˈðaʊt]	People cannot survive if they *are left without* food and water.	ohne etw. sein, dastehen
kingdom [ˈkɪŋdəm]	king → *kingdom*	Königreich
°**nobleman** [ˈnəʊblmən]		Adliger, Edelmann
Normandy [ˈnɔːməndɪ]	part of France in the northwest	*Provinz in Frankreich*
crown [kraʊn]	croWn	Krone
Norway [ˈnɔːweɪ]	~ is a North-European country.	Norwegen
°to **teach s.o. a lesson** [tiːtʃ‿ə ˈlesn]		jdm. eine Lektion erteilen
to **rule** [ruːl]		herrschen über, regieren
to **march** [mɑːtʃ]	The soldiers were ~ing down the road.	marschieren
to **be over** [bɪ ˈəʊvə]	Everybody went home at 1 o'clock because the party *was over.*	vorbei sein
invasion [ɪnˈveɪʒn]	an attack on a country by an army	Invasion, Einfall
fleet [fliːt]	a lot of ships that are sailing together	Flotte
°**favourable** [ˈfeɪvərəbl]		günstig, vorteilhaft
to **fight s.o. back** [faɪt ˈbæk]	They didn't just stand there, they *fought us back.*	jdn. zurückschlagen
to **retreat** [rɪˈtriːt]	to attack ⟷ *to retreat*	den Rückzug antreten
retreat [rɪˈtriːt]		Rückzug
to **crown s.o. (king)** [kraʊn]	All English kings and queens are ~ed in Westminster Abbey.	jdm. (zum König) krönen
rebellion [rɪˈbeljən]		Rebellion, Aufstand
to **put s.th. down** [ˈpʊt daʊn]		*hier:* etw. niederschlagen
brutal [ˈbruːtl]	Die Betonung ist anders als im Deutschen.	brutal
to **be under control** [ˈʌndə kənˌtrəʊl]	The country was ruled by the Normans. It was *under* Norman *control.*	unter Kontrolle sein
coronation [ˌkɒrəˈneɪʃn]		Krönung
to **comment on s.th.** [ˈkɒment‿ɒn]	The reporter *commented on* the situation.	etw. kommentieren

Battle words

action	*Handlung, Geschehen*	**conquest**	*Eroberung*	**leader**	*Führer/in*
advantage	*Vorteil*	**crown**	*Krone*	**legend**	*Legende*
against	*gegen*	**country**	*Land*	**to lose**	*verlieren*
armour	*Rüstung*	**to defend**	*verteidigen*	**to march**	*marschieren*
army	*Armee*	**to destroy**	*zerstören*	**plan**	*Plan*
to attack	*angreifen*	**to fight**	*kämpfen*	**retreat**	*Rückzug*
battle	*Schlacht, Kampf*	**fleet**	*Flotte*	**rebellion**	*Rebellion, Aufstand*
brutal	*brutal*	**to force**	*zwingen*	**revolution**	*Revolution*
castle	*Burg*	**to kill**	*töten*	**route**	*Weg, Route*
colony	*Kolonie*	**knight**	*Ritter*	**soldier**	*Soldat/in*
to conquer	*erobern*	**invasion**	*Invasion, Einfall*	**to trick**	*austricksen*
		kingdom	*Königreich*	**to win**	*gewinnen*

2 The Normans in control

to **order** ['ɔ:də]		befehlen; bestellen
survey ['sɜ:veɪ]	A ~ is made to find out how many of s.th. there are.	Umfrage; *hier:* Volks- und Viehzählung
monk [mʌŋk]		Mönch
county ['kaʊntɪ]		Grafschaft, Landkreis
tax [tæks]	you pay ~ on food, houses, cigarettes, petrol, the money you earn, …	Steuer
single ['sɪŋgl]		*hier:* einzig
ox, oxen *(pl)* [ɒks, oksn]	Achte auf die Schreibung.	Ochse
to **leave out** [li:v‿'aʊt]	When I cooked the meal I *left out* the salt.	auslassen, vergessen
feudal system ['fju:dl ˌsɪstəm]		Feudalsystem
system ['sɪstəm]	a way of doing things	System
society [sə'saɪətɪ]	Today we live in a modern industrial ~.	Gesellschaft
class [klɑ:s]	lower ~, middle ~, upper ~	*hier:* Gesellschaftsschicht
in return (for) [ɪn rɪ'tɜ:n fɔ:]	I will invite you to the cinema ~ your help.	als Gegenleistung (für)
°**nothing but** … ['nʌθɪŋ bʌt]		nichts als …
°**peasant** ['peznt]		Kleinbauer/-bäuerin
to **farm** [fɑ:m]		bebauen
Lord ['lɔ:d]		Herr; Meister
rent [rent]	money you pay to use s.th.	Miete; Pacht
miserable ['mɪzərəbl]	very unhappy	elend, unglücklich
overworked [ˌəʊvə'wɜ:kt]		überarbeitet
villein ['vɪlɪn]		Leibeigene/r
prayer [preə]	the words s.o. is thinking or saying when talking to the Lord	Gebet
throne [θrəʊn]	a chair that kings and queens sit on	Thron
to **carry on** [ˌkærɪ‿'ɒn]		weiterführen, fortführen
royal ['rɔɪəl]	The English ~ family lives in London.	königlich

3 The development of the English language

BC (= before Christ) [ˌbi:'si: = bɪˌfɔ: 'kraɪst]		v. Chr., a. Chr.
various ['veərɪəs]	A rainbow is made of ~ colours: green, blue, red, orange, …	verschieden; mehrere, verschiedene
AD (= Anno Domini) [ˌeɪ'di: = ˌænəʊ'dɒmɪnaɪ]		A.D., nach Chr.
to **drive** [draɪv]	Cowboys ~ cattle from one place to another.	*hier:* treiben
Viking ['vaɪkɪŋ]		Wikinger/in
calf [kɑ:f]	a young cow	Kalb
veal [vi:l]	the meat you get from a calf	Kalbfleisch
mutton ['mʌtn]	the meat you get from a sheep	Hammelfleisch
pork [pɔ:k]	the meat you get from a pig	Schweinefleisch

LANGUAGE MODULE

1 Vocabulary

individual [ˌɪndɪ'vɪdʒʊəl]		einzeln
attack [ə'tæk]		Angriff
to **invade** [ɪn'veɪd]		einmarschieren
diagram ['daɪəgræm]	He drew a ~ to show us how to get there.	Diagramm, Schaubild

5 **Bayeux** [baɪ'jɜː]		*Ort in Frankreich*
The Bayeux Tapestry [ðə baɪ'jɜː 'tæpɪstrɪ]		Teppich von Bayeux

opposites

to agree	↔	**to disagree**	**early**	↔	**late**	**to remember**	↔	**to forget**
back	↔	**front**	**empty**	↔	**full**	**right**	↔	**wrong**
better	↔	**worse**	**to give**	↔	**to take**	**to start**	↔	**to finish**
big	↔	**small**	**in**	↔	**out**	**to stop**	↔	**to go**
boy	↔	**girl**	**left**	↔	**right**	**upstairs**	↔	**downstairs**
careful	↔	**careless**	**to live**	↔	**to die**	**woman**	↔	**man**
day	↔	**night**	**loud**	↔	**quiet**			
dry	↔	**wet**	**to open**	↔	**to close**			

5 YOUR CHOICE

TEXT MODULE

1 What's in a magazine?

contents ['kɒntents]	All the words and pictures that are in a book, magazine or film.	Inhalt
°**fashion makeover** ['fæʃn 'meɪkˌəʊvə]		Typberatung
fashion ['fæʃn]	the way people dress in a certain period in time	Mode
to **break into** ['breɪk‿ ɪntʊ]	The thief *broke into* the house.	einbrechen, eindringen in
entertainment [ˌentə'teɪnmənt]	Music, film, theatre, sport, concert are all different kinds of ~.	Unterhaltung, Entertainment
to **entertain** [ˌentə'teɪn]	*to entertain* → entertainment	unterhalten
consumer [kən'sjuːmə]	~s are people who use and buy things.	Verbraucher/in, Konsument/in
°to **check out** ['tʃek‿ aʊt]	You ~ of a hotel and you ~ how good s.th. is.	sich abmelden, abreisen; *hier:* überprüfen
personal stereo [ˌpɜːsnl 'sterɪəʊ]	I listen to my cassettes on my ~.	Walkman, Discman
stereo ['sterɪəʊ]	My ~ has a a radio, a cassette recorder and a CD player.	Stereo-, Hifi, (-Anlage)
choice [tʃɔɪs]	The things you can choose from is the ~.	Auswahl, Wahl
°**roundup** ['raʊndʌp]	News ~ – the news summary	*hier:* Zusammenschau, -fassung
feature ['fiːtʃə]	important parts of a newspaper, film, person, ...	Beitrag, Bericht, Feature, Eigenschaften, Gesichtszüge
golden ['gəʊldən]	gold → *golden*	golden, Gold-
to **influence** ['ɪnflʊəns]	Consumers ~ fashion.	beeinflussen
health [helθ]	Eat fresh fruit and do lots of sport – think of your ~.	Gesundheit
Oxford Street [ˌɒksfəd 'striːt]		*große Einkaufsstraße in London*
to **make sure** [meɪk 'ʃɔː]	She *made sure* the door was locked before she left.	sicher gehen, sicher stellen, sich vergewissern

to **turn to** [tɜːn tʊ]	*Turn to* page 7 of your books.	*hier:* aufschlagen
advertising ['ædvətaɪzɪŋ]	~ is everywhere: in newspapers, on TV, on the radio, …	Werbung

Electrical products

answering machine	*Anrufbeantworter*	**dishwasher**	*Spülmaschine*
calculator	*Taschenrechner*	**fridge**	*Kühlschrank*
camcorder	*Videokamera*	**microwave**	*Mikrowelle*
camera	*Fotoapparat, Kamera*	**radio**	*Radio*
CD player	*CD-Spieler*	**TV**	*Fernsehen*
computer	*Computer*	**washing-machine**	*Waschmaschine*

2 Critical consumers

critical ['krɪtɪkl]	If you're ~, you try to see the good and bad points of s.th.	kritisch
°**beauty product** ['bjuːtɪ ˌprɒdʌkt]	You can buy ~s at the chemist's.	Kosmetikartikel
beauty ['bjuːtɪ]	*beauty* → beautiful	Schönheit
product ['prɒdʌkt]	Achte auf die Aussprache!	Produkt
the public [ðə 'pʌblɪk]	The castle is open to ~ on Sundays.	die Öffentlichkeit
cream [kriːm]	Face ~ is a beauty product.	*hier:* Creme
by the minute ['baɪ ðə ˌmɪnɪt]	from one moment to the next	*hier:* von Minute zu Minute
to **get s.o. to do s.th.** ['get sʌmwʌn tʊ ˌduː]		jdn. dazu bringen etw. zu tun
afterwards ['ɑːftəwədz]		nachher
to **judge** [dʒʌdʒ]	to form or give an opinion about s.th. or s.o.	(be)urteilen, bewerten
Wigston ['wɪgstən]		*Ort in Großbritannien*
Leicester ['lestə]		*Stadt in Großbritannien*
alcoholic [ˌælkə'hɒlɪk]	Wine is an ~ drink.	alkoholisch
juice [dʒuːs]	orange ~, apple ~, fruit ~	Saft
ignorant ['ɪgnərənt]	He's so ~. He isn't interested in knowing or learning anything.	unwissend, ungebildet, ignorant
°**alcohol content** ['ælkəhɒl ˌkɒntent]	The ~ of wine is about ten percent.	Alkoholgehalt
alcohol ['ælkəhɒl]	*alcohol* → alcoholic	Alkohol
Ruislip ['raɪslɪp]		*Stadt in Großbritannien*
Middlesex ['mɪdlseks]		*Grafschaft in Großbritannien*
to **criticize** ['krɪtɪsaɪz]	to be critical of s.th.	kritisieren
some [sʌm]		irgendein
3D Ultralite [ˌθriː‿diː 'ʌltrəlaɪt]		*Name eines Laufschuhs*
Our lightest ever running shoe. ['rʌnɪŋ ˌʃuː]		Der leichteste Laufschuh, den wir jemals gemacht haben.
light [laɪt]	heavy ⟷ *light*	leicht
spider ['spaɪdə]		Spinne
°**status symbol** ['steɪtəs ˌsɪmbl]	Big expensive cars and big houses are ~s.	Statussymbol
humour ['hjuːmə]	The English are known for their good ~.	Humor
slogan ['sləʊgən]	a short, easy-to-remember phrase which is used in ads	Slogan, Motto, Werbespruch

4	**Blackpool Pleasure Beach** ['blækpu:l ˌpleʒə bi:tʃ]		*Freizeitpark in England*
	committee [kə'mɪtɪ]	Achte auf die Schreibung! Three double letters: mm, tt, ee!	Komitee

3 *STRATEGIES* Listening

1	**booking office** ['bʊkɪŋˌɒfɪs]	Somewhere which takes reservations and sells tickets.	Vorverkaufsstelle; Kartenschalter
	Certificate 12 [sə'tɪfɪkeɪt twelv]	Films that are not for children under 12 years old.	Freigegeben ab 12
2	to **catch** [kætʃ]	He spoke so fast that I couldn't ~ what he said.	*hier:* mitbekommen
3	**radio station** ['reɪdɪəʊ ˌsteɪʃn]	where radio programmes are made	Radiosender
	to **identify** [aɪ'dentɪfaɪ]	to recognize s.th. or s.o.	identifizieren, erkennen
	background ['bækgraʊnd]	Slogans usually have ~ music.	Hintergrund; Herkunft
	comedy ['kɒmədɪ]	a funny play or film	Komödie

4 War of the worlds

	war [wɔ:]	the fighting between different armies	Krieg
	as usual [ˌəz 'ju:ʒl]	= as always	wie gewöhnlich, wie üblich
	to **turn on** [ˌtɜ:n‿'ɒn]	= to switch on	anschalten
	CBS (= Columbia Broadcasting System) [si: bi: 'es]	an American radio and TV station	*amer. Fernsehsender*
	Meridian Room [mə'rɪdɪən ˌru:m]		*Name einer Hotelbühne*
	Hotel Park Plaza [həʊ'tel ˌpɑ:k 'plɑ:zə]		*Name eines Hotels*
	downtown *(AE)* [ˌdaʊn'taʊn]	BE = town/city centre	Zentrum von ..., Innenstadt
	to **be entertained by** [ˌentə'teɪnd baɪ]	We *were entertained* by the clowns at the circus.	von jdm. unterhalten werden
	explosion [ɪk'spləʊʒn]	Did you hear about the ~? It destroyed the whole building.	Explosion
	Mars [mɑ:z]	~ is the fourth planet from the sun.	Mars (*Name eines Planeten*)
	to **approach s.th./s.o.** [ə'prəʊtʃ]	to go towards s.th. or s.o.	sich nähern, zukommen auf; anfliegen
	astronomer [ə'strɒnəmə]	An ~ studies the stars, planets and the sky.	Astronom/in, Himmelsforscher/in
	Princeton Observatory [ˌprɪnstən əb'zɜ:vətrɪ]		*Observatorium bei Princeton, USA*
	°**observatory** [əb'zɜ:vətrɪ]	a place where you can look at the stars	Observatorium, Sternwarte
	to **confirm** [kən'fɜ:m]	The youth hostel ~ed our reservation.	bestätigen
	Grovers Mill [ˌgrəʊvəz 'mɪl]		*Ort in New Jersey*
	New Jersey [nju: 'dʒɜ:zɪ]		*US-Bundesstaat*
	direct [dɪ'rekt]	going straight towards s.th. or s.o.	direkt
	metal ['metl]	Gold is a very expensive ~.	Metall
	scary ['skærɪ]		unheimlich, gruselig, gespenstisch
	to **go cold** [gəʊ 'kəʊld]		kalt werden

6 THE INDUSTRIAL REVOLUTION

TEXT MODULE

1 Changes in society

change [tʃeɪndʒ]	There was a big ~ in the way things were made during the Industrial Revolution.	Änderung, Veränderung, Wandel
to **spin, spun, spun** [spɪn, spʌn, spʌn]	Wool and cotton have to be *spun* before clothes can be made.	spinnen; drehen
cotton ['kɒtn]	~ is used for making T-shirts, trousers, sweatshirts, …	Baumwolle
by hand [baɪ 'hænd]	without using a machine	mit der Hand, von Hand
to **drive, drove, driven** [draɪv, drəʊv, 'drɪvn]	Today machines are *driven* by electricity.	*hier:* antreiben
steam engine ['stiːm ˌendʒɪn]	~s are driven by steam.	Dampfmaschine; Dampflok
invention [ɪn'venʃn]	s.th. that is completely new	Erfindung
to **look like** ['lʊk laɪk]	– What does she *look like*? – She's tall with dark hair.	aussehen
expression [ɪk'spreʃn]	I could see from the ~ on her face that she was not very happy.	Ausdruck
relation [rɪ'leɪʃn]	related, relative, *relation*	Beziehung; Verwandtschaft; Verwandte(r)

2 The Industrial Revolution

anyone ['enɪwʌn]		*hier:* jede(r)
goods [gʊdz]		Waren
they used to do s.th. [juːs‿ tʊ]	300 years ago people *used to do everything* by hand.	sie … gewöhnlich; sie pflegten zu tun
to **set** [set]		*hier:* bestimmen
cloth [klɒθ]	material used to make clothes	Stoff, Tuch
mill [mɪl]	a wind~ produces energy in an environmentally friendly way	Mühle; *hier:* Spinnerei
to **invent** [ɪn'vent]	*to invent* → invention	erfinden
to **employ** [ɪm'plɔɪ]	to give s.o. a job	beschäftigen; einstellen; beauftragen
grey [greɪ]		grau
°**grim** [grɪm]		trostlos; grimmig
chimney ['tʃɪmnɪ]	Smoke goes out of houses and factories through a ~.	Schornstein, Kamin
°**gloomy** ['gluːmɪ]		düster, finster; trübsinnig
iron ['aɪən]	a metal which is very hard	Eisen
locomotive ['ləʊkəˌməʊtɪv]	the first part of a train that pulls or pushes the other wagons	Lokomotive
trading ['treɪdɪŋ]	buying and selling things	Handel, Handels-
mining ['maɪnɪŋ]	coal ~, gold ~, salt ~	Bergbau
to **bring about** ['brɪŋ ə'baʊt]		herbeiführen, verursachen

The world of work

chimney	*Schornstein*	**inspector**	*Kontrolleur/in*	**to pollute**	*verschmutzen*
coal	*Kohle*	**to invent**	*erfinden*	**steam engine**	*Dampfmaschine; Dampflok*
company	*Firma, Unternehmen*	**invention**	*Erfindung*	**trading**	*Handel, Handelsarbeitslos*
to employ	*beschäftigen, einstellen*	**inventor**	*Erfinder/in*	**unemployed**	*arbeitslos*
factory	*Fabrik*	**locomotive**	*Lokomotive*	**workshop**	*Werkstatt*
Industrial Revolution	*Industrielle Revolution*	**machine**	*Maschine*		
industry	*Industrie*	**mill**	*Fabrik, Mühle*		
		mining	*Bergbau*		
		moving part	*beweglicher Teil*		

LANGUAGE MODULE

1 STRATEGIES Word building

1	**whenever** [wen'evə]	I wear sunglasses ~ I go out in the sun.	jedesmal wenn
	James Watt [dʒeɪmz 'wɒt]		*Personenname (Erfinder der Dampfmaschine)*
	unemployed [ˌʌnɪm'plɔɪd]	without a job	arbeitslos
	coal-mine ['kəʊlmaɪn]		Kohlenbergwerk
	parliament ['pɑ:ləmənt]	England and Germany have ~s to decide on the country's politics.	Parlament
2	**inventor** [ɪn'ventə]	to invent → *inventor*, invention	Erfinder/in
	globe [gləʊb]	 l o b e	Kugel; Globus
	pattern ['pætən]	a regularly repeated line or colour	Muster

3 REVISION Reported speech

	past [pɑ:st]	What is the present today will be the ~ tomorrow.	Vergangenheit
2	**Factory Act** ['fæktərɪ ˌækt]	a law that protects factory workers	Arbeitsschutzgesetz
	inspector [ɪn'spektə]	A factory ~ was a kind of police officer.	Kontrolleur/in
	moving part [mu:vɪŋ 'pɑ:t]	Machines have a lot of ~s in them.	beweglicher Teil

TEST YOURSELF

1	**synonym** ['sɪnənɪm]	a word or phrase that means the same as another word or phrase	Synonym, Wort mit gleicher Bedeutung
	to **underline** ['ʌndəlaɪn]		unterstreichen

False friends

Different spellings

address	*Adresse*	**indirect**	*indirekt*	**percent**	*Prozent*
bush	*Busch*	**kangaroo**	*Känguru*	**photo**	*Foto*
campaign	*Kampagne*	**kilometre**	*Kilometer*	**rhyme**	*Reim*
career	*Karriere*	**koala bear**	*Koalabär*	**rice**	*Reis*
carnival	*Karneval*	**locomotive**	*Lokomotive*	**rival**	*Rivale/Rivalin*
carrot	*Karotte*	**model**	*Modell*	**throne**	*Thron*
continent	*Kontinent*	**module**	*Modul*	**Viking**	*Wikinger/in*
crocodile	*Krokodil*	**parliament**	*Parlament*		

Different meanings

to **become** **werden**	≠	to **get** **bekommen**	**chief** **Häuptling**	≠	**boss** **Chef/in**
chips **Pommes frites**	≠	**crisps** **Kartoffelchips**	**rock** **Fels**	≠	**skirt** **Rock**
cake **Kuchen**	≠	**biscuit** **Keks**	**limo** **Stretchlimousine**	≠	**lemonade** **limo**
recipe **(Koch-)Rezept**	≠	**prescription** **(Arzt-)Rezept**	**high school** **Gesamtschule**	≠	**college** **Hochschule**

"Someday, son, all this toxic waste will be yours."

⟨FURTHER READING⟩

1 AUSTRALIA

1 Dingo

to roam [rəʊm]	herumstreunen, herumwandern
unwanted [ˌʌn'wɒntɪd]	unerwünscht, ungewollt
unloved [ˌʌn'lʌvd]	ungeliebt
affection [ə'fekʃn]	Zuneigung, Liebe
pup [pʌp]	Welpe, junger Hund
killer instinct [ˌkɪlər‿'ɪnstɪŋkt]	Instinkt zum Töten, Killerinstinkt
to trap [træp]	mit Fallen jagen; fangen
to poison [pɔɪzn]	vergiften
to wound [wu:nd]	verletzen; kränken
insult ['ɪnsʌlt]	Beleidigung
Georgina country [dʒɔ:'dʒi:nə ˌkʌntrɪ]	*Gegend in Australien*
wide open space ['waɪd ˌəʊpən 'speɪs]	weites, offenes Land
Coolibar ['ku:ləbɑ:]	*Baumart*
Gum [gʌm]	*Baumart*
Box [bɒks]	*Baumart*
parrot ['pærət]	Papagei
to rest [rest]	(sich) ausruhen
paddock ['pædək]	Koppel, Weide
movement ['mu:vmənt]	Bewegung
to herd [hɜ:d]	zusammentreiben
mob [mɒb]	Rudel, Meute
to stray [streɪ]	(umher)streunen
tucker ['tʌkə]	*austr. umg.:* Essen, Proviant
saddle bag ['sædlˌbæg]	Satteltasche
saddle ['sædl]	Sattel
noon [nu:n]	Mittag
to boil [bɔɪl]	kochen, erhitzen, zum Kochen bringen
pot [pɒt]	(Koch-)Topf
hut [hʌt]	Hütte
peacefulness ['pi:sfʊlnɪs]	Friedlichkeit, Ruhe
among [ə'mʌŋ]	unter; *hier:* zwischen
bundle ['bʌndl]	Bündel
fur [fɜ:]	Fell, Pelz
apart from [ə'pɑ:t ˌfrəm]	abgesehen von
vast [vɑ:st]	weit, riesig
to stroke [strəʊk]	streicheln
Lucky ['lʌkɪ]	*Hundename*
plenty ['plentɪ]	viel, reichlich
bone [bəʊn]	Knochen; Gräte
to repay [rɪ'peɪ]	zurückzahlen; belohnen; entschädigen
shadow ['ʃædəʊ]	Schatten
boss [bɒs]	Chef/in, Vorgesetzte/r
to growl [graʊl]	knurren
doorway ['dɔ:weɪ]	Tür, Eingang
the work in hand [ðə 'wɜ:k ɪn ˌhænd]	die anstehende Arbeit
cleanskin ['kli:nskɪn]	*ein nicht gebrandmarktes Rind*
bloody *(BE)* ['blʌdɪ]	*umg.:* verdammt
to give an order [ˌgɪv‿ən 'ɔ:də]	etw. befehlen, anweisen
to carry out [kærɪ 'aʊt]	ausführen, befolgen
to tolerate ['tɒləreɪt]	tolerieren, (er)dulden
to face [feɪs]	gegenüberstehen, ins Gesicht schauen
foolishness ['fu:lɪʃnɪs]	Dummheit, Torheit
to whistle ['wɪsl]	pfeifen (nach)
to approach [ə'prəʊtʃ]	(sich) annähern
move [mu:v]	Bewegung
gone with the wind [ˌgɒn wɪð‿ ðə 'wɪnd]	weg/fort mit dem Wind
to search [sɜ:tʃ]	suchen
to return [rɪ'tɜ:n]	zurückkehren, -kommen
bedtime ['bedtaɪm]	Schlafenszeit
milker ['mɪlkə]	*umg.:* Milchkuh
Jersey ['dʒɜ:zɪ]	*Kuhart*
Friesian ['frɪzjən]	*Kuhart*
to head for ['hed fɔ:]	sich in eine bestimmte Richtung bewegen
sight [saɪt]	Sicht; *hier:* Anblick
straggler ['stræglə]	Nachzügler/in
pack [pæk]	Rudel, Meute
(at a) distance ['dɪstəns]	(in einiger) Entfernung
to circle ['sɜ:kl]	(um)kreisen
to experience [ɪk'spɪrɪəns]	erleben, erfahren
savagery ['sævɪdʒrɪ]	Brutalität
full grown [ˌfʊl 'grəʊn]	ausgewachsen
whistle ['wɪsl]	Pfeife; *hier:* Pfiff
to lick [lɪk]	lecken
to gallop ['gæləp]	galoppieren
mate [meɪt]	*umg.:* Kumpel, Freund/in, Kollege/Kollegin
Bennett ['benɪt]	*Familienname*
abridged [ə'brɪdʒd]	gekürzt
slightly ['slaɪtlɪ]	geringfügig, leicht
setting ['setɪŋ]	Schauplatz 1
narrator [nə'reɪtə]	Erzähler/in
decision [dɪ'sɪʒn]	Entscheidung

2 From Empire to Commonwealth

Commonwealth (of Nations) ['kɒmənwelθ‿ əv 'neɪʃnz]	das Commonwealth
tie [taɪ]	Verbindung
ethnic ['eθnɪk]	ethnisch
culture ['kʌltʃə]	Kultur
to orientate ['ɔ:rɪenteɪt]	sich orientieren

colonial [kə'ləʊnjəl]	Kolonial-, kolonial
law [lɔː]	Gesetz
movement ['muːvmənt]	Bewegung; Trend
monarchy ['mɒnəkɪ]	Monarchie
head of state [ˌhed‿əv 'steɪt]	Staatsoberhaupt
to succeed [sək'siːd]	erfolgreich sein, Erfolg haben
to remain [rɪ'meɪn]	bleiben
sea power [siː 'paʊə]	Seemacht
to break away [ˌbreɪk‿ə'weɪ]	abbrechen, sich loslösen
worldwide ['wɜːldwaɪd]	weltweit
self-government [self 'gʌvnmənt]	Selbstverwaltung
background ['bækgraʊnd]	Hintergrund; Herkunft
independent [ˌɪndɪ'pendənt]	unabhängig
wealth [welθ]	Wohlstand, Reichtum
monarch ['mɒnək]	Monarch/in
Head of the Commonwealth ['hed‿əv ðə 'kɒmənwelθ]	Oberhaupt des Commonwealth
politician [ˌpɒlɪ'tɪʃn]	Politiker/in
professional [prə'feʃənl]	Berufs-, beruflich
typical ['tɪpɪkəl]	typisch

3 Australia: A song and a recipe

1 treaty ['triːtɪ]	Abkommen, Vertrag
politician [ˌpɒlɪ'tɪʃn]	Politiker/in
priceless ['praɪslɪs]	unbezahlbar
promise ['prɒmɪs]	Versprechung, Versprechen
sand [sænd]	Sand
planting of the Union Jack ['plɑːntɪŋ əv‿ðə 'juːnjən 'dʒæk]	Aufstellen der britischen Fahne
law [lɔː]	Gesetz
to run its course [kɔːs]	seinen Lauf nehmen
to separate ['sepəreɪt]	trennen
to dream [driːm]	träumen
brighter day [ˌbraɪtə‿'deɪ]	*hier:* bessere Zeiten
destiny ['destɪnɪ]	Schicksal, Vorsehung
2 Pavlova ['pævləvə]	Pawlowa
raspberry ['rɑːzbrɪ]	Himbeere
strawberry ['strɔːbrɪ]	Erdbeere
redcurrant [ˌred'kʌrnt]	(rote) Johannisbeere
whipped cream [ˌwɪpt 'kriːm]	Schlagsahne
baking paper ['beɪkɪŋ ˌpeɪpə]	Backpapier
stiff [stɪf]	steif
to spread [spred]	verteilen, streichen
to heat [hiːt]	erhitzen
oven ['ʌvn]	(Back)ofen
fan oven [ˌfæn 'ʌvn]	Umluftherd
immediately [ɪ'miːdjətlɪ]	sofort
to dry out [draɪ‿'aʊt]	austrocknen
sticky ['stɪkɪ]	klebrig
to serve [sɜːv]	servieren
method ['meθəd]	Methode

2 FROM SCHOOL TO WORK

1 How's the job then?

Sticks and stones [ˌstɪks‿ən 'stəʊnz]	*Buchtitel*
Graeme ['greɪəm]	*männl. Vorname*
soap-powder ['səʊp ˌpaʊdə]	Waschpulver
on special offer ['speʃl ˌɒfə]	Sonderangebot, im Angebot
to stack [stæk]	stapeln
Roll on twelve. ['rəʊl‿ɒn ˌtwelv]	Höchste Zeit, dass es zwölf wird.
stage [steɪdʒ]	*hier:* Stufe
Labour (= Labour Exchange) ['leɪbə]	Arbeitsamt
Bancroft's ['bænkrɒfts]	*Name eines Supermarkts*
I was to go for an interview. [wɒz tʊ 'gəʊ]	Ich sollte zu einem Vorstellungsgespräch gehen
to fancy ['fænsɪ]	mögen, gefallen
to approve of s.th. or s.o. [ə'pruːv]	billigen
mid-day ['mɪddeɪ]	Mittag
pitch-black [ˌpɪtʃ 'blæk]	pechschwarz
concrete ['kɒnkriːt]	Beton
tile [taɪl]	Kachel, Fliese
to be buried alive [bɪ 'berɪd ə'laɪv]	lebendig begraben sein
to be shut up [bɪ ˌʃʌt 'ʌp]	eingesperrt sein
gardener ['gɑːdnə]	Gärtner/in
to get fed up [get 'fed ˌʌp]	die Nase voll haben, es satt haben
shut in [ˌʃʌt 'ɪn]	eingeschlossen
electric light [ɪ'lektrɪk ˌlaɪt]	elektrisches Licht
to chew [tʃuː]	kauen
in the open [ɪn ðɪ‿'əʊpən]	im Freien
building-site ['bɪldɪŋ ˌsaɪt]	Baustelle
greenfly ['griːnflaɪ]	Blattlaus, -läuse
to roll over [ˌrəʊl 'əʊvə]	sich umdrehen, auf den Rücken rollen
youngster ['jʌŋstə]	Jugendliche/r, junger Mensch
endless ['endlɪs]	endlos
to settle ['setl]	*hier:* konzentrieren
stock-room ['stɒkruːm]	Lager, Lagerraum

to come to ['kʌm tʊ]	*hier:* jdm. einfallen, dämmern
date-stone ['deɪt stəʊn]	Dattelkern
orange-pip ['ɒrɪndʒ pɪp]	Apfelsinenkern
to suppose [sə'pəʊz]	vermuten, annehmen
bloke [bləʊk]	Kerl
rosemary ['rəʊzmərɪ]	Rosmarin
pot [pɒt]	Topf, Blumentopf
to move round in circles [ˌraʊnd‿ ɪn 'sɜːklz]	sich im Kreise bewegen/ drehen
And then he'd say … ['ən‿ ðən hiːd seɪ]	Und dann sagte er immer …
thankful ['θæŋkfʊl]	dankbar
fault [fɔːlt]	*hier:* Schuld

2 Are you obsessed with your work?

to be obsessed with [bɪ‿ əb'sest wɪð]	besessen sein von
to handle ['hændl]	*hier:* umgehen mit; fertig werden mit
pressure ['preʃə]	Druck, Stress
to crack [kræk]	zusammenbrechen, durchdrehen
to relax [rɪ'læks]	sich entspannen
perfectionist [pə'fekʃnɪst]	Perfektionist/in
to be competitive [bɪ kəm'petətɪv]	ehrgeizig sein, sich der Konkurrenz stellen
to be stressed out [bɪ 'strest 'aʊt]	gestresst, belastet sein
to push oneself ['pʊʃ wʌnˌself]	sich schinden
when it comes to work [ˌwen‿ ɪt ˌkʌmz tə 'wɜːk]	wenn es um die Arbeit geht
to get out of [get 'aʊt‿ əv]	sich vor etw. drücken
to hand s.th. in [ˌhænd 'ɪn]	etw. abgeben, einreichen
workaholic [ˌwɜːkə'hɒlɪk]	Arbeitswütige/r
slacker ['slækə]	Bummelant, Faulpelz
to pass by ['pɑːs baɪ]	vorbeigehen
to set oneself a goal [ˌset wʌnˌself ə 'gəʊl]	sich ein Ziel setzen

3 Carol Raymond, a ferry worker

Carol ['kærəl]	*weibl. Vorname*
Raymond ['reɪmənd]	*Familienname*
beverage ['bevərɪdʒ]	Getränk
fresh [freʃ]	frisch
to serve [sɜːv]	bedienen
entertainment [ˌentə'teɪnmənt]	Unterhaltung
facility [fə'sɪlətɪ]	Einrichtung, Möglichkeit
shift [ʃɪft]	Schicht
every other week ['evrɪ ˌʌðə 'wiːk]	jede zweite Woche
close group [ˌkləʊs 'gruːp]	enge Gruppe
set [set]	*hier:* Kreis, Gruppe
on shore [ˌɒn 'ʃɔː]	an Land
married ['mærɪd]	verheiratet
to get divorced [ˌget dɪ'vɔːst]	sich scheiden lassen
willing ['wɪlɪŋ]	bereit
to put up with [ˌpʊt 'ʌp wɪð]	ertragen, sich mit etw. abfinden
to receive [rɪ'siːv]	bekommen, erhalten
life saving ['laɪf ˌseɪvɪŋ]	Lebensrettung
survival [sə'vaɪvl]	Überleben
tax [tæks]	Steuer
to deduct [dɪ'dʌkt]	einbehalten, abziehen
pretty good [ˌprɪtɪ 'gʊd]	ziemlich gut
Alicante [ˌælɪ'kæntɪ]	*Stadt in Spanien*
to keep on doing s.th. ['kiːp‿ ˌɒn dʊɪŋ]	etw. weiterhin machen

4 A song: Money

getaway ['getəweɪ]	Flucht
gas [gæs]	*hier:* Mordsspaß
cash [kæʃ]	Bargeld
to stash [stæʃ]	geheimes Lager
caviar ['kævɪɑː]	Kaviar
stack [stæk]	Haufen, Stapel
hit [hɪt]	Hit, Volltreffer
Don't give me that do goody-good bullshit. [duː 'gʊdɪ ˌgud 'bʊlʃɪt]	*etwa:* Erzähl mir keinen Mist vom Bravsein.
I'm in the hi-fidelity first class travelling set [ˌhaɪfɪ'delətɪ 'fɜːst klɑːs]	*etwa:* ich reise nur erster Klasse
Lear jet ['lɪə ˌdʒet]	Learjet *(Privatflugzeug)*
slice [slaɪs]	Stück
root [ruːt]	Wurzel
evil ['iːvl]	Übel
rise [raɪz]	*hier:* Gehaltserhöhung
none [nʌn]	*hier:* nichts

3 THE WORLD AROUND US

1 Coal

underground ['ʌndəgraʊnd]	unterirdisch; *hier:* unter Tage 1
dust [dʌst]	Staub
miner ['maɪnə]	Bergarbeiter/in
coal face ['kəʊlfeɪs]	Streb *(Stollen, in dem Kohle abgebaut wird)*
pick [pɪk]	Spitzhacke, Pickel
shovel ['ʃʌvl]	Schaufel

waggon ['wægən]	Wagen
gallery ['gælərɪ]	*hier:* Stollen
low [ləʊ]	niedrig
railway line ['reɪlweɪ ˌlaɪn]	Eisenbahnlinie
earth fall ['ɜ:θ fɔ:l]	Erdrutsch
to remain [rɪ'meɪn]	übrig bleiben
Elbow gallery ['elbəʊ ˌgælərɪ]	*Name eines Stollens*
Johnson coal mine ['dʒɒnsn 'kəʊl ˌmaɪn]	*Name eines Bergwerks*
surface ['sɜ:fɪs]	Oberfläche
subsidence [səb'saɪdns]	Senkung
to sort [sɔ:t]	sortieren
to mechanise ['mekənaɪz]	mechanisieren
ton [tʌn]	Tonne
Jud [dʒʌd]	*männl. Vorname*
Moses ['məʊzɪz]	*Name eines Pferdes*
to step on ahead [ˌstep‿ɒn ə'hed]	nach vorne treten
shadow ['ʃædəʊ]	Schatten
lamp [læmp]	Lampe
to roll one's eyes [rəʊl wʌnz 'aɪz]	mit den Augen rollen
backwards ['bækwədz]	rückwärts
darkness ['dɑ:knɪs]	Dunkelheit
workmate ['wɜ:kmeɪt]	Arbeitskollege/-kollegin
to be relieved [bɪ rɪ'li:vd]	erleichtert sein
you'd have had it ['ju:d hæv 'hæd‿ ɪt]	es wäre vorbei mit dir gewesen
to block [blɒk]	blockieren, versperren
What an escape! [ɪ'skeɪp]	Das war knapp!
to kneel [ni:l]	knien
to flood [flʌd]	überschwemmen, hereinströmen
pipe [paɪp]	Rohr, Röhre
fresh [freʃ]	frisch
to last [lɑ:st]	*hier:* überleben
battery ['bætərɪ]	Batterie
far-off sound ['fɑ:r‿ ɒf saʊnd]	weit entferntes Geräusch
to tap [tæp]	klopfen
safety ['seɪftɪ]	Sicherheit

2 North Sea oil

to extract [ɪk'strækt]	fördern, gewinnen
economy [ɪ'kɒnəmɪ]	Wirtschaft
economic development [ˌi:kə'nɒmɪk dɪ'veləpmənt]	wirtschaftliche Entwicklung
Aberdeen [ˌæbə'di:n]	*Stadt in Schottland*
facility [fə'sɪlətɪ]	Einrichtung, Möglichkeit
extraction [ɪk'strækʃn]	Gewinnung, Förderung
oil platform [ɔɪl 'plætfɔ:m]	Ölbohrinsel
activist ['æktɪvɪst]	Aktivist/in
Brent Spar [brent 'spɑ:]	*Name einer Ölbohrinsel*
to occupy ['ɒkjʊpaɪ]	*hier:* besetzen
Greenpeace ['gri:nˌpi:s]	Greenpeace *(Name einer Umweltorganisation)*
Shetland ['ʃetlənd]	*schottische Insel*
to dump [dʌmp]	*hier:* versenken
Shell [ʃel]	*Name einer Mineralölgesellschaft*
to store [stɔ:]	lagern
Brent field [brent 'fi:ld]	*Name eines Ölfeldes*
to pipe [paɪp]	in Rohren leiten, pumpen
ashore [ə'ʃɔ:]	an Land
to contain [kən'teɪn]	enthalten
toxic material [ˌtɒksɪk mə'tɪərɪəl]	toxisches/giftiges Material
spokesperson ['spəʊksˌpɜ:sn]	Sprecher/in
come to rest [kʌm tʊ 'rest]	seine/ihre Ruhe finden
ton [tʌn]	Tonne
to take to pieces [teɪk tə 'pi:sɪz]	auseinandernehmen/bauen
resting place ['restɪŋ ˌpleɪs]	Ruheplatz
opposition [ˌɒpə'zɪʃn]	Opposition
to take out of service [teɪk aʊt‿ ɒv 'sɜ:vɪs]	außer Betrieb nehmen

3 Poem: 'The Battery Hen', by Pam Ayres

battery ['bætərɪ]	Batterie
hen [hen]	Huhn
Pam Ayres [pæm 'eəz]	*Personenname*
humorous ['hju:mərəs]	lustig, humorvoll
germ [dʒɜ:m]	Bazillus, Keim
to scratch [skrætʃ]	*hier:* scharren
farmyard ['fɑ:mjɑ:d]	Bauernhof
to peck [pek]	picken
worm [wɜ:m]	Wurm
the likes of you [ðə 'laɪks‿ əv 'ju:]	Leute wie du/ihr
to scramble ['skræmbl]	verrühren, zu Rührei verarbeiten
to pile up ['paɪl‿ ˌʌp]	aufhäufen
funnel ['fʌnl]	Trichter
to stick out ['stɪk ˌaʊt]	herein-/herausragen
pellet ['pelɪt]	Kügelchen
squirt [skwɜ:t]	Spritzer
beady eye ['bi:dɪ aɪ]	*hier:* Knopfauge
strategical [strə'ti:dʒɪkl]	strategisch
to place [pleɪs]	aufstellen, platzieren
to go to waste [ˌgəʊ tə 'weɪst]	verkommen, verschwendet werden
tubing ['tju:bɪŋ]	Verbindungsröhre
gangway ['gæŋweɪ]	Kanal, in dem die Eier abtransportiert werden
chick [tʃɪk]	Küken

cockerel ['kɒkərəl]	junger Hahn
fine [faɪn]	fein, prächtig
to pay one's respects to s.o. ['peɪ rɪ'spekts]	jdm. seine Aufwartung machen
to wring s.o.'s neck ['rɪŋ ˌsʌmwʌnz 'nek]	jdm. den Hals umdrehen
Time and Motion clock ['taɪm‿ ənd 'məʊʃn 'klɒk]	*hier:* Fütterungsautomat
noon [nu:n]	Mittag
'spec (= expect) [spek]	*Abk.:* ich nehme an
spray [spreɪ]	*hier:* Schauer
wire nettin' (= wire netting) ['waɪə ˌnetɪn]	Maschengitter
bloody *(BE)* ['blʌdɪ]	*umg.:* verdammt

4 THE NORMAN CONQUEST

Hereward at King William's court

Hereward ['herɪwəd]	*männl. Vorname*
the Fens [ðə 'fenz]	*Landschaft in England*
Ely [i:lɪ]	*Stadt in England*
then [ðən]	damals
to beat off [bi:t‿ 'ɒf]	wegjagen
to make sure [meɪk 'ʃɔ:]	sicher gehen, sicher stellen, sich vergewissern
impossible [ɪm'pɒsəbl]	unmöglich
Brandon ['brændən]	*Stadt in England*
to start off [stɑ:t‿ 'ɒf]	*hier:* sich auf den Weg machen
Swallow ['swɒləʊ]	*Name eines Pferdes*
awkward ['ɔ:kwəd]	unbeholfen, ungeschickt
cloak [kləʊk]	Umhang, Mantel
potter ['pɒtə]	Töpfer/in
pot [pɒt]	Topf
as well [əz 'wel]	auch (noch)
witchcraft ['wɪtʃkrɑ:ft]	Zauberkraft, Zauberei
witch [wɪtʃ]	Hexe
first-class ['fɜ:st ˌklɑ:s]	erste Klasse
servant ['sɜ:vənt]	Diener/in
the king's hall [ˌkɪŋz 'hɔ:l]	der Königssaal
daring ['dərɪŋ]	wagemutig
order ['ɔ:də]	Befehl
cook [kʊk]	Koch/Köchin
blindfold ['blaɪndfəʊld]	Augenbinde
guard [gɑ:d]	Wache
sword [sɔ:d]	Schwert
iron chain [ˌaɪən 'tʃaɪn]	Eisenkette
yard [jɑ:d]	Hof

5 YOUR CHOICE

1 What kind of reader are you?

questionnaire [ˌkwestʃə'neə]	Fragebogen
vague(ly) ['veɪglɪ]	*hier:* in etwa, ungefähr
to pretend [prɪ'tend]	tun als ob, vortäuschen
I used to have [ˌaɪ 'ju:stə ˌhæv]	ich hatte früher
to own [əʊn]	besitzen
book token ['bʊk ˌtəʊkən]	Buchgutschein
to flip through s.th. ['flɪp θru:]	durchblättern
to catch s.o.'s eye [kætʃ]	jdm. auffallen
to encourage [ɪn'kʌrɪdʒ]	anregen, ermuntern
occasional(ly) [ə'keɪʒənəlɪ]	gelegentlich, hin und wieder
past (month) [pɑ:st]	vergangen(en Monat)
to score [skɔ:]	abschneiden (bei einem Spiel oder Wettkampf)
to advise s.o. [əd'vaɪz]	jdm. raten
lazy ['leɪzɪ]	faul

2 Rap music

originally [ə'rɪdʒənəlɪ]	ursprünglich
rapper ['ræpə]	Rapper
soul (= soul music) [səʊl]	Soul *(Musikrichtung)*
jive-talk ['dʒaɪv tɔ:k]	*umg.:* junger Afro-Amerikaner
hip-hop ['hɪp ˌhɒp]	Hip-hop *(Musik- und Moderichtung)*
culture ['kʌltʃə]	Kultur
ghetto ['getəʊ]	Getto
MC (= Master of Ceremonies) [em 'si: = 'mɑ:stər‿ əv 'serɪmənɪz]	*hier:* Rap-Interpret/in
social ['səʊʃl]	sozial
category ['kætəgərɪ]	Kategorie, Art
Kurtis Blow [kɜ:rtɪs 'bləʊ]	*Personenname*
ego-trip ['egəʊ ˌtrɪp]	Egotrip; selbstsüchtig
inspirational [ˌɪnspə'reɪʃənl]	inspirierend, aufmunternd
political [pə'lɪtɪkl]	politisch
gossip ['gɒsɪp]	Klatsch, Tratsch
informative [ɪn'fɔ:mətɪv]	informativ, aufschlussreich
basically ['beɪsɪkəlɪ]	im Grunde genommen

3 Spotlight on sport

spotlight ['spɒtlaɪt]	Rampenlicht
Dennis Rodman [denɪs 'rɒdmən]	*Personenname*

NBA (= National Basketball Association) [en biː 'eɪ]	*amer. Basketball-Profiliga*
arena [ə'riːnə]	*hier:* Sporthalle
mall *(AE)* [mɔːl]	Einkaufszentrum
jersey ['dʒɜːzɪ]	*hier:* Trikot
cap [kæp]	Mütze
to dive for a ball [ˌdaɪv fːrə 'bɔːl]	nach einem Ball hechten
San Antonio [ˌsænæn'təʊnɪəʊ]	*Stadt in den US*
bleach-blond [bliːtʃ 'blɒnd]	blond gefärbt
to appreciate [ə'priːʃɪeɪt]	*hier:* anerkennen
to provide [prə'vaɪd]	liefern, zur Verfügung stellen
entertainment [ˌentə'teɪnmənt]	Unterhaltung
league [liːg]	Liga
to market ['mɑːkɪt]	vermarkten, werben
commercial [kə'mɜːʃl]	Anzeige, Werbung
role model [rəʊl 'mɒdl]	Vorbild
locker-room ['lɒkə ruːm]	Umkleidekabine
all along [ˌɔːl ə'lɒŋ]	die ganze Zeit
to matter ['mætə]	wichtig sein
guardian angel ['gɑːdjən‿'eɪndʒl]	Schutzengel
I might as well [aɪ maɪt ə'zwel]	dann kann ich auch
to be worth [bɪ 'wɜːθ]	wert sein
soul [səʊl]	Seele
to preach [priːtʃ]	predigen
ridiculous [rɪ'dɪkjʊləs]	lächerlich
response [rɪ'spɒns]	Reaktion
Bad as I wanna be [bæd‿əz aɪ 'wʌnə bɪ]	*Buchtitel*
to hit the headlines [ˌhɪt ðə 'hedlaɪnz]	Schlagzeilen machen

6 THE INDUSTRIAL REVOLUTION

1 Child labour in factories and mines

child labour ['tʃaɪld ˌleɪbə]	Kinderarbeit
labour ['leɪbə]	Arbeit
particularly [pə'tɪkjʊləlɪ]	besonders
investigation [ɪnˌvestɪ'geɪʃn]	Untersuchung
Edwin ['edwɪn]	*männl. Vorname*
lively ['laɪvlɪ]	lebhaft
straight [streɪt]	gerade
hardly ['hɑːdlɪ]	kaum
tub [tʌb]	Eimer, Wanne
bald place [bɔːld]	kahle Stelle
to thrust [θrʌst]	stoßen
underground ['ʌndəgraʊnd]	unterirdisch; unter Tage
to weigh [weɪ]	wiegen
hundredweight ['hʌndredweɪt]	Zentner
coal-digger ['kəʊl ˌdɪgə]	Bergmann/-frau
pit [pɪt]	Zeche
trapper [træpə]	*Kind, das die Klappen von Schächten öffnet und schließt*
frequently ['friːkwəntlɪ]	oft
damp [dæmp]	feucht
to vary ['veərɪ]	schwanken; sich unterscheiden
textile ['tekstaɪl]	*hier:* Textilindustrie
agriculture ['ægrɪkʌltʃə]	Landwirtschaft

2 And today

dust [dʌst]	Staub
chemical powder [ˌkemɪkl 'paʊdə]	chemisches Pulver
vapour ['veɪpə]	Dunst
storeroom ['stɔːrʊm]	Lagerraum
boiler room [bɔɪlə 'rʊm]	Heizungsraum
obvious ['ɒbvɪəs]	offensichtlich
hall [hɔːl]	Saal
row upon row ['rəʊ ʌˌpɒn 'rəʊ]	reihenweise
barely [beəlɪ]	kaum
matchstick ['mætʃstɪk]	Streichholz
share [ʃeə]	Anteil
income ['ɪŋkʌm]	Einkommen
trade union [ˌtreɪd 'juːnjən]	Gewerkschaft
right [raɪt]	Recht
data ['deɪtə]	Daten
to register ['redʒɪstə]	anmelden
housemaid ['haʊsmeɪd]	Dienstmädchen
statistic [stə'tɪstɪk]	Statistik

⟨REVISION⟩

1 Tenses

will-future [wɪl 'fjuːtʃə]	will-Futur	1
sheep-shearing ['ʃiːpˌʃɪərɪŋ]	Schafe scheren	
to shear [ʃɪə]	scheren	
Riverina ['rɪvəriːnə]	*Gegend in Australien*	
Darling Downs [ˌdɑːlɪŋ 'daʊnz]	*Gegend in Australien*	
with a break in his voice [breɪk]	mit stockender Stimme	
to bet [bet]	wetten	

2 Conditional sentences

3	conditional [kən'dɪʃənl]	das Konditional
	golf course ['gɒlfˌkɔːs]	Golfplatz
	Rigby Road [ˌrɪgbɪ 'rəʊd]	*Straßenname*
	gardener ['gɑːdnə]	Gärtner/in
	public footpath [ˌpʌblɪk 'fʊtpɑːθ]	öffentlicher Fußweg
	to close off [ˌkləʊz 'ɒf]	*hier:* zumachen
4	proper ['prɒpə]	*hier:* richtig

3 '-ing'-forms

to be afraid of [bɪ‿ ə'freɪd]	Angst haben vor	8

4 Reported speech

shampoo [ʃæm'puː]	Shampoo	9
to change one's mind ['tʃeɪndʒ wʌnz 'maɪnd]	es sich anders überlegen, seine Meinung ändern	10
to afford [ə'fɔːd]	sich leisten	

ALPHABETICAL WORD LIST

In dieser alphabetischen Liste ist das gesamte Vokabular von *Red Line New 1–5* enthalten. Namen werden in einer gesonderten Liste nach dem Vokabular aufgeführt.
Die mit einem ° gekennzeichneten Wörter zeichnen den rezeptiven Wortschatz aus. In Bundesländern, in denen nicht ausdrücklich rezeptiver Wortschatz verlangt wird, werden diese Wörter genauso behandelt wie der übrige Wortschatz. Die rezeptiv gekennzeichneten Wörter können innerhalb des Themenbereiches, in dem sie erstmalig vorkommen, eigenständig von den Schülerinnen und Schülern angewandt werden. Falls sie in späteren Themenbereichen auftauchen, werden sie nur mit Hilfe von Vorgaben verlangt.
Der Wortschatz aus Übungen und Texten, die in Spitzklammern ⟨ ⟩ stehen, ist wahlfrei.
Der Wortschatz in rechteckigen Klammern [ ] kommt in Texten bzw. Übungen vor, die nicht für alle Bundesländer verbindlich sind.
Das Zeichen * nach einem Verb bedeutet: unregelmäßiges Verb.
Die Zahlen verweisen auf das erstmalige Vorkommen der Wörter, z. B.
about [əˈbaʊt] über **I** = Red Line New Band 1
advertising [ˈædvətaɪzɪŋ] Werbung **V 5**, 51 = Red Line New Band 5, Topic 5, Seite 51

A

'A' level [ˈeɪ ˌlevl] Abschlussprüfung (*entspricht in etwa dem Abitur*) **III**
a [ə] ein/eine **I**
a deal for s.th. [diːl] ein Angebot für etw. **IV**
a hundred years ago [ə ˈhʌndrəd jɪəz əˈgəʊ] vor hundert Jahren **II**
a third [θɜːd] ein Drittel **V 1**, 12
abbreviation [əˌbriːvɪˈeɪʃn] Abkürzung **IV**
to be **able to** [bɪ ˈeɪbl tə] können **III**
Aborigine [ˌæbəˈrɪdʒəniː] *austr. Ureinwohner/in* **V 1**, 8
about [əˈbaʊt] über **I**; ungefähr **III**
to talk about [ˈtɔːk‿əˈbaʊt] reden über, sprechen über **I**
What about …? [wɒt‿əˈbaʊt] Was ist mit …? **I**
above [əˈbʌv] über **II**
⟨abridged⟩ [əˈbrɪdʒd] gekürzt **V 1**, 69
accent [ˈæksent] Akzent **III**
to **accept** [əkˈsept] akzeptieren, annehmen **V 3**, 40
accident [ˈæksɪdənt] Unfall **I**
according to [əˈkɔːdɪŋ tʊ] nach, laut, gemäß **IV**
to **accuse s.o. of s.th.** [əˈkjuːz] jdn. beschuldigen/anklagen, etw. getan zu haben **IV**
across [əˈkrɒs] über **III**
across the world [əˌkrɒs ðə ˈwɜːld] weltweit **V 3**, 35
to **act** [ækt] spielen, nachspielen **I**
to act normal [ˌækt ˈnɔːml] sich normal benehmen **III**
action [ˈækʃn] Handlung, Geschehen **II**
out of action [aʊt‿əv ˈækʃn] außer Betrieb **IV**
⟨activist⟩ [ˈæktɪvɪst] Aktivist/in **V 3**, 78
activity [ækˈtɪvɪtɪ] Tätigkeit **I**
actor [ˈæktə] Schauspieler **IV**
actually [ˈæktʃʊəlɪ] eigentlich; tatsächlich **V 1**, 8
AD (= **Anno Domini**) [ˌeɪˈdiː = ˌænəʊˈdɒmɪnaɪ] A.D., nach Chr. **V 4**, 47
to **adapt** [əˈdæpt] adaptieren, anpassen **III**
adapted [əˈdæptɪd] vereinfacht; angepasst **V 1**, 11
to **add** [æd] addieren, hinzufügen **II**
address [əˈdres] Adresse, Anschrift **III**
adjective [ˈædʒɪktɪv] Adjektiv **II**
adult [ˈædʌlt] Erwachsene/r **II**
advantage [ədˈvɑːntɪdʒ] Vorteil **IV**
adventure [ədˈventʃə] Abenteuer **II**
adverb [ˈædvɜːb] Adverb **III**
to **advertise** [ˈædvətaɪz] Werbung/Reklame machen, werben, ausschreiben **V 2**, 23
advertisement (= **ad, advert**) [ədˈvɜːtɪsment] Anzeige, Werbung **II**
advertising [ˈædvətaɪzɪŋ] Werbung **V 5**, 51
advice [ədˈvaɪs] Rat(schlag) **IV**
⟨to advise s.o.⟩ [ədˈvaɪz] jdm. raten **V 5**, 82
⟨affection⟩ [əˈfekʃn] Zuneigung, Liebe **V 1**, 68
⟨to afford⟩ [əˈfɔːd] sich leisten **V R**, 91
African [ˈæfrɪkən] afrikanisch, Afrikaner/in **III**
African-American [ˌæfrɪkən‿əˈmerɪkən] afroamerikanisch, Afroamerikaner/in **IV**
after [ˈɑːftə] nach **I**
after all [ɑːftər‿ˈɔːl] doch, doch noch **IV**
afternoon [ɑːftəˈnuːn] Nachmittag **I**
Good afternoon. [gʊd ɑːftəˈnuːn] Guten Tag. (*Anrede am Nachmittag*) **I**
in the afternoon [ɪn ðiː‿ɑːftəˈnuːn] nachmittags, am Nachmittag **I**
this afternoon [ðɪs‿ɑːftəˈnuːn] heute Nachmittag **I**
afterwards [ˈɑːftəwədz] nachher **V 5**, 52
again [əˈgen] wieder, noch einmal **I**
again and again [əˌgen‿ənd‿əˈgen] immer wieder **III**
against [əˈgenst] gegen **III**
aged [eɪdʒd] im Alter von, … Jahre alt **IV**
agency [ˈeɪdʒənsɪ] Agentur **IV**
for **ages** [fɔː ˈeɪdʒɪz] seit langem, schon ewig **IV**
ago [əˈgəʊ] vor (*nachgestellt*) **II**
to **agree** [əˈgriː] übereinstimmen **IV**
⟨agriculture⟩ [ˈægrɪkʌltʃə] Landwirtschaft **V 6**, 86
ahead [əˈhed] vorne; vorwärts **V 1**, 11
to go ahead [əˈhed] vorangehen **IV**
° **aid** [eɪd] Hilfe **V 3**, 34
aim [eɪm] Ziel **V 3**, 33
air [eə] Luft **III**
air stream travel [ˈeə striːm ˌtrævl] „Luftstromtransport" **III**
airhead [ˈeəhed] „Spinner", dumme Person **III**
airline [ˈeəlaɪn] Fluggesellschaft, Fluglinie **V 1**, 12
airport [ˈeəpɔːt] Flughafen **I**
alarm [əˈlɑːm] Alarm **IV**
alcohol [ˈælkəhɒl] Alkohol **V 5**, 52
°alcohol content [ˈælkəhɒl ˌkɒntent] Alkoholgehalt **V 5**, 52
alcoholic [ˌælkəˈhɒlɪk] alkoholisch **V 5**, 52
alive [əˈlaɪv] lebend **V 2**, 30
all [ɔːl] alle/alles **I**; ganz **I**
⟨all along⟩ [ˌɔːl əˈlɒŋ] die ganze Zeit **V 5**, 85
All in a day's work. [ˈɔːl ɪn‿ə ˈdeɪz wɜːk] *etwa:* Das gehört zu meiner täglichen Arbeit. **IV**
all over [ˈɔːl‿ˌəʊvə] überall auf **I**
all right (= alright) [ˈɒl ˈraɪt] in Ordnung **II**
all the time [ɔːl θə‿ˈtaɪm] die ganze Zeit **IV**
alligator [ˈælɪgeɪtə] Alligator **IV**
⟨to allow⟩ [əˈlaʊ] erlauben **V TP**, 92
to be allowed to [bɪ əˈlaʊd tə] dürfen **III**
almost [ˈɔːlməʊst] fast, beinahe **II**
alone [əˈləʊn] allein **II**
to leave s.o. alone [liːv ə pɜːsn əˈləʊn] jdn. in Ruhe lassen **II**
along [əˈlɒŋ] entlang **III**
alphabet [ˈælfəbɪt] Alphabet **I**
alphabetical order [ˌælfəˈbetɪkl ˈɔːdə] alphabetische Reihenfolge **II**

already [ɔ:l'redɪ] schon **II**
also ['ɔ:lsəʊ] außerdem **II**
alternative [ɔ:l'tɜ:nətɪv] Alternative, andere Möglichkeit **V 3**, 40
although [ɔ:l'ðəʊ] obwohl **III**
always ['ɔ:lweɪz] immer **I**
am [ˌeɪ 'em] 0.00–12.00 Uhr **III**
ambulance ['æmbjʊləns] Krankenwagen **I**
American [ə'merɪkən] amerikanisch, Amerikaner/in **II**
Native American ['neɪtɪv ə'merɪkən] indianisch, *amer. Ureinwohner/in* **IV**
⟨among⟩ [ə'mʌŋ] unter; zwischen **V 1**, 68
an **amount of** [ə'maʊnt‿ɒv] eine (bestimmte) Menge an **V 1**, 13
an [ən] ein/eine **I**
and [ænd] und **I**
⟨And then he'd say ...⟩ ['ən‿ðən hi:d seɪ] Und dann sagte er immer ... **V 2**, 73
angel ['eɪnʒəl] Engel **III**
angry ['æŋgrɪ] böse, verärgert **I**
animal ['ænɪml] Tier **I**
animal farming ['ænɪml ˌfɑ:mɪŋ] Viehzucht **V 3**, 33
announcement [ə'naʊnsmənt] Durchsage, Ansage, Ankündigung, Bekanntmachung **IV**
annoyed [ə'nɔɪd] verärgert **III**
anorak ['ænəræk] Anorak **I**
another [ə'nʌðə] noch einen/eine/eins **I**
answer ['ɑ:nsə] Antwort **I**
to **answer** ['ɑ:nsə] (be)antworten **I**
answering machine ['ɑ:nsərɪŋ mə'ʃi:n] Anrufbeantworter **III**
any ['enɪ] (irgend)welche **II**
not ... any more [nɒt 'enɪˌmɔ:] nicht mehr **IV**
anybody ['enɪbədɪ] (irgend)jemand **II**
anyone ['enɪwʌn] (irgend)jemand **II**; jede(r) **V 6**, 63
⟨Anyone got a wing and a prayer?⟩ ['enɪwʌn gɒt‿ə wɪŋ‿ənd‿ə ˌpreə] etwa: Kann jdm. helfen? **V 3**, 32
anything ['enɪθɪŋ] (irgend)etwas **II**
Anything else? ['enɪθɪŋ 'els] Sonst noch etwas? **I**
anyway ['enɪweɪ] sowieso; jedenfalls **III**
anywhere ['enɪweə] irgendwo **II**
Apache [ə'pætʃɪ] *Indianerstamm* **IV**
⟨apart from⟩ [ə'pɑ:t ˌfrɒm] abgesehen von **V 1**, 68
apartment (*AE*) [ə'pɑ:tmənt] Wohnung **IV**
to **appear** [ə'pɪə] erscheinen **III**
appendix [ə'pendɪks] Blinddarm **II**
apple ['æpl] Apfel **I**
apple pie [ˌæpl 'paɪ] gedeckter Apfelkuchen **IV**
applicant ['æplɪkənt] Bewerber/in **V 2**, 23
application [ˌæplɪ'keɪʃn] Bewerbung **V 2**, 23
application form [ˌæplɪ'keɪʃn 'fɔ:m] Anmeldeformular; Bewerbungsformular **IV**
to **apply for s.th.** [ə'plaɪ ˌfɔ:] sich für etw. bewerben **V 2**, 21
⟨to appreciate⟩ [ə'pri:ʃɪeɪt] anerkennen **V 5**, 84
apprenticeship [ə'prentɪʃɪp] Lehre **V 2**, 23
⟨to approach⟩ [ə'prəʊtʃ] (sich) annähern **V 1**, 68
to approach s.th./s.o. [ə'prəʊtʃ] sich nähern, zukommen auf; anfliegen **V 5**, 55
⟨to approve of s.th. or s.o.⟩ [ə'pru:v] billigen **V 2**, 72
April ['eɪprəl] April **I**
⟨architect⟩ ['ɑ:kɪtekt] Architekt/in **V TP**, 94
area ['eərɪə] Gebiet, Region, Fläche **III**
⟨arena⟩ [ə'ri:nə] Sporthalle **V 5**, 84
argument ['ɑ:gjʊment] Argument, Begründung **V 3**, 37
to have an argument [ˌhæv‿ən 'ɑ:gjʊmənt] einen Streit, eine Auseinandersetzung haben **II**
arm [ɑ:m] Arm **I**
armour ['ɑ:mə] Rüstung **III**
army ['ɑ:mɪ] Armee **IV**
⟨Arooga!⟩ [ə'ru:gə] *Warnruf der Bollin-Valley-Demonstranten* **V 3**, 36
around [ə'raʊnd] ungefähr **V 1**, 13
around [ə'raʊnd] um, herum **II**
to **arrange** [ə'reɪndʒ] arrangieren, organisieren **V 1**, 13
arrival [ə'raɪvl] Ankunft **IV**
to **arrive** [ə'raɪv] ankommen **I**
arrow ['ærəʊ] Pfeil **II**
Art [ɑ:t] Kunst **II**
work of art [wɜ:k‿əv 'ɑ:t] Kunstwerk **IV**
article ['ɑ:tɪkl] Artikel, Bericht **III**
definite article ['defɪnət ˌɑ:tɪkl] bestimmter Artikel **IV**
indefinite article [ɪn'defɪnət ˌɑ:tɪkl] unbestimmter Artikel **IV**
artist ['ɑ:tɪst] Künstler/in **IV**
as [æz] wie **II**; als **II**; da, während **IV**
(not) as ... as [æz ... æz] (nicht) so ... wie **II**
as if ... [ˌæz‿'ɪf] als ob ... **IV**
as soon as possible [əz‿su:n‿əz 'pɒsəbl] so bald wie möglich **IV**
as though [æz 'ðəʊ] als ob **IV**
as usual [ˌəz 'ju:ʒl] wie gewöhnlich, wie üblich **V 5**, 55
⟨as well⟩ [əz 'wel] auch (noch) **V 4**, 80
⟨ashore⟩ [ə'ʃɔ:] an Land **V 3**, 78
Asian ['eɪʃn] asiatisch, Asiate/Asiatin **IV**
to **ask** [ɑ:sk] fragen **I**
to ask for ['ɑ:sk fɔ:] bitten um **I**
to ask s.o. for a date [deɪt] jdn. nach einer Verabredung fragen **IV**
assembly [ə'semblɪ] Versammlung **I**
Assembly Hall [ə'semblɪ hɔ:l] Aula **II**
assembly line [ə'semblɪ ˌlaɪn] Fließband **III**
assistant [ə'sɪstənt] Helfer/in, Assistent/in **I**
astronomer [ə'strɒnəmə] Astronom/in, Himmelsforscher/in **V 5**, 55
at [æt, ət] an **I**
⟨(at a) distance⟩ ['dɪstəns] (in einiger) Entfernung **V 1**, 69
at all [ət‿'ɔ:l] überhaupt **III**
at home [ət 'həʊm] zu Hause **I**
at least [ət 'li:st] wenigstens, mindestens **II**
at once [ˌət 'wʌns] sofort **II**
⟨at present⟩ [æt 'preznt] im Moment **V TP**, 93
⟨at risk⟩ [æt 'rɪsk] in Gefahr **V TP**, 92
at the bottom of [ət ðə 'bɒtəm‿əv] unten, am unteren Ende **I**
at the moment [æt ðə‿'məʊmənt] zur Zeit **IV**
at the movies (*AE*) [ˌæt‿ðə 'mu:vɪz] im Kino **IV**
at the same time [ət ðə ˌseɪm 'taɪm] gleichzeitig **III**
at the top of [ət ðə 'tɒp‿əv] ganz oben **I**
at this time [ət 'ðɪs taɪm] um diese Zeit **II**
at ... o'clock [ət ... ə'klɒk] um ... Uhr **I**
athletics [æθ'letɪks] Leichtathletik **III**
Atishoo! [ə'tɪʃu:] Hatschi! **III**
atlas ['ætləs] Atlas **V 1**, 13
atmosphere ['ætməˌsfɪə] Atmosphäre, Stimmung **IV**
⟨to atone⟩ [ə'təʊn] sühnen, büßen **V TP**, 95
attack [ə'tæk] Angriff **V 4**, 48
to **attack** [ə'tæk] angreifen **IV**
to **attract s.o.** [ə'trækt] jdn. anziehen **V 1**, 18
attraction [ətrækʃn] Attraktion **III**
attractive [ə'træktɪv] reizvoll **V 2**, 23; schön, anziehend, attraktiv **V 3**, 40
August ['ɔ:gəst] August **I**
aunt [ɑ:nt] Tante **I**
Aunty ['ɑ:ntɪ] *Anrede für eine Tante* **I**
Aussie ['ɒzɪ] *umg.*: Australier/in **V 1**, 7
Australian [ɒ'streɪljən] australisch, Australier/in **III**
authentic [ɔ:'θentɪk] authentisch; echt **V 2**, 26
author ['ɔ:θə] Autor/in **IV**
autograph ['ɔ:təgrɑ:f] Autogramm **V 5**, 58

autumn ['ɔ:təm] Herbst **I**
[auxiliary] [ɔ:g'zɪljərɪ] Hilfs-; Hilfsverb **IV**
available [ə'veɪləbl] vorrätig, verfügbar, erhältlich **IV**
avenue ['ævənju:] Straße, Allee **IV**
⟨average⟩ ['ævərɪdʒ] Durchschnitt **V TP**, 94
to **avoid** [ə'vɔɪd] vermeiden **III**
away [ə'weɪ] weg **II**
awful ['ɔ:fʊl] schrecklich **III**
⟨awkward⟩ ['ɔ:kwəd] unbeholfen, ungeschickt **V 4**, 80
axe [æks] Axt, Beil **V 3**, 32

B

baby ['beɪbɪ] Baby **III**
babysitter ['beɪbɪˌsɪtə] Kinderbetreuer/in, Babysitter/in **IV**
babysitting ['beɪbɪˌsɪtɪŋ] Babysitten **II**
back [bæk] Rücken **V 1**, 11
back [bæk] zurück **I**
back door ['bæk 'dɔ:] Hintertür **I**
back home [bæk 'həʊm] zu Hause (damals) **V 1**, 10
back step [ˌbæk 'step] Stufe am Hintereingang **V 1**, 10
background ['bækgraʊnd] Hintergrund; Herkunft **V 5**, 54
backpack ['bækpæk] Rucksack **IV**
backpacking ['bækˌpækɪŋ] Bergtouren machen, Bergwandern; mit dem Rucksack reisen **IV**
backstage ['bæksteɪdʒ] hinter der Bühne **II**
⟨backwards⟩ ['bækwədz] rückwärts **V 3**, 76
backyard (*AE*) [ˌbæk'jɑ:d] Garten (*hinter dem Haus*) **IV**
bad [bæd] schlimm, schlecht **I**
badminton ['bædmɪntən] Federballspiel **I**
bag [bæg] Tasche **I**
bagel ['beɪgl] *jüdisches Gebäck* **IV**
bagpipes (*pl*) ['bægpaɪps] Dudelsack **II**
°**bailiff** ['beɪlɪf] Vollzugsbeamter/-beamtin **V 3**, 36
⟨baking paper⟩ ['beɪkɪŋ ˌpeɪpə] Backpapier **V 1**, 71
⟨bald place⟩ [bɔ:ld] kahle Stelle **V 6**, 86
ball [bɔ:l] Ball **I**
balloon [bə'lu:n] Luftballon **I**
banana [bə'nɑ:nə] Banane **I**
band [bænd] Gruppe, (Musik-)Kapelle **III**; [Kapelle, Musikgruppe] **II**
to **bang** [bæŋ] schlagen **V 2**, 27
bank [bæŋk] Bank **I**
bank clerk ['bæŋk‿klɑ:k] Bankangestellte/r **I**
bar [bɑ:] Tafel **I**
barbecue ['bɑ:bɪkju:] Grill, Grillfest, Barbecue **IV**
to **barbecue** ['bɑ:bɪkju:] grillen **IV**
⟨barely⟩ [beəlɪ] kaum **V 6**, 87
to **bark** [bɑ:k] bellen **I**
baseball ['beɪsbɔ:l] Baseball **IV**
basic ['beɪsɪk] Grund- **IV**
⟨basically⟩ ['beɪsɪkəlɪ] im Grunde genommen **V 5**, 83
basics ['beɪsɪks] Grundlagen **IV**
⟨basis⟩ ['beɪsɪs] Grundlage **V TP**, 93
basketball ['bɑ:skɪtbɔ:l] Basketball **IV**
°**bass** [beɪs] Bass **V 1**, 11
bat [bæt] Schläger **III**
bath [bɑ:θ] Bad, Badewanne **I**
to have a bath [hæv‿ə 'bɑ:θ] baden **I**
bathroom ['bɑ:θrʊm] Badezimmer **I**
⟨battery⟩ ['bætərɪ] Batterie **V 3**, 77
battle ['bætl] Schlacht, Kampf **III**
⟨battlefield⟩ ['bætlfi:ld] Schlachtfeld **V TP**, 95
BC (= **before Christ**) [ˌbi:'si: = bɪˌfɔ: 'kraɪst] v. Chr., a. Chr. **V 4**, 47
to **be*** [bɪ] sein **I**
Be careful! [bɪ 'keəfʊl] Pass auf!, Vorsicht! **I**
to be able to [bɪ 'eɪbl tə] können **III**
⟨to be afraid of⟩ [bɪ‿ə'freɪd] Angst haben vor **V R**, 90
to be allowed to [bɪ ə'laʊd tə] dürfen **III**
⟨to be buried alive⟩ [bɪ 'berɪd ə'laɪv] lebendig begraben sein **V 2**, 72
to be called [bɪ 'kɔ:ld] genannt werden **II**
⟨to be competitive⟩ [bɪ kəm'petətɪv] ehrgeizig sein, sich der Konkurrenz stellen **V 2**, 74
to be entertained by s.o. [ˌentə'teɪnd baɪ] von jdm. unterhalten werden **V 5**, 55
to be fair [feə] fair, gerecht sein **V 1**, 10
to be fascinated by s.th. ['fæsɪneɪtɪd] von etw. fasziniert sein **V 1**, 17
to be fluent (in a language) [bi:‿'flu:ənt] (eine Sprache) fließend sprechen **V 2**, 23
to be glued to s.th. [bɪ 'glu:d] an etw. (fest-)geklebt sein **V 3**, 32
to be good at [bɪ 'gʊd‿ət] gut sein in … **I**
to be in a hurry [bɪ ɪn‿ə'hʌrɪ] in Eile sein **III**
to be isolated ['aɪsəleɪtɪd] isoliert sein **V 1**, 9
to be jammed [bɪ 'dʒæmd] besetzt sein, belegt sein, überlastet sein **V 5**, 55
to be left without s.th. [bɪ left wɪ'ðaʊt] ohne etw. sein, dastehen **V 4**, 44
to be lucky [bɪ 'lʌkɪ] Glück haben **I**
⟨to be obsessed with⟩ [bɪ‿əb'sest wɪð] besessen sein von **V 2**, 74
to be of German nationality [bi:‿ɒv 'dʒɜ:mən ˌnæʃə'nælətɪ] deutscher Staatsangehörigkeit sein **V 2**, 23
to be on [bɪ‿'ɒn] eingeschaltet sein **I**
⟨to be open to interpretation⟩ [bɪ 'əʊpən tə ɪnˌtɜ:prɪ'teɪʃn] eine offene Frage sein **V TP**, 94
to be over [bɪ 'əʊvə] vorbei sein **V 4**, 44
to be over at … [bi:‿'əʊvər‿æt] bei … sein **IV**
to be proud of [bɪ 'praʊd‿əv] stolz sein auf **II**
⟨to be relieved⟩ [bɪ rɪ'li:vd] erleichtert sein **V 3**, 77
to be shocked [ʃɒkt] schockiert sein **IV**
⟨to be shut up⟩ [bɪ ˌʃʌt 'ʌp] eingesperrt sein **V 2**, 72
to be sick [bɪ 'sɪk] sich übergeben **IV**
to be sorry about s.th. [bɪ 'sɒrɪ əbaʊt] Leid tun, dass …, Leid tun wegen **II**
to be sorry for s.o. [bɪ 'sɒrɪ fə] Mitleid haben mit jdm. **II**
⟨to be stressed out⟩ [bɪ 'strest 'aʊt] gestresst, belastet sein **V 2**, 74
to be stuck [bɪ 'stʌk] klemmen **IV**
to be stuck with [bɪ 'stʌk wɪð] etw. am Hals haben **IV**
to be tired of s.th. [bɪ 'taɪəd‿əv] von etw. genug haben **IV**
to be trapped [bɪ 'træpt] in der Falle sein, abgeschnitten sein **III**
to be under control ['ʌndə kənˌtrəʊl] unter Kontrolle sein **V 4**, 45
to be unlucky [bɪ ʌn'lʌkɪ] kein Glück, Pech haben **III**
⟨to be worth⟩ [bɪ 'wɜ:θ] wert sein **V 5**, 85
beach [bi:tʃ] Strand **I**
⟨beady eye⟩ ['bi:dɪ aɪ] Knopfauge **V 3**, 79
bean [bi:n] Bohne **II**
bear [beə] Bär **II**
beard [bɪəd] Bart **II**
beat [bi:t] Rhythmus **III**
to **beat*** [bi:t] schlagen **IV**
to beat down [bi:t daʊn] herunterbrennen **V 5**, 61
⟨to beat off⟩ [bi:t‿'ɒf] wegjagen **V 4**, 80
beautiful ['bju:təfʊl] schön **II**
beauty ['bju:tɪ] Schönheit **V 5**, 52
°beauty product ['bju:tɪ ˌprɒdʌkt] Kosmetikartikel **V 5**, 52
because [bɪ'kɒz] weil **I**
because of [bɪ'kɒz‿əv] wegen **IV**
to **become*** [bɪ'kʌm] werden **III**
bed [bed] Bett **I**
bed and breakfast [bed‿ən 'brekfəst] Übernachtung mit Frühstück **II**

bedroom ['bedrʊm] Schlafzimmer **I**
⟨bedtime⟩ ['bedtaɪm] Schlafenszeit **V 1**, 68
beef [bi:f] Rindfleisch **II**
beetle ['bi:tl] Käfer **I**
before [bɪ'fɔ:] vorher, vor **II**
to **begin*** [bɪ'gɪn] anfangen, beginnen **II**
behind [bɪ'haɪnd] hinter **I**
from behind [frɒm bɪ'haɪnd] von hinten **II**
Belgian ['beldʒən] belgisch, Belgier/in **III**
to **believe** [bɪ'li:v] glauben **III**
bell [bel] Glocke, Klingel **III**
to **belong** (to) [bɪ'lɒŋ tʊ] dazugehören, gehören (zu) **IV**
below [bɪ'ləʊ] unten **III**
bench [bentʃ] (Park-)Bank **III**
to **bend*** [bend] biegen, beugen **II**; verbiegen **IV**
beside [bɪ'saɪd] neben **IV**
best [best] beste/bester/bestes **I**
best bit ['best bɪt] das Beste **V 2**, 22
⟨to bet⟩ [bet] wetten **V R**, 88
better ['betə] besser **I**
I hope you're better soon. [aɪ 'həʊp jʊə ˌbetə 'su:n] Ich hoffe, es geht dir bald besser. **I**
to do better [ˌdu: 'betə] besser sein **III**
between [bɪ'twi:n] zwischen **II**
⟨beverage⟩ ['bevərɪdʒ] Getränk **V 2**, 75
bicycle ['baɪsɪkl] Fahrrad **IV**
big [bɪg] groß **I**
bigger ['bɪgə] größer **II**
bike [baɪk] Fahrrad **I**
bill [bɪl] Rechnung **IV**
telephone bill ['telɪfəʊn ˌbɪl] Telefonrechnung **IV**
billboard ['bɪlbɔ:d] Reklametafel **IV**
billion ['bɪljən] Milliarde **V 1**, 12
bin [bɪn] Mülleimer **IV**
Biology [baɪ'ɒlədʒɪ] Biologie **II**
bird [bɜ:d] Vogel **II**
bird watcher ['bɜ:dˌwɒtʃə] Vogelbeobachter/in **II**
biro ['baɪrəʊ] Kugelschreiber **I**
birthday ['bɜ:θdeɪ] Geburtstag **I**
biscuit ['bɪskɪt] Keks **I**
bit [bɪt] Teil, Stück **III**
a bit [a'bɪt] etwas, ein bisschen **I**
black [blæk] schwarz **I**
she didn't **blame him** [ʃi: dɪdnt 'bleɪm hɪm] sie konnte ihn gut verstehen **IV**
⟨bleach-blond⟩ [bli:tʃ 'blɒnd] blond gefärbt **V 5**, 84
Bless you! ['bles‿ju:] Gesundheit! **III**
blind [blaɪnd] blind **IV**
⟨blindfold⟩ ['blaɪndfəʊld] Augenbinde **V 4**, 80
° **blink** [blɪŋk] Blinzeln **V 3**, 32
⟨block⟩ [blɒk] Block, Grundstück **V 1**, 10
⟨to block⟩ [blɒk] blockieren, versperren **V 3**, 77
⟨bloke⟩ [bləʊk] Kerl **V 2**, 73
blood [blʌd] Blut **III**
⟨bloody (*BE*)⟩ ['blʌdɪ] *umg.*: verdammt **V 1**, 10
to **blow*** [bləʊ] blasen **V 1**, 11
to blow s.o. away [bləʊ ə'weɪ] jdn. abknallen **IV**
blue [blu:] blau **I**
boarding school ['bɔ:dɪŋsku:l] Internat **III**
boat [bəʊt] Boot **I**
boating lake ['bəʊtɪŋ leɪk] Bootsteich **I**
body ['bɒdɪ] Körper **I**
⟨to boil⟩ [bɔɪl] kochen, erhitzen, zum Kochen bringen **V 1**, 68
⟨boiler room⟩ [bɔɪlə 'rʊm] Heizungsraum **V 6**, 87
⟨bone⟩ [bəʊn] Knochen; Gräte **V 1**, 68
book [bʊk] Buch **I**
⟨book token⟩ ['bʊk ˌtəʊkən] Buchgutschein **V 5**, 82
to **book** [bʊk] buchen, reservieren **III**
booking office ['bʊkɪŋˌɒfɪs] Vorverkaufsstelle; Kartenschalter **V 5**, 54
bookshelf ['bʊkʃelf] Bücherregal **III**
bookshop ['bʊkʃɒp] Buchhandlung **I**
border ['bɔ:də] Grenze; Rand **V 1**, 8
to get **bored** [bɔ:d] Langeweile haben/bekommen **IV**
boring ['bɔ:rɪŋ] langweilig **I**
she was **born** [ˌʃi: wəz 'bɔ:n] sie ist geboren **III**
borough ['bʌrə] Bezirk **IV**
to **borrow** ['bɒrəʊ] borgen, leihen **III**
boss [bɒs] Chef/in, Vorgesetzte/r **V 2**, 28
both [bəʊθ] beide **II**
both … and ['bəʊθ … ənd] sowohl … als auch **V 2**, 22
bottle ['bɒtl] Flasche **I**
at the **bottom of** [ət ðə 'bɒtəm‿əv] unten, am unteren Ende **II**
bow [bəʊ] Bogen **II**
to **bowl** [bəʊl] kegeln, bowlen **IV**
bowling alley ['bəʊlɪŋ ˌælɪ] Kegelbahn, Bowlingbahn **IV**
Box [bɒks] ⟨*Baumart*⟩ **V 1**, 68; Schachtel, Kiste, Dose **I**
lunch box ['lʌntʃ bɒks] *Dose für belegte Brote zum Mittagessen* **I**
boy [bɔɪ] Junge **I**
° to **boycott** ['bɔɪkɒt] boykottieren **V 3**, 37
boyfriend ['bɔɪfrend] Freund **III**
brain [breɪn] Gehirn **V 3**, 43
brainstorming ['breɪnstɔ:mɪŋ] Ideensammeln **III**
to **brake** [breɪk] bremsen **IV**
branch [brɑ:ntʃ] Ast, Zweig; Filiale, Zweigstelle **V 3**, 36
brave [breɪv] mutig, tapfer **III**
bread [bred] Brot **I**
break [breɪk] Pause **II**
⟨to break away⟩ [ˌbreɪk‿ə'weɪ] abbrechen, sich loslösen **V 1**, 70
to break into ['breɪk‿ɪntʊ] ⟨aufbrechen⟩ **V TP**, 96; einbrechen, eindringen in **V 5**, 50
to break over [breɪk 'əʊvə] hereinbrechen **III**
to break the law [ˌbreɪk ðə 'lɔ:] das Gesetz brechen **V 3**, 37
breakfast ['brekfəst] Frühstück **I**
⟨to breed⟩ [bri:d] züchten **V 1**, 10
bridge [brɪdʒ] Brücke **III**
bright [braɪt] hell, leuchtend; klug **IV**
⟨brighter day⟩ [ˌbraɪtə‿'deɪ] bessere Zeiten **V 1**, 71
[bring-and-buy sale] [brɪŋ‿ənd 'baɪ seɪl] Wohltätigkeitsbazar **II**
to **bring*** [brɪŋ] bringen **I**; mitbringen **I**
to bring about ['brɪŋ ə'baʊt] herbeiführen, verursachen **V 6**, 63
[to bring down (trees)] [brɪŋ daʊn] abknicken, ausreißen **IV**
British ['brɪtɪʃ] britisch **I**
Britons ['brɪtnz] Briten, *(Ur-)Einwohner von Großbritannien* **III**
brochure ['brəʊʃə] Broschüre, Prospekt **III**
broken ['brəʊkən] kaputt, zerbrochen **I**
brother ['brʌðə] Bruder **I**
brown [braʊn] braun **I**
brutal ['bru:tl] brutal **V 4**, 45
bubble bath ['bʌbl ˌbɑ:θ] Schaumbad **I**
bucket ['bʌkɪt] Eimer **I**
⟨budget⟩ ['bʌdʒɪt] Budget **V TP**, 93
budgie (= budgerigar) ['bʌdʒɪ = 'bʌdʒərɪgɑ:] Wellensittich **II**
buffalo ['bʌfələʊ] Büffel, Bison **IV**
to **build*** [bɪld] bauen **III**
building [bɪldɪŋ] Gebäude **IV**
⟨building-site⟩ ['bɪldɪŋ ˌsaɪt] Baustelle **V 2**, 73
bully ['bʊlɪ] Rabauke, Rüpel, Tyrann **II**
to **bump into s.o./s.th.** [bʌmp] gegen jdn./etw. stoßen, mit jdm. zusammenstoßen **IV**

⟨bundle⟩ ['bʌndl] Bündel **V 1**, 68
bungee-jumping ['bʌndʒɪ ˌdʒʌmpɪŋ] „Bungee"-Springen *(an einem Gummiseil aus großer Höhe springen)* **III**
⟨bureau⟩ [bjʊə'rəʊ] Behörde **V 5**, 55
burglar ['bɜ:glə] Einbrecher/in **I**
to **burn*** [bɜ:n] (an)brennen, verbrennen **IV**
burrito [bə'ri:təʊ] *mexikanisches Gericht (gefüllte Pfannkuchen)* **IV**
bus [bʌs] Bus **I**
bus shelter ['bʌs ˌʃeltə] überdachte Bushaltestelle **III**
bus stop ['bʌs stɒp] Bushaltestelle **I**
bush [bʊʃ] Busch **IV**; Busch *(freies oder offenes Land)* **V 1**, 10
⟨bush-style⟩ ['bʊʃ staɪl] im Outback-Stil **V TP**, 94
bushman ['bʊʃmən] jmd. der im Busch lebt und arbeitet **V 1**, 7
business ['bɪznɪs] Geschäft **IV**
Business French [ˌbɪznɪs 'frentʃ] Wirtschaftsfranzösisch **V 2**, 23
busy ['bɪzɪ] beschäftigt **I**
but [bʌt] außer, abgesehen von **V 1**, 10
but [bʌt] aber **I**
butter ['bʌtə] Butter **I**
button [bʌtn] Knopf **IV**
to **buy*** [baɪ] kaufen **I**
by [baɪ] mit **I**; von, vom *(in Passivsätzen)*; bis **IV**
by hand [baɪ 'hænd] mit der Hand, von Hand **V 6**, 62
by mistake [baɪ mɪ'steɪk] aus Versehen **V 2**, 22
by the minute ['baɪ ðə ˌmɪnɪt] von Minute zu Minute **V 5**, 52
Bye! [baɪ] Tschüs! *(kurze gesprochene Form von* Goodbye) **I**
bye-bye [baɪ 'baɪ] auf Wiedersehen **IV**

C

cab [kæb] Taxi **IV**
cabbage ['kæbɪdʒ] Kohl **II**
cabin ['kæbɪn] Blockhaus **IV**
café ['kæfeɪ] Café **IV**
cafeteria [ˌkæfɪ'tɪərɪə] Cafeteria **III**
cage [keɪdʒ] Käfig **II**
cake [keɪk] Kuchen, Torte **I**
to **calculate** ['kælkjʊleɪt] (aus)rechnen, kalkulieren **V 1**, 10
calculator ['kælkjʊleɪtə] Taschenrechner **V 3**, 35
calendar ['kælɪndə] Kalender **I**
calf [kɑ:f] Kalb **V 4**, 47
call [kɔ:l] Anruf **III**
to **call** [kɔ:l] rufen, anrufen **I**; nennen **III**
to be called [bɪ 'kɔ:ld] genannt werden **II**
calm [kɑ:m] ruhig **III**
camcorder ['kæmkɒ:də] Videokamera **II**
camera ['kæmərə] Fotoapparat, Kamera **I**
camp [kæmp] Lager **IV**
to go to camp [gəʊ tə 'kæmp] ins Ferienlager fahren **IV**
to set up camp [set‿ʌp 'kæmp] ein Lager aufschlagen, lagern **V 3**, 36
to **camp** [kæmp] zelten, kampieren **IV**
campaign [kæm'peɪn] Kampagne, Feldzug **V 3**, 33
to **campaign** [kæm'peɪn] sich einsetzen, sich stark machen **V 3**, 33
campground *(AE)* ['kæmpgraʊnd] Campingplatz **IV**
campus ['kæmpəs] Campus, Schul-, Universitätsgelände **IV**
can [kæn] Dose **IV**
can [kæn] können **I**
cancellation [ˌkænsə'leɪʃn] Stornierung, Absage **III**
candle ['kændl] Kerze **I**
candy *(AE) (sg + pl)* ['kændɪ] Süßigkeit, Süßigkeiten **IV**
canoe [kə'nu:] Kanu **IV**
canyon ['kænjən] Schlucht, Cañon **IV**
⟨cap⟩ [kæp] Mütze **V 5**, 84
capital ['kæpɪtl] Hauptstadt **III**
captain ['kæptɪn] Hauptmann; Kapitän **IV**
car [kɑ:] Auto **I**
car park ['kɑ: ˌpɑ:k] Parkplatz, -haus **II**
caravan ['kærəvæn] Wohnwagen **II**
card [kɑ:d] Karte **I**
to take **care of s.th.** [teɪk 'keər‿ɒv ˌsʌmθɪŋ] etw. erledigen; nach etw. schauen; sich um etw. kümmern **IV**
to **care (about)** [keə] sich kümmern (um) **V 3**, 32
career [kə'rɪə] Berufsweg, Karriere **V 2**, 22
careers officer [kə'rɪəz ˌɒfɪsə] Berufsberater/in **V 2**, 28
careful ['keəfʊl] vorsichtig, sorgfältig **III**
Be careful! [bɪ 'keəfʊl] Pass auf!, Vorsicht! **I**
careless ['kɜəlɪs] nachlässig **III**; unvorsichtig **III**
carnival ['kɑ:nɪvl] Karneval, Volksfest **III**
⟨carpet industry⟩ ['kɑ:pɪt ˌɪndəstrɪ] Teppichindustrie **V TP**, 97
carrot ['kærət] Karotte, Möhre **II**
to **carry** ['kærɪ] tragen **III**
to carry on [ˌkærɪ‿'ɒn] weiterführen, fortführen **V 4**, 46
⟨to carry out⟩ [kærɪ 'aʊt] ausführen, befolgen **V 1**, 68
case [keɪs] Etui, Hülle **I**
pencil case ['pensl keɪs] Federmäppchen **I**
⟨cash⟩ [kæʃ] Bargeld **V 2**, 75
cashier [kæ'ʃɪə] Kassierer/in **IV**
cassette [kæ'set] Kassette **II**
castle ['kɑ:sl] Burg **I**
cat [kæt] Katze **I**
to **catch*** [kætʃ] fangen **II**; mitbekommen **V 5**, 54
⟨to catch s.o.'s eye⟩ [kætʃ] jdm. auffallen **V 5**, 82
to catch up with s.o. [ˌkætʃ‿'ʌp wɪð] jdn. einholen **III**
catchy ['kætʃɪ] eingängig **III**
⟨category⟩ ['kætəgərɪ] Kategorie, Art **V 5**, 83
cathedral [kə'θi:drəl] Kathedrale **III**
cattle *(pl)* ['kætl] Rind(-vieh) **IV**
cattle rancher ['kætl rɑ:ntʃə] Rancher/in, Viehzüchter/in **IV**
cattle ranching ['kætl ˌrɑ:ntʃɪŋ] Rinderzucht **V 3**, 33
cause [kɔ:z] Ursache **V 3**, 35
to **cause** [kɔ:z] verursachen **V 3**, 35
cave [keɪv] Höhle **II**
⟨caviar⟩ ['kævɪɑ:] Kaviar **V 2**, 75
CD [si: 'di:] CD **I**
CD player [si: 'di: pleɪə] CD-Spieler **I**
CD-ROM [si: di: 'rɒm] CD-ROM **V 3**, 34
to **celebrate** ['selɪbreɪt] feiern **IV**
center *(AE)* ['sentə] Mitte, Zentrum **IV**
central ['sentrl] in der Mitte, zentral, Zentral-, Mittel- **IV**
centre ['sentə] Mitte, Zentrum **I**
century ['sentʃʊrɪ] Jahrhundert **III**
certain ['sɜ:tn] sicher, bestimmt **V 1**, 10
certainly ['sɜ:tnlɪ] gewiss, bestimmt **III**
certificate [sə'tɪfɪkət] Bescheinigung, Nachweis **V 1**, 13
Certificate 12 [sə'tɪfɪkeɪt twelv] Freigegeben ab 12 **V 5**, 54
chair [tʃeə] Stuhl **I**
chance [tʃɑ:ns] Chance, Möglichkeit **III**
change [tʃeɪndʒ] Änderung, Veränderung, Wandel **V 6**, 62; Wechselgeld, Kleingeld **IV**
to **change** [tʃeɪndʒ] (sich) (ver)ändern, wechseln **II**
to change onto [tʃeɪndʒ] umsteigen auf **III**
⟨to change one's mind⟩ ['tʃeɪndʒ wʌnz 'maɪnd] es sich anders überlegen, seine Meinung ändern **V R**, 91
channel ['tʃænl] (Fernseh-)Kanal, Programm **III**
character ['kærəktə] Figur, Person **III**
charity ['tʃærətɪ] Wohltätigkeitsverein **V 5**, 59
to have a **chat** [tʃæt] sich unterhalten, plaudern **V 1**, 13
cheap [tʃi:p] billig **II**

to **cheat** [tʃi:t] schummeln **III**
to **check** [tʃek] überprüfen, kontrollieren **I**
to check in [ˌtʃek‿ˈɪn] einchecken, anmelden **III**
°to check out [ˈtʃek‿aʊt] sich abmelden, abreisen; überprüfen **V 5**, 50
checklist [ˈtʃeklɪst] Checkliste **III**
Cheer up! [ˈtʃɪər‿ʌp] Kopf hoch! **III**
cheerleader [ˈtʃɪəli:də] Cheerleader/in **IV**
cheese [tʃi:z] Käse **I**
chemical [ˈkemɪkl] Chemikalie; chemisch **V 3**, 42
⟨chemical powder⟩ [ˌkemɪkl ˈpaʊdə] chemisches Pulver **V 6**, 87
chemist's [ˈkemɪsts] Apotheke **II**
chess [tʃes] Schach **IV**
⟨to chew⟩ [tʃu:] kauen **V 2**, 73
⟨chick⟩ [tʃɪk] Küken **V 3**, 79
chicken [tʃɪkɪn] Huhn **II**
chief [tʃi:f] (Indianer-)Häuptling **IV**
child [tʃaɪld] Kind **I**
⟨child labour⟩ [ˈtʃaɪld ˌleɪbə] Kinderarbeit **V 6**, 86
children *(pl)* [ˈtʃɪldrən] Kinder **I**
chimney [ˈtʃɪmnɪ] Schornstein, Kamin **V 6**, 63
Chinese [ˌtʃaɪˈni:z] chinesisch, Chinesisch, Chinese/Chinesin **II**
chips *(pl)* [tʃɪps] Pommes frites **I**
⟨chock-a-block⟩ [ˈtʃɒk‿ə‿ˌblɒk] *umg.*: gerammelt voll, überfüllt **V 1**, 11
chocolate [ˈtʃɒkələt] Schokolade **I**
choice [tʃɔɪs] Auswahl, Wahl **V 5**, 50
choir [ˈkwaɪə] Chor **IV**
to **choose*** [tʃu:z] wählen, aussuchen **II**
chopstick [ˈtʃɒpstɪk] (Ess-)Stäbchen **IV**
chopsuey [ˌtʃɒpˈsu:ɪ] *chinesisches Gericht* **IV**
chorus [ˈkɔ:rəs] Refrain **II**
Christmas [ˈkrɪsməs] Weihnachten **II**
church [tʃɜ:tʃ] Kirche **I**
cinema [ˈsɪnɪmə] Kino **I**
circle [ˈsɜ:kl] Kreis **IV**
⟨to circle⟩ [ˈsɜ:kl] (um)kreisen **V 1**, 69
circus [ˈsɜ:kəs] Zirkus, Ring **III**
citizen [ˈsɪtɪzn] Bürger/in **IV**
city [ˈsɪtɪ] (Groß-)Stadt **I**
⟨civilization⟩ [ˌsɪvɪlaɪˈzeɪʃn] Zivilisation **V TP**, 93
civilized [ˈsɪvɪlaɪzd] zivilisiert **IV**
to **claim** [kleɪm] Anspruch erheben auf, beanspruchen **V 1**, 16
to **clap** [klæp] klatschen **II**
[Clap'n' Rap] [ˌklæp‿n ˈræp] Klatschen und „Rappen" **II**
class [klɑ:s] Gesellschaftsschicht **V 4**, 46; Klasse *(in einer deutschen Schule)* **I**
classroom [ˈklɑ:srʊm] Klassenzimmer **I**
to **clean** [kli:n] putzen **II**
to clean out [ˌkli:n‿ˈaʊt] sauber machen; ausmisten **V 2**, 21
to clean up [kli:n‿ˈʌp] putzen, aufwischen, aufräumen **IV**
clean [kli:n] sauber **II**
⟨cleanskin⟩ [ˈkli:nskɪn] *ein nicht gebrandmarktes Rind* **V 1**, 68
[to clear] [klɪə] roden **V 3**, 41
clear [klɪə] klar, deutlich **III**
clerk [klɑ:k] Büroangestellte/r **I**
bank clerk [ˈbæŋk‿klɑ:k] Bankangestellte/r **I**
clever [ˈklevə] intelligent, klug **I**
to **click on** [ˈklɪk‿ˌɒn] „anklicken", mit der Maus auswählen **III**
cliff [klɪf] Klippe, Fels **III**
climate [ˈklaɪmɪt] Klima **III**
to **climb** [klaɪm] klettern **III**; steigen **V 3**, 32
to climb up [ˌklaɪm ˈʌp] hochklettern, erklettern **I**
climbing [ˈklaɪmɪŋ] Bergsteigen, Klettern **II**
⟨cloak⟩ [kləʊk] Umhang, Mantel **V 4**, 80
clock [klɒk] Uhr **II**
⟨close group⟩ [ˌkləʊs ˈgru:p] enge Gruppe **V 2**, 75
to **close** [kləʊz] schließen, zumachen **I**
⟨to close off⟩ [ˌkləʊz ˈɒf] zumachen **V R**, 89
close (to) [kləʊs] nah (bei) **III**
closed [kləʊzd] geschlossen **III**
cloth [klɒθ] Stoff, Tuch **V 6**, 63
clothes *(pl)* [ˈkləʊðz] Kleider **I**
cloud [klaʊd] Wolke **IV**
clown [ˈklaʊn] Clown **III**
club [klʌb] Klub, Verein **II**
clue [klu:] Hinweis **III**
coach [kəʊtʃ] Trainer/in **IV**
coal [kəʊl] Kohle **III**
⟨coal face⟩ [ˈkəʊlfeɪs] Streb *(Stollen, in dem Kohle abgebaut wird)* **V 3**, 76
⟨coal-digger⟩ [ˈkəʊl ˌdɪgə] Bergmann/-frau **V 6**, 86
coal-mine [ˈkəʊlmaɪn] Kohlenbergwerk **V 6**, 64
coast [kəʊst] Küste **III**
on the coast [ˌɒn ðə ˈkəʊst] an der Küste **III**
coastguard [ˈkəʊstgɑ:d] Küstenwache **III**
coat [kəʊt] Mantel **II**
⟨cockerel⟩ [ˈkɒkərəl] junger Hahn **V 3**, 79
coconut [ˈkəʊkənʌt] Kokosnuss **II**
coconut shy [ˈkəʊkənʌt ˈʃaɪ] Wurfbude mit Kokosnüssen **II**
coffee [ˈkɒfɪ] Kaffee **II**
coke [kəʊk] Cola **IV**
coke float [ˌkəʊk ˈfləʊt] *amer. Getränk* **IV**
cold [kəʊld] Erkältung **II**
cold [kəʊld] kalt **I**
collar [ˈkɒlə] Halsband **IV**
colleague [ˈkɒli:g] Kollege/Kollegin **V 2**, 24
to **collect** [kəˈlekt] (ein)sammeln **I**; abholen **I**
college [ˈkɒlɪdʒ] College, Hochschule **V 2**, 22
⟨colonial⟩ [kəˈləʊnjəl] Kolonial-, kolonial **V 1**, 70
colony [ˈkɒlənɪ] Kolonie **IV**
color *(AE)* [ˈkʌlə] Farbe **IV**
colour [ˈkʌlə] Farbe **I**
°colour scheme [ˈkʌlə ˌski:m] Farbzusammenstellung **V 2**, 22
colourful [ˈkʌləfʊl] bunt **III**
to **come*** [kʌm] kommen **I**
⟨c'mon (= come on)⟩ [k‿ˈmɒn] ach komm, komm schon **V 1**, 10
Come on! [kəm‿ˈɒn] Komm schon!, Kommt schon! **I**
⟨come to rest⟩ [kʌm tʊ ˈrest] seine/ihre Ruhe finden **V 3**, 78
to come along [kʌm əˈlɒŋ] gedeihen **IV**
to come down [kʌm ˈdaʊn] hierher kommen **V 1**, 10
to come home [kʌm ˈhəʊm] nach Hause kommen **I**
to come off [kʌm‿ˈɒf] abgehen **II**
to come over to s.o. [ˌkʌm‿ˈəʊvə] auf jdn. zukommen **III**
to come round [kʌm ˈraʊnd] vorbeikommen **III**
⟨to come to⟩ [ˈkʌm tʊ] jdm. einfallen, dämmern **V 2**, 73
⟨comeback⟩ [ˈkʌmbæk] Rückkehr **V TP**, 93
comedy [ˈkɒmədɪ] Komödie **V 5**, 54
comfortable [ˈkʌmfətəbl] bequem **V 1**, 18
comic [ˈkɒmɪk] Comic **I**
comma [ˈkɒmə] Komma **III**
comment [ˈkɒment] Bemerkung, Kommentar **III**
to **comment on s.th.** [ˈkɒment‿ɒn] etw. kommentieren **V 4**, 45
⟨commercial⟩ [kəˈmɜ:ʃl] Anzeige, Werbung **V 5**, 84; geschäftlich; kommerziell **V TP**, 93
committee [kəˈmɪtɪ] Komitee **V 5**, 53
common [ˈkɒmən] gemeinsam; häufig, weit verbreitet **V 1**, 13

⟨Commonwealth (of Nations)⟩ ['kɒmənwelθ‿əv 'neɪʃnz] das Commonwealth **V 1**, 70
to **communicate** [kə'mju:nɪkeɪt] kommunizieren, Informationen austauschen, sich verständigen **IV**
communication [kə,mju:nɪ'keɪʃn] Kommunikation, Informationsaustausch, Verständigung **IV**
community service [kə'mju:nətɪ ,sɜ:vɪs] Zivildienst **V 2**, 22
company ['kʌmpənɪ] Firma, Unternehmen **IV**
to **compare** [kəm'peə] vergleichen **II**
comparison [kəm'pærɪsn] Vergleich **III**
to **compete in** [kəm'pi:t‿ɪn] teilnehmen an (*Wettbewerb*) **III**
to compete for [kəm'pi:t] konkurrieren um **V 5**, 60
competition [kɒmpə'tɪʃn] Wettbewerb, Preisausschreiben **I**
to **complete** [kəm'pli:t] vervollständigen, ausfüllen, durchmachen **III**
complete [kəm'pli:t] vollständig **III**
complicated ['kɒmplɪkeɪtɪd] kompliziert **III**
compound word [kəm'paʊnd wɜ:d] zusammengesetztes Wort **IV**
comprehensive (school) [,kɒmprɪ'hensɪv ,sku:l] Gesamtschule **III**
computer [kəm'pju:tə] Computer **I**
Computer Science [kəm'pju:tə 'saɪəns] Informatik **IV**
to **concentrate** (on) ['kɒnsəntreɪt‿,ɒn] sich konzentrieren (auf) **III**
concert ['kɒnsət] Konzert **III**
⟨concrete⟩ ['kɒnkri:t] Beton **V 2**, 72
condition [kən'dɪʃn] Bedingung, Umstand; Verhältnis **IV**
⟨conditional⟩ [kən'dɪʃənl] das Konditional **V R**, 89
conference ['kɒnfərəns] Konferenz, Tagung **III**
confidence ['kɒnfɪdəns] Vertrauen; Selbstvertrauen **V 1**, 13
to **confirm** [kən'fɜ:m] bestätigen **V 5**, 55
confused [kən,fju:zd] durcheinander, verwirrt **IV**
to **connect** [kə'nekt] verbinden **III**
connecting [kə'nektɪŋ] verbindend **III**
to **conquer** ['kɒŋkə] erobern **III**
conquest ['kɒŋkwest] Eroberung **V 4**, 44
pros and **cons** [,prəʊz‿ənd 'kɒnz] Vor- und Nachteile **V 1**, 13
⟨consequently⟩ ['kɒnsɪkwəntlɪ] folglich **V TP**, 92
construction [kən'strʌkʃn] Bau, Konstruktion **V 2**, 22
consumer [kən'sju:mə] Verbraucher/in, Konsument/in **V 5**, 50
⟨to contain⟩ [kən'teɪn] enthalten **V 3**, 78
contents ['kɒntents] Inhalt **V 5**, 50
context ['kɒntekst] Kontext, Zusammenhang **III**
continent ['kɒntɪnənt] Kontinent, Erdteil **V 1**, 8
to **continue** [kən'tɪnju:] weitermachen, fortfahren **IV**
⟨contour⟩ ['kɒn,tʊə] Kontur, Umrisslinie **V 3**, 32
contrast ['kɒntrɑ:st] Gegenüberstellung; Gegensatz, Kontrast **V 1**, 8
control module [kən'trəʊl ,mɒdju:l] Fernsteuerung **IV**
conversation [,kɒnvə'seɪʃn] Unterhaltung, Gespräch **IV**
convict ['kɒnvɪkt] Strafgefangener/Strafgefangene **V 1**, 9
⟨cook⟩ [kʊk] Koch/Köchin **V 4**, 80
to **cook** [kʊk] kochen **II**
cookie (*AE*) ['kʊkɪ] Keks **IV**
cool [ku:l] kühl **V 1**, 11; toll, klasse, cool, super **IV**
⟨Coolibar⟩ ['ku:ləbɑ:] *Baumart* **V 1**, 68
copy ['kɒpɪ] Kopie **V 2**, 30
to **copy** ['kɒpɪ] abschreiben, kopieren **III**
° **coral** (*sg + pl*) ['kɒrəl] Koralle(n) **V 1**, 14
corner ['kɔ:nə] Ecke **II**
cornflakes (*pl*) ['kɔ:nfleɪks] Cornflakes **I**
coronation [,kɒrə'neɪʃn] Krönung **V 4**, 45
to **correct** [kə'rekt] korrigieren, verbessern **I**
to **cost*** [kɒst] kosten **I**
costume ['kɒstju:m] Kostüm **IV**
cotton ['kɒtn] Baumwolle **V 6**, 62
to **count** [kaʊnt] zählen **I**
countable ['kaʊntəbl] zählbar **V 2**, 26
countdown ['kaʊntdaʊn] Countdown **IV**
counter ['kaʊntə] Theke, Ladentisch **IV**
country ['kʌntrɪ] Land **III**
in the country [ɪn ðə 'kʌntrɪ] auf dem Lande **III**
countryside ['kʌntrɪsaɪd] Landschaft **III**
county ['kaʊntɪ] Grafschaft, Landkreis **V 4**, 46
courier ['kʊrɪə] Bote/Botin; Kurier **IV**
course [kɔ:s] Kurs, Lehrgang **III**
of course [əv‿'kɔ:s] natürlich, selbstverständlich **I**
court [kɔ:t] Hof **II**
cousin ['kʌzn] Cousin/e **I**
⟨to cover⟩ ['kʌvə] abdecken; einnehmen **V TP**, 94
covered wagon ['kʌvəd ,wægən] Planwagen **IV**
cow [kaʊ] Kuh **I**
crab [kræb] Krebs **I**
⟨to crack⟩ [kræk] zusammenbrechen, durchdrehen **V 2**, 74
crash [kræʃ] Unfall, Zusammenstoß; Absturz **IV**
to **crash** [kræʃ] schlagen, krachen **III**
to crash into s.th. [kræʃ] in etw. hineinkrachen **IV**
Crash! [kræʃ] Rums! **I**
to **crawl** [krɔ:l] krabbeln **V 3**, 42
to crawl out [krɔ:l‿'aʊt] herauskriechen **V 3**, 36
crayon ['kreɪən] Buntstift **I**
crazy ['kreɪzɪ] verrückt **I**
cream [kri:m] Sahne **II**; Creme **V 5**, 52
to **create** [kri:'eɪt] schaffen, verursachen; kreieren **V 3**, 35
creative [kri:'eɪtɪv] kreativ, schöpferisch **IV**
creature ['kri:tʃə] Geschöpf, Lebewesen, Kreatur **V 5**, 55
cricket ['krɪkɪt] *englischer Rasensport* **I**
crime [kraɪm] Kriminalität; Verbrechen **IV**
criminal ['krɪmɪnl] kriminell; Straftäter/in **IV**
crisps (*pl*) [krɪsps] Kartoffelchips **I**
critical ['krɪtɪkl] kritisch **V 5**, 52
to **criticize** ['krɪtɪsaɪz] kritisieren **V 5**, 52
crocodile ['krɒkədaɪl] Krokodil **V 1**, 8
° to **cross** [krɒs] kreuzen; überqueren **V 1**, 8
crowd [krəʊd] Menschenmenge **II**
crowded ['kraʊdɪd] voll mit Leuten, überfüllt **IV**
crown [kraʊn] Krone **V 4**, 44
to **crown s.o.** (*king*) [kraʊn] jdm. (zum König) krönen **V 4**, 45
to **cry** [kraɪ] weinen **II**
⟨culture⟩ ['kʌltʃə] Kultur **V 1**, 70
cup [kʌp] Tasse **II**; Pokal, Kelch **III**
cupboard ['kʌbəd] Schrank **I**
CV (= Curriculum Vitae) [si: 'vi: = kə,rɪkjələm 'vi:taɪ] Lebenslauf **V 2**, 23
curry ['kʌrɪ] Curry (*indisches Gericht*) **II**
customer ['kʌstəmə] Kunde/Kundin **IV**
customer service [,kʌstəmə 'sɜ:vɪs] Kundenservice, -dienst **V 2**, 23
to **cut*** [kʌt] schneiden **II**
to cut off [kʌt'ɒf] abbrechen, abschneiden **V 5**, 55
to cut out [,kʌt‿'aʊt] ausschneiden **III**
⟨cutout doll⟩ ['kʌtaʊt dɒl] ausgeschnittene Puppe **V 1**, 11
CV (= **Curriculum Vitae**) [si: 'vi: = kə,rɪkjələm 'vi:taɪ] Lebenslauf **V 2**, 23
to **cycle** ['saɪkl] Rad fahren **III**
cycling ['saɪklɪŋ] Fahrradfahren **II**
cyclist ['saɪklɪst] Radfahrer/in **III**

D

Dad [dæd] Vati, Papa **I**
to do **damage** ['dæmɪdʒ] Schaden anrichten **IV**

to **damage** ['dæmɪdʒ] beschädigen **IV**
damn [dæm] verdammt **IV**
Damn idiot! [dæm‿'ɪdɪət] Verdammter Idiot! **IV**
Damn you! ['dæm‿ju:] Zur Hölle mit dir/Ihnen! **IV**
⟨damp⟩ [dæmp] feucht **V 6**, 86
dance [dɑ:ns] Tanz **III**
to **dance** [dɑ:ns] tanzen **I**
dancer [dɑ:nsə] Tänzer/in **III**
danger ['deɪndʒə] Gefahr **V 3**, 33
dangerous ['deɪndʒərəs] gefährlich **II**
Danish ['deɪnɪʃ] dänisch, Dänisch **III**
⟨daring⟩ ['dərɪŋ] wagemutig **V 4**, 80
dark [dɑ:k] dunkel **IV**
⟨darkness⟩ ['dɑ:knɪs] Dunkelheit **V 3**, 77
⟨data⟩ ['deɪtə] Daten **V 6**, 87
date [deɪt] Datum **I**
date of birth [ˌdeɪt‿əv 'bɜ:θ] Geburtsdatum **V 2**, 24
⟨date-stone⟩ ['deɪt stəʊn] Dattelkern **V 2**, 73
to ask s.o. for a date [deɪt] jdn. nach einer Verabredung fragen **IV**
daughter ['dɔ:tə] Tochter **II**
day [deɪ] Tag **I**
day off [ˌdeɪ 'ɒf] freier Tag, Urlaubstag **III**
in ... days [ɪn ... deɪz] in ... Tagen **I**
dead [ded] tot **I**
dear [dɪə] liebe/lieber/liebes **I**
Oh dear! [əʊ 'dɪə] Oh je! **I**
death [deθ] Tod **IV**
December [dɪ'sembə] Dezember **I**
to **decide** [dɪ'saɪd] sich entscheiden, beschließen **III**
decimal number [ˌdesɪml 'nʌmbə] Dezimalzahl **III**
⟨decision⟩ [dɪ'sɪʒn] Entscheidung **V 1**, 69
⟨to deduct⟩ [dɪ'dʌkt] einbehalten, abziehen **V 2**, 75
deep [di:p] tief **III**
deer (*sg + pl*) [dɪə] Reh, Hirsch; Rotwild **IV**
to **defend** [dɪ'fend] verteidigen **III**
definite article ['definət ˌɑ:tɪkl] bestimmter Artikel **IV**
definitely ['defɪnɪtlɪ] hundertprozentig, ganz sicher; endgültig, definitiv **IV**
to **deliver** [dɪ'lɪvə] liefern **IV**
delivery [dɪ'lɪvərɪ] Lieferung **V 2**, 23
⟨deodorant⟩ [di:'əʊdərənt] Deodorant **V TP**, 93
department [dɪ'pɑ:tmənt] Abteilung **V 2**, 23
department store [dɪ'pɑ:tment 'stɔ:] Warenhaus **II**
to **depend on s.th.** [dɪ'pend‿ɒn] abhängig sein von; sich verlassen auf **V 3**, 35
⟨dependable⟩ [dɪ'pendəbl] zuverlässig, verläßlich **V 3**, 39
⟨derby⟩ ['dɑ:bɪ] Derby **V TP**, 93
to **describe** [dɪ'skraɪb] beschreiben **III**
description [dɪ'skrɪpʃn] Beschreibung **IV**
desert ['dezət] Wüste **V 1**, 8
desk [desk] Schreibtisch, Pult **I**
dessert [dɪ'zɜ:t] Nachtisch **IV**
⟨destiny⟩ ['destɪnɪ] Schicksal, Vorsehung **V 1**, 71
to **destroy** [dɪ'strɔɪ] zerstören **III**
detail ['di:teɪl] Einzelheit, Detail **II**
to get **detention** [dɪ'tenʃn] nachsitzen müssen **III**
to **develop** [dɪ'veləp] (sich) entwickeln **V 1**, 9
development [dɪ'veləpmənt] Entwicklung **V 3**, 40
diagram ['daɪəgræm] Diagramm, Schaubild **V 4**, 49
to **dial** ['daɪəl] wählen, eintippen (*Telefonnummer*) **III**
dialogue ['daɪəlɒg] Dialog, Gespräch **I**
diary ['daɪərɪ] Tagebuch, Terminkalender **II**
dice (*sg + pl*) [daɪs] Würfel **I**
dictionary ['dɪkʃənrɪ] Wörterbuch **II**
° **didgeridoo** [ˌdɪdʒerɪ'du:] Didgeridoo *(Musikinstrument der Aborigines)* **V 1**, 8
to **die** [daɪ] sterben **I**
diet ['daɪət] Ernährungsweise; Nahrung; Diät **V 3**, 34
° to **differ** ['dɪfə] sich unterscheiden **V 1**, 13
difference ['dɪfrəns] Unterschied **III**
different ['dɪfrənt] unterschiedlich, anders **I**
difficult ['dɪfɪkəlt] schwierig **II**
to **dig*** [dɪg] graben **V 3**, 36
digit ['dɪdʒɪt] Zahl, Ziffer **IV**
dingo, dingoes (*pl*) ['dɪŋgəʊ] *Hundeart* **V 1**, 7
dinner ['dɪnə] Mittagessen, Abendessen **III**
dinner lady ['dɪnə ˌleɪdɪ] *Dame an der Essensausgabe* **III**
diploma [dɪ'pləʊmə] Diplom **V 2**, 22
direct [dɪ'rekt] direkt **V 5**, 55
dirty ['dɜ:tɪ] schmutzig, dreckig **I**
disadvantage [ˌdɪsəd'vɑ:ntɪdʒ] Nachteil **IV**
to **disagree** [ˌdɪsə'gri:] nicht übereinstimmen; anderer Meinung sein **IV**
to **disappear** [ˌdɪsə'pɪə] verschwinden **III**
disappointed [ˌdɪsə'pɔɪntɪd] enttäuscht **III**
disappointing [ˌdɪsə'pɔɪntɪŋ] enttäuschend **III**
disco ['dɪskəʊ] [Disko, Tanzveranstaltung mit Popmusik] **II**; Diskothek **III**
to **discuss** [dɪ'skʌs] besprechen, diskutieren **IV**
discussion [dɪ'skʌʃn] Diskussion, Besprechung **V 3**, 38
disease [dɪ'zi:z] Krankheit **IV**
dishwasher ['dɪʃˌwɒʃə] Spülmaschine **V 3**, 34
⟨to dislike⟩ [dɪs'laɪk] nicht mögen **V 3**, 39
display [dɪ'spleɪ] Ausstellung; Anzeige **V 2**, 22
to **display** [dɪ'spleɪ] ausstellen; zeigen **IV**
⟨to disturb⟩ [dɪ'stɜ:b] stören **V TP**, 92
⟨disused⟩ ['dɪsju:zd] nicht mehr benützt **V 3**, 40
to **dive** [daɪv] ins Wasser springen; tauchen **IV**
⟨to dive for a ball⟩ [ˌdaɪv f:rə 'bɔ:l] nach einem Ball hechten **V 5**, 84
to **divide** [dɪ'vaɪd] teilen, aufteilen **III**
to **do*** [du:] tun, machen **I**
do it yourself [ˌdu: ɪt jɔ:'self] heimwerken **III**
Do you? ['du: ju:] Oder?, Nicht wahr? **III**
⟨Don't give me that do goody-good bullshit.⟩ [du: 'gʊdɪ ˌgud 'bʊlʃɪt] *etwa:* Erzähl mir keinen Mist vom Brav-sein. **V 2**, 75
So do I. [ˌsəʊ du: 'aɪ] Ich auch. **II**
to do a paper round ['peɪpə ˌraʊnd] Zeitungen austragen **V 2**, 21
to do better [ˌdu: 'betə] besser sein **III**
to do the washing-up ['dʊ ðə ˌwɒʃɪŋ'ʌp] spülen, abwaschen **I**
to do well [ˌdu: 'wel] gut sein, gut abschneiden **III**
doctor ['dɒktə] Arzt/Ärztin **I**
dodgem car ['dɒdʒəm kɑ:] Autoscooter **II**
dog [dɒg] Hund **I**
dog biscuit ['dɒg ˌbɪskɪt] Hundekuchen **I**
dog-free zone ['dɒgfri: 'zəʊn] hundefreie Zone **I**
How are you **doing?** Wie geht es dir/euch/Ihnen? **IV**
dollar (= **$**) ['dɒlə] Dollar (*amer. Geldeinheit*) **IV**
dolphin ['dɒlfɪn] Delphin **IV**
door [dɔ:] (Garagen-)Tor **I**; Tür **I**
back door ['bæk 'dɔ:] Hintertür **I**
front door ['frʌnt 'dɔ:] Haustür **I**
⟨doorway⟩ ['dɔ:weɪ] Tür, Eingang **V 1**, 68
double ['dʌbl] zweimal, Doppel- **I**
double decker ['dʌbl ˌdekə] Doppeldecker **I**
down [daʊn] herunter, hinunter **I**
to sit down [sɪt 'daʊn] sich hinsetzen **I**
down under [daʊn‿'ʌndə] *umg.:* Australien; Ozeanien **V 1**, 7
downstairs [ˌdaʊn'steəz] unten (*im Gebäude*) **I**
downtown (*AE*) [ˌdaʊn'taʊn] Zentrum von ..., Innenstadt **V 5**, 55
Dr ['dɒktə] Doktor (*Anrede*) **II**
to **drag** [dræg] schleppen, ziehen **IV**
dragon ['drægən] Drache **III**

drama group ['drɑːmə gruːp] Theatergruppe **I**
to **draw*** [drɔː] zeichnen **I**
dream [driːm] Traum **II**
⟨to dream⟩ [driːm] träumen **V 1**, 71
dress [dres] Kleid **II**
drink [drɪŋk] Getränk **III**
to **drink*** [drɪŋk] trinken **I**
drive-in restaurant [draɪv‿ɪn 'restərɔnt] Autorestaurant **IV**
to **drive*** [draɪv] fahren **I**; treiben **V 4**, 47; antreiben **V 6**, 62
driver ['draɪvə] Fahrer/in **I**
driver's license (*AE*) ['draɪvəz ˌlaɪsəns] Führerschein **IV**
[drop] [drɒp] Tropfen **II**
to **drop** [drɒp] fallen (lassen) **II**
to **drown** [draʊn] ertrinken, ertränken **II**
drug [drʌg] Droge, Rauschgift; Medikament **V 5**, 57
° **drum** [drʌm] Trommel, (*Pl.* Schlagzeug) **V 1**, 11
to **dry** [draɪ] trocknen **IV**
⟨to dry out⟩ [draɪ‿'aʊt] austrocknen **V 1**, 71
dry [draɪ] trocken **IV**
duck [dʌk] Ente **I**
to **dump** [dʌmp] abladen, fallen lassen **V 3**, 37; ⟨versenken⟩ **V 3**, 78
during ['djʊərɪŋ] während **IV**
⟨dust⟩ [dʌst] Staub **V 3**, 76
Dutch [dʌtʃ] niederländisch, Niederländisch **III**
⟨dweller⟩ ['dwelə] Bewohner/in **V 3**, 40

E

e-mail ['iːmeɪl] E-Mail (*elektronischer Briefverkehr*) **III**
each [iːtʃ] jede/jeder/jedes **II**
each other [ˌiːtʃ‿'ʌðə] einander, sich gegenseitig **III**
eagle ['iːgl] Adler **IV**
ear [ɪə] Ohr **II**
early ['ɜːlɪ] früh **I**
to **earn** [ɜːn] verdienen **V 2**, 21
earth [ɜːθ] Erde **III**
⟨earth fall⟩ ['ɜːθ fɔːl] Erdrutsch **V 3**, 76
What on earth ...? [ˌwɒt ɒn 'ɜːð] Was um alles in der Welt ...? **II**
earthquake ['ɜːθkweɪk] Erdbeben **IV**
easily [iːzɪlɪ] leicht (*Adverbialform*) **III**
east [iːst] östlich, Ost-, Osten **II**
Easter ['iːstə] Ostern **II**
easy ['iːzɪ] einfach, leicht **I**
to **eat*** [iːt] essen **I**
⟨economic development⟩ [ˌiːkə'nɒmɪk dɪ'veləpmənt] wirtschaftliche Entwicklung **V 3**, 78
⟨economy⟩ [ɪ'kɒnəmɪ] Wirtschaft **V 3**, 78
⟨edge⟩ [edʒ] Kante **V TP**, 92
editor ['edɪtə] Herausgeber/in; Redakteur/in **V 2**, 28
effect [ɪ'fekt] Wirkung, Effekt **V 5**, 56
egg [eg] Ei **I**
⟨ego-trip⟩ ['egəʊ ˌtrɪp] Egotrip; selbstsüchtig **V 5**, 83
Egyptian [ɪ'dʒɪpʃn] ägyptisch, Ägypter/in **III**
⟨electric light⟩ [ɪ'lektrɪk ˌlaɪt] elektrisches Licht **V 2**, 72
electricity [ˌɪlek'trɪsətɪ] Elektrizität, Strom **V 3**, 35
elephant ['elɪfənt] Elefant **II**
elevator (*AE*) ['elɪveɪtə] Aufzug, Fahrstuhl **IV**
else [els] sonst (noch) **I**
emergency [ɪ'mɜːdʒənsɪ] Notfall **III**
to **employ** [ɪm'plɔɪ] beschäftigen; einstellen; beauftragen **V 6**, 63
employer [ɪm'plɔɪə] Arbeitgeber/in **V 2**, 23
to **empty** ['emptɪ] (sich) leeren **V 5**, 56
empty ['emptɪ] leer **II**
to **enclose** [ɪn'kləʊz] beilegen, beifügen **IV**
⟨to encourage⟩ [ɪn'kʌrɪdʒ] anregen, ermuntern **V 5**, 82

end [end] Ende **I**
ending ['endɪŋ] Ende, Schluss (*bei Geschichten*) **I**
⟨endless⟩ ['endlɪs] endlos **V 2**, 73
enemy ['enəmɪ] Feind/in **II**
energy ['enədʒɪ] Energie **III**
engine ['endʒɪn] Motor **III**
engineer [ˌendʒɪ'nɪə] Ingenieur/in **IV**
engineering [ˌendʒɪ'nɪərɪŋ] Technik; Maschinenbau **V 2**, 28
English ['ɪŋglɪʃ] englisch, Englisch **I**
to **enjoy** [ɪn'dʒɔɪ] genießen, gern tun **II**
enjoyable [ɪn'dʒɔɪəbl] nett; unterhaltsam, amüsant **IV**
enormous [ɪ'nɔːməs] riesig **III**
enough [ɪ'nʌf] genug **I**
to **enter** ['entə] eintreten **III**
to **entertain** [ˌentə'teɪn] unterhalten **V 5**, 50
entertainment [ˌentə'teɪnmənt] Unterhaltung, Entertainment **V 5**, 50
entry ['entrɪ] Eingang, Einfahrt **IV**
environment [ɪn'vaɪərənmənt] Umwelt **III**
environmental [ɪnˌvaɪərən'mentl] Umwelt- **V 3**, 33
equal opportunities employer ['iːkwəl ˌɒpə'tjuːnətɪz ɪm'plɔɪə] Arbeitgeber/in, der/die Chancengleichheit bietet **V 2**, 23
equipment [ɪ'kwɪpmənt] Ausstattung, Ausrüstung **IV**
equivalent [ɪ'kwɪvələnt] Gleichwertiges, Entsprechendes **V 2**, 23
error ['erə] Fehler **IV**
escalator ['eskəleɪtə] Rolltreppe **II**
to **escape** [ɪ'skeɪp] entkommen, entfliehen **V 2**, 30
especially [ɪ'speʃəlɪ] insbesondere **III**
etc. [ɪt'setərə] usw. **III**
⟨ether⟩ ['iːθə] Äther **V 3**, 32
⟨ethnic⟩ ['eθnɪk] ethnisch **V 1**, 70
European [ˌjʊərə'piːən] europäisch, Europäer/in **III**
even ['iːvn] sogar **II**
evening ['iːvnɪŋ] Abend **I**
°evening class ['iːvnɪŋ ˌklɑːs] Abendschule, Unterricht am Abend **V 2**, 23
in the evening [ɪn‿ðiː‿'iːvnɪŋ] abends, am Abend **I**
event [ɪ'vent] Ereignis **V 3**, 36; Veranstaltung **III**
ever ['evə] jemals **II**
every ['evrɪ] jede/jeder/jedes **I**
⟨every other week⟩ ['evrɪ ˌʌðə 'wiːk] jede zweite Woche **V 2**, 75
everybody ['evrɪbədɪ] jede/jeder **II**
everyone ['evrɪwʌn] jede/jeder **I**
everything ['evrɪθɪŋ] alles **I**
everywhere ['evrɪweə] überall **IV**
° to **evict** [ɪ'vɪkt] zur Räumung zwingen **V 3**, 36
⟨evil⟩ ['iːvl] Übel **V 2**, 75
⟨evolution⟩ [ˌiːvə'luːʃn] Evolution **V TP**, 93
exact [ɪg'zækt] genau, exakt **IV**
exam [ɪg'zæm] Prüfung **III**
to **examine** [ɪg'zæmɪn] untersuchen **I**
example [ɪg'zɑːmpl] Beispiel **I**
excellent ['eksələnt] ausgezeichnet, hervorragend **IV**
except [ɪk'sept] außer **V 1**, 8
exchange [ɪks'tʃeɪndʒ] Austausch **III**
excited [ɪk'saɪtɪd] aufgeregt **II**
exciting [ɪk'saɪtɪŋ] aufregend, spannend **I**
excursion [ɪk'skɜːʃn] Ausflug, Exkursion **V 1**, 11
excuse [ɪk'skjuːs] Ausrede **III**
Excuse me, please. [ɪk'skjuːz mɪ pliːz] Entschuldigung., Entschuldigen Sie bitte. **I**
exercise ['eksəsaɪz] Übung, Aufgabe **I**
exercise book ['eksəsaɪz ˌbʊk] Heft **I**
⟨exhibition⟩ [ˌeksɪ'bɪʃn] Austellung **V TP**, 95
to **exist** [ɪg'zɪst] existieren **IV**
exit ['eksɪt] Ausgang; Ausfahrt **V 1**, 11

to **expect** [ɪk'spekt] erwarten **IV**
expensive [ɪk'spensɪv] teuer **II**
experience [ɪk'spɪərɪəns] Erfahrung, Erlebnis **III**
experience in selling [ɪk'spɪərɪəns‿ɪn ˌselɪŋ] Verkaufserfahrung **V 2**, 23
⟨to experience⟩ [ɪk'spɪrɪəns] erleben, erfahren **V 1**, 69
experiment [ɪk'sperɪmənt] Experiment, Versuch **III**
to **explain** [ɪk'spleɪn] erklären **II**
explorer [ɪk'splɔːrə] Forscher/in **V 1**, 16
explosion [ɪk'spləʊʒn] Explosion **V 5**, 55
to **export** ['ɪkspɔːt] exportieren **V 1**, 9
express (train) [ɪk'spres] Schnellzug **III**
expression [ɪk'spreʃn] Ausdruck **V 6**, 62
extra ['ekstrə] zusätzlich **I**
extract ['ekstrækt] Auszug **IV**
⟨to extract⟩ [ɪk'strækt] fördern, gewinnen **V 3**, 78
⟨extraction⟩ [ɪk'strækʃn] Gewinnung, Förderung **V 3**, 78
eye [aɪ] Auge **I**
° **eyesore** ['aɪsɔː] Schandfleck **V 3**, 35

F

face [feɪs] Gesicht **II**
face to face [ˌfeɪs tə 'feɪs] von Angesicht zu Angesicht **III**
⟨to face⟩ [feɪs] gegenüberstehen, ins Gesicht schauen **V 1**, 68
⟨facility⟩ [fə'sɪlətɪ] Einrichtung, Möglichkeit **V 2**, 75
fact [fækt] Tatsache, Fakt **II**
⟨factor⟩ ['fæktə] Faktor **V 1**, 13
factory ['fæktərɪ] Fabrik **III**
Factory Act ['fæktərɪ ˌækt] Arbeitsschutzgesetz **V 6**, 66
fair [feə] Volksfest, Jahrmarkt **II**
to **fall*** [fɔːl] fallen **III**
to fall down [ˌfɔːl 'daʊn] umfallen, hinfallen, herunterfallen **III**
to fall off [ˌfɔːl‿'ɒf] (von etwas) herunterfallen **III**
to fall over [fɔːl‿'əʊvə] hinfallen **I**
false friends [ˌfɔːls 'frendz] „falsche Freunde" **III**
familiar [fə'mɪljə] gewohnt, vertraut; bekannt **V 5**, 58
family ['fæməlɪ] Familie **I**
famous ['feɪməs] berühmt **III**
fan [fæn] Fan **II**
⟨fan oven⟩ [ˌfæn 'ʌvn] Umluftherd **V 1**, 71
⟨to fancy⟩ ['fænsɪ] mögen, gefallen **V 2**, 72
fantastic [fæn'tæstɪk] fantastisch, toll **II**
⟨far-off sound⟩ ['fɑːr‿ɒf saʊnd] weit entferntes Geräusch **V 3**, 77
far [fɑː] weit **II**
farm [fɑːm] Bauernhof **I**
to **farm** [fɑːm] bebauen **V 4**, 46
farmer ['fɑːmə] Bauer/Bäuerin **III**
farmland ['fɑːmlænd] Ackerland **IV**
⟨farmyard⟩ ['fɑːmjɑːd] Bauernhof **V 3**, 79
farther ['fɑːðə] weiter **IV**
to be **fascinated by s.th.** ['fæsɪneɪtɪd] von etw. fasziniert sein **V 1**, 17
fascinating ['fæsɪneɪtɪŋ] faszinierend **III**
fashion ['fæʃn] Mode **V 5**, 50
°fashion makeover ['fæʃn 'meɪkˌəʊvə] Typberatung **V 5**, 50
fast [fɑːst] schnell **II**
father ['fɑːðə] Vater **I**
⟨fault⟩ [fɔːlt] Schuld **V 2**, 73
favorite (*AE*) ['feɪvərɪt] Lieblings- **IV**
° **favourable** ['feɪvərəbl] günstig, vorteilhaft **V 4**, 44
favourite ['feɪvərɪt] Lieblings- **I**
fax [fæks] Telefax **IV**
fear [fɪə] Angst, Furcht **IV**
feather ['feðə] Feder **IV**
feature ['fiːtʃə] Beitrag, Bericht, Feature, Eigenschaften, Gesichtszüge **V 5**, 51
February ['februərɪ] Februar **I**
to **feed*** [fiːd] füttern **I**
to **feel*** [fiːl] fühlen, sich fühlen **I**
to feel sick [ˌfiːl 'sɪk] sich schlecht, krank fühlen **II**
to feel well [ˌfiːl 'wel] sich wohl fühlen **II**
feeler ['fiːlə] Fühler **I**
feeling ['fiːlɪŋ] Gefühl **III**
foot, **feet** (= **ft.**) (*pl*) [fʊt, fiːt] Fuß (*Maßeinheit*) **IV**
fence [fens] Zaun **V 1**, 7
ferry ['ferɪ] Fähre **I**
festival ['festəvl] Fest, Festival **IV**
fete [feɪt] Schulfest, Stadtfest **II**
⟨feudal system⟩ ['fjuːdl ˌsɪstəm] Feudalsystem **V 4**, 46
a **few** [ə 'fjuː] [(einige) wenige] **II**; ein paar **III**
field [fiːld] Feld, Wiese **III**
to **fight*** [faɪt] kämpfen **III**
to fight s.o. back [faɪt 'bæk] jdn. zurückschlagen **V 4**, 45
figure ['fɪgə] Figur, Gestalt **III**
to **figure out** ['fɪgər‿aʊt] (heraus)finden **IV**
to **fill** [fɪl] stopfen **IV**
to fill in [ˌfɪl‿'ɪn] ausfüllen **III**
film [fɪlm] Film **II**
to **film** [fɪlm] filmen **II**
⟨final⟩ ['faɪnl] Endspiel, Finale **V TP**, 93
financial [faɪ'nænʃəl] finanziell **IV**
to **find*** [faɪnd] finden **I**
to find out [faɪnd‿'aʊt] herausfinden **I**
⟨fine⟩ [faɪn] fein, prächtig **V 3**, 79
I'm fine. [aɪm 'faɪn] Mir geht's gut. **I**
finger ['fɪŋgə] Finger **II**
to **finish** ['fɪnɪʃ] beenden, aufhören **I**
fire ['faɪə] Feuer **IV**
fire brigade ['faɪə brɪˌgeɪd] Feuerwehr **I**
firefighter ['faɪəˌfaɪtə] Feuerwehrmann/-frau **IV**
fireman ['faɪəmən] Feuerwehrmann **I**
fireworks (*pl*) ['faɪəwɜːks] Feuerwerk **IV**
firm [fɜːm] Firma **I**
firm [fɜːm] fest **IV**
first [fɜːst] erste/erster/erstes **I**; zuerst, als Erste/r/s **II**
at first [ət 'fɜːst] zuerst **II**
⟨first-class⟩ ['fɜːst ˌklɑːs] erste Klasse **V 4**, 80
fish [fɪʃ] Fisch **I**
fish finger [fɪʃ 'fɪŋgə] Fischstäbchen **I**
fish tank ['fɪʃ ˌtæŋk] Aquarium **II**
fishing ['fɪʃɪŋ] Fischen, Fischfang, Angeln **III**
fit [fɪt] fit **V 2**, 22
flag ['flæg] Fahne, Flagge **IV**
flame [fleɪm] Flamme **IV**
flat [flæt] Wohnung **I**
flat [flæt] flach, platt **I**
flat tyre [ˌflæt 'taɪə] platter Reifen, Platten **I**
fleet [fliːt] Flotte **V 4**, 44
flight [flaɪt] Flug **III**
⟨to flip through s.th.⟩ ['flɪp θruː] durchblättern **V 5**, 82
° to **float** [fləʊt] schweben; schwimmen; treiben **V 3**, 32
⟨to flood⟩ [flʌd] überschwemmen, hereinströmen **V 3**, 77
floor [flɔː] Boden **I**; Stockwerk, Etage **II**
⟨to flop⟩ [flɒp] sich fallen lassen **V 1**, 10
flour ['flaʊə] Mehl **IV**
flow chart ['fləʊ tʃɑːt] Flussdiagramm **V 1**, 14
to **flow** [fləʊ] fließen **IV**
flower ['flaʊə] Blume **II**
flowerpot ['flaʊəpɒt] Blumentopf **I**
flu [fluː] Grippe **II**
to **fly*** [flaɪ] fliegen **II**
to fly high ['flaɪ ˌhaɪ] gute Laune haben **IV**
to **fold** [fəʊld] falten **II**
folder ['fəʊldə] Mappe, Hefter **I**

folk [fəʊk] Folk (*Musikrichtung*) **III**
folk dancing ['fəʊkdɑ:nsɪŋ] Volkstanzen **V 1**, 11
to **follow** ['fɒləʊ] folgen, verfolgen **III**
food [fu:d] Nahrung, Essen **II**
⟨foolishness⟩ ['fu:lɪʃnɪs] Dummheit, Torheit **V 1**, 68
foot, feet (*pl*) [fʊt] Fuß, Füße **II**
football ['fʊtbɔ:l] Fußball **I**; American Football **IV**
for [fɔ:, fə] für **I**
°for a rainy day [ə 'reɪnɪ deɪ] *umg.*: für schlechte Zeiten **V 5**, 59
for ages [fɔ: 'eɪdʒɪz] seit langem, schon ewig **IV**
for sale [fə 'seɪl] zum Verkauf, zu verkaufen **II**
to ask for ['ɑ:sk fɔ:] bitten um **I**
force [fɔ:s] Kraft, Macht **III**
to **force** [fɔ:s] zwingen **IV**
to force s.o. to do s.th. [fɔ:s] jdn. zwingen etw. zu tun **IV**
foreigner ['fɒrənə] Ausländer/in **IV**
forest ['fɒrɪst] Wald **II**
⟨forever⟩ [fə'revə] für immer **V TP**, 95
to **forget*** [fə'get] vergessen **II**
fork [fɔ:k] Gabel **II**
form [fɔ:m] Art **III**; Form **I**
application form [ˌæplɪ'keɪʃn 'fɔ:m] Anmeldeformular; Bewerbungsformular **IV**
to **form** [fɔ:m] bilden, formen **IV**
formal ['fɔ:ml] formell, förmlich **IV**
fortunately ['fɔ:tʃnətlɪ] glücklicherweise, zum Glück **IV**
fortune ['fɔ:tʃu:n] Schicksal **IV**
fortune cookie ['fɔ:tʃu:n ˌkʊkɪ] *Keks, der eine Art Lebensweisheit enthält* **IV**
four-wheel drive (= **4WD**) [ˌfɔ:wi:l 'draɪv] Fahrzeug mit Allradantrieb **V 1**, 10
fourteen-year-old [fɔ:'ti:n jiər‿əʊld] vierzehnjährig **III**
free [fri:] frei **I**; kostenlos **I**
freedom ['fri:dəm] Freiheit **III**
French [frentʃ] französisch, Französisch **III**
⟨frequently⟩ ['fri:kwəntlɪ] oft **V 6**, 86
⟨fresh⟩ [freʃ] frisch **V 2**, 75
⟨freshwater⟩ ['freʃˌwɔ:tə] Süßwasser **V TP**, 92
Friday ['fraɪdeɪ] Freitag **I**
fridge (= **refrigerator**) [frɪdʒ] Kühlschrank **IV**
friend [frend] Freund/in **I**
friendly ['frendlɪ] freundlich **II**
⟨Friesian⟩ ['frɪzjən] *Kuhart* **V 1**, 69
to **frighten** ['fraɪtn] erschrecken, Angst einjagen **V 5**, 55
to get **frightened** ['fraɪtnd] Angst bekommen **IV**
frightening ['fraɪtnɪŋ] erschreckend, Furcht erregend **II**
frog [frɒg] Frosch **I**
from [frɒm] aus, von **I**
from behind [frɒm bɪ'haɪnd] von hinten **II**
from time to time [frəm 'taɪm tə 'taɪm] von Zeit zu Zeit **IV**
from top to bottom [frəm 'tɒp tə ˌbɒtəm] von oben bis unten **III**
from ... to [frəm ... tu:] von ... nach **I**
at the **front** [ət ðə 'frʌnt] vorn **II**
front door ['frʌnt 'dɔ:] Haustür **I**
in **front of** [ɪn 'frʌnt əv] vor **I**
fruit (*sg + pl*) [fru:t] Frucht, Früchte, Obst **II**
full [fʊl] voll **II**
⟨full grown⟩ [ˌfʊl 'grəʊn] ausgewachsen **V 1**, 69
fun [fʌn] Spaß **I**
⟨funnel⟩ ['fʌnl] Trichter **V 3**, 79
funny ['fʌnɪ] lustig, komisch **I**
⟨fur⟩ [fɜ:] Fell, Pelz **V 1**, 68
to **furnish** ['fɜ:nɪʃ] einrichten, möblieren **V 2**, 22
furniture (*sg + pl*) ['fɜ:nɪtʃə] Möbel **V 2**, 22
further ['fɜ:ðə] weiter **IV**
future ['fju:tʃə] Zukunft **II**

G

gallery ['gælərɪ] Kunstgalerie **IV**; ⟨Stollen⟩ **V 3**, 76
⟨to gallop⟩ ['gæləp] galoppieren **V 1**, 69
gallows ['gæləʊz] Galgen **II**
game [geɪm] Spiel **I**
gameboy ['geɪmbɔɪ] *Computerspiel* **III**
gang [gæŋ] Bande, Gang **IV**
⟨gangway⟩ ['gæŋweɪ] Kanal, in dem die Eier abtransportiert werden **V 3**, 79
garage ['gærɑ:dʒ] Garage **I**
garbage (*AE*) ['gɑ:bɪdʒ] Abfall **IV**
garbage can (*AE*) ['gɑ:bɪdʒ kæn] Abfalleimer **IV**
garden ['gɑ:dən] Garten **I**
⟨gardener⟩ ['gɑ:dnə] Gärtner/in **V 2**, 72
gas [gæs] Gas **V 1**, 8; ⟨Mordsspaß⟩ **V 2**, 75
⟨gas explosion⟩ [gæs ɪk'spləʊʒn] Gasexplosion **V TP**, 97
gate [geɪt] Tor **V 3**, 37
⟨gateway⟩ ['geɪtweɪ] Tor **V TP**, 94
GCSE (= **General Certificate of Secondary Education**) [ˌdʒi: si: es i:, ˌdʒenərəl sə'tɪfɪkət‿əv 'sekəndərɪ ˌedʒʊ'keɪʃn] Abschlussprüfung (*entspricht in etwa Mittlerer Reife*) **III**
° **G'day** [gə'deɪ] Guten Tag (*austr. Begrüßung*) **V 1**, 7
general ['dʒenərəl] allgemein **V 1**, 15
generation [ˌdʒenə'reɪʃn] Generation **V 3**, 40
genitive ['dʒenɪtɪv] Genitiv **III**
gentleman ['dʒentlmən] Herr **V 5**, 55
geographical [dʒɪə'græfɪkəl] geografisch **IV**
Geography [dʒɪ'ɒgrəfɪ] Erdkunde **II**
⟨germ⟩ [dʒɜ:m] Bazillus, Keim **V 3**, 79
German ['dʒɜ:mən] deutsch, Deutsch, Deutsche/r **I**
gerund ['dʒerənd] Gerundium **V 2**, 26
to **get*** [get] bekommen **I**; holen **I**
to get + adj. [get] werden **III**
to get around [ə'raʊnd] sich fortbewegen **III**
to get at s.th. ['get æt] auf etw. hinauswollen **IV**
to get bored [bɔ:d] Langeweile haben/bekommen **IV**
⟨to get divorced⟩ [ˌget dɪ'vɔst] sich scheiden lassen **V 2**, 75
⟨to get fed up⟩ [get 'fed ˌʌp] die Nase voll haben, es satt haben **V 2**, 72
to get frightened ['fraɪtnd] Angst bekommen **IV**
to get hurt [hɜ:t] sich weh tun, sich verletzen **V 3**, 36
to get in line (*AE*) [ˌget ɪn 'laɪn] sich anstellen **IV**
to get into the mood [get‿ˌɪntə ðə 'mu:d] sich einstimmen **III**
to get lost [get 'lɒst] verloren gehen, sich verirren **I**
to get off [ˌget‿'ɒf] aussteigen **III**
to get on with s.o. [get‿'ɒn wɪð] sich mit jdm. gut verstehen **III**
Get out! [get 'aʊt] Hinaus mit dir!, Hinaus mit euch! **I**
⟨to get out of⟩ [get 'aʊt‿əv] sich vor etw. drücken **V 2**, 74
to get ready [get 'redɪ] (sich) vorbereiten **I**
°Get real! [get 'ri:əl] *etwa:* Komm auf den Boden! **V 3**, 33
to get s.o. to do s.th. ['get sʌmwʌn tʊ ˌdu:] jdn. dazu bringen etw. zu tun **V 5**, 52
to get s.th. ready [get 'sʌmθɪŋ 'redɪ] etw. fertig machen, vorbereiten **II**
to get some time off [taɪm‿'ɒf] frei bekommen **V 2**, 22
to get stuck [get 'stʌk] stecken bleiben **I**
to get the bus [ˌget ðə 'bʌs] den Bus nehmen **I**
to get there ['get ðeə] hinkommen **I**
to get through [get 'θru:] durchkommen (*am Telefon*) **V 5**, 55
[to get tired] [get 'taɪəd] müde werden **II**
to get to know s.o. [get tʊ‿'nəʊ] jdn. kennen lernen **V 1**, 11

to get up [get‿'ʌp] aufstehen **I**
Get well soon! ['get wel 'su:n] Gute Besserung! **I**
⟨getaway⟩ ['getəweɪ] Flucht **V 2**, 75
⟨ghetto⟩ ['getəʊ] Getto **V 5**, 83
ghost [gəʊst] Geist, Gespenst **II**
ghost train ['gəʊst 'treɪn] Geisterbahn **II**
giant ['dʒaɪənt] Riese; riesig, Riesen- **IV**
girl [gɜ:l] Mädchen **I**
gist [dʒɪst] Wesentliches **IV**
to **give*** [gɪv] geben **I**
to give a talk [ˌgɪv‿ə 'tɔ:k] eine Rede/ein Referat halten **III**
⟨to give an order⟩ [ˌgɪv‿ən 'ɔ:də] etw. befehlen, anweisen **V 1**, 68
to give away [gɪv ə'weɪ] weggeben **II**
give my love to ... [ˌgɪv maɪ 'lʌv tə] grüß/grüßt ... recht herzlich **I**
to give s.o. a message [gɪv ə 'mesɪdʒ] jdm. etw. ausrichten **III**
to give up [ˌgɪv‿'ʌp] aufgeben **III**
to give ... a lift [lɪft] ... im Auto mitnehmen **I**
glad [glæd] froh **I**
glass [glɑ:s] Glas **II**
glasses ['glɑ:sɪz] Brille **III**
global warming ['gləʊbl ˌwɔ:mɪŋ] globale Erwärmung, Treibhauseffekt **V 3**, 33
globe [gləʊb] Kugel; Globus **V 6**, 64
°**gloomy** ['glu:mɪ] düster, finster; trübsinnig **V 6**, 63
to **go*** [gəʊ] gehen, fahren **I**
to go across ['gəʊ əˌkrɒs] überqueren **III**
⟨to go bush⟩ ['gəʊ bʊʃ] in den Outback gehen **V TP**, 94
to go cold [gəʊ 'kəʊld] kalt werden **V 5**, 55
to go down on one's knees [gəʊ ˌdaʊn‿ɒn wʌnz 'ni:z] sich hinknien **III**
to go for a walk [ˌgəʊ fər‿ə 'wɔ:k] spazieren gehen **I**
to go home [gəʊ 'həʊm] nach Hause gehen **I**
to go on [gəʊ‿'ɒn] weitermachen **I**
to go (out) with s.o. [gəʊ 'aʊt wɪð] mit jdm. (aus)gehen **IV**
to go shopping [gəʊ 'ʃɒpɪŋ] einkaufen gehen **II**
to go swimming [gəʊ 'swɪmɪŋ] schwimmen gehen **I**
[to be going to] [bi: 'gəʊɪŋ tu:] vorhaben zu ... **II**
to go to bed [gəʊ tə 'bed] ins Bett gehen, schlafen gehen **I**
to go to the shops [gəʊ tə ðə 'ʃɒps] einkaufen gehen **I**
⟨to go to waste⟩ [ˌgəʊ tə 'weɪst] verkommen, verschwendet werden **V 3**, 79
to go together [gəʊ tə'geðə] zusammenpassen **I**
°to go veggie ['vedʒɪ] *umg.:* Vegetarier/in werden **V 3**, 33
to go wrong [gəʊ 'rɒŋ] schief gehen **II**; sich verfahren **II**
goal [gəʊl] Tor *(beim Sport)* **I**
goalkeeper ['gəʊlˌki:pə] Torwart **III**
God [gɒd] Gott **III**
God bless you! [ˌgɒd 'bles‿ju:] Gott segne Dich/Euch! *(veraltete Grußform)* **III**
gold [gəʊld] (aus) Gold **III**; [Gold] **II**
golden ['gəʊldən] golden, Gold- **V 5**, 51
golf [gɒlf] Golf **IV**
⟨golf course⟩ ['gɒlfˌkɔ:s] Golfplatz **V R**, 89
⟨gone with the wind⟩ [ˌgɒn wɪð‿ðə 'wɪnd] weg/fort mit dem Wind **V 1**, 68
good [gʊd] gut **I**
Good afternoon. [gʊd ɑ:ftə'nu:n] Guten Tag. *(Anrede am Nachmittag)* **I**
good-looking [ˌgʊd'lʊkɪŋ] gut aussehend **V 5**, 57
Good morning. [gʊd 'mɔ:nɪŋ] Guten Morgen. **I**
good working knowledge ['gʊd ˌwɜ:kɪŋ nɒlɪdʒ] gute Grundkenntnis **V 2**, 24
It's good to see you. [ɪts ˌgʊd tə 'si: jʊ] Schön, dich/euch zu sehen. **I**
It's no good ... [ɪts nəʊ 'gʊd] Es bringt nichts, ..., Es hat keinen Sinn, ... **II**
to be good at [bɪ 'gʊd‿ət] gut sein in ... **I**
Goodbye. [gʊd'baɪ] Auf Wiedersehen., Tschüs. **I**
Thank **goodness!** [θæŋk 'gʊdnɪs] Gott sei Dank! **IV**
goods [gʊdz] Waren **V 6**, 63
goose, geese *(pl)* [gu:s] Gans, Gänse **II**
Gosh! [gɒʃ] *Ausruf des Erstaunens* **II**
⟨gossip⟩ ['gɒsɪp] Klatsch, Tratsch **V 5**, 83
gotten *(AE)* ['gɒtn] bekommen **IV**
government ['gʌvnment] Regierung **IV**
to **grab** [græb] greifen, schnappen, packen **IV**
grade *(AE)* [greɪd] Note *(in der Schule)*; Klasse **IV**
gradually ['grædʒʊəlɪ] nach und nach, allmählich **IV**
graffiti [grə'fi:tɪ] Wandmalereien, Graffiti **IV**
grammar ['græmə] Grammatik **III**
Grandma ['grænmɑ:] Oma **I**
Grandpa ['grænpɑ:] Opa **I**
graphics *(pl)* ['græfɪks] Bilder, Grafik **III**
grass [grɑ:s] Gras **IV**
grave [greɪv] schlimm; ernst **V 5**, 55
great [greɪt] toll, großartig **I**
Greek [gri:k] griechisch, Griechisch **I**
green [gri:n] grün **I**
⟨greenfly⟩ ['gri:nflaɪ] Blattlaus, -läuse **V 2**, 73
⟨greenhouse gases⟩ ['gri:nhaʊs ˌgæsɪz] Treibhausgas **V TP**, 95
grey [greɪ] grau **V 6**, 63
grid [grɪd] Tabelle **IV**
°**grim** [grɪm] trostlos; grimmig **V 6**, 63
grin [grɪn] Lächeln, Grinsen **V 1**, 15
⟨to grin⟩ [grɪn] grinsen **V 1**, 11
ground [graʊnd] Boden **III**
group [gru:p] Gruppe **I**
tutor group ['tju:tə ˌgru:p] Klasse *(in einer englischen Schule)* **I**
to **group** [gru:p] gruppieren, in Gruppen einteilen **IV**
to **grow*** [grəʊ] (an)pflanzen, wachsen **II**
⟨to growl⟩ [graʊl] knurren **V 1**, 68
[grumpy] ['grʌmpɪ] mürrisch, schlecht gelaunt **II**
⟨guard⟩ [gɑ:d] Wache **V 4**, 81
⟨guardian angel⟩ ['gɑ:djən‿'eɪndʒl] Schutzengel **V 5**, 85
to **guess** [ges] raten **III**
Guess what! [ges 'wɒt] Rate mal! **V 2**, 29
guest [gest] Gast **I**
guest house ['gest haʊs] Pension, Gästehaus **I**
guide [gaɪd] Führer/in **IV**; Reiseführer *(Buch)* **IV**
guided tour [ˌgaɪdɪd 'tʊə] Führung **IV**
guitar [gɪ'tɑ:] Gitarre **I**
⟨Gum⟩ [gʌm] *Baumart* **V 1**, 68
gun [gʌn] Schusswaffe, Pistole, Gewehr **IV**
guy *(AE)* [gaɪ] Mann, Kerl **IV**
gym [dʒɪm] Turnhalle, Sporthalle **III**; Fitnessstudio **IV**

H

hair [heə] Haar(e) **II**
haircut ['heəkʌt] Haarschnitt, Frisur **II**
hairdresser ['heəˌdresə] Friseur/in **V 2**, 21
half [hɑ:f] halb; Hälfte **I**
hall [hɔ:l] Diele, Flur **I**; ⟨Saal⟩ **V 6**, 87
Halloween [ˌhæləʊ'i:n] *Halloween* **IV**
ham [hæm] gekochter Schinken **I**
hammer ['hæmə] Hammer **III**
hamster ['hæmstə] Hamster **II**
hand [hænd] Hand **I**
to give s.o. a hand [gɪv‿ə 'hænd] jdm. helfen **IV**
⟨to hand s.th. in⟩ [ˌhænd 'ɪn] etw. abgeben, einreichen **V 2**, 74

⟨to handle⟩ ['hændl] umgehen mit; fertig werden mit **V 2**, 74
handout ['hændaʊt] *zusammenfassendes Papier, Handout* **V 1**, 14
handwriting ['hænd,raɪtɪŋ] Handschrift **IV**
to **hang*** [hæŋ] hängen **V 3**, 36
to hang around [hæŋ‿ə'raʊnd] warten, herumhängen **V 5**, 59
hangman ['hæŋmən] Henker **II**
to **happen** ['hæpən] passieren, geschehen **II**
happy ['hæpɪ] fröhlich, glücklich **I**
Happy birthday! [,hæpɪ 'bɜːθdeɪ] Herzlichen Glückwunsch zum Geburtstag! **I**
⟨to harass⟩ ['hærəs] belästigen **V TP**, 92
harbour ['hɑːbə] Hafen **V 1**, 11
hard [hɑːd] hart **III**; schwer **IV**
⟨hardly⟩ ['hɑːdlɪ] kaum **V 6**, 86
[hardwood] ['hɑːdwʊd] Hartholz **V 3**, 41
harmless ['hɑːmles] harmlos **IV**
harvest ['hɑːvɪst] Ernte **IV**
hat [hæt] Hut **II**
⟨to hatch⟩ [hætʃ] ausschlüpfen **V 1**, 10
to **hate** [heɪt] hassen, nicht leiden können **II**
to **have*** [hæv] haben **I**
have got ['hæv gɒt] haben, besitzen **I**
haven't got ... ['hævnt gɒt] nicht haben **I**
Let's have a go. [hæv‿ə 'gəʊ] Probieren wir es mal. **II**
So have you. ['səʊ hæv‿juː] Du auch. **II**
to have a bath [hæv‿ə 'bɑːθ] baden **I**
to have a chat [tʃæt] sich unterhalten, plaudern **V 1**, 13
to have a good time [hæv‿ə,gʊd 'taɪm] Spaß haben **II**
to have a ride [hæv‿ə 'raɪd] fahren **II**
to have a word with s.o. [,hæv‿ə'wɜːd‿wɪð] mit jdm. sprechen **III**
to have an argument [,hæv‿ən 'ɑːgjʊmənt] einen Streit, eine Auseinandersetzung haben **II**
to have to ['hæv tə] müssen **III**
he [hiː] er **I**
head [hed] Kopf **I**
⟨head of state⟩ [,hed‿əv 'steɪt] Staatsoberhaupt **V 1**, 70
⟨Head of the Commonwealth⟩ ['hed‿əv ðə 'kɒmənwelθ] Oberhaupt des Commonwealth **V 1**, 70
⟨to head for⟩ ['hed fɔː] sich in eine bestimmte Richtung bewegen **V 1**, 69
headache ['hedeɪk] Kopfschmerzen **II**
heading ['hedɪŋ] Überschrift **IV**
headline ['hedlaɪn] Titel, Überschrift, Schlagzeile **V 3**, 38
headphones ['hedfəʊnz] Kopfhörer **III**
headteacher [,hed'tiːtʃə] Schuldirektor/in **I**
headword ['hedwɜːd] Stichwort **IV**
health [helθ] Gesundheit **V 5**, 51
healthy living ['helθɪ 'lɪvɪŋ] gesunde Lebensweise **I**
to **hear*** [hɪə] hören **II**
heart [hɑːt] Herz **IV**
heat [hiːt] Hitze **V 1**, 11
⟨to heat⟩ [hiːt] erhitzen **V 1**, 71
heating ['hiːtɪŋ] Heizung **III**
heavy ['hevɪ] schwer **III**
heavy metal [hevɪ 'metl] Heavy Metal (*Musikrichtung*) **III**
heavy traffic [,hevɪ 'træfɪk] viel Verkehr **III**
⟨hectare⟩ ['hekteə] Hektar **V TP**, 95
height [haɪt] Höhe **IV**
helicopter ['helɪkɒptə] Hubschrauber **IV**
Hello. [hə'ləʊ] Hallo., Guten Tag. **I**
to say hello ['seɪ hə'ləʊ] grüßen **I**
helmet ['helmɪt] Helm **II**
help [help] Hilfe **III**
Help! [help] Hilfe! **I**
to **help** [help] helfen **I**
helper ['helpə] Helfer/in **II**
helpful ['helpfʊl] hilfsbereit **III**
helpless ['helplɪs] hilflos **III**
hen [hen] Henne **I**; ⟨Huhn⟩ **V 3**, 79
her [hɜː] ihr/ihre **I**; ihr/sie **I**
⟨to herd⟩ [hɜːd] zusammentreiben **V 1**, 68
here [hɪə] hier **I**
Here we come! ['hɪə wiː ,kʌm] Jetzt kommen wir! **IV**
Here you are. ['hɪə jʊ‿ɑː] Hier, bitte schön. **I**
hero, heroes (*pl*) ['hɪərəʊ] Held, Helden **III**
herself [hɜː'self] (sie/ihr) selbst **III**
Hey! [heɪ] He! **I**
Hey there! He da!, Hallo! **IV**
Hi! [haɪ] Hallo! **I**
Hi there! ['haɪ ,ðeə] Hallo! **II**
to **hide*** [haɪd] (sich) verstecken **II**
high [haɪ] hoch **II**
⟨high altar⟩ [haɪ 'ɔːltə] Hochaltar **V TP**, 95
high jump ['haɪdʒʌmp] Hochsprung **III**
high school (*AE*) ['haɪ ,skuːl] Gesamtschule **IV**
hiker ['haɪkə] Wanderer/Wanderin **IV**
to go **hiking** [,gəʊ 'haɪkɪŋ] wandern gehen **IV**
hill [hɪl] Hügel **I**
him [hɪm] ihm/ihn **I**
himself [hɪm'self] (ihn/ihm) selbst **III**
Hindu ['hɪnduː] hinduistisch, Hindu **III**
⟨hip-hop⟩ ['hɪp ,hɒp] Hip-hop *(Musik- und Moderichtung)* **V 5**, 83
his [hɪz] sein/seine **I**
Hispanic [hɪ'spænɪk] hispanisch, *Amerikaner/in lateinamer. Herkunft* **IV**
History ['hɪstərɪ] Geschichte **II**
⟨hit⟩ [hɪt] Hit, Volltreffer **V 2**, 75
to **hit*** [hɪt] treffen, schlagen **II**; angreifen **V 3**, 36
⟨to hit the headlines⟩ [,hɪt ðə 'hedlaɪnz] Schlagzeilen machen **V 5**, 85
to hit the trail [hɪt ðə 'treɪl] *umg.:* sich auf den Weg machen **IV**
Hmm. [hm] Hm., Tja. **I**
hobby ['hɒbɪ] Hobby **II**
hockey ['hɒkɪ] Rasenhockey **I**
to **hold*** [həʊld] halten **III**
Hold on! [,həʊld‿'ɒn] Halt dich fest!, Halten Sie sich fest! **III**
to hold up [,həʊld‿'ʌp] (hoch)halten **III**
hole [həʊl] Loch **I**
holiday ['hɒlədeɪ] Urlaub, Ferien **III**
on holiday [,ɒn 'hɒlədeɪ] im Urlaub, in den Ferien **III**
home [həʊm] Heim, Zuhause **I**
at home [ət 'həʊm] zu Hause **I**
°home furnishings [həʊm 'fɜːnɪʃɪŋz] Inneneinrichtung **V 2**, 22
to come home [kʌm 'həʊm] nach Hause kommen **I**
to go home [gəʊ 'həʊm] nach Hause gehen **I**
hometown [,həʊm'taʊn] Heimatstadt **IV**
homework ['həʊmwɜːk] Hausaufgaben **I**
honey ['hʌnɪ] Honig; Liebling (*Kosename*) **IV**
hood [hʊd] Kapuze **II**
to **hope** [həʊp] hoffen **I**
⟨hopeless⟩ ['həʊplɪs] hoffnungslos **V 3**, 39
horrible ['hɒrəbl] grauenhaft, schrecklich **IV**
horror ['hɒrə] Horror **III**
horse [hɔːs] Pferd **II**
hospital ['hɒspɪtl] Krankenhaus **I**
host [həʊst] Gastgeber; Moderator/in **IV**
hot dog [,hɒt 'dɒg] Hot dog (*heißes Würstchen in einem Brötchen*) **II**
hot [hɒt] heiß **I**
hotel [həʊ'tel] Hotel **II**
hotline ['hɒt,laɪn] Hotline, „heißer Draht" **IV**

hour ['aʊə] Stunde **I**
house [haʊs] Haus **I**
housekeeper ['haʊs,ki:pə] Haushälter/in **II**
⟨housemaid⟩ ['haʊsmeɪd] Dienstmädchen **V 6**, 87
housework ['haʊswɜ:k] Hausarbeit **I**
housing unit ['haʊzɪŋ‿ju:nɪt] Wohneinheit **IV**
hovercraft ['hɒvəkrɑ:ft] Luftkissenboot **I**
how [haʊ] wie **I**
How about …? [haʊ‿ə'baʊt] Wie steht's mit …?, Wie wär's mit …? **II**
How are you doing? Wie geht es dir/euch/Ihnen? **IV**
How are you? [haʊ‿'ɑ: ju:] Wie geht es dir/euch/Ihnen? **I**
How many? [haʊ 'menɪ] Wie viele? **I**
How much? [haʊ 'mʌtʃ] Wie viel? **I**
however [haʊ'evə] jedoch, aber **V 2**, 28
hug [hʌg] Umarmung **II**
huge [hju:dʒ] riesig **IV**
human ['hju:mən] Mensch **III**
human ['hju:mən] menschlich **IV**
Humanities *(pl)* [hju:'mænətɪz] Erdkunde und Geschichte *(in der Schule)* **II**
⟨humorous⟩ ['hju:mərəs] lustig, humorvoll **V 3**, 79
humour ['hju:mə] Humor **V 5**, 53
⟨hundredweight⟩ ['hʌndredweɪt] Zentner **V 6**, 86
hunger ['hʌŋgə] Hunger **V 3**, 34
hungry ['hʌŋgrɪ] hungrig **I**
to **hunt** [hʌnt] jagen **III**
hunter ['hʌntə] Jäger/in **IV**
°to **hurl** [hɜ:l] schleudern **V 1**, 11
hurricane ['hʌrɪkən] Wirbelsturm **IV**
to **hurry** ['hʌrɪ] (sich) (be)eilen **II**
to be in a **hurry** [bɪ ɪn‿ə'hʌrɪ] in Eile sein **III**
to **hurt*** [hɜ:t] weh tun, schmerzen **I**
husband ['hʌzbənd] Ehemann **III**
⟨hut⟩ [hʌt] Hütte **V 1**, 68
hyphen ['haɪfn] Bindestrich **IV**
°**hypocrite** ['hɪpəkrɪt] Heuchler/in, Scheinheilige/r **V 3**, 37

I

I [aɪ] ich **I**
⟨I might as well⟩ [aɪ maɪt ə'zwel] dann kann ich auch **V 5**, 85
⟨I used to have⟩ [,aɪ 'ju:stə ,hæv] ich hatte früher **V 5**, 82
⟨I was to go for an interview.⟩ [wɒz tʊ 'gəʊ] Ich sollte zu einem Vorstellungsgespräch gehen **V 2**, 72
I'd like … [aɪd laɪk] Ich hätte gern … **II**
°I'll also help … [help] Normalerweise helfe ich auch dabei … **V 2**, 22
⟨I'm in the hi-fidelity first class travelling set⟩ [,haɪfɪ'delətɪ 'fɜ:st klɑ:s] *etwa:* ich reise nur erster Klasse **V 2**, 75
I've got … ['aɪv gɒt] Ich habe … **I**
ice cream [,aɪs 'kri:m] Eiskrem **I**
ice rink ['aɪs ,rɪŋk] Eisbahn **II**
ice-skating ['aɪs'skeɪtɪŋ] Schlittschuhlaufen **II**
idea [aɪ'dɪə] Idee **I**
ideal [aɪ,dɪəl] ideal, besonders geeignet **II**
to **identify** [aɪ'dentɪfaɪ] identifizieren, erkennen **V 5**, 54
idiot ['ɪdɪət] Idiot/in, Dummkopf **III**
if [ɪf] ob **IV**
if [ɪf] wenn, falls **II**
ignorant ['ɪgnərənt] unwissend, ungebildet, ignorant **V 5**, 52
ill [ɪl] krank **II**
illegal [ɪ'li:gəl] illegal, ungesetzlich **IV**
image ['ɪmɪdʒ] Bild, Figur **IV**
to **imagine** [ɪ'mædʒɪn] sich vorstellen **III**
⟨immediately⟩ [ɪ'mi:djətlɪ] sofort **V 1**, 71
immigrant ['ɪmɪgrənt] Einwanderer/Einwanderin **IV**
important [ɪm'pɔ:tnt] wichtig **II**
⟨impossible⟩ [ɪm'pɒsəbl] unmöglich **V 4**, 80
impression [ɪm'preʃn] Eindruck **IV**
to **improve** [ɪm'pru:v] verbessern **IV**
in [ɪn] in **I**
in a fun way [ɪn‿ə fʌn 'weɪ] auf unterhaltsame Art **III**
in front of [ɪn 'frʌnt əv] vor **I**
⟨in particular⟩ [ɪn pə'tɪkjʊlə] besonders, vor allem **V TP**, 92
in return (for) [ɪn rɪ'tɜ:n fɔ:] als Gegenleistung (für) **V 4**, 46
in the afternoon [ɪn ði:‿ɑ:ftə'nu:n] nachmittags, am Nachmittag **I**
in the evening [ɪn‿ði:‿'i:vnɪŋ] abends, am Abend **I**
in the meantime [ɪn ðə‿'mi:ntaɪm] in der Zwischenzeit **V 3**, 36
in the morning [ɪn ðə 'mɔ:nɪŋ] morgens, am Vormittag **I**
⟨in the open⟩ [ɪn ðɪ‿'əʊpən] im Freien **V 2**, 73
in turn [ɪn 'tɜ:n] der Reihe nach, abwechselnd **IV**
in … days [ɪn … 'deɪz] in … Tagen **I**
incident ['ɪnsɪdent] Vorfall, Ereignis **IV**
⟨income⟩ ['ɪŋkʌm] Einkommen **V 6**, 87
indeed [ɪn'di:d] *(nachgestellt)* sehr **III**
indefinite article [ɪn'defɪnət ,ɑ:tɪkl] unbestimmter Artikel **IV**
Independence Day [,ɪndɪ'pendəns deɪ] *Unabhängigkeitstag* **IV**
⟨independent⟩ [,ɪndɪ'pendənt] unabhängig **V 1**, 70
index ['ɪndeks] Inhaltsverzeichnis **IV**
Indian ['ɪndjən] indianisch, Indianer/in **IV**
Indian ['ɪndjən] indisch, Inder/in **II**
indirect [,ɪndɪ'rekt] indirekt **V 2**, 29
individual [,ɪndɪ'vɪdʒʊəl] einzeln **V 4**, 48
indivisible [,ɪndɪ'vɪzəbl] unteilbar **IV**
Industrial Revolution [ɪn'dʌstrɪəl ,revə'lu:ʃn] Industrielle Revolution **V 3**, 35
industrial [ɪn'dʌstrɪəl] Industrie-, industriell **V 6**, 62
industry ['ɪndəstrɪ] Industrie **III**
infinitive [ɪn'fɪnətɪv] Infinitiv, Grundform **II**
influence ['ɪnflʊəns] Einfluss **V 1**, 12
to **influence** ['ɪnflʊəns] beeinflussen **V 5**, 51
to **inform** [ɪn'fɔ:m] benachrichtigen, informieren **IV**
information *(sg + pl)* [,ɪnfə'meɪʃn] Information(en), Auskunft/Auskünfte **II**
⟨informative⟩ [ɪn'fɔ:mətɪv] informativ, aufschlussreich **V 5**, 83
-ing-form ['ɪŋ fɔ:m] -ing-Form, Gerundium **IV**
inhabitant [ɪn'hæbɪtənt] Einwohner/in **V 1**, 7
⟨inner⟩ ['ɪnə] innere/r/s **V 3**, 40
to **input** ['ɪnpʊt] eingeben **IV**
inside [ɪn'saɪd] drinnen **I**
inspector [ɪn'spektə] Kontrolleur/in **V 6**, 66
⟨inspirational⟩ [,ɪnspə'reɪʃənl] inspirierend, aufmunternd **V 5**, 83
to **install** [ɪn'stɔ:l] installieren **IV**
instead [ɪn'sted] statt **III**
instructions *(pl)* [ɪn'strʌkʃnz] Betriebsanleitung, Anweisungen **IV**
⟨insult⟩ ['ɪnsʌlt] Beleidigung **V 1**, 68
⟨interactive audio tour⟩ [,ɪntər'æktɪv ɔ:dɪəʊ tɔ:] interaktiver Rundgang mit Geräuschkulisse **V TP**, 95
interest ['ɪntrəst] Interesse **III**
to be **interested in s.th.** [bɪ 'ɪntrəstɪd ɪn] interessiert sein an **IV**
interesting ['ɪntrɪstɪŋ] interessant **II**
to **interfere** (with) [,ɪntə'fɪə wɪð] sich einmischen (in) **IV**
international [,ɪntə'næʃənl] international **III**
Internet ['ɪntənet] Internet **V 1**, 9
to **interrupt** [,ɪntə'rʌpt] unterbrechen **V 1**, 14

interview ['ɪntəvju:] Interview, Gespräch **III**
to **interview** ['ɪntəvju:] interviewen **IV**
into ['ɪntʊ] in, hinein **I**
to **introduce** (-self) [ɪntrə'dju:s] (sich) vorstellen; einführen **III**
introduction [ˌɪntrə'dʌkʃn] Einführung, Einleitung **III**
to **invade** [ɪn'veɪd] einmarschieren **V 4**, 48
invasion [ɪn'veɪʒn] Invasion, Einfall **V 4**, 44
to **invent** [ɪn'vent] erfinden **V 6**, 63
invention [ɪn'venʃn] Erfindung **V 6**, 62
inventor [ɪn'ventə] Erfinder/in **V 6**, 64
⟨investigation⟩ [ɪnˌvestɪ'geɪʃn] Untersuchung **V 6**, 86
invitation [ˌɪnvɪ'teɪʃn] Einladung **I**
to **invite** [ɪn'vaɪt] einladen **I**
to **involve** [ɪn'vɒlv] ⟨beinhalten⟩ **V 1**, 13; beteiligen **IV**
involvement [ɪn'vɒlvmənt] Engagement, Mitarbeit **IV**
Irish ['aɪrɪʃ] irisch, Irisch **III**
iron ['aɪən] Eisen **V 6**, 63
⟨iron chain⟩ [ˌaɪən 'tʃaɪn] Eisenkette **V 4**, 81
irregular [ɪ'regjʊlə] unregelmäßig **I**
irresponsible [ˌɪrɪ'spɒnsəbl] unverantwortlich **V 5**, 56
is [ɪz] ist **I**
island ['aɪlənd] Insel **II**
it [ɪt] es/er/sie **I**; ihn/sie/es; ihm/ihr **I**
Italian [ɪ'tæljən] italienisch, Italienisch, Italiener/in **I**
its [ɪts] sein, seine/ihr, ihre **I**
it's [ɪts] er, sie, es ist **I**
It's no good ... [ɪts nəʊ 'gʊd] Es bringt nichts, ...; Es hat keinen Sinn, ... **II**
It's up to you. [ɪts‿ˌʌp tə 'ju:] Es liegt an dir., Du entscheidest. **III**
itself [ɪt'self] (sich) selbst **III**

J

jacket ['dʒækɪt] Jacke **II**
January ['dʒænjʊərɪ] Januar **I**
Japanese [ˌdʒæpə'ni:z] japanisch, Japanisch, Japaner/in **III**
jazz [dʒæs] Jazz **III**
jealous ['dʒeləs] eifersüchtig **III**
jeans (*sg + pl*) [dʒi:nz] Jeans **I**
⟨Jersey⟩ ['dʒɜ:zɪ] *Kuhart* **V 1**, 69; Trikot **V 5**, 84
⟨jive-talk⟩ ['dʒaɪv tɔ:k] *umg.*: junger Afroamerikaner **V 5**, 83
job [dʒɒb] Beruf, Arbeit **I**
to **jog** [dʒɒg] joggen **IV**
to **join** [dʒɔɪn] eintreten, sich anschließen **II**
joke [dʒəʊk] Witz **II**
journey ['dʒɜ:nɪ] (lange) Reise **IV**
joyful ['dʒɔɪfʊl] freudig, froh **V 1**, 11
⟨joyriding⟩ ['dʒɔɪraɪdɪŋ] eine Spritztour/Vergnügungsfahrt machen **V TP**, 96
to **judge** [dʒʌdʒ] (be)urteilen, bewerten **V 5**, 52; ⟨urteilen⟩ **V TP**, 96
juice [dʒu:s] Saft **V 5**, 52
July [dʒu:'laɪ] Juli **I**
to **jump** [dʒʌmp] springen **II**
junction ['dʒʌŋkʃn] Straßenkreuzung **III**
June [dʒu:n] Juni **I**
junior ['dʒu:njə] Unterstufen- **II**
just [dʒʌst] eben, gerade, nur **I**
justice ['dʒʌstɪs] Gerechtigkeit **IV**

K

kangaroo [ˌkæŋgə'ru:] Känguru **V 1**, 8
to **keep*** [ki:p] halten, behalten **II**
⟨Keep it up!⟩ ['ki:p‿ɪt ˌʌp] Weiter so!, Dran bleiben! **V TP**, 93
Keep out! ['ki:p‿aʊt] ⟨Zutritt verboten!⟩ **V TP**, 93
⟨to keep away⟩ [ki:p‿ə'weɪ] wegbleiben **V TP**, 92
⟨to keep on doing s.th.⟩ ['ki:p‿ˌɒn dʊɪŋ] etw. weiterhin machen **V 2**, 75
to keep out [ki:p‿'aʊt] draußen halten **V 1**, 7
to keep up [ˌki:p 'ʌp] aufrechterhalten, beibehalten **V 1**, 18
kettle ['ketl] Kessel **II**
key [ki:] Schlüssel **III**
key word [ˌki: 'wɜ:d] Schlüsselwort, wichtigster Begriff **III**
° **keyboard** ['ki:bɔ:d] Keyboard **V 1**, 11
⟨keyring⟩ ['ki:rɪŋ] Schlüsselbund **V TP**, 96
to **kick** [kɪk] treten, mit dem Fuß stoßen **I**
kid [kɪd] Kind **III**
to **kill** [kɪl] töten **IV**
⟨killer instinct⟩ [ˌkɪlər‿'ɪnstɪŋkt] Instinkt zum Töten, Killerinstinkt **V 1**, 68
kilometre (= **km**) ['kɪləʊˌmi:tə] Kilometer **V 1**, 7
kilt [kɪlt] Schottenrock **II**
kind [kaɪnd] Art **III**
kindergarten ['kɪndəˌgɑ:tn] Kindergarten **V 1**, 11
king [kɪŋ] König **III**
kingdom ['kɪŋdəm] Königreich **V 4**, 44
kiss [kɪs] Kuss **IV**
kit [kɪt] Kätzchen **II**
kitchen ['kɪtʃɪn] Küche **I**
kite [kaɪt] Drachen **I**
knee [ni:] Knie **II**
⟨to kneel⟩ [ni:l] knien **V 3**, 77
knife, knives (*pl*) [naɪf] Messer **I**
knight [naɪt] Ritter **III**
to **knit** [nɪt] stricken **IV**
⟨to knock down⟩ [ˌnɒk'daʊn] umfahren **V TP**, 96
to knock over ['nɒk ˌəʊvə] umwerfen, umstoßen **III**
to **know*** [nəʊ] wissen, kennen **I**
knowledge ['nɒlɪdʒ] Kenntnis(se), Wissen **V 2**, 23
good working knowledge ['gʊd ˌwɜ:kɪŋ nɒlɪdʒ] gute Grundkenntnis **V 2**, 24
koala bear [kəʊ'ɑ:lə‿ˌbeə] Koalabär **V 1**, 8
Korean [kə'rɪən] koreanisch, Koreanisch, Koreaner/in **IV**

L

laboratory (= **lab**) [lə'bɒrətərɪ] Labor **V 3**, 41
⟨labour⟩ ['leɪbə] Arbeit **V 6**, 86
⟨Labour (= Labour Exchange)⟩ ['leɪbə] Arbeitsamt **V 2**, 72
lace [leɪs] Spitze (*Gewebeart*) **II**
ladder ['lædə] Leiter **I**
lady ['leɪdɪ] Dame **II**
lake [leɪk] (der) See, Teich **I**
lamb [læm] Lamm **I**
lambing time ['læmɪŋ taɪm] Zeit, in der Lämmer geboren werden **I**
⟨lamp⟩ [læmp] Lampe **V 3**, 76
lance [lɑ:ns] Lanze **III**
land [lænd] Boden, Grundstück, Land **III**
to **land** [lænd] landen; an Land gehen **V 1**, 16
landscape ['lænskeɪp] Landschaft **IV**
language ['læŋgwɪdʒ] Sprache **III**
large [lɑ:dʒ] groß **III**
to **last** [lɑ:st] (noch) reichen; dauern **V 3**, 35; ⟨überleben⟩ **V 3**, 77
last [lɑ:st] letzter/letzte/letztes **I**
last but not least [ˌlɑ:st bʌt nɒt 'li:st] nicht zuletzt **IV**
late [leɪt] spät, zu spät **I**

to work late ['wɜ:k leɪt] länger arbeiten **I**
sooner or **later** ['su:nər‿ɔ: ˌleɪtə] früher oder später **V 3**, 36
to **laugh** [lɑ:f] lachen **I**
to laugh at s.o. ['lɑ:f ət] über jdn. lachen **II**
law ['lɔ:] Gesetz **V 3**, 37
to break the law [ˌbreɪk ðə 'lɔ:] das Gesetz brechen **V 3**, 37
to **lay*** [leɪ] legen **I**
⟨lazy⟩ ['leɪzɪ] faul **V 5**, 82
lb (= **pound**) [paʊnd] *Abkürzung für* pound (*Gewicht*) **I**
to **lead*** [li:d] führen **IV**
leader ['li:də] Führer/in **III**
leaflet ['li:flɪt] Prospekt, Informationsblatt **II**
⟨league⟩ [li:g] Liga **V 5**, 84
⟨Lear jet⟩ ['lɪə ˌdʒet] Learjet *(Privatflugzeug)* **V 2**, 75
to **learn*** [lɜ:n] lernen **I**
at **least** [ət 'li:st] wenigstens, mindestens **II**
to **leave*** [li:v] abfahren **I**; verlassen **II**
to leave on [ˌli:v‿'ɒn] anlassen, laufen lassen **III**
to leave out [li:v‿'aʊt] auslassen, vergessen **V 4**, 46
to leave s.o. alone [li:v ə'ləʊn] jdn. in Ruhe lassen **II**
[to leave s.th. open] [li:v 'əʊpən] etw. offen lassen **II**
left [left] (nach) links **I**
on the left/right [ɒn ðə 'left, ɒn ðə 'raɪt] links/rechts, auf der linken/rechten Seite **I**
leg [leg] Bein **I**
legend ['ledʒənd] Legende **III**
lemonade [lemə'neɪd] Limonade **I**
to **lend*** [lend] leihen, verleihen **I**
⟨length⟩ [leŋθ] Länge **V TP**, 95
less [les] weniger **IV**
lesson [lesn] Unterrichtsstunde **I**
private lesson [ˌpraɪvɪt 'lesn] Nachhilfeunterricht **IV**
°to teach s.o. a lesson [ti:tʃ‿ə 'lesn] jdm. eine Lektion erteilen **V 4**, 44
to **let*** [let] lassen, erlauben **III**
let's [lets] lasst uns **I**
to let s.o. know [let 'nəʊ] jdm. Bescheid geben/sagen; wissen lassen **IV**
to let the dirt fly [let ðə 'dɜ:t flaɪ] Spaß haben **IV**
letter ['letə] Brief **I**; Buchstabe **I**
level ['levl] Niveau, Stufe **III**
liberty ['lɪbətɪ] Freiheit **IV**
library ['laɪbrərɪ] Bibliothek, Bücherei **III**
⟨to lick⟩ [lɪk] lecken **V 1**, 69
lie [laɪ] Lüge **III**
to **lie*** [laɪ] liegen **I**
life [laɪf] Leben **III**
⟨life saving⟩ ['laɪf ˌseɪvɪŋ] Lebensrettung **V 2**, 75
way of life [ˌweɪ‿əv 'laɪf] Lebensstil **IV**
life-sized [ˌlaɪf'saɪzd] lebensgroß **IV**
lifeboat ['laɪfbəʊt] Seenotrettungsboot **III**
lifeboatman/woman ['laɪfbəʊtmæn/wʊmən] Seenotrettungsmann/-frau **III**
⟨lifeless⟩ ['laɪflɪs] leblos **V 3**, 39
lifelike ['laɪflaɪk] lebensecht **III**
lifestyle [laɪfˌstaɪl] Lebensstil **IV**
lift [lɪft] Aufzug, Fahrstuhl **II**
to **lift** [lɪft] (hoch)heben **IV**
to **give** ... **a lift** [lɪft] ... im Auto mitnehmen **I**
light [laɪt] Licht **III**
to **light** [laɪt] anzünden; beleuchten **IV**
light [laɪt] leicht **V 5**, 52
lightning ['laɪtnɪŋ] Blitz **II**
to **like** [laɪk] mögen, gern haben **I**
like [laɪk] (so) wie **I**
What's ... like? [wɒts ... laɪk] Wie ist ...? **I**
⟨limerick⟩ ['lɪmərɪk] Limerick *(Gedichtform)* **V 3**, 43
to **limit** ['lɪmɪt] begrenzen, limitieren **IV**
limo ['lɪməʊ] Stretchlimousine **IV**

line [laɪn] Zeile **II**; Linie **III**; Telefonleitung **V 5**, 55
to get in line (*AE*) [ˌget ɪn 'laɪn] sich anstellen **IV**
to **link** [lɪŋk] verbinden **V 3**, 36
link [lɪŋk] Verbindung **V 3**, 39
lion ['laɪən] Löwe **II**
lipstick ['lɪpstɪk] Lippenstift **III**
list [lɪst] Liste **I**
to **listen** ['lɪsn] zuhören **I**
listening practice ['lɪsnɪŋ ˌpræktɪs] Hörverstehensübung **I**
listener ['lɪsnə] Zuhörer/in **V 5**, 56
little [lɪtl] klein **I**; ⟨wenig⟩ **V 1**, 13
to **live** [lɪv] leben, wohnen **I**
to live on [ˌlɪv‿'ɒn] weiterleben **III**
to live on s.th. [lɪv‿ɒn] von etw. leben **V 2**, 28
live [laɪv] live, direkt **II**
⟨lively⟩ ['laɪvlɪ] lebhaft **V 6**, 86
living-room ['lɪvɪŋrʊm] Wohnzimmer **I**
° **local councillor** [ˌləʊkl 'kaʊnsələ] Stadtrat/Stadträtin **V 3**, 37
local ['ləʊkl] örtlich, hiesig, lokal- **V 1**, 13
⟨lock⟩ [lɒk] Schloss **V TP**, 96
to **lock** [lɒk] abschließen, verschließen **III**
locked [lɒkt] abgeschlossen **I**
locker ['lɒkə] Schließfach **IV**
⟨locker-room⟩ ['lɒkə ru:m] Umkleidekabine **V 5**, 85
locomotive ['ləʊkəˌməʊtɪv] Lokomotive **V 6**, 63
lonely ['ləʊnlɪ] einsam **V 1**, 8
long [lɒŋ] lang **I**
longhouse ['lɒŋhaʊs] *langes Holzhaus der Indianer des amer. Nordwestens* **IV**
look [lʊk] Blick **IV**
to **look** [lʊk] aussehen **I**; sehen, anschauen **I**
to look after s.o. [ˌlʊk‿'ɑ:ftə 'sʌmwʌn] sich um jdn. kümmern **II**
to look at ['lʊk‿ət] anschauen **I**
to look for ['lʊk ˌfɔ:] etw. suchen **II**
to look forward to s.th. [lʊk 'fɔ:wəd] sich auf etw. freuen **IV**
to look like ['lʊk laɪk] aussehen **V 6**, 62
to look nice [lʊk 'naɪs] nett, schön aussehen **II**
to look s.o. up [lʊk‿'ʌp] bei jdm. vorbeischauen **IV**
to look up [lʊk‿ʌp] hochschauen, aufsehen **IV**; nachschlagen **III**
Lord ['lɔ:d] Herr; Meister **V 4**, 46
lorry ['lɒrɪ] Lastwagen **II**
to **lose*** [lu:z] verlieren **III**
to lose s.o. [lu:z] jdn. abhängen **IV**
lots of [lɒts‿əv] eine Menge, viel(e) **II**
a lot of [ə'lɒt‿əv] viel/viele, eine Menge **I**
lottery ['lɒtərɪ] Lotterie **V 5**, 59
loud [laʊd] laut **II**
love [lʌv] alles Liebe (*als Briefschluss*) **I**; ⟨Schatz⟩ **V 1**, 10
to **love** [lʌv] lieben **II**
lovely ['lʌvlɪ] schön, herrlich **II**
low [ləʊ] niedrig **V 5**, 56
low rate [ləʊ 'reɪt] günstig **IV**
lower ['ləʊə] der/die/das untere **II**
luck [lʌk] Glück **IV**
lucky ['lʌkɪ] glücklich, Glücks- **I**
to be lucky [bɪ 'lʌkɪ] Glück haben **I**
lunch [lʌntʃ] Mittagessen **I**
lunch box ['lʌntʃ bɒks] *Dose für belegte Brote zum Mittagessen* **I**
lunchbreak ['lʌntʃˌbreɪk] Mittagspause **V 2**, 30
° to **lurch** [lɜ:tʃ] torkeln; sich ruckartig bewegen **V 5**, 61

M

machine [mə'ʃi:n] Maschine, Gerät **III**
mad [mæd] verrückt; böse, verärgert **IV**
Madam ['mædəm] *Anrede für eine Dame* **IV**
magazine [ˌmægə'zi:n] Zeitschrift **I**
mail [meɪl] Post **IV**
main [meɪn] Haupt- **III**
mainly ['meɪnlɪ] hauptsächlich **III**
to **make*** [meɪk] machen **I**
made in Wales [ˌmeɪd‿ɪn 'weɪlz] hergestellt in Wales **III**
to make friends with s.o. [ˌmeɪk 'frendz‿wɪð] sich mit jdm. anfreunden **III**
to make it ['meɪk‿ɪt] Erfolg haben; es rechtzeitig schaffen **IV**
[to make money] [meɪk 'mʌnɪ] Geld verdienen **II**
to make notes [meɪk 'nəʊts] sich Notizen machen **II**
to make sure [meɪk 'ʃɔ:] sicher gehen, sicher stellen, sich vergewissern **V 5**, 51
⟨mall (*AE*)⟩ [mɔ:l] Einkaufszentrum **V 5**, 84
man, men (*pl*) [mæn] Mann, Männer **I**
to **manage to do s.th.** ['mænɪdʒ] schaffen etw. zu tun **IV**
management ['mænɪdʒmənt] Führung, Leitung, Management **IV**
manager ['mænɪdʒə] Geschäftsführer/in, Manager/in **IV**
How **many?** [haʊ 'menɪ] Wie viele? **I**
map [mæp] Landkarte **I**
marathon [ˌmærəθn] Marathon **III**
March [mɑ:tʃ] März **I**
to **march** [mɑ:tʃ] marschieren **V 4**, 44
marital status [ˌmærɪtl 'steɪtəs] Familienstand **V 2**, 24
mark [mɑ:k] Note **III**
marked [mɑ:kt] markiert **III**
market ['mɑ:kɪt] Markt **I**
⟨to market⟩ ['mɑ:kɪt] vermarkten, werben **V 5**, 84
⟨married⟩ ['mærɪd] verheiratet **V 2**, 75
Martian ['mɑ:ʃn] Marsmensch **V 5**, 55
mascot ['mæskət] Maskottchen **I**
match [mætʃ] Spiel **III**
to **match s.th. with s.th.** [mætʃ] das Passende zu etw. finden **IV**
⟨matchstick⟩ ['mætʃstɪk] Streichholz **V 6**, 87
⟨mate⟩ [meɪt] *umg.:* Kumpel, Freund/in, Kollege/Kollegin **V 1**, 69
material [mə'tɪərɪəl] Material, Stoff **IV**
Math (*AE*) [mæθ] Mathe, Mathematikunterricht **IV**
Maths [mæθs] Mathe **II**
⟨to matter⟩ ['mætə] wichtig sein **V 5**, 85
it doesn't **matter** [ɪt ˌdʌznt 'mætə] es macht nichts, es ist egal **II**
May [meɪ] Mai **I**
may [meɪ] dürfen **III**; vielleicht tun **III**
maybe ['meɪbi:] vielleicht **I**
⟨MC (= Master of Ceremonies)⟩ [em 'si: = 'mɑ:stər‿əv 'serɪmənɪz] Rap-Interpret/in **V 5**, 83
me [mi:] mir/mich **I**
meal [mi:l] Mahlzeit, Essen **II**
to **mean*** [mi:n] bedeuten, meinen **II**; wollen **IV**
meaning ['mi:nɪŋ] Bedeutung **III**
What's it **meant to do?** [ment tʊ] Was soll er/sie/es eigentlich tun/machen? **IV**
meat [mi:t] Fleisch **II**
mechanic [mɪ'kænɪk] Mechaniker/in **I**
⟨to mechanise⟩ ['mekənaɪz] mechanisieren **V 3**, 76
medal ['medəl] Orden, Medaille **III**
⟨medical⟩ ['medɪkl] ärztliche Untersuchung **V 1**, 13
medicine ['medsɪn] Medizin **II**
to **meet*** [mi:t] (sich) treffen **I**; sich kennen lernen **IV**
meeting [mi:tɪŋ] Treffen, Besprechung **II**; Begegnung **III**
member ['membə] Mitglied, Angehörige/r **III**
memory ['meməri] Gedächtnis **II**
to **mend** [mend] reparieren, flicken **III**
mess [mes] Unordnung **I**
to **mess s.th. up** [mes‿'ʌp] etw. durcheinander bringen **V 2**, 22
message ['mesɪdʒ] Botschaft, Nachricht **III**
to give s.o. a message [gɪv ə 'mesɪdʒ] jdm. etw. ausrichten **III**
⟨messed up⟩ [mest‿'ʌp] durcheinander (gebracht) **V 3**, 32
metal ['metl] Metall **V 5**, 55
meter (*AE*) ['mi:tə] Meter **IV**
⟨method⟩ ['meθəd] Methode **V 1**, 71
metre ['mi:tə] Meter **III**
Mexican ['meksɪkn] mexikanisch, Mexikaner/in **IV**
micro ['maɪkrəʊ] Mikro- **IV**
microwave (oven) ['maɪkrəweɪv] Mikrowelle(nherd) **IV**
⟨mid-day⟩ ['mɪddeɪ] Mittag **V 2**, 72
middle ['mɪdl] Mitte **IV**
midnight ['mɪdnaɪt] Mitternacht **IV**
might [maɪt] könnte **III**
⟨mighty⟩ ['maɪtɪ] stark, mächtig **V 3**, 32
mile [maɪl] Meile **III**
military service ['mɪlɪtərɪ ˌsɜ:vɪs] Wehrdienst **V 2**, 22
milk [mɪlk] Milch **I**
⟨milker⟩ ['mɪlkə] *umg.:* Milchkuh **V 1**, 69
milkman ['mɪlkmən] Milchmann **II**
milkshake ['mɪlkʃeɪk] Milchmixgetränk **I**
mill [mɪl] Mühle; Spinnerei **V 6**, 63
million ['mɪljən] Million **III**
millionaire [ˌmɪljə'neə] Millionär/in **IV**
mince [mɪns] Hackfleisch **II**
mind map ['maɪnd ˌmæp] Wörternetz **IV**
to **mind** [maɪnd] jdm. etw. ausmachen **II**
Do you mind if …? [də‿ju: maɪnd‿ɪf] Macht es dir/Ihnen etwas aus, wenn …? **III**
Never mind. ['nevə ˌmaɪnd] Mach dir nichts daraus., Macht euch nichts daraus. **I**
mine [maɪn] Mine, Bergwerk **III**
to **mine** [maɪn] fördern, abbauen **V 3**, 35
⟨miner⟩ ['maɪnə] Bergarbeiter/in **V 3**, 76
minigolf ['mɪnɪgɒlf] Minigolf **V 5**, 58
mining ['maɪnɪŋ] Bergbau **V 6**, 63
minute ['mɪnɪt] Minute **I**
In a minute. [ɪn‿ə 'mɪnɪt] Augenblick noch!, Warte/t mal einen Moment. **I**
mirror ['mɪrə] Spiegel **II**
miserable ['mɪzərəbl] elend, unglücklich **V 4**, 46
to **miss** [mɪs] verpassen, vermissen, übersehen **III**
missing ['mɪsɪŋ] fehlend **III**
mistake [mɪ'steɪk] Fehler **III**
⟨mob⟩ [mɒb] Rudel, Meute **V 1**, 68
model ['mɒdl] Modell **III**
modern ['mɒdən] modern **III**
module ['mɒdju:l] Modul **V 1**, 8
mom (*AE*) [mɑ:m] Mutter, Mutti, Mama **IV**
moment ['məʊmənt] Moment, Augenblick **II**
⟨monarch⟩ ['mɒnək] Monarch/in **V 1**, 70
⟨monarchy⟩ ['mɒnəkɪ] Monarchie **V 1**, 70
Monday ['mʌndeɪ] Montag **I**
money ['mʌnɪ] Geld **I**
monk [mʌŋk] Mönch **V 4**, 46
monkey ['mʌŋkɪ] Affe **II**
monster ['mɒnstə] Ungeheuer, Monster **II**
month [mʌnθ] Monat **I**
mood [mu:d] Stimmung **III**
moon [mu:n] Mond **V 3**, 32
more [mɔ:] mehr, weitere **I**
more interesting [mɔ: 'ɪntrəstɪŋ] interessanter **II**
more … than ever [ˌmɔ: ðən‿'evə] mehr …/…-er denn je **III**

morning ['mɔ:nɪŋ] Morgen **I**
Good morning. [gʊd 'mɔ:nɪŋ] Guten Morgen. **I**
in the morning [ɪn ðə 'mɔ:nɪŋ] morgens, am Vormittag **I**
most [məʊst] am meisten **II**
most exciting [məʊst ɪk'saɪtɪŋ] am aufregendsten **II**
motel [məʊ'tel] Motel **IV**
mother ['mʌðə] Mutter **I**
mother tongue ['mʌðə ˌtʌŋ] Muttersprache **V 1**, 12
motorbike ['məʊtəbaɪk] Motorrad **III**
motorhome ['məʊtəhəʊm] Wohnmobil **IV**
motorway ['məʊtəweɪ] Autobahn **III**
mountain ['maʊntɪn] Berg **II**
mountain biking ['maʊntɪn ˌbaɪkɪŋ] Mountainbike fahren **III**
mountain rescue ['maʊntɪn 'reskju:] Bergwacht **II**
mouse, mice (*pl*) [maʊs] Maus, Mäuse **II**
mouth [maʊθ] Mund **I**
⟨move⟩ [mu:v] Bewegung **V 1**, 68; Umzug **V 1**, 11
to **move** [mu:v] (sich) bewegen **III**; umziehen **III**
to move out [ˌmu:v‿'aʊt] ausziehen **V 2**, 27
⟨to move round in circles⟩ [ˌraʊnd‿ɪn 'sɜ:klz] sich im Kreise bewegen/drehen **V 2**, 73
⟨movement⟩ ['mu:vmənt] Bewegung **V 1**, 68; Bewegung; Trend **V 1**, 70
movie (*AE*) ['mu:vɪ] Film **IV**
moving part [mu:vɪŋ 'pɑ:t] beweglicher Teil **V 6**, 66
MP (= **Member of Parliament**) [ˌem 'pi: = ˌmembər‿ɒv 'pɑ:ləmənt] Abgeordnete/r *(im Parlament)* **V 3**, 37
Mr ['mɪstə] Herr *(Anrede für Männer)* **I**
Mrs ['mɪsɪz] Frau *(Anrede für verheiratete Frauen)* **I**
Ms [məz] Frau *(Anrede für Frauen, ob verheiratet oder nicht)* **V 1**, 10
Mt. (= **Mount**) [ˌmaʊnt] Berg (*bei Namen*) **IV**
mud ball ['mʌd bɔ:l] Schlammball **IV**
mugger ['mʌgə] Straßenräuber/in **IV**
multi- ['mʌltɪ] multi- **IV**
multi-cultural [ˌmʌltɪ‿'kʌltʃərəl] multikulturell **IV**
multi-ethnic [ˌmʌltɪ‿'eθnɪk] multiethnisch, Vielvölker- **IV**
⟨multimedia⟩ [ˌmʌltɪ'mi:djə] Multimedia **V TP**, 93
Mum [mʌm] Mama, Mutti **I**
mummy ['mʌmɪ] Mumie **III**
museum [mju:'zɪəm] Museum **II**
music ['mjʊzɪk] Musik **I**
pop music ['pɒp 'mju:zɪk] Popmusik **I**
musical ['mju:zɪkəl] Musical **IV**
Muslim ['mʊslɪm] islamisch, Moslem/Moslime **III**
must [mʌst] müssen **I**
mutton ['mʌtn] Hammelfleisch **V 4**, 47
my [maɪ] mein/meine **I**
myself [maɪ'self] (mich/mir) selbst **III**
mystery ['mɪstrɪ] Geheimnis, Rätsel **IV**

N

nacho ['nʌtʃəʊ] *mexikanische Vorspeise* **IV**
name [neɪm] Name **I**
My name is … ['maɪ neɪm‿ɪz] Ich heiße … **I**
named [neɪmd] namens, mit dem Namen **IV**
⟨narrator⟩ [nə'reɪtə] Erzähler/in **V 1**, 69
nasty ['nɑ:stɪ] scheußlich, übel, gemein **II**
nation ['neɪʃn] Nation **V 3**, 32
national ['næʃənl] national **III**
national park ['næʃənl 'pɑ:k] Nationalpark **IV**
nationality [ˌnæʃə'nælətɪ] Nationalität, Staatsangehörigkeit **V 2**, 23
native ['neɪtɪv] einheimisch, Einheimische/r, Eingeborene/r, Ureinwohner/in **V 1**, 16
Native American ['neɪtɪv ə'merɪkən] indianisch, *amer. Ureinwohner/in* **IV**
natural ['nætʃrəl] Natur-, natürlich **V 1**, 16
natural resource [ˌnætʃrəl rɪ'sɔ:s] (natürliche) Rohstoffe, Bodenschätze **V 3**, 33
natural science [ˌnætʃrəl 'saɪəns] Naturwissenschaft **V 3**, 43
⟨natural waterway⟩ ['nætʃrəl ˌwɔ:təweɪ] natürliches Gewässer **V TP**, 92
⟨natural wood⟩ ['nætʃrəl ˌwʊd] Naturholz **V TP**, 94
naturally ['nætʃrəlɪ] natürlich; selbstverständlich **IV**
nature ['neɪtʃə] Natur **IV**
near [nɪə] in der Nähe von **I**
nearly ['nɪəlɪ] fast **III**
necessary ['nesəsərɪ] nötig **V 2**, 21
to **need** [ni:d] brauchen, benötigen **I**
negative ['negətɪv] verneinter Satz; negativ **III**
neighbor (*AE*) ['neɪbə] Nachbar/in **IV**
neighborhood (*AE*) ['neɪbəhʊd] Nachbarschaft, Wohnviertel **IV**
neighborhood watch (*AE*) [ˌneɪbəhʊd 'wɒtʃ] *Nachbarschaftshilfe zum Schutz vor Kriminalität* **IV**
neighbour ['neɪbə] Nachbar/in **I**
neither ['naɪðə] auch nicht **IV**
neon sign [ˌnɪɒn 'saɪn] Leuchtreklame **IV**
nervous ['nɜ:vəs] aufgeregt, nervös **II**
nest [nest] Nest **V 1**, 16
⟨neutral⟩ ['nju:trəl] neutral **V TP**, 93
° **never-never land** [nevə‿'nevə ˌlænd] *austr. Ausdruck für weit abgelegene Gegend* **V 1**, 8
never ['nevə] nie **I**
Never mind. ['nevə ˌmaɪnd] Mach dir nichts daraus., Macht euch nichts daraus. **I**
new [nju:] neu **I**
news (*sg* + *pl*) [nju:z] Nachricht(en) **II**
newsagent's ['nju:z ˌeɪdʒənts] Laden für Zeitungen, Zeitschriften, Tabakwaren, Süßigkeiten, etc. **II**
newspaper ['nju:sˌpeɪpə] Zeitung **III**
next [nekst] nächste/r/s **I**
next door [ˌnekst 'dɔ:] nebenan **V 1**, 10
next to [nekst tʊ] neben **II**
nice [naɪs] nett, schön **I**
(the) **nicest** [ðə 'naɪsɪst] am schönsten, der/die/das schönste **II**
night [naɪt] Nacht **I**
nightmare ['naɪtmeə] Alptraum **III**
no [nəʊ] nein **I**
no longer [nəʊ 'lɒŋgə] nicht mehr **V 3**, 34
° **nobleman** ['nəʊblmən] Adliger, Edelmann **V 4**, 44
nobody ['nəʊbədɪ] niemand, keiner **I**
to **nod** [nɒd] nicken **IV**
noise [nɔɪz] Lärm, Krach, Geräusch **I**
noisy ['nɔɪzɪ] laut, lärmend **II**
non-swimmers ['nɒnˌswɪmməz] Nichtschwimmer **II**
[non-uniform day] [nɒn 'ju:nɪfɔ:m deɪ] *Tag, an dem keine Uniform getragen werden muss* **II**
⟨none⟩ [nʌn] nichts **V 2**, 75
nonsense ['nɒnsəns] Quatsch, Unsinn **III**
⟨noon⟩ [nu:n] Mittag **V 1**, 68
normal ['nɔ:ml] normal **III**
north [nɔ:θ] nördlich, Nord-, Norden **II**
northern ['nɔ:ðn] nördlich **V 3**, 35
nose [nəʊz] Nase **II**
nosy ['nəʊzɪ] neugierig **I**
not [nɒt] nicht **I**
not … any more [nɒt 'enɪˌmɔ:] nicht mehr **IV**
not … either ['aɪðə] auch nicht **IV**
not … yet [nɒt … jet] noch nicht **I**
note [nəʊt] Zettel **III**
notebook (*AE*) ['nəʊtbʊk] (Übungs-)Heft **IV**

to make **notes** [meɪk 'nəʊts] sich Notizen machen **II**
to take notes [teɪk 'nəʊts] Notizen machen **II**
nothing ['nʌθɪŋ] nichts **I**
°nothing but ... ['nʌθɪŋ bʌt] nichts als ... **V 4**, 46
notice ['nəʊtɪs] Aushang, Schild **II**
to **notice** ['nəʊtɪs] bemerken **III**
noun [naʊn] Substantiv **II**
November [nəʊ'vembə] November **I**
now [naʊ] jetzt, nun **I**
nuclear ['nju:klɪə] Kern-, Atom- **V 3**, 35
number ['nʌmbə] Nummer, Zahl **I**
nurse [nɜ:s] Krankenschwester/Krankenpfleger **I**
nursery school ['nɜ:sərɪ ˌsku:l] Kindergarten **I**
nursing course ['nɜ:sɪŋ ˌkɔ:s] Krankenschwester/-pflegerausbildung **V 3**, 36

O

o [əʊ] null (*bei Telefonnummern*) **I**
oak [əʊk] Eiche **II**
object ['ɒbdʒɪkt] Gegenstand, Objekt **V 2**, 22
° **observatory** [əb'zɜ:vətrɪ] Observatorium, Sternwarte **V 5**, 55
⟨obvious⟩ ['ɒbvɪəs] offensichtlich **V 6**, 87
⟨occasional(ly)⟩ [ə'keɪʒənəlɪ] gelegentlich, hin und wieder **V 5**, 82
⟨to occupy⟩ ['ɒkjʊpaɪ] besetzen **V 3**, 78
ocean ['əʊʃən] Ozean **V 1**, 8
at ... o'clock [ət ... ə'klɒk] um ... Uhr **I**
October [ɒk'təʊbə] Oktober **I**
of [ɒv , əv] von **I**
of course [əv‿'kɔ:s] natürlich, selbstverständlich **I**
Off you go! [ˌɒf ju: 'gəʊ] Fort mit dir/euch! **II**
to **offer** ['ɒfə] (an)bieten **IV**
office ['ɒfɪs] Büro, Amt **I**
booking office ['bʊkɪŋˌɒfɪs] Vorverkaufsstelle; Kartenschalter **V 5**, 54
police **officer** [pə'li:s‿ˌɒfɪsə] Polizist/in **I**
official [ə'fɪʃl] offiziell **V 1**, 12
often ['ɒfn] oft **I**
oh [əʊ] oh **I**
Oh dear! [əʊ 'dɪə] Oh je! **I**
oil [ɔɪl] Öl **III**
⟨oil platform⟩ [ɔɪl 'plætfɔ:m] Ölbohrinsel **V 3**, 78
oil rig ['ɔɪl rɪg] Ölplattform, Ölbohrinsel **III**
⟨oil spill⟩ ['ɔɪl spɪl] Ölteppich, Ölschlick **V 3**, 32
OK [əʊ'keɪ] OK, in Ordnung **I**
old [əʊld] alt **I**
on-the-job training [ˌɒn ðə‿dʒɒb 'treɪnɪŋ] Schulung bei der Arbeit **V 2**, 23
on [ɒn] auf **I**
on (the radio) [ɒn] im (Rundfunk) **I**
°on board [ɒn 'bɔ:d] an Bord **V 1**, 13
on business [ɒn 'bɪznɪs] geschäftlich **IV**
⟨on edge⟩ ['ɒn‿edʒ] nervös, unruhig **V TP**, 93
on foot [ɒn 'fʊt] zu Fuß **IV**
⟨on one's own⟩ [ˌɒn wʌnz 'əʊn] allein **V 2**, 22
⟨on shore⟩ [ˌɒn 'ʃɔ:] an Land **V 2**, 75
⟨on special offer⟩ ['speʃl ˌɒfə] Sonderangebot, im Angebot **V 2**, 72
on the coast [ˌɒn ðə 'kəʊst] an der Küste **III**
on the left/right [ɒn ðə 'left, ɒn ðə 'raɪt] links/rechts, auf der linken/rechten Seite **I**
on the other hand [ɒn ðɪ 'ʌðə ˌhænd] auf der anderen Seite **V 1**, 9
on the phone [ɒn ðə 'fəʊn] am Telefon **IV**
on the seventh of [ɒn ðə 'sevnθ‿əv] am siebten **I**
on the telephone [ɒn ðə 'telɪfəʊn] am Telefon **I**
⟨on the very spot⟩ [spɒt] genau an der Stelle **V TP**, 95

to be on [bɪ‿'ɒn] eingeschaltet sein **I**
once [wʌns] (früher) einmal **V 1**, 12
at once [ˌət 'wʌns] sofort **II**
once again [wʌns ə'gen] noch einmal **V 3**, 32
one [wʌn] ein/eine/eins **I**
the **one** [ðə wʌn] derjenige/diejenige/dasjenige **III**
the **only** [ðɪ‿'əʊnlɪ] der/die/das einzige **V 1**, 10
only ['əʊnlɪ] nur, erst **I**
Oops! [u:ps] Hoppla! **I**
to **open** ['əʊpən] öffnen, aufmachen **I**
open ['əʊpən] offen, geöffnet **I**
⟨open water⟩ ['əʊpən wɔ:tə] offenes Meer **V 1**, 13
open-air museum [ˌəʊpn‿'eə mju:'zɪəm] Freilichtmuseum **IV**
operation [ˌɒpə'reɪʃn] Operation **II**; Arbeitsgang; Bedienung **IV**
opinion [ə'pɪnjən] Meinung **III**
in my opinion [ɪn 'maɪ əˌpɪnjən] meiner Meinung (nach) **III**
opponent [ə'pəʊnənt] Gegner/in **III**
opportunity [ˌɒpə'tju:nətɪ] Gelegenheit, Chance **V 2**, 23
opposite ['ɒpəzɪt] Gegenteil **I**
opposite ['ɒpəzɪt] gegenüber **II**
⟨opposition⟩ [ˌɒpə'zɪʃn] Opposition **V 3**, 78
or [ɔ:] oder **I**
⟨orange-pip⟩ ['ɒrɪndʒ pɪp] Apfelsinenkern **V 2**, 73
orange ['ɒrɪndʒ] Orange **II**
orchestra ['ɔ:kɪstrə] Orchester **III**
order ['ɔ:də] ⟨Befehl⟩ **V 4**, 80; Reihenfolge; Ordnung **I**
word order ['wɜ:d ˌɔ:də] Satzstellung **I**
to **order** ['ɔ:də] befehlen; bestellen **V 4**, 46
to order s.o. to do s.th ['ɔ:də] jdm. befehlen etw. zu tun **V 2**, 27
organization [ˌɔ:gənaɪ'zeɪʃn] Organisation **IV**
to **organize** ['ɔ:gənaɪz] organisieren **III**
⟨to orientate⟩ ['ɔ:rɪenteɪt] sich orientieren **V 1**, 70
origin ['ɒrɪdʒɪn] Ursprung, Herkunft **IV**
⟨originally⟩ [ə'rɪdʒənəlɪ] ursprünglich **V 5**, 83
other ['ʌðə] andere, weitere **I**
on the other hand [ɒn ðɪ 'ʌðə ˌhænd] auf der anderen Seite **V 1**, 9
Ouch! [aʊtʃ] Aua! **II**
ought to ['ɔ:t‿tʊ] sollte, solltest, solltet, sollten **IV**
our ['aʊə] unser/unsere **I**
Our lightest ever running shoe. ['rʌnɪŋ ˌʃu:] Der leichteste Laufschuh, den wir jemals gemacht haben. **V 5**, 52
ourselves [ˌaʊə'selvz] (uns) selbst **III**
out [aʊt] draußen, heraus **I**
out of ['aʊt‿əv] aus **II**
out of action [aʊt‿əv 'ækʃn] außer Betrieb **IV**
out of work [ˌaʊt‿əv 'wɜ:k] arbeitslos **III**
to find out [faɪnd‿'aʊt] herausfinden **I**
outback ['aʊtbæk] *austr. Hinterland* **V 1**, 7
outdoor ['aʊtdɔ:] draußen, im Freien, Freiluft- **IV**
⟨outer⟩ ['aʊtə] äußere/r/s **V 1**, 13
outlaw ['aʊtlɔ:] Gesetzlose/r, Vogelfreie/r, Bandit/in **II**
outside [ˌaʊt'saɪd] draußen **I**
⟨oven⟩ ['ʌvn] (Back)ofen **V 1**, 71
over ['əʊvə] über **I**
over there [əʊvə 'ðeə] da drüben, dort **I**
to be over at ... [bi:‿'əʊvər‿æt] bei ... sein **IV**
"Over 60s" [ˌəʊvə 'sɪkstɪz] Über Sechzigjährige **II**
overworked [ˌəʊvə'wɜ:kt] überarbeitet **V 4**, 46
⟨to own⟩ [əʊn] besitzen **V 5**, 82
own [əʊn] eigen **II**
owner ['əʊnə] Besitzer/in **V 3**, 41
ox, oxen (*pl*) [ɒks, ɒksn] Ochse **V 4**, 46

P

P.A. system (= **public address system**) [piː eɪ ˈsɪstəm = ˈpʌblɪk əˈdres sɪstəm] Lautsprecheranlage **IV**
⟨pack⟩ [pæk] Rudel, Meute **V 1**, 69
package [ˈpækɪdʒ] Paket **IV**
packed lunch [ˌpækt ˈlʌntʃ] Lunchpaket **III**
packet [ˈpækɪt] Päckchen **I**
⟨to paddle⟩ [ˈpædl] waten, plantschen **V TP**, 92
⟨paddock⟩ [ˈpædək] Koppel, Weide **V 1**, 68
page [peɪdʒ] Seite **I**
paint [peɪnt] Farbe, Lack **III**
to **paint** [peɪnt] (be)malen, streichen **II**
painting [ˈpeɪntɪŋ] Bild, Gemälde **IV**
pair [peə] Paar **I**
panic [ˈpænɪk] Panik **V 5**, 55
to **panic** [ˈpænɪk] in Panik geraten **V 5**, 56
pants (*AE*) (*sg* + *pl*) [pænts] Hose, Hosen **IV**
paper [ˈpeɪpə] Papier **II**; Zeitung **IV**
test paper (*AE*) [test ˈpeɪpə] Klassenarbeit **IV**
parade [pəˈreɪd] Umzug, Parade **IV**
paragraph [ˈpærəgrɑːf] Absatz, Abschnitt **IV**
parcel [ˈpɑːsl] Paket, Päckchen **V 2**, 23
parcel service [ˈpɑːsl ˌsɜːvɪs] Paketdienst **V 2**, 23
Pardon? [ˈpɑːdn] Wie bitte? **III**
parents (*pl*) [ˈpeərənts] Eltern **I**
park [pɑːk] Park **I**
national park [ˈnæʃənl ˈpɑːk] Nationalpark **IV**
park-and-ride [ˌpɑːk‿ənˈraɪd] „Park-and-Ride"-System **III**
to **park** [pɑːk] parken **III**
parliament [ˈpɑːləmənt] Parlament **V 6**, 64
⟨parrot⟩ [ˈpærət] Papagei **V 1**, 68
part [pɑːt] Teil, Rolle **II**
part-time job [ˌpɑːt taɪm ˈdʒɒb] Teilzeitstelle **IV**
⟨particular⟩ [pəˈtɪkjʊlə] eigen, pingelig **V TP**, 93
⟨particularly⟩ [pəˈtɪkjʊləlɪ] besonders **V 6**, 86
⟨particulars⟩ [pəˈtɪkjʊləz] Näheres, Einzelheiten **V TP**, 93
partner [ˈpɑːtnə] Partner/in **I**
party [ˈpɑːtɪ] Party, Feier **I**
to **pass** [pɑːs] reichen, weitergeben **I**; vorbeigehen; bestehen **IV**
⟨to pass by⟩ [ˈpɑːs baɪ] vorbeigehen **V 2**, 74
passenger [ˈpæsɪndʒə] Passagier/in; Beifahrer/in **IV**
passive [ˈpæsɪv] passiv **V 2**, 26; [Passiv-] **IV**
passport [ˈpɑːspɔːt] Reisepass **IV**
past [pɑːst] Vergangenheit **V 6**, 66
past participle [pɑːst ˈpɑːtɪsɪpl] Partizip Perfekt **II**
[past progressive] [ˈpɑːst prəʊˈgresɪv] Verlaufsform der Vergangenheit **II**
past tense [ˈpɑːst tens] *Vergangenheitsform im Englischen* **II**
⟨past (month)⟩ [pɑːst] vergangen(en Monat) **V 5**, 82
past [pɑːst] nach (*bei Uhrzeiten*) **I**
pastrami [pəˈstrɑːmɪ] *Wurstsorte* **IV**
patchwork quilt [ˌpætʃˌwɜːk ˈkwɪlt] aus bunten Flicken zusammengesetzte Decke **IV**
path [pɑːθ] Pfad, Weg **II**
patient [ˈpeɪʃnt] Patient/in **II**
pattern [ˈpætən] Muster **V 6**, 64
paved [peɪvd] gepflastert **IV**
⟨Pavlova⟩ [ˈpævləvə] Pawlowa **V 1**, 71
pay [peɪ] Bezahlung **V 2**, 21
to **pay*** [peɪ] (be)zahlen **III**; [zahlen, bezahlen] **II**
⟨to pay one's respects to s.o.⟩ [ˈpeɪ rɪˈspekts] jdm. seine Aufwartung machen **V 3**, 79
PE (= **Physical Education**) [ˌpiː ˈiː = ˈfɪzɪkl ˌedjuːˈkeɪʃn] Sportunterricht **II**
peaceful [ˈpiːsfʊl] friedlich **IV**
⟨peacefulness⟩ [ˈpiːsfʊlnɪs] Friedlichkeit, Ruhe **V 1**, 68
° **peasant** [ˈpeznt] Kleinbauer/-bäuerin **V 4**, 46
⟨to peck⟩ [pek] picken **V 3**, 79
to **peel** [piːl] schälen **II**
⟨pellet⟩ [ˈpelɪt] Kügelchen **V 3**, 79
pen [pen] Füller **I**
pence (= **p**) (*pl*) [pens] Pfennige (*britisches Geld*) **I**
pencil [ˈpensl] Bleistift **I**
pencil case [ˈpensl keɪs] Federmäppchen **I**
penfriend [ˈpenfrend] Brieffreund/in **III**
people (*pl*) [ˈpiːpl] Leute **I**
pepper [ˈpepə] Pfeffer **III**
per [pɜː] pro **III**
percent [pəˈsent] Prozent **IV**
perfect [ˈpɜːfɪkt] vollkommen **IV**
⟨perfectionist⟩ [pəˈfekʃnɪst] Perfektionist/in **V 2**, 74
perhaps [pəˈhæps] vielleicht **II**
period (*AE*) [ˈpɪərɪəd] Unterrichtsstunde **IV**; Zeit **V 2**, 22
° **perk** [pɜːk] Vergünstigung **V 2**, 23
permanent [ˈpɜːmənənt] ständig, dauerhaft **V 1**, 12
person [ˈpɜːsn] Person **I**
personal stereo [ˌpɜːsnl ˈsterɪəʊ] Walkman, Discman **V 5**, 50
personal [ˈpɜːsnl] persönlich **V 2**, 23
°personal attention [ˌpɜːsnl əˈtenʃn] persönliche Betreuung **V 1**, 13
personal interview [ˌpɜːsnl ˈɪntəvjuː] persönliches Vorstellungsgespräch **V 2**, 23
personalized [ˈpɜːsnəlaɪzd] auf eine bestimmte Person bezogen **IV**
° **personnel manager** [ˌpɜːsəˈnel ˈmænɪdʒə] Personalleiter/in **V 2**, 23
pet [pet] Haustier **I**
petrol [ˈpetrəl] Benzin **III**
petrol station [ˈpetrəl ˌsteɪʃn] Tankstelle **III**
phone booth (*AE*) [ˈfəʊn ˌbuːð] Telefonzelle **IV**
to **phone** [fəʊn] anrufen **I**
photo [ˈfəʊtəʊ] Foto **I**
to take a photo of [teɪk‿əˈfəʊtəʊ‿əv] ein Foto machen von **I**
photocopy [ˈfəʊtəʊˌkɒpɪ] Fotokopie **V 1**, 13
phrase [freɪz] Ausdruck, Satzteil **II**
piano [pɪˈænəʊ] Klavier **II**
⟨pick⟩ [pɪk] Spitzhacke, Pickel **V 3**, 76
to **pick** (out) [ˌpɪk‿ˈaʊt] (her)aussuchen, herausholen; herauspicken **V 1**, 13
to **pick up** [ˈpɪk‿ʌp] aufheben, aufnehmen, abholen **II**; kaufen, holen **IV**
picnic [ˈpɪknɪk] Picknick **III**
picture [ˈpɪktʃə] Bild **I**
pie [paɪ] Kuchen; Pastete **IV**
piece [piːs] Stück **II**
pig [pɪg] Schwein **I**
pigeon [ˈpɪdʒɪn] Taube **III**
⟨to pile up⟩ [ˈpaɪl‿ʌp] aufhäufen **V 3**, 79
pillow [ˈpɪləʊ] Kopfkissen **II**
pink [pɪŋk] rosa, pink **II**
pint [paɪnt] *etwa 0,5l* **I**
pipe [paɪp] Pfeife **IV**; ⟨Rohr, Röhre⟩ **V 3**, 77
⟨to pipe⟩ [paɪp] in Rohren leiten, pumpen **V 3**, 78
⟨pit⟩ [pɪt] Zeche **V 6**, 86
pitch [pɪtʃ] Feld (*für Sport*) **III**
⟨pitch-black⟩ [ˌpɪtʃ ˈblæk] pechschwarz **V 2**, 72
pizza [ˈpiːtsə] Pizza **II**
place [pleɪs] ⟨Gegend⟩ **V TP**, 94; Ort, Stelle **II**
to go places [ˌgəʊ ˈpleɪsɪz] herumfahren, herumreisen **IV**
⟨to place⟩ [pleɪs] aufstellen, platzieren **V 3**, 79; bringen **V TP**, 92
° **plain** [pleɪn] Ebene, Flachland **V 3**, 32
plan [plæn] Plan **I**
to **plan** [plæn] planen **IV**

plane [pleɪn] Flugzeug **I**
planet ['plænɪt] Planet **V 3**, 32
⟨planner⟩ ['plænə] Planer/in **V 3**, 40
plant [plɑ:nt] Pflanze **IV**
[plantation] [plæn'teɪʃn] Plantage **V 3**, 41
⟨planting of the Union Jack⟩ ['plɑ:ntɪŋ əv‿ðə 'ju:njən 'dʒæk] Aufstellen der britischen Fahne **V 1**, 71
plastic ['plæstɪk] Plastik, Kunststoff **III**
plate [pleɪt] Teller **II**
play [pleɪ] Theaterstück **II**
to **play** [pleɪ] spielen **I**
to play tricks on [,pleɪ 'trɪks] jdm. einen Streich spielen **II**
player ['pleɪə] Spieler/in **III**
playground ['pleɪgraʊnd] Schulhof, Spielplatz **I**
please [pli:z] bitte **I**
pleased [pli:zd] erfreut **III**
to **pledge allegiance** [pledʒ ə'li:dʒns] Treue geloben **IV**
⟨plenty⟩ ['plentɪ] viel, reichlich **V 1**, 68
plus [plʌs] und, plus **V 2**, 23
pm [,pi:'em] 12.00–24.00 Uhr **III**
pocket ['pɒkɪt] Tasche *(bei Kleidung)* **I**
pocket money ['pɒkɪt ,mʌnɪ] Taschengeld **I**
poem ['pəʊɪm] Gedicht **III**
point [pɔɪnt] Punkt **III**
point of view [,pɔɪnt‿əv 'vju:] Standpunkt, Sicht **V 5**, 58
to **point s.th. at s.o.** [pɔɪnt] etw. auf jdn. richten **IV**
⟨to poison⟩ [pɔɪzn] vergiften **V 1**, 68
police [pə'li:s] Polizei **I**
police officer [pə'li:s‿ɒfɪsə] Polizist/in **I**
Polish ['pəʊlɪʃ] polnisch, Polnisch **III**
polite [pə'laɪt] höflich **II**
⟨political⟩ [pə'lɪtɪkl] politisch **V 5**, 83
⟨politician⟩ [,pɒlɪ'tɪʃn] Politiker/in **V 1**, 70
politics *(sg + pl)* ['pɒlətɪks] Politik, politische Ansichten **V 5**, 57
to **pollute** [pə'lu:t] verschmutzen **III**
pollution [pə'lu:ʃn] Umweltverschmutzung **V 3**, 33
Pom [pɒm] *austr. umg.:* Engländer/in **V 1**, 7
pond [pɒnd] Teich **I**
pony ['pəʊnɪ] Pony **II**
poor [pɔ:] arm **I**; schlecht **III**
popcorn ['pɒpkɔ:n] Popcorn **II**
pop music ['pɒp 'mju:zɪk] Popmusik **I**
pop star ['pɒp 'stɑ:] Popstar **III**
popular ['pɒpjʊlə] beliebt **I**
population [pɒpjʊ'leɪʃn] Bevölkerung **V 1**, 12
pork [pɔ:k] Schweinefleisch **V 4**, 47
porridge ['pɒrɪdʒ] Haferbrei **II**
position [pə'zɪʃn] Position, Stelle **V 1**, 8
positive ['pɒzətɪv] positiv **V 1**, 11
possible ['pɒsəbl] möglich **III**
post office ['pəʊst ,ɒfɪs] Post, Postamt **I**
postcard ['pəʊstkɑ:d] Postkarte **I**
poster ['pəʊstə] Poster, Plakat **I**
⟨pot⟩ [pɒt] (Koch-)Topf **V 1**, 68; Topf **V 4**, 80; Blumentopf **V 2**, 73
potato, potatoes *(pl)* [pə'teɪtəʊ] Kartoffel, Kartoffeln **I**
⟨potter⟩ ['pɒtə] Töpfer/in **V 4**, 80
pound (= **lb**) [paʊnd] Pfund *(Gewicht)* **I**
pound (= **£**) [paʊnd] Pfund *(britisches Geld)* **I**
power ['paʊə] Kraft; Stärke; Macht; Energie **V 3**, 35
power station ['paʊə ,steɪʃn] Kraftwerk **V 3**, 35
Word power ['wɜ:d ,paʊə] Die Kraft der Wörter **I**
to **power** ['paʊə] antreiben, betreiben **V 3**, 35
powerful ['paʊəfʊl] stark, kraftvoll, kräftig **IV**
practice ['præktɪs] Übung, Training **I**
listening practice ['lɪsnɪŋ ,præktɪs] Hörverstehensübung **I**
sound practice ['saʊnd ,præktɪs] Ausspracheübung **I**

to **practise** ['præktɪs] üben **II**
prairie ['preərɪ] Prärie **IV**
prayer [preə] Gebet **V 4**, 46
⟨to preach⟩ [pri:tʃ] predigen **V 5**, 85
⟨predator⟩ ['predətər] Raubtier **V TP**, 92
to **prefer** [prɪ'fɜ:] lieber haben, vorziehen **III**
prejudice ['predʒʊdɪs] Vorurteil **IV**
to **prepare** [prɪ'peə] (sich) vorbereiten, zubereiten **V 1**, 13
preposition [,prepə'zɪʃn] Präposition **III**
prescription [prɪ'skrɪpʃn] Rezept *(vom Arzt)* **II**
present ['prezənt] Geschenk **I**
to **present** [prɪ'zent] präsentieren, vorstellen **V 1**, 13
⟨to present s.o. to s.o.⟩ [prə'zent] jdn. vorstellen **V TP**, 93
⟨present⟩ ['preznt] anwesend, vorhanden **V TP**, 92
present perfect ['preznt 'pɜ:fɪkt] *englische Vergangenheitsform* **II**
present progressive [,preznt prəʊ'gresɪv] *Verlaufsform* **IV**
present tense ['preznt tens] Präsens **II**
⟨to preserve⟩ [prɪ'zɜ:v] konservieren, schützen, gut erhalten **V 3**, 40
to **press** [pres] drücken **IV**
⟨pressure⟩ ['preʃə] Druck, Stress **V 2**, 74
⟨to pretend⟩ [prɪ'tend] tun als ob, vortäuschen **V 5**, 82
pretty [prɪtɪ] hübsch **II**; ziemlich **V 1**, 8
price [praɪs] Preis **III**
⟨priceless⟩ ['praɪslɪs] unbezahlbar **V 1**, 71
primary school ['praɪmərɪ ,sku:l] Grundschule **III**
principal *(AE)* ['prɪnsəpl] Schuldirektor/in **IV**
prison ['prɪzn] Gefängnis **V 1**, 9
prisoner ['prɪznə] Gefangene/r **II**
private lesson [,praɪvɪt 'lesn] Nachhilfeunterricht **IV**
prize [praɪz] Preis, Gewinn **I**
probability [,prɒbə'bɪlətɪ] Wahrscheinlichkeit **IV**
probably ['prɒbəblɪ] wahrscheinlich **II**
problem ['prɒbləm] Aufgabe **IV**; Problem **I**
to **produce** [prə'dju:s] produzieren **V 3**, 35
producer [prə'dju:sə] Produzent/in **IV**
product ['prɒdʌkt] Produkt **V 5**, 52
⟨professional⟩ [prə'feʃənl] Berufs-, beruflich **V 1**, 70
program *(AE)* ['prəʊgræm] Sendung *(im Radio oder TV)*; Programm **IV**
to **program** ['prəʊgræm] programmieren **IV**
programme ['prəʊgræm] [Programm] **II**; Sendung **III**
progress *(sg + pl)* ['prəʊgres] Fortschritt **III**
project ['prɒdʒekt] Projekt **III**
promenade [,prɒmə'nɑ:d] Promenade **I**
⟨promise⟩ ['prɒmɪs] Versprechung, Versprechen **V 1**, 71
to **promise** ['prɒmɪs] versprechen **III**
prompter ['prɒmptə] Souffleur/Souffleuse *(Stichwortgeber/in beim Theater)* **II**
pronoun ['prəʊnaʊn] Pronomen **III**
to **pronounce** [prə'naʊns] aussprechen **IV**
⟨pronunciation⟩ [prə'nʌnsɪ'eɪʃn] Aussprache **V TP**, 92
⟨proper⟩ ['prɒpə] richtig **V R**, 89
pros and cons [,prəʊz‿ənd 'kɒnz] Vor- und Nachteile **V 1**, 13
⟨prostitute⟩ ['prɒstɪtju:t] Prostituierte/r **V TP**, 97
to **protect** [prə'tekt] schützen, beschützen **IV**
protest ['prəʊtest] Protest **V 3**, 33
protest march ['prəʊtest ,mɑ:tʃ] Protestmarsch, Demonstration **V 3**, 37
to **protest** [prəʊ'test] protestieren **IV**
protester [prə'testə] Protestierende/r, Demonstrant/in **V 3**, 36
proud [praʊd] stolz **II**
to be proud of [bɪ 'praʊd‿əv] stolz sein auf **II**
⟨to provide⟩ [prə'vaɪd] liefern, zur Verfügung stellen **V 5**, 84

PS (= **postscript**) [piː ˈes] PS, Postskriptum **IV**
public [ˌpʌblɪk] öffentlich **III**
⟨public footpath⟩ [ˌpʌblɪk ˈfʊtpɑːθ] öffentlicher Fußweg **V R**, 89
public meeting [ˌpʌblɪk ˈmiːtɪŋ] öffentliche Versammlung **V 3**, 37
to **pull** [pʊl] ziehen **II**
to pull up [pʊl‿ˈʌp] hochziehen **V 3**, 36
pullover [ˈpʊlˌəʊvə] Pullover **I**
pump [pʌmp] Luftpumpe **I**
⟨pup⟩ [pʌp] Welpe, junger Hund **V 1**, 68
pupil [ˈpjuːpl] Schüler/in **I**
puppet [ˈpʌpɪt] Marionette **II**
purse [pɜːs] Geldbeutel, Portmonee **II**
to **push** [pʊʃ] schieben **III**
⟨to push oneself⟩ [ˈpʊʃ wʌnˌself] sich schinden **V 2**, 74
to **put*** [pʊt] setzen, stellen, legen **I**
to put down [pʊt ˈdaʊn] hinlegen, hinstellen; auflegen *(Telefon)* **IV**
to put in [ˈpʊt‿ɪn] einsetzen, hineintun **I**
to put on [ˈpʊt‿ɒn] anziehen, aufsetzen **II**
to put s.th. down [ˈpʊt daʊn] etw. niederschlagen **V 4**, 45
to put up [ˌpʊt‿ˈʌp] aufhängen, montieren **III**
⟨to put up with⟩ [ˌpʊt ˈʌp wɪð] ertragen, sich mit etw. abfinden **V 2**, 75
puzzle [ˈpʌzl] Rätsel **II**
⟨pylon⟩ [ˈpaɪlən] Mast **V 1**, 11

Q

qualifications [ˌkwɒlɪfɪˈkeɪʃnz] Qualifikationen; Abschluss **V 2**, 23
quality [ˈkwɒlətɪ] Qualität **III**
quarter [ˈkwɔːtə] Viertel **I**
queen [kwiːn] Königin **III**
question [ˈkwestʃən] Frage **I**
⟨questionnaire⟩ [ˌkwestʃəˈneə] Fragebogen **V 5**, 82
queue [kjuː] Schlange **III**
quick [kwɪk] schnell **II**
quickly [ˈkwɪklɪ] schnell *(Adverbialform)* **III**
quiet [ˈkwaɪət] still, ruhig **I**
quite [kwaɪt] ganz **II**
quite a [kwaɪt‿ə] ziemlich, ein/e ziemliche/r/s **IV**
quiz [kwɪz] Quiz, Ratespiel **I**

R

rabbit [ˈræbɪt] Kaninchen **II**
race [reɪs] Rennen **III**
to **race** [reɪs] rennen, rasen **IV**
racket [ˈrækɪt] Schläger **III**
radio [ˈreɪdɪəʊ] Radio **I**
radio station [ˈreɪdɪəʊ ˌsteɪʃn] Radiosender **V 5**, 54
raffle [ˈræfl] Verlosung, Tombola **II**
raft [rɑːft] Floß **V 1**, 9
railroad *(AE)* [ˈreɪlrəʊd] Eisenbahn **IV**
railway [ˈreɪlweɪ] Eisenbahn **III**
⟨railway line⟩ [ˈreɪlweɪ ˌlaɪn] Eisenbahnlinie **V 3**, 76
rain [reɪn] Regen **II**
to **rain** [reɪn] regnen **I**
[to rain hard] [reɪn ˈhɑːd] heftig regnen **II**
rainforest [ˈreɪnˌfɒrɪst] Regenwald **V 1**, 18
rainstorm [ˈreɪnstɔːm] heftiger Regenguss, Wolkenbruch **III**
ranch [rɑːntʃ] Ranch, Viehfarm **V 3**, 41
ranger [ˈreɪndʒə] Aufseher/in, Ranger/in **IV**
rap [ræp] Rap *(Musikrichtung)* **III**
[to rap] [ræp] „rappen" **II**

rapid [ˈræpɪd] schnell, rasch **V 6**, 64
rapids *(sg + pl)* [ˈræpɪds] Stromschnellen **IV**
⟨rapper⟩ [ˈræpə] Rapper **V 5**, 83
rare [reə] selten, rar **IV**
⟨raspberry⟩ [ˈrɑːzbrɪ] Himbeere **V 1**, 71
rather than [ˈrɑːðə] eher **IV**
would rather [ˈrɑːðə] lieber **IV**
rating [ˈreɪtɪŋ] Einschaltquote **V 5**, 56
raw [rɔː] roh **IV**
RE (= Religious Education) [ˌɑː r‿iː = rɪˈlɪdʒəs ˌedjuːˈkeɪʃn] Religionsunterricht **II**
to **reach** [riːtʃ] erreichen, greifen (nach) **IV**
to reach for s.th. [ˈriːtʃ fɔː] nach etw. greifen **IV**
⟨to reach out⟩ [ˈriːtʃ‿aʊt] ausstrecken **V TP**, 96
to **react** [rɪˈækt] reagieren **IV**
to **read*** [riːd] lesen **I**
to read out [ˌriːd‿ˈaʊt] vorlesen **III**
reader [ˈriːdə] Leser/in **III**
ready [ˈredɪ] fertig, bereit **I**
to get ready [get ˈredɪ] (sich) vorbereiten **I**
real [rɪəl] echt, wirklich **III**
realistic [ˌrɪəˈlɪstɪk] realistisch **V 5**, 56
really [ˈrɪəlɪ] wirklich **I**
to **rearrange** [ˌriːəˈreɪndʒ] umstellen **V 2**, 22
reason [ˈriːzn] Grund, Ursache **IV**
reasonable [ˈriːznəbl] vernünftig, angemessen **IV**
rebellion [rɪˈbeljən] Rebellion, Aufstand **V 4**, 45
⟨to receive⟩ [rɪˈsiːv] bekommen, erhalten **V 2**, 75
reception [rɪˈsepʃn] Rezeption **IV**
receptionist [rɪˈsepʃənɪst] Empfangschef/-dame **IV**
recipe [ˈresɪpɪ] (Koch-)Rezept **II**
to **reckon** [ˈrekən] glauben, damit rechnen **V 1**, 10
to **recognize** [ˈrekəgnaɪz] erkennen **III**; °anerkennen **V 1**, 13
to **recommend** [ˌrekəˈmend] empfehlen **IV**
to **record** [rɪˈkɔːd] aufnehmen **III**; ⟨messen⟩ **V 5**, 55
recording [rɪˈkɔːdɪŋ] Aufnahme **II**
⟨to recreate⟩ [ˌriːkriːˈeɪt] nachschaffen, wiederschaffen **V TP**, 95
to **recycle** [ˌriːˈsaɪkl] wieder verwerten **V 3**, 39
recycling bin [ˌriːˈsaɪklɪŋ bɪn] Recyclingtonne **IV**
red [red] rot **I**
⟨redcurrant⟩ [ˌredˈkʌrnt] (rote) Johannisbeere **V 1**, 71
reduced in size [rɪˌdjuːst‿ɪn ˈsaɪz] verkleinert **I**
redwood [ˈredwʊd] *Baumart* **IV**
reef [riːf] Riff **V 1**, 8
reference [ˈrefrəns] Empfehlungsschreiben, Referenz **V 2**, 21
region [ˈriːdʒən] Region **IV**
register [ˈredʒɪstə] Klassenbuch **III**
⟨to register⟩ [ˈredʒɪstə] anmelden **V 6**, 87
regular [ˈregjʊlə] regelmäßig **II**
related [rɪˈleɪtɪd] verwandt; zusammenhängend **IV**
relation [rɪˈleɪʃn] Beziehung; Verwandtschaft; Verwandte(r) **V 6**, 62
relative [ˈrelətɪv] Verwandte/r **IV**
relative clause [ˌrelətɪv ˈklɔːz] Relativsatz **III**
⟨to relax⟩ [rɪˈlæks] sich entspannen **V 2**, 74
reliable [rɪˈlaɪəbl] zuverlässig **V 2**, 21
religion [rɪˈlɪdʒən] Religion **IV**
⟨to remain⟩ [rɪˈmeɪn] bleiben **V 1**, 70; übrig bleiben **V 3**, 76
to **remember** [rɪˈmembə] behalten, sich merken, sich erinnern **I**
to **remind s.o. to do s.th.** [rɪˈmaɪnd] jdm. daran erinnern etw. zu tun **V 2**, 27
remote [rɪˈməʊt] entfernt, abgelegen **IV**
renewable [rɪˈnjuːəbl] erneuerbar **V 3**, 35
rent [rent] Miete; Pacht **V 4**, 46
to **rent** *(AE)* [rent] mieten **IV**

to **repair** [rɪ'peə] reparieren **I**
⟨to repay⟩ [rɪ'peɪ] zurückzahlen; belohnen; entschädigen **V 1**, 68
to **repeat** [rɪ'pi:t] wiederholen **III**
to **replace** [rɪ'pleɪs] ersetzen **V 3**, 42
to **reply** [rɪ'plaɪ] antworten **IV**
report [rɪ'pɔ:t] Bericht, Reportage **II**; Zeugnis **III**
to **report** [rɪ'pɔ:t] berichten **IV**
reported speech [rɪ,pɔ:tɪd 'spi:tʃ] indirekte Rede **V 2**, 27
reporter [rɪ'pɔ:tə] Reporter/in, Journalist/in **III**
republic [rɪ'pʌblɪk] Republik **IV**
request [rɪ'kwest] Bitte, Wunsch **I**
to **require** [rɪ'kwaɪə] benötigen, brauchen; erfordern **IV**
rescue ['reskju:] Rettung **III**
rescue service ['reskju: sɜ:vɪs] Rettungsdienst **III**
to **rescue** ['reskju:] retten, bergen **II**
reservation [,rezə'veɪʃn] Reservat **IV**; Reservierung **IV**
reserve [rɪ'zɜ:v] Reserve **V 3**, 35
reservoir ['rezəvwɑ:] Stausee, Reservoir **V 3**, 35
resources [rɪ'sɔ:sɪz] Mittel, Ressourcen **V 3**, 33
to **respond** [rɪ'spɒnd] antworten, reagieren auf **IV**
⟨response⟩ [rɪ'spɒns] Reaktion **V 5**, 85
rest [rest] Rest **IV**
⟨to rest⟩ [rest] (sich) ausruhen **V 1**, 68
restaurant ['restərɒnt] Restaurant **I**
⟨resting place⟩ ['restɪŋ ,pleɪs] Ruheplatz **V 3**, 78
result [rɪ'zʌlt] Ergebnis, Resultat; Folge **IV**
⟨to result in⟩ [rɪ'zʌlt‿ɪn] führen zu **V 3**, 40
° **retailing** [ri:'teɪlɪŋ] Einzelhandel **V 2**, 23
to **retell** [,ri:'tel] nacherzählen **III**
retreat [rɪ'tri:t] Rückzug **V 4**, 45
to **retreat** [rɪ'tri:t] den Rückzug antreten **V 4**, 45
⟨to return⟩ [rɪ'tɜ:n] zurückkehren, -kommen **V 1**, 68
review [rɪ'vju:] Kritik, Besprechung (eines Buches, Filmes, einer CD) **III**
to **revise** [rɪ'vaɪz] wiederholen **III**
revolution [,revə'lu:ʃn] Revolution **V 6**, 62
⟨to rewrite⟩ [,ri:'raɪt] umschreiben **V 3**, 39
rhyme [raɪm] Reim **I**
rice [raɪs] Reis **V 2**, 30
rich [rɪtʃ] reich **IV**
ride [raɪd] Fahrt **II**
to **ride*** [raɪd] reiten, fahren **II**
⟨ridiculous⟩ [rɪ'dɪkjʊləs] lächerlich **V 5**, 85
riding school ['raɪdɪŋ ,sku:l] Reitschule **II**
right [raɪt] (nach) rechts **I**; ⟨Recht⟩ **V 6**, 87
on the left/right [ɒn ðə 'left, ɒn ðə 'raɪt] links/rechts, auf der linken/rechten Seite **I**
right [raɪt] richtig **I**
right away ['raɪt‿ə'weɪ] sofort **I**
ring [rɪŋ] Ring **I**
to **ring*** [rɪŋ] klingeln (lassen) **III**
⟨rise⟩ [raɪz] Gehaltserhöhung **V 2**, 75
⟨to rise⟩ [raɪz] sich erheben **V 1**, 10
to **rise up*** ['raɪz‿ʌp] aufstehen **IV**
rival ['raɪvl] Rivale/Rivalin, Konkurrent/in, Konkurrenz- **V 5**, 56
river [rɪvə] Fluss **IV**
river-rafting ['rɪvə‿rɑ:ftɪŋ] Schlauchboot fahren (*auf einem Fluss*) **IV**
road (= **Rd.**) [rəʊd] Straße **I**
roadworks ['rəʊdwɜ:ks] Baustelle **III**
⟨to roam⟩ [rəʊm] herumstreunen, herumwandern **V 1**, 68
roar [rɔ:] Gebrüll; Donner **V 1**, 15
to **roar** [rɔ:] brüllen; donnern **V 1**, 11
roast beef ['rəʊst ,bi:f] Rinderbraten **II**
rock [rɒk] Fels **I**
⟨role model⟩ [rəʊl 'mɒdl] Vorbild **V 5**, 85
role play ['rəʊl pleɪ] Rollenspiel **I**
to **roll away** [,rəʊl ə'weɪ] wegrollen **V 3**, 32
⟨Roll on twelve.⟩ ['rəʊl‿ɒn ,twelv] Höchste Zeit, dass es zwölf wird. **V 2**, 72
⟨to roll one's eyes⟩ [rəʊl wʌnz 'aɪz] mit den Augen rollen **V 3**, 76
⟨to roll over⟩ [,rəʊl 'əʊvə] sich umdrehen, auf den Rücken rollen **V 2**, 73
Roman ['rəʊmən] Römer/in, römisch **III**
⟨roof⟩ [ru:f] Dach **V TP**, 94
room [ru:m] Platz **I**; Raum, Zimmer **I**
⟨root⟩ [ru:t] Wurzel **V 2**, 75
rope [rəʊp] Seil **III**
rope ladder [rəʊp 'lædə] Strickleiter **V 3**, 36
⟨rosemary⟩ ['rəʊzmərɪ] Rosmarin **V 2**, 73
rough [rʌf] rau, aufgewühlt **III**; grob **IV**
round [raʊnd] rund **III**
round [raʊnd] in … herum **III**; um … herum **I**
roundabout ['raʊndəbaʊt] Karussell **II**; Kreisverkehr **III**
° **roundup** ['raʊndʌp] Zusammenschau, -fassung **V 5**, 50
route [ru:t] Weg, Route **IV**
⟨row upon row⟩ ['rəʊ ʌ,pɒn 'rəʊ] reihenweise **V 6**, 87
to **row** [rəʊ] rudern **II**
royal ['rɔɪəl] königlich **V 4**, 46
rubbish ['rʌbɪʃ] Abfall, Müll **I**
rude [ru:d] unhöflich, grob **IV**
rugby ['rʌgbɪ] Rugby **III**
rule [ru:l] Regel **III**
to **rule** [ru:l] herrschen über, regieren **V 4**, 44
ruler ['ru:lə] Lineal; Herrscher/in **V 1**, 12
to **run*** [rʌn] rennen, laufen **II**
⟨to run its course⟩ [kɔ:s] seinen Lauf nehmen **V 1**, 71
to run off, ran off [ræn ɒf] rannte weg **II**
to run out [,rʌn 'aʊt] zu Ende gehen, ausgehen **V 3**, 34
runway ['rʌnweɪ] Start-/Landebahn **V 3**, 33
Russian ['rʌʃən] russisch, Russisch **III**

S

sack [sæk] Sack **II**
sad [sæd] traurig **IV**
⟨saddle⟩ ['sædl] Sattel **V 1**, 68
⟨saddle bag⟩ ['sædl,bæg] Satteltasche **V 1**, 68
safe [seɪf] sicher **III**
safely [seɪflɪ] sicher **III**
⟨safety⟩ ['seɪftɪ] Sicherheit **V 3**, 77
to **sail** [seɪl] segeln **IV**
salad ['sæləd] gemischter Salat **I**
salary ['sælərɪ] Gehalt **V 2**, 22
[sale] [seɪl] Verkauf **II**
⟨sales slip⟩ ['seɪlz ,slɪp] Kassenzettel, Quittung, Beleg **V TP**, 96
salt [sɔ:lt] Salz **V 1**, 8
saltwater [sɔ:lt'wɔ:tə] Salzwasser **V 1**, 8
same [seɪm] gleich **I**
at the same time [ət ðə ,seɪm 'taɪm] gleichzeitig **III**
⟨sand⟩ [sænd] Sand **V 1**, 71
sandcastle ['sændkɑ:sl] Sandburg **I**
sandwich ['sænwɪdʒ] belegtes Brot **I**
Saturday ['sætədeɪ] Samstag, Sonnabend **I**
sauerkraut ['saʊəkraʊt] Sauerkraut **II**
sausage ['sɒsɪdʒ] Würstchen, Wurst **I**
savage ['sævɪdʒ] Wilde/r **IV**
⟨savagery⟩ ['sævɪdʒrɪ] Brutalität **V 1**, 69
to **save** [seɪv] retten **I**; sparen **I**
saw [sɔ:] Säge **V 3**, 36
to **say*** [seɪ] sagen **I**
It doesn't say. [ɪt ,dʌznt 'seɪ] Das wird nicht gesagt., Das steht nicht darauf. **II**
to say hello ['seɪ hə'ləʊ] grüßen **I**
to be **scared of** [bɪ 'skeəd əv] Angst haben vor **II**

scarf, scarves (*pl*) [skɑːf] Schal, Schals **III**
scary ['skærɪ] unheimlich, gruselig, gespenstisch **V 5**, 55
scene [siːn] Szene **II**
schedule (*AE*) ['ʃedjuːl] Stundenplan; Fahrplan **IV**
school [skuːl] Schule **I**
boarding school ['bɔːdɪŋ ˌskuːl] Internat **III**
Science ['saɪəns] Naturwissenschaft(en) **II**
scientist ['saɪəntɪst] Wissenschaftler/in **V 3**, 35
to **score** [skɔː] ⟨abschneiden (bei einem Spiel oder Wettkampf)⟩ **V 5**, 82; ein Tor erzielen **III**
Scottish ['skɒtɪʃ] schottisch **II**
to **scowl** [skaʊl] ein böses Gesicht machen **IV**
⟨to scramble⟩ ['skræmbl] verrühren, zu Rührei verarbeiten **V 3**, 79
⟨to scratch⟩ [skrætʃ] scharren **V 3**, 79
scream [skriːm] Schrei **IV**
to **scream** [skriːm] schreien **III**
screen [skriːn] Bildschirm, Leinwand **III**
⟨to scribble⟩ ['skrɪbl] hinkritzeln **V 1**, 10
° **scuba diving** ['skuːbə‿ˌdaɪvɪŋ] Tauchen **V 1**, 13
sea [siː] Meer **I**
⟨sea power⟩ [siː 'paʊə] Seemacht **V 1**, 70
seal [siːl] Robbe **II**
⟨to search⟩ [sɜːtʃ] suchen **V 1**, 68
seaside ['siːsaɪd] an der Küste, am Meer **III**
at the seaside [ət ðə 'siːsaɪd] am Meer, an der See **I**
season ['siːzn] Jahreszeit **I**
seat [siːt] Sitz, Sitzplatz **I**
second ['sekənd] Sekunde **III**
secondary school ['sekəndərɪ ˌskuːl] weiterführende Schule **III**
secondary modern (school) ['sekəndərɪ ˌmɒdən] *brit. Schultyp, entspricht etwa einer Realschule* **V 2**, 24
section ['sekʃn] Abteilung, Teil **III**
⟨sediment⟩ ['sedɪmənt] Ablagerung, Sediment **V 3**, 32
to **see*** [siː] sehen **I**
You only see the fun side. [jʊ 'əʊnlɪ siː ðə 'fʌn saɪd] Du siehst nur dein Vergnügen. **IV**
See you! *umg.*: Tschüs!, Bis bald!, Bis dann! **IV**
to **seem** [siːm] scheinen **II**
to **select** [sɪ'lekt] auswählen **IV**
⟨self-government⟩ [self 'gʌvnmənt] Selbstverwaltung **V 1**, 70
to **sell*** [sel] verkaufen **I**
to **send*** [send] schicken **II**
sentence ['sentəns] Satz **I**
separate entry ['seprət‿ˌentrɪ] eigener Eintrag **IV**
⟨to separate⟩ ['sepəreɪt] trennen **V 1**, 71
September [sep'tembə] September **I**
series (*sg* + *pl*) ['sɪəriːz] Serie **V 5**, 56
serious ['sɪərɪəs] ernsthaft **III**
⟨servant⟩ ['sɜːvənt] Diener/in **V 4**, 80
⟨to serve⟩ [sɜːv] bedienen **V 2**, 75; servieren **V 1**, 71
service ['sɜːvɪs] Dienst, Dienstleistung **III**
service station ['sɜːvɪs ˌsteɪʃn] Raststätte **III**
⟨set⟩ [set] Kreis, Gruppe **V 2**, 75
to **set** [set] bestimmen **V 6**, 63
⟨to set oneself a goal⟩ [ˌset wʌnˌself ə 'gəʊl] sich ein Ziel setzen **V 2**, 74
to set up camp [set‿ʌp 'kæmp] ein Lager aufschlagen, lagern **V 3**, 36
⟨setting⟩ ['setɪŋ] Schauplatz **V 1**, 69
to **settle** ['setl] (be)siedeln, sich niederlassen **IV**; ⟨konzentrieren⟩ **V 2**, 73
settlement ['setlmənt] Siedlung **IV**
settler ['setlə] Siedler/in **IV**
several ['sevrl] mehrere, einige **IV**
⟨shadow⟩ ['ʃædəʊ] Schatten **V 1**, 68
to **shake*** ['ʃeɪk] zittern, schütteln **IV**
⟨shampoo⟩ [ʃæm'puː] Shampoo **V R**, 91
⟨share⟩ [ʃeə] Anteil **V 6**, 87
to **share** [ʃeə] teilen **V 1**, 18
shark [ʃɑːk] Hai **V 1**, 8
she [ʃiː] sie **I**
⟨to shear⟩ [ʃɪə] scheren **V R**, 88
shed [ʃed] Stall, Schuppen **I**
sheep (*sg* + *pl*) [ʃiːp] Schaf, Schafe **I**
⟨sheep-shearing⟩ ['ʃiːpˌʃɪərɪŋ] Schafe scheren **V R**, 88
sheepdog ['ʃiːpdɒg] Hirtenhund **I**
sheet [ʃiːt] Blatt; Scheibe; Laken **V 1**, 10
shelf, shelves (*pl*) [ʃelf] Regal, Regale **I**
sheriff ['ʃerɪf] Sheriff **II**
⟨shift⟩ [ʃɪft] Schicht **V 2**, 75
ship [ʃɪp] Schiff **III**
shirt [ʃɜːt] Hemd(bluse) **I**
to **shiver** ['ʃɪvə] zittern, erschauern **V 3**, 36
shock [ʃɒk] [Schock] **II**; Schock(zustand) **IV**
to be **shocked** [ʃɒkt] schockiert sein **IV**
shoe [ʃuː] Schuh **I**
to **shoot*** [ʃuːt] schießen **II**
shop [ʃɒp] Geschäft, Laden **I**
shop assistant ['ʃɒp‿əˌsɪstənt] Verkäufer/in **I**
to go to the shops [gəʊ tə ðə 'ʃɒps] einkaufen gehen **I**
shopping ['ʃɒpɪŋ] Einkaufs-, Einkaufen **I**
shopping centre ['ʃɒpɪŋ ˌsentə] Einkaufszentrum **I**
shopping list ['ʃɒpɪŋ lɪst] Einkaufsliste **I**
short cut ['ʃɔːt kʌt] Abkürzung **II**
short [ʃɔːt] kurz **I**
shorts (*sg* + *pl*) [ʃɔːts] Shorts, kurze Hose, kurze Hosen **IV**
shotgun ['ʃɒtgʌn] Schrotflinte **IV**
should [ʃʊd] sollte, sollten, solltest, solltet **III**
shoulder ['ʃəʊldə] Schulter **II**
shout [ʃaʊt] Schrei **IV**
to **shout** [ʃaʊt] rufen **II**
⟨shovel⟩ ['ʃʌvl] Schaufel **V 3**, 76
show [ʃəʊ] Vorstellung, Vorführung **III**; Schau; Ausstellung **V 1**, 10
to **show*** [ʃəʊ] zeigen **I**
to show s.th. off [ʃəʊ‿'ɒf] mit etw. protzen, mit etw. angeben **IV**
⟨to shrink*⟩ [ʃrɪŋk] schrumpfen **V TP**, 96
to **shut*** [ʃʌt] schließen **II**
⟨shut in⟩ [ˌʃʌt 'ɪn] eingeschlossen **V 2**, 72
to be **sick** [bɪ 'sɪk] sich übergeben **IV**
to feel sick [ˌfiːl 'sɪk] sich schlecht, krank fühlen **II**
side [saɪd] Seite **II**
° **sigh** [saɪ] Seufzen **V 3**, 32
sight [saɪt] Sehenswürdigkeit **III**; ⟨Sicht; Anblick⟩ **V 1**, 69
sign [saɪn] Schild, Zeichen **II**
signal ['sɪgnl] Signal, Zeichen **II**
silence ['saɪləns] Stille, Schweigen **V 5**, 55; Ruhe, Stille **IV**
silent ['saɪlənt] still, stumm, geräuschlos; schweigsam **IV**
silly ['sɪlɪ] dumm, albern **I**
similar ['sɪmɪlə] ähnlich **V 3**, 40
[simple past] ['sɪmpl ˌpɑːst] einfache Vergangenheit **II**
simple present [ˌsɪmpl 'preznt] Präsens **III**
since [sɪns] seit **IV**
Sincerely, [sɪn'sɪəlɪ] Mit freundlichen Grüßen (*Schlussformel in Briefen*) **IV**
Sincerely yours, (*AE*) [sɪn'sɪəlɪ jɔːz] Mit freundlichen Grüßen (*Schlussformel in Briefen*) **IV**
to **sing*** [sɪŋ] singen **I**
⟨to sing along⟩ [sɪŋ‿ə'lɒŋ] mitsingen **V 1**, 11
singer ['sɪŋə] Sänger/in **III**
single ['sɪŋgl] einzeln; ledig **V 2**, 24; einzig **V 4**, 46
sir [sɜː] *höfliche Anrede für einen Mann* **V 2**, 30
Sir [sɜː] *Anrede/Titel eines Ritters* **III**
sister ['sɪstə] Schwester **I**
to **sit*** [sɪt] sitzen **I**

Sit down. [sɪt 'daʊn] Setz dich., Setzt euch. **I**
to sit down [sɪt 'daʊn] sich hinsetzen **I**
⟨site⟩ [saɪt] Stelle, Platz **V TP**, 95
situation [ˌsɪtjʊ'eɪʃn] Situation, Lage **III**
size [saɪz] Größe **I**
to **skate** [skeɪt] Rollschuh/Schlittschuh laufen **IV**
skateboard ['skeɪtbɔ:d] Skateboard **I**
skater ['skeɪtə] Schlitt-/Rollschuhläufer/in, Skateboard-fahrer/in **II**
skates [skeɪts] Schlittschuhe **II**
skill [skɪl] Fertigkeit, Fähigkeit **IV**
skin [skɪn] Haut **I**
skirt [skɜ:t] Rock **II**
sky [skaɪ] Himmel **V 3**, 32
skyscraper ['skaɪˌskreɪpə] Wolkenkratzer **IV**
⟨slacker⟩ ['slækə] Bummelant, Faulpelz **V 2**, 74
⟨slaughter⟩ ['slɔ:tə] Gemetzel **V TP**, 95
slave [sleɪv] Sklave/Sklavin **IV**
to **sleep*** [sli:p] schlafen **I**
⟨to sleep over⟩ ['sli:p‿ˌaʊvə] bei jdm. übernachten **V 1**, 10
sleeping bag ['sli:pɪŋ bæg] Schlafsack **IV**
sleepless ['sli:plɪs] schlaflos **III**
⟨slice⟩ [slaɪs] Stück **V 2**, 75
⟨slightly⟩ ['slaɪtlɪ] geringfügig, leicht **V 1**, 69
slippery ['slɪpərɪ] rutschig, glatt **II**
slogan ['sləʊgən] Slogan, Motto, Werbespruch **V 5**, 53
slow [sləʊ] langsam **III**
slow-moving traffic [ˌsləʊmu:vɪŋ 'træfɪk] zähfließender Verkehr **III**
small [smɔ:l] klein **I**
to **smell*** [smel] riechen **IV**
smile [smaɪl] Lächeln **IV**
to **smile** [smaɪl] lächeln **II**
smoke [sməʊk] Rauch **III**
to **smoke** [sməʊk] rauchen **IV**
no **smoking** [nəʊ 'sməʊkɪŋ] Rauchen verboten **II**
snack bar ['snæk bɑ:] Imbissstube **I**
snake [sneɪk] Schlange **I**
snow [snəʊ] Schnee **I**
So what? [səʊ 'wɒt] Na und? **IV**
so [səʊ] also **I**; so (viel) **II**
so (that) ['səʊ ðæt] damit **IV**
soap [səʊp] Seife **I**
⟨soap-powder⟩ ['səʊp ˌpaʊdə] Waschpulver **V 2**, 72
soccer ['sɒkə] Fußball **IV**
⟨social⟩ ['səʊʃl] sozial **V 5**, 83
society [sə'saɪətɪ] Gesellschaft **V 4**, 46
sock [sɒk] Socke **II**
⟨sofa⟩ ['səʊfə] Sofa **V 1**, 10
soft [sɒft] weich; leise **V 3**, 32
software ['sɒftweə] Software **IV**
soil [sɔ:l] Erde **V 3**, 41
solar ['səʊlə] Sonnen-, Solar- **V 3**, 35
soldier ['səʊldʒə] Soldat/in **IV**
to **solve** [sɒlv] lösen **V 1**, 10
some [sʌm] einige, etwas **II**
some [sʌm] irgendein **V 5**, 52
somebody ['sʌmbədɪ] jemand **II**
someone ['sʌmwʌn] jemand **III**
something ['sʌmθɪŋ] etwas **II**
sometimes ['sʌmtaɪmz] manchmal **I**
somewhere ['sʌmweə] irgendwo **II**
son [sʌn] Sohn **II**
song [sɒŋ] Lied **I**
soon [su:n] bald **I**
as soon as possible [əz‿su:n‿əz 'pɒsəbl] so bald wie möglich **IV**
sooner or later ['su:nər‿ɔ: ˌleɪtə] früher oder später **V 3**, 36
sore [sɔ:] schmerzend **II**
Sorry. ['sɒrɪ] Entschuldigung., Tut mir Leid. **I**
to be **sorry about s.th.** [bɪ 'sɒrɪ əbaʊt] Leid tun, dass ..., Leid tun wegen **II**
to be sorry for s.o. [bɪ 'sɒrɪ fə] Mitleid haben mit jdm. **II**
⟨to sort⟩ [sɔ:t] sortieren **V 3**, 76
⟨soul⟩ [səʊl] Seele **V 5**, 85
⟨soul (= soul music)⟩ [səʊl] Soul *(Musikrichtung)* **V 5**, 83
sound ['saʊnd] Geräusch, Laut **II**
sound effect ['saʊnd ɪˌfekt] Geräuscheffekt **II**
sound practice ['saʊnd ˌpræktɪs] Ausspracheübung **I**
to **sound** [saʊnd] klingen, sich anhören **III**
soup [su:p] Suppe **III**
source [sɔ:s] Quelle **V 3**, 35
south [saʊθ] südlich, Süd-, Süden **II**
southern ['sʌðən] südlich **V 1**, 11
souvenir [ˌsu:və'nɪə] Souvenir, Andenken, Mitbringsel **I**
space [speɪs] Weltraum, All **V 3**, 35
spade [speɪd] Spaten **I**
Spanish ['spænɪʃ] spanisch, Spanisch **I**
spare room ['speə‿ru:m] Gästezimmer **V 1**, 10
spare [speə] Ersatz- **V 1**, 10
to **speak*** [spi:k] sprechen **I**
to speak up [spi:k 'ʌp] sich äußern, die Meinung sagen; lauter sprechen **IV**
speaker ['spi:kə] Sprecher/in **V 1**, 12
⟨'spec (= expect)⟩ [spek] *Abk.:* ich nehme an **V 3**, 79
special ['speʃl] besondere/r/s; Spezialität des Hauses **I**
⟨species (*sg* + *pl*)⟩ ['spi:ʃi:z] Art, Spezies **V TP**, 92
speech [spi:tʃ] Rede **IV**
speech bubble ['spi:tʃ bʌbl] Sprechblase **V 3**, 42
speed [spi:d] Geschwindigkeit, Schnelligkeit, Tempo **IV**
to **spell*** [spel] buchstabieren **I**
spelling ['spelɪŋ] Rechtschreibung **III**
to **spend*** [spend] verbringen, ausgeben **II**
spider ['spaɪdə] Spinne **V 5**, 52
to **spin*** [spɪn] spinnen; drehen **V 6**, 62
⟨spokesperson⟩ ['spəʊksˌpɜ:sn] Sprecher/in **V 3**, 78
spoon [spu:n] Löffel **I**
sports [spɔ:ts] Sport(arten) **II**
Sports Day ['spɔ:tsdeɪ] Sportfest **III**
sportsfield ['spɔ:tsfi:ld] Sportplatz **III**
sportsperson ['spɔ:tsˌpɜ:sn] Sportler/in **III**
spot [spɒt] Fleck, Pickel **II**
⟨spotlight⟩ ['spɒtlaɪt] Rampenlicht **V 5**, 84
⟨spray⟩ [spreɪ] Schauer **V 3**, 79
to **spray** [spreɪ] sprühen **IV**
to **spread*** [spred] sich verbreiten; sich ausbreiten; ausbreiten **V 1**, 11; verteilen, streichen **V 1**, 71
spring [sprɪŋ] Frühling **I**
square ['skweə] Platz **I**
square kilometre ['skweə 'kɪləʊˌmi:tə] Quadratkilometer **V 1**, 9
⟨squirt⟩ [skwɜ:t] Spritzer **V 3**, 79
stable ['steɪbl] Stall **IV**
stack [stæk] ⟨Haufen⟩ **V 2**, 75; Stapel **IV**
⟨to stack⟩ [stæk] stapeln **V 2**, 72
staff [stɑ:f] Mitarbeiterteam, Personal **IV**
stage [steɪdʒ] Bühne **II**; ⟨Stufe⟩ **V 2**, 72
to be on the **stage** [bɪ ɒn ðə 'steɪdʒ] auf der Bühne sein, stehen **II**
stairs [steəz] Treppe, Treppenhaus **III**
stall [stɔ:l] Bude **II**
stamp [stæmp] Briefmarke **II**
to **stand*** [stænd] stehen **I**
I can't stand ... [aɪ 'kɑ:nt 'stænd] ich kann ... nicht leiden, ausstehen **II**
to stand back [ˌstænd 'bæk] zurückbleiben **III**
star [stɑ:] Star; Stern **IV**
to **start** [stɑ:t] anfangen, beginnen **I**

Let's start. [ˌlets ˈstɑːt] Lass uns anfangen. **I**
⟨to start off⟩ [stɑːt‿ˈɒf] sich auf den Weg machen **V 4**, 80
⟨to stash⟩ [stæʃ] geheimes Lager **V 2**, 75
state [steɪt] (Bundes-)Staat **IV**
statement [ˈsteɪtmənt] Aussage, Aussagesatz **II**
station [ˈsteɪʃn] Bahnhof **I**; *Vieh-/Schaffarm im austr. Outback* **V 1**, 8
⟨statistic⟩ [stəˈtɪstɪk] Statistik **V 6**, 87
statue [ˈstætʃuː] Statue, Denkmal **I**
° **status symbol** [ˈsteɪtəs ˌsɪmbl] Statussymbol **V 5**, 52
to **stay** [steɪ] (zu Besuch) wohnen **I**; bleiben **I**
to stay in touch with [ɪn ˈtʌtʃ] in Verbindung bleiben mit **V 1**, 14
steak [steɪk] Steak **IV**
to **steal*** [stiːl] stehlen **III**
steam engine [ˈstiːm ˌendʒɪn] Dampfmaschine; Dampflok **V 6**, 62
steep [stiːp] steil **II**
step [step] Schritt, Stufe **I**
to **step** [step] treten **III**
to step between [step bɪˈtwiːn] dazwischentreten **IV**
⟨to step on ahead⟩ [ˌstep‿ɒn əˈhed] nach vorne treten **V 3**, 76
to step on s.o.'s toes [ˈstep‿ɒn …ˈtəʊz] jdm. auf die Füße treten; jdn. beleidigen **III**
stereo [ˈsteriəʊ] Stereo-, Hifi, (-Anlage) **V 5**, 50
⟨to stick out⟩ [ˈstɪk ˌaʊt] herein-/herausragen **V 3**, 79
⟨sticky⟩ [ˈstɪki] klebrig **V 1**, 71
⟨stiff⟩ [stɪf] steif **V 1**, 71
still [stɪl] regungslos **IV**
still [stɪl] (immer) noch **II**
⟨stock-room⟩ [ˈstɒkruːm] Lager, Lagerraum **V 2**, 73
stomach [ˈstʌmək] Magen **II**
stomach-ache [ˈstʌməkeɪk] Bauchschmerzen **II**
stone [stəʊn] Stein **I**
to **stop** [stɒp] anhalten **I**; aufhören **II**
Stop it! [ˈstɒp‿ɪt] Hör/Hört auf! **II**
store (*AE*) [stɔː] Geschäft, Laden **IV**
⟨to store⟩ [stɔː] lagern **V 3**, 78
⟨storeroom⟩ [ˈstɔːrʊm] Lagerraum **V 6**, 87
storm [stɔːm] Sturm **III**
stormy [ˈstɔːmi] stürmisch **III**
story [ˈstɔːri] Geschichte, Erzählung **I**
storyline [ˈstɔːrilaɪn] (Verlauf einer) Geschichte **III**
⟨straggler⟩ [ˈstræglə] Nachzügler/in **V 1**, 69
⟨straight⟩ [streɪt] gerade **V 6**, 86
straight on [streɪt‿ˈɒn] geradeaus **I**
strange [streɪndʒ] seltsam, merkwürdig **II**
⟨strategical⟩ [strəˈtiːdʒɪkl] strategisch **V 3**, 79
strategy [ˈstrætɪdʒi] Strategie, Vorgehensweise **V 1**, 13
straw [strɔː] ⟨Stroh⟩ **V TP**, 94; Strohhalm, Trinkhalm **IV**
⟨strawberry⟩ [ˈstrɔːbri] Erdbeere **V 1**, 71
⟨to stray⟩ [streɪ] (umher)streunen **V 1**, 68
street [striːt] Straße **I**
stress [stres] Betonung; Stress **V 3**, 40
to **stress** [stres] betonen **V 3**, 40
string [strɪŋ] Saite, Bindfaden **III**
⟨to stroke⟩ [strəʊk] streicheln **V 1**, 68
strong [strɒŋ] stark **III**
to be **stuck** [bi ˈstʌk] klemmen **IV**
to be stuck with [bi ˈstʌk wɪð] etw. am Hals haben **IV**
student (*AE*) [ˈstjuːdnt] Schüler/in; Student/in **IV**
Student Council (*AE*) [ˌstjuːdnt ˈkaʊnsl] Schülermitverwaltung **IV**
to **study** [stʌdi] studieren; beobachten; lesen **IV**
stuff [stʌf] Zeug; Stoff **IV**
stupid [ˈstjuːpɪd] dumm **II**
style [staɪl] Stil, Richtung **III**
subject [ˈsʌbdʒɪkt] Fach **II**; Thema **III**
⟨subsidence⟩ [səbˈsaɪdns] Senkung **V 3**, 76
⟨subtropical⟩ [ˌsʌbˈtrɒpɪkl] subtropisch **V TP**, 93
⟨suburban⟩ [səˈbɜːbən] Vororts- **V 1**, 11
subway (*AE*) [ˈsʌbweɪ] U-Bahn **IV**
⟨to succeed⟩ [səkˈsiːd] erfolgreich sein, Erfolg haben **V 1**, 70
success [səkˈses] Erfolg **III**
such a [sʌtʃ‿ə] solch ein/e, ein/e solche/r **IV**
suddenly [ˈsʌdnli] plötzlich **II**
sugar [ˈʃʊgə] Zucker **I**
to **suggest** [səˈdʒest] vorschlagen; andeuten, hindeuten auf **IV**
suggestion [səˈdʒestʃn] Vorschlag **IV**
suit [suːt] Anzug, Kostüm **III**
suitable [ˈsuːtəbl] geeignet, passend **IV**
summary [ˈsʌməri] Zusammenfassung **II**
summer [ˈsʌmə] Sommer **I**
sun [sʌn] Sonne **III**
sundae [ˈsʌndeɪ] Eisbecher **IV**
Sunday [ˈsʌndeɪ] Sonntag **I**
sunglasses (*sg + pl*) [ˈsʌnglɑːsɪz] Sonnenbrille, Sonnenbrillen **IV**
sunny [ˈsʌni] sonnig **I**
[sunroof] [ˈsʌnruːf] Schiebedach **II**
sunshine [ˈsʌnʃaɪn] Sonnenschein **III**
⟨superb⟩ [suːˈpɜːb] großartig **V TP**, 92
⟨superhuman⟩ [ˌsuːpəˈhjuːmən] übermenschlich **V 3**, 39
supermarket [ˈsuːpəˌmɑːkɪt] Supermarkt **I**
superstar [ˌsuːpəˈstɑː] Superstar **III**
to **support** [səˈpɔːt] unterstützen **V 3**, 37
⟨to suppose⟩ [səˈpəʊz] vermuten, annehmen **V 2**, 73
sure [ʃɔː] sicher **I**
I'm not sure. [aɪm nɒt ˈʃɔː] Ich bin mir nicht sicher. **I**
to **surf** [sɜːf] surfen, Wellen reiten **III**
⟨surface⟩ [ˈsɜːfɪs] Oberfläche **V 3**, 76
° **surfie** [ˈsɜːfi] *austr. umg.:* Wellenreiter/in **V 1**, 7
surprise [səˈpraɪz] Überraschung **I**
surprised [səˈpraɪzd] überrascht **III**
survey [ˈsɜːveɪ] Umfrage; Volks- und Viehzählung **V 4**, 46
⟨survival⟩ [səˈvaɪvl] Überleben **V 2**, 75
to **survive** [səˈvaɪv] überleben **IV**
sushi [ˈsuːʃi] *japanisches Fischgericht* **IV**
swampland [ˈswɒmplænd] Sumpf(gebiet) **IV**
to **swear*** [sweə] schwören; fluchen **IV**
sweater [ˈswetə] Pullover **IV**
sweatshirt [ˈswetʃɜːt] Sweatshirt **I**
sweet [swiːt] Bonbon **I**
sweet [swiːt] süß, niedlich **II**
to **swim*** [swɪm] schwimmen **II**
swimmer [ˈswɪmə] Schwimmer/in **III**
to go **swimming** [gəʊ ˈswɪmɪŋ] schwimmen gehen **I**
swimming pool [ˈswɪmɪŋpuːl] Schwimmbad **II**
Swiss [swɪs] schweizerisch **IV**
to **switch on** [swɪtʃ‿ˈɒn] einschalten **III**
⟨sword⟩ [sɔːd] Schwert **V 4**, 81
synonym [ˈsɪnənɪm] Synonym, Wort mit gleicher Bedeutung **V 6**, 67
system [ˈsɪstəm] System **V 4**, 46

T

T-shirt [ˈtiːʃɜːt] T-Shirt **I**
table [ˈteɪbl] Tisch **I**
table setting [ˈteɪbl ˌsetɪŋ] Tischdekoration **V 2**, 22
to **tackle** [ˈtækl] angreifen (*beim Sport*) **III**
to **take*** [teɪk] nehmen **I**; bringen **I**; erfordern; dauern **IV**
to take a photo of [teɪk‿əˈfəʊtəʊ‿əv] ein Foto machen von **I**
to take action [teɪk ˈækʃn] Schritte unternehmen **V 3**, 37

to take care of s.th. [teɪk 'keər‿ɒv ˌsʌmθɪŋ] etw. erledigen; nach etw. schauen; sich um etw. kümmern **IV**
to take home [teɪk 'həʊm] nach Hause bringen **I**
to take notes [teɪk 'nəʊts] Notizen machen **II**
to take off, took off ['teɪk ɒf, 'tʊk ɒf] ausziehen, wegnehmen **II**
to take out [teɪk 'aʊt] hinaustragen **IV**
⟨to take out of service⟩ [teɪk aʊt‿ɒv 'sɜːvɪs] außer Betrieb nehmen **V 3**, 78
to take part in s.th. [ˌteɪk 'pɑːt‿ɪn] an etw. teilnehmen **III**
to take place [ˌteɪk 'pleɪs] stattfinden **III**
⟨to take to pieces⟩ [teɪk tə 'piːsɪz] auseinander nehmen/bauen **V 3**, 78
⟨to take to the air⟩ [ˌteɪk tʊ ðɪ‿eə] abheben, in die Luft steigen **V 3**, 32
takeaway ['teɪkəweɪ] *Imbissstube, Schnellgaststätte mit Straßenverkauf* **II**
tale [teɪl] Geschichte, Sage **II**
talk [tɔːk] Referat, Rede, Gespräch **III**
talk-radio program (*AE*) [tɔːk 'reɪdɪəʊ prəʊgræm] *Radiosendung, bei der die Hörer und Hörerinnen anrufen können* **IV**
to give a talk [ˌgɪv‿ə 'tɔːk] eine Rede/ein Referat halten **III**
to **talk about** ['tɔːk‿əˌbaʊt] reden über, sprechen über **I**
tall story [tɔːl 'stɔːrɪ] Lügengeschichte **IV**
tall [tɔːl] groß; hoch **IV**
⟨to tap⟩ [tæp] klopfen **V 3**, 77
tape [teɪp] Band, Kassette **IV**
task [tɑːsk] Aufgabe **V 2**, 26
to **taste** [teɪst] schmecken, probieren **II**
tax [tæks] Steuer **V 4**, 46
taxi ['tæksɪ] Taxi **III**
tea [tiː] Mahlzeit am frühen Abend **I**; Tee **I**
tea-cosy [ˌtiː'kəʊzɪ] Teewärmer **II**
to **teach*** [tiːtʃ] lehren, unterrichten **III**
°to teach s.o. a lesson [tiːtʃ‿ə 'lesn] jdm. eine Lektion erteilen **V 4**, 44
teacher ['tiːtʃə] Lehrer/in **I**
team [tiːm] Mannschaft **I**
teamwork ['tiːmwɜːk] Teamarbeit **V 2**, 20
⟨technical⟩ ['teknɪkl] technisch **V TP**, 93
techno [tek'nəʊ] Techno (*Musikrichtung*) **III**
Technology [tek'nɒlədʒɪ] Informatik (*Computerunterricht*) **II**; Technologie **III**
teddy ['tedɪ] Teddybär **II**
teenager ['tiːnˌeɪdʒə] Jugendliche/r; Teenager **IV**
teepee [tiː'piː] Tipi (*kegelförmiges Zelt der Prärie-Indianer*) **IV**
tel. [tel] Telefonnummer (*Abkürzung*) **III**
telephone ['telɪfəʊn] Telefon **I**
(telephone) call [kɔːl] Anruf **III**
on the telephone [ɒn ðə 'telɪfəʊn] am Telefon **I**
telephone bill ['telɪfəʊn ˌbɪl] Telefonrechnung **IV**
to **telephone** ['telɪfəʊn] telefonieren, anrufen **III**
teletext ['telɪtekst] Videotext **IV**
to **tell*** [tel] erzählen **I**; sagen, mitteilen **I**
to tell lies [ˌtel 'laɪz] lügen **III**
to tell the time ['tel ðə 'taɪm] die Uhrzeit angeben **I**
to have a **temperature** [ˌhæv‿ə 'temprətʃə] Fieber haben **II**
temple ['templ] Tempel **III**
tennis ['tenɪs] Tennis **I**
tennis court ['tenɪskɔːt] Tennisplatz **III**
tense [tens] Zeit **III**
tent [tent] Zelt **V 3**, 36
term [tɜːm] Schuljahresabschnitt **III**
terrible ['terəbl] schrecklich, furchtbar **I**
territory ['terətərɪ] Gebiet, Territorium **V 1**, 8
test [test] Prüfung, Klassenarbeit **III**
test paper (*AE*) [test 'peɪpə] Klassenarbeit **IV**
to **test** [test] prüfen **III**
text [tekst] Text **I**
⟨textile⟩ ['tekstaɪl] Textilindustrie **V 6**, 86
than [ðən] als (*bei Vergleichen*) **II**
to **thank s.o.** [θæŋk] jdm. danken **IV**
Thank goodness! [θæŋk 'gʊdnɪs] Gott sei Dank! **IV**
Thank you. ['θæŋk‿jʊ] Danke schön. **I**
⟨thankful⟩ ['θæŋkfʊl] dankbar **V 2**, 73
Thanks! [θæŋks] Danke! **I**
Thanksgiving ['θænksˌgɪvɪŋ] Erntedankfest **IV**
that [ðæt] dass **II**
that [ðæt] der/die/das **III**
that well [ðæt 'wel] besonders gut **IV**
⟨that's fine by me⟩ [ðæts 'faɪn baɪ 'miː] ich habe nichts dagegen **V 1**, 10
the [ðiː] der/die/das **I**
⟨the king's hall⟩ [ˌkɪŋz 'hɔːl] der Königssaal **V 4**, 80
⟨the likes of you⟩ [ðə 'laɪks‿əv 'juː] Leute wie du/ihr **V 3**, 79
the public [ðə 'pʌblɪk] die Öffentlichkeit **V 5**, 52
⟨the thin blue line⟩ ['ðə θɪn bluː ˌlaɪn] Linie, die nicht überschritten werden darf **V 3**, 32
⟨the work in hand⟩ [ðə 'wɜːk ɪn ˌhænd] die anstehende Arbeit **V 1**, 68
the wrong way round [ðə ˌrɒŋ weɪ 'raʊnd] falsch herum **V 1**, 7
the ... the ... ['ðə ... ðə ...] je ... desto ... **V 1**, 7
theater (*AE*) [θɪ'etə] Theater **IV**
theatre ['θɪətə] Theater **II**
their [ðeə] ihr/ihre (*Pl.*) **I**
them [ðem] sie/ihnen **I**
theme park ['θiːm ˌpɑːk] Freizeitpark, Erlebnispark **III**
themselves [ðəm'selvz] (sich) selbst **III**
then [ðen] dann **I**
⟨then⟩ [ðən] damals **V 4**, 80
there [ðeə] da, dort **I**
over there [əʊvə 'ðeə] da drüben, dort **I**
there are [ðeər‿'ɑː] es gibt, es sind **I**
there is [ðeər‿'ɪz] es gibt, es ist **I**
these [ðiːz] diese hier **I**
they [ðeɪ] sie (*Pl.*) **I**
thief, thieves (*pl*) [θiːf] Dieb/Diebin, Diebe/Diebinnen **II**
thin [θɪn] dünn **V 3**, 32
thing [θɪŋ] Ding, Sache **I**
to **think*** [θɪŋk] denken, glauben **I**
to think of ['θɪnk‿əv] ausdenken **I**
I think so. [aɪ 'θɪŋk səʊ] Ich denke schon. **II**
thirsty ['θɜːstɪ] durstig **II**
this [ðɪs] dies/dieser/diese/dieses **I**
this afternoon [ðɪs‿ɑːftə'nuːn] heute Nachmittag **I**
this suggests ... [ðɪs sə'dʒests] das legt den Schluss nahe **IV**
those [ðəʊz] die da drüben **I**
though [ðəʊ] jedoch; aber **IV**
a **thousand** ['θaʊznd] (ein)tausend **II**
throat [θrəʊt] Hals, Rachen **II**
throne [θrəʊn] Thron **V 4**, 46
through [θruː] durch **I**
throw [θrəʊ] Wurf **II**
to **throw*** [θrəʊ] werfen **I**
to throw off [θrəʊ ɒf] abwerfen, wegwerfen **II**
⟨to thrust⟩ [θrʌst] stoßen **V 6**, 86
thunder ['θʌndə] Donner **II**
°to **thunder** ['θʌndə] donnern **V 1**, 11
thunderstorm ['θʌndəstɔːm] Gewitter **III**
Thursday ['θɜːzdeɪ] Donnerstag **I**
ticket ['tɪkɪt] Fahrkarte **I**
the **tide**(*s*) [taɪd] Gezeiten, Ebbe, Flut **III**
to **tidy** ['taɪdɪ] aufräumen **II**
to tidy up ['taɪdɪ‿ʌp] aufräumen **I**

tidy ['taɪdɪ] ordentlich, aufgeräumt **I**
⟨tie⟩ [taɪ] Verbindung **V 1**, 70
to **tie** [taɪ] (fest)binden, anbinden **IV**
tiger ['taɪgə] Tiger **II**
tights (*sg +pl*) [taɪts] Strumpfhose, Strumpfhosen **II**
⟨tile⟩ [taɪl] Kachel, Fliese **V 2**, 72
till (= **until**) [tɪl] bis **IV**
time [taɪm] Zeit **I**; Mal **III**
all the time [ɔ:l θə‿'taɪm] die ganze Zeit **IV**
from time to time [frəm 'taɪm tə 'taɪm] von Zeit zu Zeit **IV**
ten times [ˌten 'taɪmz] zehnmal **II**
⟨Time and Motion clock⟩ ['taɪm‿ənd 'məʊʃn 'klɒk] Fütterungsautomat **V 3**, 79
to tell the time ['tel ðə 'taɪm] die Uhrzeit angeben **I**
What time is it? [ˌwɒt 'taɪm‿ɪz‿ɪt] Wie spät ist es?, Wie viel Uhr ist es? **I**
timetable ['taɪmteɪbl] Fahrplan **I**; Stundenplan **II**
tin [tɪn] Zinn, Blech **IV**
tip [tɪp] Tipp, Hinweis **III**; Trinkgeld **IV**
tired ['taɪəd] müde **I**
to be tired of s.th. [bɪ 'taɪəd‿əv] von etw. genug haben **IV**
title ['taɪtl] Titel **II**
to [tʊ] vor **I**; zu **I**
from ... to [frəm ... tə] von ... nach **I**
tobacco [tə'bækəʊ] Tabak **IV**
today [tə'deɪ] heute **I**
toe [təʊ] Zehe **II**
together [tə'geðə] zusammen **I**
toilet ['tɔɪlɪt] Toilette **I**
⟨to tolerate⟩ ['tɒləreɪt] tolerieren, (er)dulden **V 1**, 68
tomato, tomatoes (*pl*) [tə'mɑ:təʊ] Tomate, Tomaten **I**
tomorrow [tə'mɒrəʊ] morgen **I**
⟨ton⟩ [tʌn] Tonne **V 3**, 76
tone [təʊn] Ton **III**
tongue [tʌŋ] Zunge; Sprache **V 1**, 12
mother tongue ['mʌðə ˌtʌŋ] Muttersprache **V 1**, 12
tonight [tə'naɪt] heute Abend, heute Nacht **III**
too [tu:] allzu, zu **I**; auch **I**
tooth, teeth (*pl*) [tu:θ] Zahn, Zähne **III**
top [tɒp] oberer Teil; Gipfel **III**
at the **top of** [ət ðə 'tɒp‿əv] ganz oben **I**
topic ['tɒpɪk] Thema **V 1**, 13
tour ['tʊə] Rundfahrt, Rundgang **III**
guided tour [ˌgaɪdɪd 'tʊə] Führung **IV**
to **tour around** [tʊə ə'raʊnd] eine Tour/(Rund-)Reise machen, herumreisen **IV**
tourist ['tʊərɪst] Tourist/in **III**
tournament ['tɔ:nəmənt] Turnier **III**
towards [tə'wɔ:dz] auf ... zu **II**
tower ['taʊə] Turm **III**
town [taʊn] Stadt **I**
⟨toxic material⟩ [ˌtɒksɪk mə'tɪərɪəl] toxisches/giftiges Material **V 3**, 78
toy [tɔɪ] Spielzeug **III**
tractor ['træktə] Traktor, Trecker **I**
⟨trade union⟩ [ˌtreɪd 'ju:njən] Gewerkschaft **V 6**, 87
trading ['treɪdɪŋ] Handel, Handels- **V 6**, 63
tradition [trə'dɪʃn] Tradition, Brauch **IV**
traditional [trə'dɪʃənl] traditionell **V 2**, 28
traffic ['træfɪk] Verkehr **III**
traffic lights (*sg + pl*) ['træfɪk ˌlaɪts] Verkehrsampel, Verkehrsampeln **III**
heavy traffic [ˌhevɪ 'træfɪk] viel Verkehr **III**
slow-moving traffic [ˌsləʊmu:vɪŋ 'træfɪk] zähfließender Verkehr **III**
traffic jam ['træfɪk ˌdʒæm] Stau **III**
trail (*AE*) [treɪl] Spur; Weg, Pfad **IV**
to hit the trail [hɪt ðə 'treɪl] *umg.:* sich auf den Weg machen **IV**

train [treɪn] Zug **I**
to **train** [treɪn] trainieren **III**
trainee [treɪ'ni:] Auszubildende/r **V 2**, 31
trainers ['treɪnəz] Turnschuhe **II**
training ['treɪnɪŋ] Ausbildung, Schulung **V 2**, 23
°training site ['treɪnɪŋ ˌsaɪt] Übungsplatz **V 1**, 13
to **translate** [træns'leɪt] übersetzen **III**
transparency [træns'pærənsɪ] Folie **V 1**, 14
transport ['trænspɔ:t] Verkehrsmittel, Transport **III**
trap [træp] Falle **III**
⟨to trap⟩ [træp] mit Fallen jagen; fangen **V 1**, 68
to be **trapped** [bɪ 'træpt] in der Falle sein, abgeschnitten sein **III**
trapper ['træpə] Fallensteller/in, Trapper/in **IV**; ⟨*Kind, das die Klappen von Schächten öffnet und schließt*⟩ **V 6**, 86
travel ['trævl] Reisen **V 3**, 36
to **travel** ['trævl] reisen **II**
travel diary ['trævl ˌdaɪərɪ] Reisetagebuch **II**
traveled (*AE*) ['trævld] reiste, reistest, reisten **IV**
⟨to tread water⟩ ['tred ˌwɔ:tə] sich über Wasser halten **V 1**, 13
to **treat** [tri:t] behandeln **IV**
⟨treaty⟩ ['tri:tɪ] Abkommen, Vertrag **V 1**, 71
tree [tri:] Baum **I**
tribal land [ˌtraɪbl 'lænd] Stammesland **IV**
tribe [traɪb] Stamm **IV**
trick [trɪk] Trick, Kunstgriff **I**
trick-or-treat [trɪk‿ɔ:‿'tri:t] *etwa:* „Streich-oder-Leckerei" **IV**
to **trick** [trɪk] austricksen **I**
tricky ['trɪkɪ] schwierig **IV**
trip [trɪp] Ausflug, Reise **II**
to **trip** ['trɪp] stolpern **I**
trouble ['trʌbl] Schwierigkeiten **I**
to be in trouble [bɪ‿ɪn 'trʌbl] Schwierigkeiten haben **I**
trousers (*sg +pl*) ['traʊzəz] Hose, Hosen **I**
truck (*AE*) [trʌk] Lkw, Lastwagen **IV**
true [tru:] wahr **IV**
[trumpet] ['trʌmpɪt] Trompete **II**
truth [tru:θ] Wahrheit **IV**
to **try** [traɪ] (aus)probieren, versuchen **II**
to try harder [traɪ 'hɑ:də] sich mehr anstrengen **III**
to try on [traɪ‿'ɒn] anprobieren **I**
to try out for [ˌtraɪ 'aʊt fɔ:] vorsingen, vorspielen **IV**
⟨tub⟩ [tʌb] Eimer, Wanne **V 6**, 86
the **tube** [ðə tju:b] *gängiger Ausdruck für die Londoner U-Bahn* **III**
⟨tubing⟩ ['tju:bɪŋ] Verbindungsröhre **V 3**, 79
⟨tucker⟩ ['tʌkə] *austr. umg.:* Essen, Proviant **V 1**, 68
Tuesday ['tju:zdeɪ] Dienstag **I**
°**tuition** [tju:'ɪʃn] Unterricht **V 1**, 13
tune [tju:n] Melodie **III**
tunnel ['tʌnl] Tunnel **I**
°**turbine** ['tɜ:baɪn] Turbine **V 3**, 35
turkey ['tɜ:kɪ] Pute/r, Truthahn/Truthenne **IV**
Turkish ['tɜ:kɪʃ] türkisch, Türkisch **I**
Your **turn.** ['jɔ: tɜ:n] Du bist an der Reihe. **I**
to **turn** [tɜ:n] (sich) drehen, wenden **V 3**, 32; abbiegen **I**
to turn down [ˌtɜ:n 'daʊn] herunterschalten **III**
to turn off [ˌtɜ:n‿'ɒf] ausschalten **III**
to turn on [ˌtɜ:n‿'ɒn] anschalten **V 5**, 55
to turn over [ˌtɜ:n 'əʊvə] umkippen, umdrehen **III**
[to turn s.th. into s.th.] ['tɜ:n ˌɪntʊ] ... in etwas verwandeln **V 3**, 41
to turn to [tɜ:n tʊ] aufschlagen **V 5**, 51
to turn up [tɜ:n 'ʌp] lauter drehen, hoch drehen **IV**
tutor ['tju:tə] Klassenlehrer/in, Betreuungslehrer/in **I**
tutor group ['tju:tə ˌgru:p] Klasse (*in einer englischen Schule*) **I**

TV [tiː'viː] Fernsehen **I**
twice [twaɪs] zweimal **II**
twin [twɪn] Zwilling **I**
twin town ['twɪn 'taʊn] Partnerstadt **I**
Twinning Office ['twɪnɪŋ ˌɒfɪs] Städtepartnerschaftsbüro **I**
type [taɪp] Typ; Art, Sorte **IV**
to **type** [taɪp] tippen **IV**
⟨typical⟩ ['tɪpɪkəl] typisch **V 1**, 70
tyre ['taɪə] Reifen **I**

U

ugly ['ʌglɪ] hässlich **IV**
umbrella [ʌm'brelə] Regenschirm **III**
uncle ['ʌŋkl] Onkel **I**
great uncle ['greɪt ˌʌŋkl] Großonkel **II**
under ['ʌndə] unter **I**
⟨underbelly⟩ ['ʌndəˌbelɪ] Bauch **V 1**, 11
the **underground** [ðɪ 'ʌndəgraʊnd] U-Bahn **III**; ⟨unterirdisch; unter Tage⟩ **V 3**, 76
⟨underground⟩ ['ʌndəgraʊnd] unterirdisch; unter Tage **V 6**, 86
to **underline** ['ʌndəlaɪn] unterstreichen **V 6**, 67
to **understand*** [ʌndə'stænd] verstehen **I**
⟨to undo⟩ [ˌʌn'duː] aufmachen, öffnen, auseinander nehmen **V 3**, 39
unemployed [ˌʌnɪm'plɔɪd] arbeitslos **V 6**, 64
unfriendly [ʌn'frendlɪ] unfreundlich **III**
unhappy [ʌn'hæpɪ] unglücklich **II**
uniform ['juːnɪfɔːm] Uniform **I**
unit ['juːnɪt] Lektion, Kapitel **I**
unless [ən'les] es sei denn; außer **V 1**, 10
⟨unloved⟩ [ˌʌn'lʌvd] ungeliebt **V 1**, 68
to be **unlucky** [bɪ ʌn'lʌkɪ] kein Glück, Pech haben **III**
untidy [ʌn'taɪdɪ] unordentlich **I**
until [ʌn'tɪl] bis **II**
⟨unwanted⟩ [ˌʌn'wɒntɪd] unerwünscht, ungewollt **V 1**, 68
up to ['ʌp ˌtʊ] bis **III**
It's up to you. [ɪts‿ˌʌp tə 'juː] Es liegt an dir., Du entscheidest. **III**
upon [ə'pɒn] auf **V 3**, 32
upper ['ʌpə] der/die/das obere **II**
upside down [ˌʌpsaɪd 'daʊn] auf dem Kopf **V 1**, 7
upstairs [ˌʌp'steəz] oben (im Gebäude) **I**
us [ʌs] uns **I**
use of s.th. [juːs‿ɒv] Gebrauch von etw. **IV**
to **use** [juːz] benutzen **I**
they used to do s.th. [juːs‿tʊ] sie … gewöhnlich; sie pflegten zu tun **V 6**, 63
to be **used to s.th.** [bɪ 'juːst tʊ] gewöhnt sein an **IV**
useful ['juːsfʊl] nützlich **II**
useless ['juːslɪs] nutzlos **III**
usually ['juːʒʊəlɪ] gewöhnlich, normalerweise **I**

V

vacancy ['veɪkənsɪ] offene/freie Stelle **V 2**, 23
vacation (*AE*) [və'keɪʃn] Ferien, Urlaub **IV**
⟨vague(ly)⟩ ['veɪglɪ] in etwa, ungefähr **V 5**, 82
Valentine ['væləntaɪn] *Freund/in, dem/der man am Valentinstag einen Gruß schickt* **IV**
Valentine's card ['væləntaɪnz kaːd] Valentinskarte **IV**
Valentine's Day ['væləntaɪnz deɪ] Valentinstag **IV**
valley ['vælɪ] Tal **III**
van [væn] Lieferwagen, Transporter **II**
vanilla [və'nɪlə] Vanille **IV**
⟨vapour⟩ ['veɪpə] Dunst **V 6**, 87
various ['veərɪəs] verschieden; mehrere, verschiedene **V 4**, 47
⟨to vary⟩ ['veərɪ] schwanken; sich unterscheiden **V 6**, 86
⟨vast⟩ [vɑːst] weit, riesig **V 1**, 68
veal [viːl] Kalbfleisch **V 4**, 47
vegetable ['vedʒtəbl] Gemüse **II**
vegetarian [ˌvedʒɪ'teərɪən] Vegetarier/in **V 3**, 33
vehicle ['vɪəkl] Fahrzeug **V 1**, 11
⟨to venture out⟩ ['ventʃər‿aʊt] sich hinauswagen **V 1**, 13
verb [vɜːb] Verb **I**
very ['verɪ] sehr **I**
vet [vet] Tierarzt/Tierärztin **I**
vet's assistant ['vets‿ə'sɪstənt] Tierarzthelfer/in **I**
⟨victory⟩ ['vɪktərɪ] Sieg **V TP**, 95
video ['vɪdɪəʊ] Video **I**
view [vjuː] Blick, Aussicht **IV**
to **view** [vjuː] anschauen, betrachten **IV**
viewer ['vjuːə] Zuschauer/in **V 5**, 61
Viking ['vaɪkɪŋ] Wikinger/in **V 4**, 47
village ['vɪlɪdʒ] Dorf **III**
⟨villein⟩ ['vɪlɪn] Leibeigene/r **V 4**, 46
violence ['vaɪələns] Gewalt **III**
to **visit** ['vɪzɪt] besuchen, besichtigen **II**
visitor ['vɪzɪtə] Besucher/in **III**
⟨vitality⟩ [vaɪ'tælətɪ] Energie, Vitalität **V TP**, 93
⟨vivid⟩ ['vɪvɪd] lebhaft **V TP**, 95
vocabulary [vəʊ'kæbjʊlərɪ] Wortschatz, Vokabular **III**
voice [vɔɪs] Stimme **II**
volleyball ['vɒlɪbɔːl] Volleyball **II**
voluntary ['vɒləntərɪ] freiwillig **V 2**, 20
⟨to vow⟩ [vaʊ] geloben **V TP**, 95
vowel ['vaʊəl] Vokal **II**

W

wage, wages (*pl*) [weɪdʒ, weɪdʒɪz] Lohn **V 2**, 21
⟨waggon⟩ ['wægən] Wagen **V 3**, 76
wagon ['wægən] Planwagen **IV**
covered wagon ['kʌvəd ˌwægən] Planwagen **IV**
wagon train ['wægən ˌtreɪn] Planwagentreck **IV**
to **wait** [weɪt] warten **I**
to wait for ['weɪt fɔː] warten auf **I**
wake boarding (*AE*) ['weɪk ˌbɔːdɪŋ] *Wassersportart* **IV**
to wake up* ['weɪk‿ʌp] aufwachen **II**
walk [wɔːk] Spaziergang **I**
to go for a walk [ˌgəʊ fər‿ə 'wɔːk] spazieren gehen **I**
to **walk** [wɔːk] (zu Fuß) gehen **I**
to walk down [wɔːk 'daʊn] hinuntergehen **IV**
walkway ['wɔːkweɪ] Fußweg **IV**
wall [wɔːl] Wand, Mauer **IV**
⟨wall-to-wall people⟩ [wɔːl ˌtə‿wɔːl 'piːpl] von Menschen überfüllt **V 1**, 11
wallet (*AE*) ['wɒlɪt] Geldbeutel, Portmonee **IV**
to **want** [wɒnt] (haben) wollen **I**
war [wɔː] Krieg **V 5**, 55
ward [wɔːd] Station (*in einem Krankenhaus*) **II**
warden ['wɔːdn] Jugendherbergsvater/mutter **III**
to **warm up** [wɑːm‿'ʌp] aufwärmen **IV**
warm [wɔːm] warm **I**
to **warn** [wɔːn] warnen **II**
warrior ['wɒrɪə] Krieger/in **IV**
to **wash** [wɒʃ] waschen **IV**
to wash up [wɒʃ‿'ʌp] abwaschen, (Geschirr) spülen **I**
washable ['wɒʃəbl] waschbar **IV**
washing machine ['wɒʃɪŋ məˌʃiːn] Waschmaschine **V 3**, 34
washing-up [ˌwɒʃɪŋ'ʌp] Abwasch **I**
waste [weɪst] Müll, Abfall **III**; Verschwendung **V 3**, 34

⟨wasteland⟩ ['weɪstlænd] Ödland **V 3**, 40
watch [wɒtʃ] Armbanduhr **IV**
to **watch** [wɒtʃ] (zu)schauen, gucken **I**
Watch out! [ˌwɒtʃ‿'aʊt] Pass auf! **III**
water ['wɔ:tə] Wasser **I**
to **water** ['wɔ:tə] zu trinken geben; gießen **V 1**, 10
waterfall ['wɔ:təfɔ:l] Wasserfall **IV**
wave [weɪv] Welle **III**
to **wave** [weɪv] wehen; winken **IV**
waxwork ['wækswɜ:k] Wachs- **III**
way [weɪ] Weg **I**; Weise **III**
in different ways [ɪn ˌdɪfrənt 'weɪz] auf verschiedene Weise **III**
[no way] [nəʊ 'weɪ] auf keinen Fall **II**
way of life [ˌweɪ‿əv 'laɪf] Lebensstil **IV**
we [wi:] wir **I**
weak [wi:k] schwach **III**
⟨wealth⟩ [welθ] Wohlstand, Reichtum **V 1**, 70
weapon ['wepən] Waffe **III**
to **wear*** [weə] tragen, anhaben **I**
weather ['weðə] Wetter **I**
weather forecast ['weðə ˌfɔ:kɑ:st] Wettervorhersage **II**
Wednesday ['wenzdeɪ] Mittwoch **I**
week [wi:k] Woche **I**
weekend [ˌwi:k'end] Wochenende **II**
⟨to weigh⟩ [weɪ] wiegen **V 6**, 86
weight [weɪt] Gewicht **IV**
to **welcome** ['welkəm] begrüßen, willkommen heißen **V 3**, 38
Welcome to ... ['welkəm tʊ] Willkommen in ... **I**
Welcome back. [ˌwelkəm 'bæk] Willkommen zurück. **II**
well [wel] gut, nun, na ja **I**
well [wel] gut *(Adverbialform)* **III**
Get well soon! ['get wel 'su:n] Gute Besserung! **I**
to do well [ˌdu: 'wel] gut sein, gut abschneiden **III**
to feel well [ˌfi:l 'wel] sich wohl fühlen **II**
Well done! [wel 'dʌn] Gut gemacht!, Bravo! **I**
Welsh [welʃ] walisisch, Walisisch **II**
west [west] westlich, West-, Westen **II**
West Indian [ˌwest‿'ɪndjən] westindisch, Westinder/in **III**
wet [wet] nass **I**
what [wɒt] was **I**
So what? [səʊ 'wɒt] Na und? **IV**
What a ... ['wɒt‿ə] Was für ein/e ... **I**
What about ...? ['wɒt‿əˌbaʊt] Wie wär's mit ...? **II**
⟨What an escape!⟩ [ɪ'skeɪp] Das war knapp! **V 3**, 77
What if ...? ['wɒt‿ɪf] Was wäre, wenn ...? **II**
What on earth ...? [ˌwɒt‿ɒn 'ɜ:θ] Was um alles in der Welt ...? **II**
whatever [wɒt'evə] was (auch immer), egal was **IV**
What's up? Was gibt's Neues?, Was ist los? **IV**
What's going on? [wɒts ˌgəʊɪŋ‿'ɒn] Was geht hier vor? **V 3**, 36
What's ... like? [wɒts ... 'laɪk] Wie ist ...? **I**
whatsit ['wɒtsɪt] Wieheißtesnochmal, Dingsda **III**
wheel [wi:l] Rad **II**
when [wen] wann **I**
⟨when it comes to work⟩ [ˌwen‿ɪt ˌkʌmz tə 'wɜ:k] wenn es um die Arbeit geht **V 2**, 74
whenever [wen'evə] jedesmal wenn **V 6**, 64
where [weə] wo **I**
wherever [weər'evə] wo auch immer, egal wo **IV**
whether ['weðə] ob **V 2**, 25
which [wɪtʃ] der/die/das **III**; welche/welcher/welches **II**
while [waɪl] Weile **III**
while [waɪl] während **II**
⟨whipped cream⟩ [ˌwɪpt 'kri:m] Schlagsahne **V 1**, 71
to **whisper** ['wɪspə] flüstern **III**
⟨whistle⟩ ['wɪsl] Pfeife; Pfiff **V 1**, 69
to **whistle** ['wɪsl] pfeifen **V 3**, 36; ⟨pfeifen (nach)⟩ **V 1**, 68
white [waɪt] weiß **I**
whitewater rafting [ˌwaɪt'wɔ:tə 'rɑ:ftɪŋ] Wildwasser-Rafting **IV**
who [hu:] der/die/das **III**; wen/wem **I**; wer **I**
Who's a pretty boy, then? *etwa:* Ach, bist du niedlich! **IV**
on the **whole** [ˌɒn ðə 'həʊl] im Großen und Ganzen **III**
whole [həʊl] ganz **III**
(to) **whom** [(tə) hu:m] (an) wen **III**
whose [hu:z] dessen, deren **III**; wessen **III**
why [waɪ] warum **I**
wide [waɪd] weit, breit **IV**
⟨wide open space⟩ ['waɪd ˌəʊpən 'speɪs] weites, offenes Land **V 1**, 68
wife, wives *(pl)* [waɪf] Ehefrau, Ehefrauen **II**
wig [wɪg] Perücke **II**
wild [waɪld] wild, unberührt **III**
wilderness ['wɪldənes] Wildnis **IV**
⟨will-future⟩ [wɪl 'fju:tʃə] will-Futur **V R**, 88
will [wɪl] werden **II**
⟨willing⟩ ['wɪlɪŋ] bereit **V 2**, 75
to **win*** [wɪn] gewinnen **II**
wind [wɪnd] Wind **III**
wind power ['wɪnd ˌpaʊə] Windkraft **V 3**, 35
window ['wɪndəʊ] Fenster **I**
window display ['wɪndəʊ dɪˌspleɪ] Auslage, Schaufensterdekoration **V 2**, 22
window dresser ['wɪndəʊ ˌdresə] Schaufensterdekorateur/in **V 2**, 22
°window-dressing ['wɪndəʊ ˌdresɪŋ] Schaufenster dekorieren **V 2**, 22
window-shopping ['wɪndəʊʃɒpɪŋ] Schaufensterbummel **II**
° **window-like** ['wɪndəʊ ˌlaɪk] fensterähnlich **V 2**, 22
windy ['wɪndɪ] windig **I**
wine [waɪn] Wein **II**
winner ['wɪnə] Gewinner/in **I**
winter ['wɪntə] Winter **I**
⟨wire nettin' (= wire netting)⟩ ['waɪə ˌnetɪn] Maschengitter **V 3**, 79
to **wish** [wɪʃ] wünschen **V 3**, 32
⟨witch⟩ [wɪtʃ] Hexe **V 4**, 80
⟨witchcraft⟩ ['wɪtʃkrɑ:ft] Zauberkraft, Zauberei **V 4**, 80
with [wɪð] bei, mit **I**
⟨with a break in his voice⟩ [breɪk] mit stockender Stimme **V R**, 88
within [wɪð'ɪn] innen **V 2**, 21; innerhalb **IV**
without [wɪð'aʊt] ohne **I**
woman, women *(pl)* ['wʊmən] Frau, Frauen **I**
wonderful ['wʌndəfl] wunderbar **III**
wood [wʊd] Holz; Wald **V 3**, 36
wool [wʊl] Wolle **IV**
word [wɜ:d] Wort **I**
word order ['wɜ:d ˌɔ:də] Satzstellung **I**
Word power ['wɜ:d ˌpaʊə] Die Kraft der Wörter **I**
work [wɜ:k] Arbeit **III**
All in a day's work. [ɔ:l ɪn‿ə 'deɪz wɜ:k] *etwa:* Das gehört zu meiner täglichen Arbeit. **IV**
work experience [ˌwɜ:k ɪk'spɪərɪəns] Praktikum **V 2**, 21
work of art [wɜ:k‿əv 'ɑ:t] Kunstwerk **IV**
to **work** [wɜ:k] arbeiten **I**; funktionieren, klappen **III**
to work hard [wɜ:k 'hɑ:d] hart, schwer arbeiten **II**
⟨workaholic⟩ [ˌwɜ:kə'hɒlɪk] Arbeitswütige/r **V 2**, 74
⟨workmate⟩ ['wɜ:kmeɪt] Arbeitskollege/-kollegin **V 3**, 77
worksheet ['wɜ:kʃi:t] Arbeitsblatt **III**
workshop ['wɜ:kʃɒp] Kurs, Schulung, Werkstatt **III**
world [wɜ:ld] Welt **II**
across the world [əˌkrɒs ðə 'wɜ:ld] weltweit **V 3**, 35
worldwide ['wɜ:ldwaɪd] weltweit **V 2**, 23
⟨worm⟩ [wɜ:m] Wurm **V 3**, 79

worried ['wʌrɪd] besorgt, beunruhigt **I**
worry ['wʌrɪ] Sorge **IV**
to **worry** ['wʌrɪ] sich Sorgen machen **II**
Don't worry. [ˌdəʊnt 'wʌrɪ] Mach dir/Macht euch keine Sorgen. **II**
worse [wɜːs] schlechter, schlimmer **III**
worst bit ['wɜːst bɪt] das Schlechteste **V 2**, 22
(the) worst [ðə wɜːst] am schlechtesten, am schlimmsten **III**
to be **worth + gerund** [bɪ 'wɜːθ] sich lohnen etw. zu machen **III**
would rather ['rɑːðə] lieber **IV**
Would you like …? ['wʊd‿jʊ laɪk] Hättest du/Hätten Sie gern …? **II**
⟨to wound⟩ [wuːnd] verletzen; kränken **V 1**, 68
Wow! [waʊ] Toll!, Super! (*Ausruf der Begeisterung*) **II**
wrestling ['reslɪŋ] Ringen **IV**
⟨to wring s.o.'s neck⟩ ['rɪŋ ˌsʌmwʌnz 'nek] jdm. den Hals umdrehen **V 3**, 79
to **write*** [raɪt] schreiben **I**
writer ['raɪtə] Autor/in, Schriftsteller/in **III**
wrong [rɒŋ] falsch **I**
S.th. is wrong. [rɒŋ] Es stimmt etw. nicht. **IV**
to be wrong about [biː 'rɒŋ ə'baʊt] Unrecht haben mit **II**
What's wrong with you? [wɒts 'rɒŋ wɪð 'juː] Was fehlt dir/Ihnen? **II**

Y

⟨yacht⟩ [jɒt] Jacht **V TP**, 93
yard [jɑːd] ° amer./brit. Längenmaß. ca. 91,5 cm **V 5**, 55; ⟨Hof⟩ **V 4**, 81
Yeah! [jeə] *umg.:* Ja! **IV**
year [jɪə] Jahr, Jahrgang **I**
yearbook (*AE*) ['jɪəbʊk] Jahrbuch *(einer Schule)* **IV**
to **yell** [jel] *umg.:* schreien, brüllen **V 3**, 36
yellow ['jeləʊ] gelb **I**
yes [jes] ja **I**
yesterday ['jestədɪ] gestern **II**
yet [jet] schon **III**
not … yet [nɒt … jet] noch nicht **I**
YHA (= **Youth Hostel Association**) [waɪ eɪtʃ‿'eɪ] Jugendherbergsverband **III**
you [jʊ] dich/euch/Sie; dir/euch/Ihnen **I**; du, Sie **I**; ihr/Sie **I**; man, einen **II**
Thank you. ['θæŋk‿jʊ] Danke schön. **I**
⟨you'd have had it⟩ ['juːd hæv 'hæd‿ɪt] es wäre vorbei mit dir gewesen **V 3**, 77
young [jʌŋ] jung **II**
⟨youngster⟩ ['jʌŋstə] Jugendliche/r, junger Mensch **V 2**, 73
your [jɔː] dein/deine; Ihr/Ihre; euer/eure; Ihr/Ihre **I**
yourself [jɔː'self] dich selbst **II**
do it yourself [ˌduː ɪt jɔː'self] heimwerken **III**
youth [juːθ] Jugend **III**
youth centre ['juːθ sentr] Jugendzentrum **II**
youth hostel ['juːθ ˌhɒstl] Jugendherberge **III**
Yuck! [jʌk] Igitt!, Pfui!, Bäh! (*Ausruf des Ekels*) **IV**

Z

zero ['zɪərəʊ] Null **IV**
zipper (*AE*) ['zɪpə] Reißverschluss **IV**
zoo [zuː] Zoo **II**

Boys' names

Alan ['ælən]
Alex ['æˌlɪks]
Andrew ['ændruː]
Arthur ['ɑːθə]
Asim ['æziːm]
Barry ['bærɪ]
Bill [bɪl]
Bruce [bruːs]
Charlie ['tʃɑːlɪ]
Colin ['kɒlɪn]
Daniel ['dænjəl]
Darren ['dærən]
Daryl ['dærɪl]
Dave ['deɪv]
David ['deɪvɪd]
Eddy ['edɪ]
Edward ['edwəd]
⟨Edwin⟩ ['edwɪn]
Florian ['flɔːrɪən]
Frank [fræŋk]
Fred [fred]
George [dʒɔːdʒ]
⟨Graeme⟩ ['greɪəm]
Herbert ['hɜːbət]
⟨Hereward⟩ ['herɪwəd]
Hugh [hjuː]
Ike [aɪk]
Jack [dʒæk]
Jackie ['dʒækɪ]
James [dʒeɪmz]
Jerry ['dʒerɪ]
Jez ['dʒez]
Jim [dʒɪm]
John [dʒɒn]
Jonah ['dʒəʊnə]
Josh [dʒɒʃ]
⟨Jud⟩ [dʒʌd]
Ken [ken]
Kevin ['kevɪn]
Lee [liː]
Lenny ['lenɪ]
Leo ['liːəʊ]
Mal [mæl]
Mark [mɑːk]
Michael ['maɪkəl]
Mick [mɪk]
Mike [maɪk]
Nick [nɪk]
Paul [pɔːl]
Percival ['pɜːsɪvl]
Pete [piːt]
Peter ['piːtə]
Rajiv ['rɑːdʒiːv]
⟨Raymond⟩ ['reɪmənd]
Rick [rɪk]
Robert ['rɒbət]
Rodney ['rɒdnɪ]
Ryan ['raɪən]
Sam [sæm]
Seymour ['siːmɔː]
Shane [ʃeɪn]
Simon ['saɪmən]
Stan [stæn]
Steve [stiːv]
Thomas ['tɒməs]
Tim [tɪm]
Tom [tɒm]
Tony ['təʊnɪ]

Troy [trɔɪ]
Washington ['wɒʃɪŋtən]
Wayne [weɪn]
William ['wɪljəm]

Girls' names

Anna ['ænə]
Annabel ['ænəbel]
Anne ['æn]
Audrey [ɔ:drɪ]
Becky ['bekɪ]
Betsy ['betsɪ]
Candy ['kændɪ]
⟨Carol⟩ ['kærəl]
Carrie ['kærɪ]
Cass ['kæs]
Cathy [kæθɪ]
Cindy ['sɪndɪ]
Claudia ['klɔ:djə]
Daisy ['deɪzɪ]
Debbie ['debɪ]
Dee [di:]
Ed ['ed]
Elizabeth [ɪ'lɪzəbəθ]
Ellen ['elɪn]
Emma ['emə]
Fran [fræn]
Gwen [gwen]
Hannah ['hænə]
Heather ['heðə]
Helen ['helɪn]
Holly ['hɒlɪ]
Isi (= **Isadorella**) [ɪzɪ]
Jackie ['dʒækɪ]
Jane [dʒeɪn]
Janet ['dʒænɪt]
Janine [dʒəni:n]
Jenny ['dʒenɪ]
Jill [dʒɪl]
Joanna [dʒəʊ'ænə]
Judy ['dʒu:dɪ]
Julie ['dʒu:lɪ]
Karen [kə'ren]
Kate [keɪt]
Kelly ['kelɪ]
Kim [kɪm]
Kittie ['kɪtɪ]
Kristy ['krɪstɪ]
Lucy ['lu:sɪ]
Lynn [lɪn]
Margaret ['mɑ:grɪt]
Mary ['meərɪ]
Megan ['megən]
Mel [mel]
Mildred ['mɪldrɪd]
Miriam ['mɪrɪəm]
Nina ['ni:nə]
Nora ['nɔ:rə]
Pam [pæm]
Pat [pæt]
Patricia [pə'trɪʃə]
Polly ['pɒlɪ]
Rachel ['reɪtʃl]
Rebecca [rɪ'bekə]
Sally [ˌsælɪ]
Samira [sə'mɪərə]
Sarah ['seərə]
Shabina [ʃə'bɪnə]
Shawna [ʃɔ:nə]
Shelley ['ʃelɪ]
Soo [su:]
Sophie ['səʊfɪ]
Stacey (= **Stace**) ['steɪsɪ]
Stella ['stelə]
Sue [su:]
Sukey ['su:kɪ]
Susan ['su:zn]
Suvina [sə'vi:nə]
Tammy ['tæmɪ]
Tori ['tɔ:rɪ]
Tricia ['trɪʃə]
Trudi ['tru:dɪ]
Victoria [vɪk'tɔ:rɪə]
Virginia [və'dʒɪnjə]
Wilma ['wɪlmə]
Yasmin ['jæzmɪn]

Surnames

Abbott ['æbət]
Adib [ə'dɪb]
Alburg ['ælˌbɜ:rg]
Barker ['bɑ:kə]
⟨Bennett⟩ ['benɪt]
Benson ['bensn]
Blackwell [blækwəl]
Braddock ['brædək]
Broadwood ['brɔ:dwʊd]
Brown [braʊn]
Burton ['bɜ:tn]
Cameron ['kæmərən]
Campbell ['kæmbl]
Canterville ['kæntəvɪl]
Carlson ['kɑ:lsən]
Chang [tʃæŋ]
Cho [tʃɔ:]
Chung [tʃʌng]
Clark [klɑ:k]
Cooper ['ku:pə]
Crane [kreɪn]
Croft [krɒft]
Dane [deɪn]
Davis ['deɪvɪs]
Dixon ['dɪksn]
Duncan ['dʌŋkən]
Gibson ['gɪbsn]
Golightly [gəʊ'laɪtlɪ]
Grant [grɑ:nt]
[Haritonidis] ['hærɪtɒnˌɪdɪs]
Hilton ['hɪltən]
Hunt ['hʌnt]
Ismaili [ɪz'meɪlɪ]
Jackson ['dʒæksən]
Jenkins ['dʒeŋkɪnz]
Jessop ['dʒesəp]
Jonker ['jɒŋkə]
Kishi [kɪʃɪ]
Leadham ['ledəm]
Lomu ['ləʊmu:]
MacTavish [mək'tævɪʃ]
Martin ['mɑ:tɪn]
Mason ['meɪsn]
Matthews ['mæθju:z]
Mc Carthy [mə'kɑ:θɪ]
McCracken [mə'krækn]
McLean [mə'kleɪn]
Mikhailovich ['mɪkhæləvɪtʃ]

Miller ['mɪlə]
Moreno [mɒri:nəʊ]
Morgan ['mɔ:gən]
Mushnick ['mʌʃnɪk]
Nosy ['nəʊzɪ]
O'Hara [ə'hɑ:rə]
O'Reilly [əʊ‿'raɪlɪ]
Otis ['əʊtɪs]
Parker ['pɑ:kə]
Patel [pə'təl]
Patterson ['pætəsn]
Penrose ['penrəʊz]
Percy ['pɜ:sɪ]
Price [praɪs]
Pritchard ['prɪtʃəd]
Reynolds ['renldz]
Richards ['rɪtʃədz]
Ross [rɒs]
Schweitzer ['ʃwaɪtsə]
Sheikh [ʃeɪk]
Singh [sɪŋ]
Smith [smɪθ]
Smyth [smɪθ]
Spencer ['spensə]
Stevenson ['sti:vnzn]
Stuart ['stju:ət]
Taylor ['teɪlə]
Umney ['ʌmnɪ]
Underwood ['ʌndəwʊd]
Upstone [ˌʌp'stəʊn]
Walker ['wɔ:kə]
Wall [wɔ:l]
Weston [westən]
White [waɪt]
Wilder ['waɪldə]
[Wilson] ['wɪlsn]
Wood [wʊd]
Zorzi [zɔ:zɪ]

Geographical names

⟨Aberdeen⟩ [ˌæbə'di:n]
Aberystwyth [ˌæbə'rɪstwɪθ]
Adelaide ['ædəleɪd]
Africa ['æfrɪkə]
Alaska [ə'læskə]
Alaska Range [ə'læskə reɪndʒ]
⟨Alicante⟩ [ˌælɪ'kæntɪ]
Alice Springs ['ælɪs 'sprɪŋz]
the **Alps** [ælps]
Ambleside ['æmblsaɪd]
America [ə'merɪkə]
Antarctica [ænt'ɑ:ktɪkə]
⟨Arizona⟩ [ˌærɪ'zəʊnə]
Arkansas River ['ɑ:kənsɔ: ˌrɪvə]
Asia ['eɪʃə]
Athens ['æθɪnz]
Australia [ɒ'streɪljə]
⟨Ayers Rock⟩ [eəz 'rɒk]
Baker Street ['beɪkə ˌstri:t]
The **Bakerloo Line** [ðə ˌbeɪkə'lu: ˌlaɪn]
⟨Battle⟩ ['bætl]
Bayeux [baɪ'jɜ:]
Belfast [ˌbel'fɑ:st]
Belgium ['beldʒəm]
Ben Nevis [ˌben 'nevɪs]
Berlin [bɜ:'lɪn]
Big Ben [ˌbɪg 'ben]
The **Big Apple** [ðə ˌbɪg 'æpl]
Birmingham ['bɜ:mɪŋəm]
Bollin Valley [ˌbɒlɪn 'vælɪ]
Bondi Beach ['bɒndaɪ ˌbi:tʃ]
⟨Brandon⟩ ['brændən]
Brisbane ['brɪzbən]
Britain ['brɪtn]
Great **Britain** [ˌgreɪt 'brɪtn]
the **British Isles** [ðə ˌbrɪtɪʃ‿'aɪlz]
Broad Haven ['brɔ:d heɪvn]
the **Bronx** [ðə 'brɒŋks]
Brooklyn ['brʊklɪn]
Buckingham Palace [ˌbʌkɪŋəm 'pælɪs]
Caerleon [kɑ:'li:ən]
Cairns [keənz]
California [ˌkælɪ'fɔ:njə]
Camden Market [ˌkæmdən 'mɑ:kɪt]
Camelot ['kæmɪlɒt]
Cardiff ['kɑ:dɪf]
The **Caribbean** [ðə ˌkærɪ'bi:ən]
Castleton ['kɑ:sltən]
Central Park [ˌsentrl 'pɑ:k]
Channel Tunnel ['tʃænl 'tʌnl]
Chelsea ['tʃelsɪ]
Chester ['tʃestə]
Chicago [ʃi:'kɑ:gəʊ]
China ['tʃaɪnə]
Chinatown ['tʃaɪnəˌtaʊn]
The **Circle Line** [ðə 'sɜ:kl ˌlaɪn]
Colorado [ˌkɒlə'rɑ:dəʊ]
Conway ['kɒnweɪ]
Cornwall ['kɔ:nwəl]
Covent Garden [ˌkɒvənt 'gɑ:dn]
Coventry ['kɒvəntrɪ]
Cowden ['kaʊden]
⟨Darling Downs⟩ [ˌdɑ:lɪŋ 'daʊnz]
[Darwin] ['dɑ:wɪn]
Denali [de'nɑ:lɪ]
Denmark ['denmɑ:k]
Denver ['denvə]
Dover ['dəʊvə]
Druidston ['dru:ɪdstən]
Dungog ['dʌngɒg]
East Cheam [ˌi:st 'tʃi:m]
Edinburgh ['edɪnbrə]
Elf Row [ˌelf 'rəʊ]
⟨Ely⟩ [i:lɪ]
England ['ɪŋglənd]
Europe ['jʊərəp]
Everglades ['evəgleɪdz]
Fishguard ['fɪʃgɑ:d]
Florida ['flɒrɪdə]
Fort William [ˌfɔ:t 'wɪljəm]
France [frɑ:ns]
⟨Georgina country⟩ [dʒɔ:'dʒi:nə ˌkʌntrɪ]
Germany ['dʒɜ:mənɪ]
Glenarm [glen'ɑ:m]
Golden ['gəʊldən]
Grand Canyon [ˌgrænd 'kænjən]
Great Barrier Reef [ˌgreɪt bærɪə 'ri:f]
Greece [gri:s]
Greenwich Village [ˌgrenɪdʒ 'vɪlɪdʒ]
Grovers Mill [ˌgrəʊvəz 'mɪl]
Harlem ['hɑ:ləm]
Harrod's ['hærədz]
Hastings ['heɪstɪŋs]
Hawaii [hə'waɪi:]
Heathrow [ˌhi:θ'rəʊ]
Holyhead ['hɒlɪhed]
The **Houses of Parliament** [ðə ˌhaʊzɪz‿əv 'pɑ:ləmənt]
Hull [hʌl]

Humberside [ˈhʌmbəsaɪd]
Hyde Park [ˌhaɪd ˈpɑːk]
India [ˈɪndjə]
Northern Ireland [ˈnɔːθən‿ˈaɪələnd]
the Republic of Ireland [ðə rɪˌpʌblɪk‿ɒv‿ˈaɪələnd]
Isle of Wight [ˌaɪl‿əv ˈwaɪt]
Issaquah [ˈɪzəˌkwɑː]
Istanbul [ˌɪstænˈbʊl]
Italy [ˈɪtəlɪ]
Jamaica [dʒəˈmeɪkə]
Japan [dʒəˈpæn]
Kakadu [ˈkækədu:]
Kansas [ˈkænzəs]
Kings Canyon [ˌkɪŋz ˈkænjən]
Korea [kəˈrɪə]
Lake District [ˈleɪk ˌdɪstrɪkt]
Lake View Drive [ˌleɪk vju: ˈdraɪv]
Lake Windermere [ˌleɪk ˈwɪndəˌmɪə]
Latin America [ˌlætɪn əˈmerɪkə]
Leeds [li:dz]
Leicester [ˈlestə]
Leicester Square [ˌlestə ˈskweə]
Little Italy [ˌlɪtl ˈɪtəlɪ]
Little Ukraine [ˌlɪtl ju:ˈkreɪn]
Loch Lomond [lɒk ˈləʊmənd]
Loch Ness [lɒk ˈnes]
London [ˈlʌndən]
London Bridge [ˌlʌndən ˈbrɪdʒ]
London Zoo [ˌlʌndən ˈzu:]
The **London Dungeon** [ðə ˌlʌndən ˈdʌnʒən]
Luton [ˈlu:tn]
Madame Tussaud's [ˌmædəm təˈsɔ:dz]
Malham [ˈmæləm]
Malibu [ˈmælɪbʊ]
Manchester [ˈmæntʃɪstə]
Manhattan [mænˈhætn]
Melbourne [ˈmelbən]
Mesa Verde [ˌmesə ˈvɜdɪ]
The **Metropolitan Line** [ðə ˌmetrəˈpɒlɪtən ˌlaɪn]
Mexico [ˈmeksɪkəʊ]
Middlesex [ˈmɪdlseks]
Milford Haven [ˌmɪlfəd ˈheɪvn]
Mississippi [ˌmɪsɪˈsɪpɪ]
Mt. McKinley [ˌmaʊnt məˈkɪnlɪ]
Mt. Rainier [ˌmaʊnt reɪˈnɪər]
Museum of the Moving Image [mju:ˌzɪəm‿əv‿ðə ˌmu:vɪŋ‿ɪmɪdʒ]
Neasden [ˈni:zdən]
Nebraska [nɪˈbræskə]
The **Netherlands** [ðə ˈneðələndz]
New Holland [nju: ˈhɒlənd]
New Jersey [nju: ˈdʒɜ:zɪ]
New South Wales [ˌnju: saʊθ ˈweɪlz]
New York [ˌnju: ˈjɔ:k]
New York City [ˌnju: ˈjɔ:k sɪtɪ]
New Zealand [ˌnju: ˈzi:lənd]
Newstead Abbey [ˌnju:stɪd‿ˈæbɪ]
Nolton Haven [ˌnɒltən ˈheɪvn]
Normandy [ˈnɔ:məndɪ]
North Sea [ˌnɔ:θ ˈsi:]
Northallerton [nɔ:ˈθælətən]
Northumberland [nɔ:ˈθʌmbələnd]
Norway [ˈnɔ:weɪ]
Notting Hill Gate [ˌnɒtɪŋhɪl ˈgeɪt]
Nottingham [ˈnɒtɪŋəm]
Oz [ɒz]
Pacific Northwest [pəˌsɪfɪk nɔ:θˈwest]
Paddington [ˈpædɪŋtən]
Pakistan [ˌpɑ:kɪˈstɑ:n]
Paris [ˈpærɪs]
Peak District [ˈpi:k ˌdɪstrɪkt]
Perth [pɜ:θ]
Piccadilly Circus [ˌpɪkəˈdɪlɪ ˈsɜ:kəs]
The **Piccadilly Line** [ðə ˌpɪkəˈdɪlɪ ˌlaɪn]
Pike [paɪk]
Pittsburgh [ˈpɪtsbɜ:g]
Poland [ˈpəʊlənd]
Puerto Rico [ˈpwɜ:təʊ ˈri:kəʊ]
Queens [kwi:nz]
Queensland [ˈkwi:nzlənd]
Regent's Park [ˌri:dʒənts ˈpɑ:k]
The **River Thames** [ðə ˌrɪvə ˈtemz]
⟨Riverina⟩ [ˈrɪvəri:nə]
Rock Circus [ˌrɒk ˈsɜ:kəs]
Roman Wall [ˌrəʊmən ˈwɔ:l]
Rotterdam [ˌrɒtəˈdæm]
Royal Gorge [ˌrɔɪəl ˈgɔ:dʒ]
Ruislip [ˈraɪslɪp]
Russia [ˈrʌʃə]
⟨San Antonio⟩ [ˌsænænˈtəʊnɪəʊ]
Scarborough [ˈskɑ:brə]
Scotland [ˈskɒtlənd]
Seattle [sɪˈætl]
Sequoia [sɪˈkwɔɪə]
Shadwell [ˈʃædwəl]
Shenandoah [ˌʃenənˈdəʊə]
Sherwood [ˈʃɜ:wʊd]
Siberia [saɪˈbɪərɪə]
Skegness [skegˈnes]
Snoqualmie Falls [snəʊˌkwɑ:lmɪ ˈfɔ:lz]
Snowdon [ˈsnəʊdn]
Snowdonia [snəʊˈdəʊnjə]
South Africa [ˌsaʊθ‿ˈæfrɪkə]
Spain [speɪn]
Speaker's Corner [ˌspi:kəz ˈkɔ:nə]
Spokane [spɒˈkæn]
Staten Island [ˌstætn‿ˈaɪlənd]
Stratford [ˈstrætfəd]
Suquamish [sʊˈkwɑ:mɪʃ]
Surfers Paradise [ˌsɜ:fəz ˈpærədaɪs]
Swansea [ˈswɒnzɪ]
Switzerland [ˈswɪtsələnd]
Sydney [ˈsɪdnɪ]
Tasmania [tæzˈmeɪnjə]
Tenby [ˈtenbɪ]
⟨Texas⟩ [ˈteksəs]
⟨Thailand⟩ [taɪlænd]
⟨the Fens⟩ [ðə ˈfenz]
Thessalonica [ˌθesələˈnaɪkə]
Times Square [ˌtaɪmz ˈskweə]
Tonga [ˈtɒŋgə]
The **Tower of London** [ðə ˌtaʊər‿əv ˈlʌndən]
Tower Bridge [ˌtaʊə ˈbrɪdʒ]
Tower Hill [ˌtaʊə ˈhɪl]
Trafalgar Square [trəˈfælgə ˈskweə]
Trinidad [ˈtrɪnɪdæd]
Truro [ˈtrʊərəʊ]
Turkey [ˈtɜ:kɪ]
The **UK** (= **The United Kingdom**) [ju: ˈkeɪ = ju:ˈnaɪtɪd ˈkɪŋdəm]
USA (= **United States of America, US**) [ˌju:esˈeɪ = ju:ˈnaɪtɪd steɪts‿əv‿əˈmerɪkə, ˌju: ˈes]
Vietnam [ˌvjetˈnæm]
Virginia [vəˈdʒɪnjə]
WA (= **Washington**) [ˈdʌblju: eɪ = ˈwɒʃɪŋtən]
Wales [weɪlz]
Waterloo Bridge [ˌwɔ:təlu: ˈbrɪdʒ]
Waterloo Station [ˌwɔ:təlu: ˈsteɪʃn]
The **West Indies** [ðə ˌwest‿ˈɪndɪz]
Westminster Abbey [ˌwestmɪnstər‿ˈæbɪ]

Wigston ['wɪgstən]
York [jɔ:k]
Yorkshire ['jɔ:kʃə]
Yorkshire Dales [ˌjɔ:kʃə 'deɪlz]
Yorkshire Moors [ˌjɔ:kʃə 'mɔ:z]
Yorkshire Wolds [ˌjɔ:kʃə 'wəʊldz]
Yosemite [jəʊ'semɪtɪ]

Other names

1015 [ˌten fɪf'ti:n]
Alton Towers [ˌɔ:ltən 'taʊəz]
American Adventure Centre [ə'merɪkən əd'ventʃə 'sentə]
the **Angles and Saxons** [ˌðɪ ˌæŋglz‿ən 'sæksnz]
Animal Aid ['ænɪml ˌeɪd]
Apple Tours [æpl 'tɔ:z]
Arty ['ɑ:tɪ]
Asterix ['æstərɪks]
⟨Bad as I wanna be⟩ [bæd‿əz aɪ 'wʌnə bɪ]
⟨Bancroft's⟩ ['bænkrɒfts]
Batman ['bætmæn]
⟨Battle Abbey⟩ ['bætl ˌæbɪ]
Beowulf ['beɪəʊwʊlf]
Big Wheel [ˌbɪg 'wi:l]
Bill Neidje [bɪl 'ni:dʒə]
Blackpool Pleasure Beach ['blækpu:l ˌpleʒə bi:tʃ]
All **Blacks** [ˌɔ:l 'blæks]
⟨Brent field⟩ [brent 'fi:ld]
⟨Brent Spar⟩ [brent 'spɑ:]
The **British Library** [ðə ˌbrɪtɪʃ 'laɪbrərɪ]
The **British Museum** [ðə ˌbrɪtɪʃ mju:'zɪəm]
Broadway ['brɔ:dweɪ]
° **BTEC diploma** ['bi:tek dɪ'pləʊmə]
Bugs Bunny [ˌbʌgz 'bʌnɪ]
Camelot ['kæmɪlɒt]
Captain Cook [ˌkæptɪn 'kʊk]
Captain Courage [ˌkæptɪn 'kʌrɪdʒ]
CBS (= **Columbia Broadcasting System**) [si: bi: 'es]
Charlie Brown [tʃɑ:lɪ 'braʊn]
Charlie Chaplin ['tʃɑ:lɪ 'tʃæplɪn]
Chicago Bulls [ʃɪ'kɑ:gəʊ 'bʊlz]
Christopher Columbus ['krɪstəfə kə'lʌmbəs]
Columbus [kə'lʌmbəs]
Commando [kə'mɑ:ndəʊ]
Crocodile Dundee ['krɒkədaɪl dʌnˌdi:]
3D Ultralite [ˌθri:‿di: 'ʌltrəlaɪt]
Daily News ['deɪlɪ ˌnju:z]
Denise Lewis [dəˌni:z 'lu:ɪs]
⟨Dennis Rodman⟩ [denɪs 'rɒdmən]
Double Quick ['dʌbl ˌkwɪk]
Dracula ['drækjʊlə]
Edward I [ˌedwəd ðə 'fɜ:st]
Edward the Confessor ['edwəd ðə ˌkɒnfesə]
⟨Elbow gallery⟩ ['elbəʊ ˌgælərɪ]
the **Empire State Building** [ˌempaɪə 'steɪt ˌbɪldɪŋ]
Eurostar ['jʊərəʊˌstɑ:]
Factcenter ['fæktˌsentə]
Food Court ['fu:d ˌkɔ:t]
Friar Tuck [ˌfraɪə 'tʌk]
Friends of the Earth ['frendz‿əv ðɪ ˌɜ:θ]
Gala apples ['gɑ:lə]
General Grant Tree [ˌdʒenrl ˌgrɑ:nt 'tri:]
Gilman Village [ˌgɪlmən 'vɪlɪdʒ]
Goose Fair ['gu:s feə]
The **Great Spirit** [ðə greɪt 'spɪrɪt]
⟨Greenpeace⟩ ['gri:nˌpi:s]
Greenwood ['gri:nwʊd]
Guy Fawkes [gaɪ 'fɔ:ks]
H. G. Wells [eɪtʃ dʒi: 'welz]
Harald Hardraada [hærəld 'hɑ:drɑ:də]
Harbour Bridge ['hɑ:bə ˌbrɪdʒ]
the **Hard Rock Café** [ˌhɑ:d rɒk‿'kæfeɪ]
Harold Godwineson [hærəld 'gɒdwɪnsən]
Haywood School ['heɪwʊd 'sku:l]
Hotel Park Plaza [həʊ'tel ˌpɑ:k 'plɑ:zə]
Hydro [ˌhaɪdrə]
IHS (= **Issaquah High School**) [ˌaɪ‿eɪtʃ‿'es = 'ɪzəˌkwɑ: 'haɪ sku:l]
the **International District** [ˌɪntə'næʃənl 'dɪstrɪkt]
The **Jackals** [ðə 'dʒækɔ:lz]
James Bond [ˌdʒeɪmz 'bɒnd]
James Cook [dʒeɪmz kʊk]
James Watt [dʒeɪmz 'wɒt]
Jan Mark ['dʒæn ˌmɑ:k]
Jeff Pitt [ˌdʒef 'pɪt]
Jill North [ˌðʒɪl 'nɔ:θ]
Jimi Hendrix [ˌdʒɪmɪ 'hendrɪks]
Jo Lawson [ˌdʒəʊ 'lɔ:sn]
John Lennon [dʒɒn 'lenən]
⟨Johnson coal mine⟩ ['dʒɒnsn 'kəʊl ˌmaɪn]
the **Joker** [ðə 'dʒəʊkə]
Kermit ['kɜ:mɪt]
King Arthur [ˌkɪŋ 'ɑ:θə]
King's Park ['kɪŋz ˌpɑ:k]
⟨Kurtis Blow⟩ [kɜ:rtɪs 'bləʊ]
Lake Sammamish [ˌleɪk sə'mæmɪʃ]
Lance [lɑ:ns]
Lancelot ['lɑ:nsəlɒt]
Lincoln Center [ˌlɪŋkən 'sentə]
Lois Lane [ˌləʊɪs 'leɪn]
Londoner ['lʌndənə]
⟨Lucky⟩ ['lʌkɪ]
M6 [ˌem 'sɪks]
Madison Avenue [ˌmædɪsən 'ævənju:]
London **Marathon** ['lʌndən ˌmærəθn]
Mars [mɑ:z]
Mercury Theater of the Air ['mɜ:kjʊrɪ θɪ'etər‿əv ðɪ‿'eə]
Meridian Room [mə'rɪdɪən ˌru:m]
Midnight Oil ['mɪdnaɪt ˌɔɪl]
Miss Piggy [mɪs 'pɪgɪ]
⟨Moses⟩ ['məʊzɪz]
⟨NBA (= National Basketball Association)⟩ [en bi: 'eɪ]
Norman ['nɔ:mən]
The **Odeon** [ðɪ 'əʊdjən]
Opera House ['ɒprə ˌhaʊs]
Orson Welles [ˌɔ:sn 'welz]
Oxford Street [ˌɒksfəd 'stri:t]
Pablo Garc ĭa [ˌpʌbləʊ gɑ:'si:ə]
⟨Pam Ayres⟩ [pæm 'eəz]
the **Pike Place Market** [paɪk pleɪs 'mɑ:kɪt]
the **Pilgrims** [ðə 'pɪlgrɪmz]
Pioneer Square [paɪəˌnɪə 'skweə]
Plaza Hotel [ˌplɑ:zə həʊ'tel]
Princeton Observatory [ˌprɪnstən əb'zɜ:vətrɪ]
Pug [pʌg]
Pugwacket ['pʌgwækɪt]
the **Queen** [ðə 'kwi:n]
Rainier Road [ˌreɪni:ər 'rəʊd]
Ramon Raquello [ræmɒn 'rækeləʊ]
red-eye flight (*AE*) ['red‿aɪ‿flaɪt]
⟨Rigby Road⟩ [ˌrɪgbɪ 'rəʊd]
Ringo Starr [rɪŋəʊ 'stɑ:]
Robin Hood ['rɒbɪn 'hʊd]
The **Romans** [ˌðə 'rəʊmənz]
The **Round Table** [ðə ˌraʊnd 'teɪbl]
⟨Shell⟩ [ʃel]
Sherlock Holmes [ˌʃɜ:lɒk 'həʊmz]
⟨Shetland⟩ ['ʃetlənd]
⟨Shetland pony⟩ ['ʃetlənd ˌpəʊnɪ]

Sioux [su:]
Sizz [ˈsɪz]
Skyline Drive [ˌskaɪlaɪn ˈdraɪv]
The **Sonics** (= **The Seattle Supersonics**) [ˌdə ˈsɒnɪks]
the **Space Needle** [ðə ˈspeɪs ˌni:dl]
Spiderman [ˈspaɪdəmæn]
St Paul's Cathedral [sənt ˌpɔ:lz kəˈθi:drəl]
St. John's School [snt ˈdʒɒnz ˌsku:l]
⟨Sticks and stones⟩ [ˌstɪks‿ən ˈstəʊnz]
Superbowl [ˈsu:pəbəʊl]
Superman [ˈsu:pəmæn]
⟨Swallow⟩ [ˈswɒləʊ]
The **Taj Mahal Restaurant** [ðə ˌtʌdʒ məˈhɑ:l ˈrestərɒnt]
Taplow High [ˈtæpˌləʊ haɪ]
the (Botanical) Gardens [ðə bəˈtænɪkl ˈgɑ:dnz]
The Australian Open [ðɪ ɒˌstreɪljən ˈaʊpən]
The Bayeux Tapestry [ðə baɪˈjɜ: ˈtæpɪstrɪ]
The British Empire [ˈempaɪə]
⟨The Christian Science Monitor⟩ [ðə ˈkrɪstʃən saɪəns ˌmɒnɪtə]
Thunder Looper [ˌθʌndə ˈlu:pə]
Tricky situations [ˈtrɪkɪ ˌsɪtjʊˈeɪʃnz]
Trocadero [ˌtrɒkəˈdɪərəʊ]
Twycross zoo [ˈtwaɪkrɒs ˈzu:]
⟨UNICEF⟩ [ˈju:nɪsef]
Walker Colt [ˌwɔ:kə ˈkəʊlt]
Walt Disney [wɔ:lt ˈdɪznɪ]
Wembley Stadium [ˌwemblɪ ˈsteɪdjəm]
Wild West [waɪld ˈwest]
William the Conqueror [ˌwɪljəm ðə ˈkɒŋkərə]
Wimbledon [ˈwɪmbldən]
Winchester [ˈwɪnʃɪstə]
World Cup [ˌwɜ:ld ˈkʌp]
the **World Trade Center** [wɜ:ld ˈtreɪd ˌsentə]
Worldfest [wɜ:ldˈfest]
Yothu Yindi [ˈjɒtu: ˌjɪndɪ]
Ziontree [ˈzaɪəntrɪ]

IRREGULAR VERBS

infinitive	simple past	past participle	German
be [bi:]	was [wɒz]	been [bi:n]	sein
beat [bi:t]	beat [bi:t]	beat [bi:t]	schlagen
become [bɪ'kʌm]	became [bɪ'keɪm]	become [bɪ'kʌm]	werden
begin [bɪ'gɪn]	began [bɪ'gæn]	begun [bɪ'gʌn]	beginnen
bend [bend]	bent [bent]	bent [bent]	(sich) bücken, biegen
blow [bləʊ]	blew [blu:]	blown [bləʊn]	blasen
bring [brɪŋ]	brought [brɔ:t]	brought [brɔ:t]	bringen
build [bɪld]	built [bɪlt]	built [bɪlt]	bauen
burn [bɜ:n]	burnt [bɜ:nt]	burnt [bɜ:nt]	brennen
buy [baɪ]	bought [bɔ:t]	bought [bɔ:t]	kaufen
catch [kætʃ]	caught [kɔ:t]	caught [kɔ:t]	fangen
choose [tʃu:z]	chose [tʃəʊz]	chosen ['tʃəʊzn]	auswählen
come [kʌm]	came [keɪm]	come [kʌm]	kommen
cost [kɒst]	cost [kɒst]	cost [kɒst]	kosten
cut [kʌt]	cut [kʌt]	cut [kʌt]	schneiden
dig [dɪg]	dug [dʌg]	dug [dʌg]	graben
do [du:]	did [dɪd]	done [dʌn]	machen, tun
draw [drɔ:]	drew [dru:]	drawn [drɔ:n]	zeichnen, ziehen
drink [drɪŋk]	drank [dræŋk]	drunk [drʌŋk]	trinken
drive [draɪv]	drove [drəʊv]	driven ['drɪvn]	fahren; antreiben
eat [i:t]	ate [et]	eaten ['i:tn]	essen
fall [fɔ:l]	fell [fel]	fallen ['fɔ:ln]	fallen
feed [fi:d]	fed [fed]	fed [fed]	füttern
feel [fi:l]	felt [felt]	felt [felt]	fühlen
fight [faɪt]	fought [fɔ:t]	fought [fɔ:t]	kämpfen
find [faɪnd]	found [faʊnd]	found [faʊnd]	finden
fly [flaɪ]	flew [flu:]	flown [fləʊn]	fliegen
forget [fə'get]	forgot [fə'gɒt]	forgotten [fə'gɒtn]	vergessen
get [get]	got [gɒt]	got [gɒt]	holen, bekommen
give [gɪv]	gave [geɪv]	given ['gɪvn]	geben
go [gəʊ]	went [went]	gone [gɒn]	gehen
grow [grəʊ]	grew [gru:]	grown [grəʊn]	(an)pflanzen, wachsen
hang [hæŋ]	hung [hʌŋ]	hung [hʌŋ]	hängen
have [hæv]	had [hæd]	had [hæd]	haben
hear [hɪə]	heard [hɜ:d]	heard [hɜ:d]	hören
hide [haɪd]	hid [hɪd]	hidden ['hɪdn]	(sich) verstecken
hit [hɪt]	hit [hɪt]	hit [hɪt]	schlagen, treffen
hold [həʊld]	held [held]	held [held]	halten
hurt [hɜ:t]	hurt [hɜ:t]	hurt [hɜ:t]	verletzen, weh tun
keep [ki:p]	kept [kept]	kept [kept]	(be)halten
know [nəʊ]	knew [nju:]	known [nəʊn]	wissen, kennen
lay [leɪ]	laid [leɪd]	laid [leɪd]	legen
lead [li:d]	led [led]	led [led]	führen
learn [lɜ:n]	learned [lɜ:nt], learnt [lɜ:nt]	learned [lɜ:nt], learnt [lɜ:nt]	lernen
leave [li:v]	left [left]	left [left]	(ver)lassen

infinitive	simple past	past participle	German
lend [lend]	lent [lent]	lent [lent]	(ver)leihen
let [let]	let [let]	let [let]	lassen
lie [laɪ]	lay [leɪ]	lain [leɪn]	liegen
lose [lu:z]	lost [lɒst]	lost [lɒst]	verlieren
make [meɪk]	made [meɪd]	made [meɪd]	machen
mean [mi:n]	meant [ment]	meant [ment]	bedeuten
meet [mi:t]	met [met]	met [met]	treffen, begegnen
pay [peɪ]	paid [peɪd]	paid [peɪd]	zahlen, bezahlen
put [pʊt]	put [pʊt]	put [pʊt]	setzen, stellen, legen
read [ri:d]	read [red]	read [red]	lesen
ring [rɪŋ]	rang [ræŋ]	rung [rʌŋ]	klingeln, anrufen
ride [raɪd]	rode [rəʊd]	ridden ['rɪdn]	reiten, fahren
rise [raɪz]	rose [rəʊz]	risen ['rɪzn]	aufstehen
run [rʌn]	ran [ræn]	run [rʌn]	laufen, rennen
say [seɪ]	said [sed]	said [sed]	sagen
see [si:]	saw [sɔ:]	seen [si:n]	sehen
sell [sel]	sold [səʊld]	sold [səʊld]	verkaufen
send [send]	sent [sent]	sent [sent]	schicken, senden
shake [ʃeɪk]	shook [ʃʊk]	shaken [ʃeɪkn]	schütteln, zittern
shoot [ʃu:t]	shot [ʃɒt]	shot [ʃɒt]	schießen
show [ʃəʊ]	showed [ʃəʊd]	shown [ʃəʊn]	zeigen
sing [sɪŋ]	sang [sæŋ]	sung [sʌŋ]	singen
sit [sɪt]	sat [sæt]	sat [sæt]	sitzen
sleep [sli:p]	slept [slept]	slept [slept]	schlafen
smell [smel]	smelt [smelt]	smelt [smelt]	riechen
speak [spi:k]	spoke [spəʊk]	spoken ['spəʊkn]	sprechen
spell [spel]	spelled [spelt], spelt [spelt]	spelled [spelt], spelt [spelt]	buchstabieren
spend [spend]	spent [spent]	spent [spent]	ausgeben, verbringen
spin [spɪn]	span [spæn]	spun [spʌn]	spinnen; drehen
spread [spred]	spread [spred]	spread [spred]	ausbreiten, verbreiten
stand [stænd]	stood [stʊd]	stood [stʊd]	stehen
steal [sti:l]	stole [stəʊl]	stolen ['stəʊlən]	stehlen
swear [sweə]	swore [swɔ:]	sworn [swɔ:n]	schwören, fluchen
swim [swɪm]	swam [swæm]	swum [swʌm]	schwimmen
take [teɪk]	took [tʊk]	taken ['teɪkn]	nehmen, bringen
teach [ti:tʃ]	taught [tɔ:t]	taught [tɔ:t]	lehren
tell [tel]	told [təʊld]	told [təʊld]	erzählen, sagen
think [θɪnk]	thought [θɔ:t]	thought [θɔ:t]	denken
throw [θrəʊ]	threw [θru:]	thrown [θrəʊn]	werfen
understand [ˌʌndə'stænd]	understood [ˌʌndə'stʊd]	understood [ˌʌndə'stʊd]	verstehen
wake [weɪk]	woke [wəʊk]	woken ['wəʊkn]	wecken, aufwachen
wear [weə]	wore [wɔ:]	worn [wɔ:n]	tragen (Kleidung)
win [wɪn]	won [wʌn]	won [wʌn]	gewinnen
write [raɪt]	wrote [rəʊt]	written ['rɪtn]	schreiben

⟨CLASSROOM PHRASES⟩

Arriving and leaving

I'm sorry I'm late.	Tut mir Leid, dass ich mich verspätet habe.
I've forgotten my exercise book.	Ich habe mein Heft vergessen.
What's for homework?	Was haben wir als Hausaufgabe auf?
See you next time.	Bis zum nächsten Mal.
Have a nice weekend.	Schönes Wochenende!

If there is a problem ...

Are you feeling OK?	Ist alles in Ordnung?
I'm fine, thank you.	Gut, danke.
What's the matter with you?	Was fehlt dir denn?
I'm not feeling well.	Ich fühle mich nicht gut.
I've got a headache.	Ich habe Kopfweh.

Asking for help

What do we have to do?	Was müssen wir denn machen?
What's that in English/German?	Was heißt das auf Englisch/Deutsch?
Can I say: ...?/What does ... mean?	Kann ich sagen: ...?/Was bedeutet ...?
How do you do this exercise?	Wie macht man diese Übung?
Did you understand what he/she said?	Hast du verstanden, was er/sie sagte?
No, I didn't understand it either.	Nein, ich habe das auch nicht verstanden.
Could you write it on the board, please?	Könnten Sie das bitte an die Tafel schreiben?
Sorry? Can you repeat the question/ sentence, please?	Wie bitte? Können Sie die Frage/den Satz bitte wiederholen?
Can you play the cassette again, please?	Können Sie die Kassette bitte nochmal abspielen?
Could you play it with pauses, please?	Könnten Sie sie bitte mit Pausen abspielen?
Can we do another example, please?	Können wir noch ein Beispiel machen?

Working together

Do we do this in groups/with partners?	Machen wir dies in Gruppen-/Partnerarbeit?
Whose turn is it?	Wer ist dran?
What are we going to do first?	Was machen wir als Erstes?
Who is going to write down our results?	Wer schreibt unsere Ergebnisse auf?
I'd like to present our results.	Ich möchte unsere Ergebnisse vorstellen.

Working at a computer

My computer has crashed.	Mein Rechner ist abgestürzt.
I can't understand this message on the screen.	Ich verstehe diese Meldung auf dem Bildschirm nicht.
It won't accept my username/password.	Mein Benutzername/Kennwort wird nicht angenommen.
What's the website address ?	Wie ist die Internet-Adresse für diese Seite(n)?
Which option shall I click on?	Auf welches Feld soll ich klicken?
What am I supposed to type in here?	Was soll ich hier eintippen?
I have saved it on disk.	Ich habe es auf Diskette gespeichert.

Talking about stories, poems, songs, ...

I liked/didn't like the story.	Diese Geschichte gefiel mir/gefiel mir nicht.
I thought it was brilliant/interesting/ funny/really exciting.	Ich fand sie toll/interessant/ witzig/wirklich spannend.
I thought it was sad/terrible/boring.	Ich fand sie traurig/schrecklich/langweilig.
It was OK, but I've read better ones.	Sie war OK, aber ich habe schon bessere gelesen.
I enjoyed it very much.	Ich habe sie gern gelesen/gehört/gesehen.
It was hard to follow.	Sie war schwer verständlich.
There wasn't much action in the story.	Es passierte nicht viel in der Geschichte.
The ending was unexpected/predictable.	Der Schluß war unerwartet/vorauszusagen.
The main/minor characters ...	Die Haupt-/Nebenfiguren ...
The plot/setting/theme ...	Die Handlung/der Schauplatz/das Thema ...
What is the writer/poet trying to tell us?	Was will uns der Autor/Dichter damit sagen?
I like the music but the words aren't very original.	Ich finde die Musik gut, aber der Text ist nicht besonders originell.

Having a discussion ...

What do you think?	Was meinst du?
I disagree.	Ich bin anderer Meinung.
In my opinion ...	Meiner Meinung nach .../Meines Erachtens ...
I can see your point, but ...	Ich verstehe dein Argument, aber ...
I think you are right/wrong.	Ich denke, du hast Recht/Unrecht.
That's one way of looking at it.	So kann man's auch sehen.
I don't follow you.	Ich verstehe nicht, was du meinst.
On the one hand ..., on the other hand ...	Einerseits ..., andererseits ...
I don't think that's relevant.	Das finde ich nicht wichtig.

What the teacher might say to you

Let's have a look at the text on page	Schlagt bitte Seite ... auf.
Please turn to page	Bitte blättert auf Seite ... um.
I'd like someone to write the answers on a transparency.	Ich brauche jemanden, der die Lösungen auf eine Folie schreibt.
You're going to hear the recording twice.	Ihr werdet die Aufnahme zweimal hören.
Would you collect the exercise books/ worksheets, please?	Würdest du bitte die Übungshefte/Arbeitsblätter einsammeln?
Do this exercise for homework.	Macht diese Übung als Hausaufgabe.
Try to find some more information about this topic on the Internet.	Versuch/Versucht, weitere Informationen über dieses Thema im Internet zu finden.
Please speak up.	Sprich bitte lauter.
No prompting, please.	Nicht vorsagen, bitte.
Please don't interrupt him/her.	Bitte unterbrich ihn/sie nicht.
Let him/her finish.	Lass ihn/sie ausreden.
Excellent!/Spot on!	Prima! Genau richtig!
Not quite. Think again.	Nicht ganz richtig. Denk nochmal nach.
Have another go.	Versuch es noch einmal.

Bildquellen:

Cover: Mauritius - Weyer
p. 7: Mauritius - Kerscher (Tricia); Mauritius - Westlight (Sydney); Mauritius - SST (Surfie); Medford Taylor/NGM (dingo fence)
p. 8: J. Carnemoll/ZEFA-APL (outback with cattle); Rogan Coles/Redferns (Yothu Yindi); Mauritius (shark); Klein & Hubert (Koala); Murray View, Gympie, Queensland (crocodile)
p. 14: Mauritius - Age (diving on the Barrier Reef)
p. 17: Okapia(bird)
p. 19: Mary Evans Picture Library (raising of the British flag at Sydney)
p. 20: Erica Macmillan, Sutton Coldfield (Save the children shop); Department for Education and Employment © Crown Copyright (scene at a Job Centre); Sally and Richard Greenhill (mechanics with spraypainting machine); Rene Burri/ Magnum/Focus (child labour); dpa (film crew)
p. 21: dpa (Anke Huber signing autographs); Jürgen Kleine, Ammerbuch (teenagers cleaning stable)
p. 22: Mauritius - Kupka (window dresser)
p. 24: Senta Herkle, Hochberg (passport photo of a teenage girl)
p. 27: Jürgen Kleine, Ammerbuch (Martin on phone; Heather on phone)
p. 28: Mauritius Superstock (teenage girl); Sally and Richard Greenhill (teenage boy; teenage girl); Sally and Richard Greenhill (teenage girl); Michael Mattison, Stuttgart (Jeff Pitt); Jürgen Kleine, Ammerbuch (Martin on the phone; Heather on the phone)
p. 29: Erica Macmillan, Sutton Coldfield (Chinese supermarket)
p. 31: PhotoDisk (business woman)
p. 32: Tony Stone-Nigel Dickinson (rainforest Guatemala)
p. 33: Greenpeace (environmental protest); Jürgen Kleine, Ammerbuch (Stella and Carrie)
p. 35: PhotoDisk (solar panels, coal mine, hydroelectric power station, wind turbines); Mauritius - ACE (nuclear power station); Tony Stone (oil rig under construction);
p. 36: PA News Photo Library (Bollin Valley protest camp)
p. 42: Mauritius - C. Bayer (teenage boy); Mauritius-Mitterer (teenage boy)
p. 46: J. Allan Cash Ltd., London (White Tower)
p. 49: Klett-Archiv (Bayeux Tapestry)
p. 50: dpa (Heptathlete Denise Lewis); Mauritius - AGE (teenage girls); Mauritius - Nitz (girl with purses); Sony (discman); Mauritius - Fact (go-cart)
p. 51: Mauritius - Hubatka (teenage girl); J. Allan Cash Ltd., London (Selfridges); Jürgen Kleine, Ammerbuch (party scene)
p. 53: Topham Picturepoint, Edenbridge (Blackpool Pleasure Beach)
p. 62: Bridgeman Art Library, London (cotton hand spinning); Mansell Collection, London (children working in a factory)
p. 63: The Royal Collection (view of Manchester by Wyld)
p. 65: Mary Evans Picture Library, London (slum scene)
p. 66: Mary Evans Picture Library, London (boy carrying heavy wet clay)
p. 68: A. Compost/BIOS/Okapia (dingo)
p. 69: NAS/T. McHugh/Okapia (group of dingoes)
p. 70: dpa (Queen Elizabeth II visiting India)
p. 71: Robert Harding Picture Library (Pavlova)
p. 76: Mary Evans Picture Library, London (mining scenes)
p. 78: Greenpeace - Sims (Greenpeace boat); J. Allan Cash Ltd., London (newsreader)
p. 81: Bridgeman Art Library, London (scenes from Bayeux Tapestry)
p. 83: Laima Druskis/Stock, Boston/PNI (African American boy with radio). Steve Hopkins/Black Star/PNI (breakdancer); Musik&Show (rap musician Ice-T)
p. 84: Sportimage (Dennis Rodman)
p. 86: Mary Evans Picture Library (children working in mine)
p. 87: Bilderberg - Renate v. Forster (boy baking bread); Bilderberg - Hans Jürgen Burkhard (children carrying fruit); Bilderberg - M. Kirchgessner (boy stacking up newspapers); Bilderberg (child wiping windscreen); Bilderberg - Thomas Ernsting (woman and child working in mine)
p. 92: Bilderberg - Wolfgang Kunz (crocodile)

Textquellen:

p. 10: Extract from the novel *„Love Me, Love Me Not“*, by Libby Gleeson. © Penguin Books, Australia, 1993
p. 13: Extract from *Lonely Planet Travel Survival Kit “Australia”*, 5th edition 1989, p. 452; © Lonely Planet Publications, Hawthorn, Victoria 3122, Australia, 1989; reproduced by permission of Lonely Planet Publications
p. 14: Extract from travel guide *DER- Tours: „Australien, Neuseeland, Südsee,* 1.04.97-31.03.98, 2. Auflage. Deutsches Reisebüro, Emil-von- Behring- Str. 6, 60439 Frankfurt/ Main
p. 22: Newspaper article *„Careering: Window dresser“* © The Times, 1015, 15.02.97
p. 24: Cartoon: „Hobbies: Swimming ...“ by Robert Thompson © The Spectator

p. 29: Cartoon: „I told you, ...“ © The Spectator, 24.03.1993
p. 32: Song: „Earth and Sun and Moon“ by Midnight Oil (Moginie). Warner Chappell Music/Sprint Music
p. 34: Brochure „Meat eating is ...“ © Animal Aid, Tonbridge, Kent
p. 38: Cartoon: „Take it easy, dear ...“ © The Spectator, 11.01.1997
p. 39: Cartoon: „No fish“ © Ken Pyne, London
p. 46: Cartoon: „The feudal system“ from: *Horrible Histories – The Measly Middle Ages* by Terry Deary and Martin Brown. © Scholastic Children's Books – Hippo, London, 1996
p. 52: Letters to '1015' from: "The Times"
p. 52: Advertisement: „3D Ultralite“ from: Men's Health International, Market Harborough, Leicestershire
p. 71: Song: „Treaty“ by Yothu Yindi. Yunupingu, M./Mununggurr,M./Williams, C.S./Yunupingu G./Kelly P.M./Kellaway S.A./Marika, W.P., © Mushroom Music Pty, Ltd., c/o Global, München und Sony/ATV Music Publishing GmbH, Frankfurt
p. 72: „How's the job then?“ Extract from the novel „Sticks and Stones“ by Susan Price. Faber & Faber, London. Cover © Derek Brazell
p. 74: Quiz: „Are you obsessed with your work?“ © BLISS, Nr. 102, April 1997
p. 75: Song: „Money“ by Pink Floyd. © 1973 Pink Floyd Music Publishers Ltd. 1994 EMI Records Ltd.
p. 76: Extract from short story „Half a mile down“ by Arthur Catherall from: The Third Eagle Annual. Ed. by Marcus Morris. Hutton Press Ltd., London
p. 78: Extract from a newspaper article: Protesters occupy oil platform. "The Times" 01.05.95
p. 79: Poem: „Battery hen“ by Pam Ayres from "All Pam's Poems", Hutchinson & Co (Publishers) Ltd., London
p. 82: Quiz: „What kind of reader are you?“ from: Letts Study Guide: GSCE English by Shelagh Hubbard and Jim Sweetman, Letts Educational 1993
p. 83: Kurtis Blow quotes from: „Bringing it all back home“ by Robbie Woliver, Pantheon Books, New York
p. 84: Extract from 'Bad as I wanna be' by Dennis Rodman. © 1996 by Dennis Rodman. Used by permission of Dell Books, a division of Bantam Doubleday Dell Publishing Group, Inc.
p. 86: Quotes from child labourers from „Industrial Britain“ by Christine Counsell and Chris Steer; Cambridge History Programme, Cambridge University Press, Cambridge, 1993
p. 86: Table: Factory Acts from 'Industrial Britain' by Christine Counsell and Chris Steer; Cambridge History Programme, Cambridge University Press, 1993
p. 88: 'The way the Aussies do it' by P. Shindler. From: '100 Favourite After-Dinner Stories' by P. Shindler © Judy Piatkus Ltd., London
p. 91: Brochure: Kakadu National Park Visitor Guide © Northern Territory Government Tourist Bureau, Darwin, Australia
p. 92: Extract from PONS Kompaktwörterbuch Englisch-Deutsch, Deutsch-Englisch, Stuttgart, 1997
p. 94: 'What's hot, dry and big?' Extract from an article from 'The Christian Science Monitor' © Christian Science Publishing Society A 72, Boston MA, USA
p. 95: Brochure: Explore England's History - Battle Abbey © English Heritage, London
p. 96: 'Joyriding' from: Shout Magazine © D.C. Thomson & Co. Ltd., Dundee, UK
p. 97: Extract from a UNICEF report: "Child labour" from UNICEF Jahresbericht 1995. © UNICEF, Köln
p. 105: Cartoon: „I don't know how to say this ...“ © Syndication International, London
p. 128: Cartoon: 'I wasn't born here ...' from Punch 19.02.1988
p. 132: Cartoon: 'Can Jennifer come out and work?' by Cheney from The New Yorker, 22.07.1996
p. 136: Cartoon: 'I see the pollution levels are up again.' from The Times (Diary), 21.08.1996
p. 136: Cartoon: 'You're not thinking ...' from The Spectator Cartoon Book. Ed. by Michael Heath. John Murray Publishers, London 1994
p. 136: Cartoon: 'Do not drop litter. ...' © Private Eye, London
p. 143: Cartoon: 'I'm so sorry. Are you really a TV star?' from Punch 15.01.1991

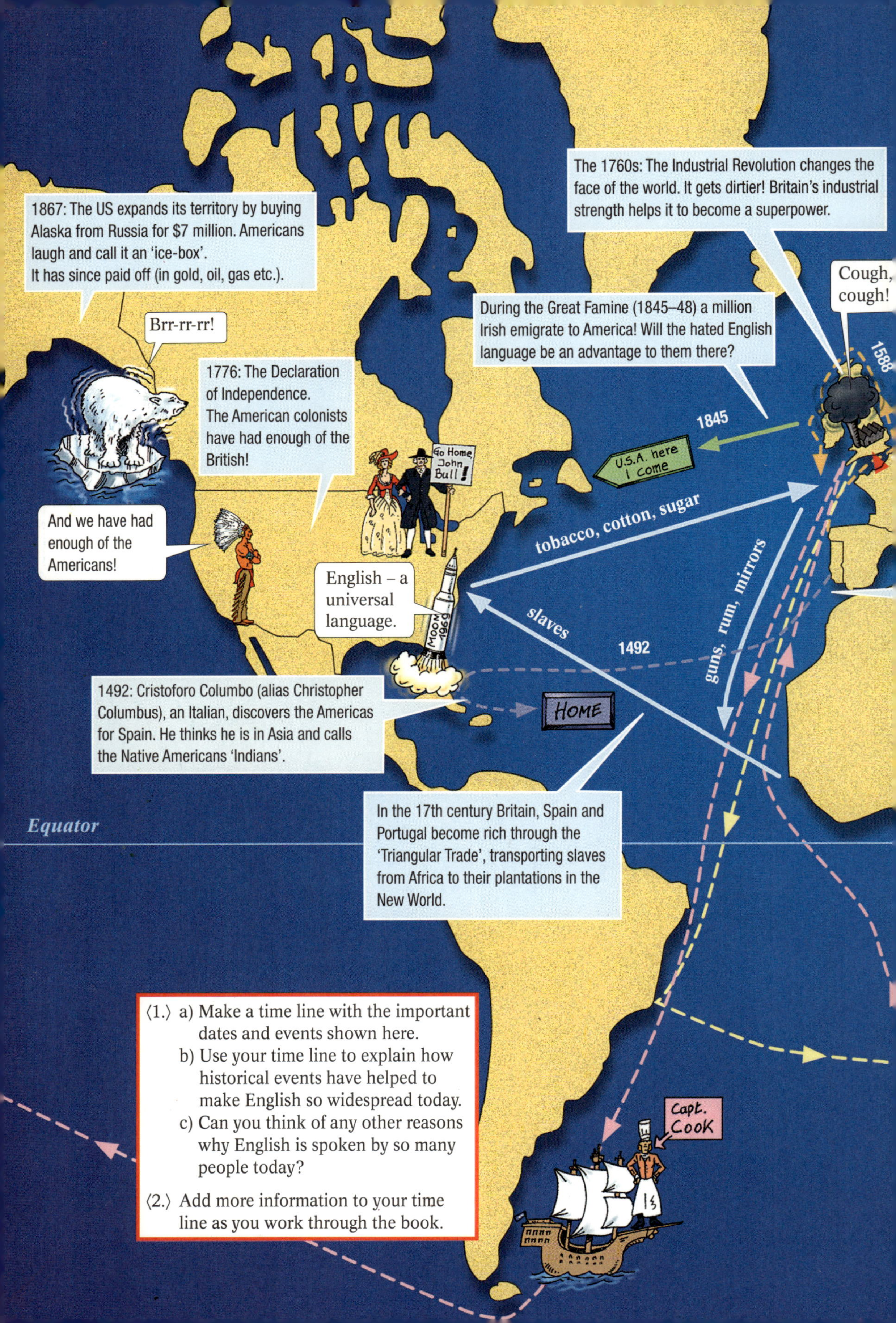

⟨1.⟩ a) Make a time line with the important dates and events shown here.
b) Use your time line to explain how historical events have helped to make English so widespread today.
c) Can you think of any other reasons why English is spoken by so many people today?

⟨2.⟩ Add more information to your time line as you work through the book.